The Art of Avaz and Mohammad Reza Shajarian

The Art of Avaz and Mohammad Reza Shajarian

Foundations and Contexts

Rob Simms and Amir Koushkani

LEXINGTON BOOKS
Lanham • Boulder • New York • Toronto • Plymouth, UK

Published by Lexington Books
A wholly owned subsidary of The Rowman & Littlefield Publishing Group, Inc.
4501 Forbes Boulevard, Suite 200, Lanham, Maryland 20706
http://www.lexingtonbooks.com

Estover Road, Plymouth PL6 7PY, United Kingdom

Pari Azarm Motamedi has generously given permission to use her artwork and selections
from copyrighted English translations of the poetry of Mohammadreza Sharafii Kadkani.

Ostad Mohammad Reza Shajarian has generously given permission to use music and
lyrics from his recordings of Rabbana, Golha-ye Tāze #37 and selected photographs and
interview materials.

British Library Cataloguing in Publication Information Available

Library of Congress Cataloging-in-Publication Data

Library of Congress Cataloging-in-Publication Data Available
ISBN 978-0-7391-7211-7 (cloth : alk. paper) — ISBN 978-0-7391-7212-4

♾™ The paper used in this publication meets the minimum requirements of American
National Standard for Information Sciences—Permanence of Paper for Printed Library
Materials, ANSI/NISO Z39.48-1992.

Printed in the United States of America

*Dedicated to
the spirit and freedom
of the people of Iran*

Contents

Chapter 4: Performing Avaz

Preface

This book is the first volume of a three-part study that examines the music and public profile of Mohammad Reza Shajarian as a major Iranian figure through the tumultuous late-twentieth/early-twenty-first century. Shajarian's achievement is generally regarded as nothing less than "perfecting" avaz (pronounced `ā • vāz)—the traditional art of singing Persian classical poetry—and personally functioning as an icon of contemporary Iran, both nationally and globally. Among other things, his powerful music provides a uniquely revealing window into Iranian culture and recent history; beyond Iran he may be regarded as simply one of the greatest voices of our time. This book centers on the historical and social context of sung poetry in Iran, Shajarian's artistic life up to the Islamic Revolution of 1979, as well as presenting a detailed examination of his creative process and musical materials. Our companion volume, *Mohammad Reza Shajarian's Avaz in Iran and Beyond, 1979–2010* (Simms and Koushkani 2012), examines Shajarian's work from the period of the revolution to the present. These monographs are complemented by musical transcriptions of complete performances of the avaz from Shajarian's major albums discussed throughout our study (forthcoming).

The study began as a revision of my dissertation (Simms 1996)—which, due to circumstances at the time, I consciously had left as unfinished business—and turned into something quite different and very much improved. Interviews with Shajarian himself redressed the greatest weakness of the previous work, which I recognized at the time to stand as a decent preliminary analysis awaiting such collaboration. My dissertation also called for co-authorship to bypass various methodological, epistemological, and ethical issues we face in ethnomusicology, especially to continue decolonizing the latter and be more transparent in our work. We need to seriously, fully, and directly include artists in the discourse and power-brokering of ethnomusicology as we move forward in the twenty-first century.

Enhancing Ostad Shajarian's substantial contribution here, co-authorship with Amir Koushkani is another major strength of the present study. I have known Amir since 1991, when I studied setar performance and radif with him in Toronto for two years upon his first arrival to Canada from Iran. Amir brings much to this study: he is a cultural insider, an eyewitness to the revolution and Iranian society through the 1980s; he is a tar virtuoso with valuable insights as a professional musician into the Iranian music business; he is part of a vast network of musicians and is a major source of oral tradition regarding myriad aspects of musical culture and transmission; he is an accomplished composer in both Western and Iranian idioms (and is meticulous about matters of notation), a music theorist and master of radif, and a gifted teacher of tar and setar performance in keeping with the finest line of the tradition; he has a deep knowledge of Persian poetry, language and poetic symbolism; and he has extensive experience with Sufi culture, literature, history, and practice. Amir has known Shajarian personally for many years, in which they have had many casual but meaningful conversations about Iranian musical culture. A long-standing fan and connoisseur of Shajarian's music, he has developed an uncanny understanding of Shajarian, frequently identifying or hypothesizing things that were later confirmed in interviews. The present study also goes far beyond my dissertation in presenting the larger context of avaz in Iranian culture and history, situating Shajarian as a highly significant individual exponent of this massive legacy.

The text unfolds as a continuous "trialogue" of our very different perspectives and subjective experiences regarding each theme or topic (an approach taken in varying degrees by Locke 1989, 1991, During et al. 1991, and During 1994 among others), with our voices clearly differentiated and identified through the use of contrasting fonts and the inclusion of our respective initials at the opening of individual statements:

> OS: *Ostad Shajarian*
> AK: Amir Koushkani
> RS: Rob Simms

Individual discussions from various dates are collated and juxtaposed under a progression of themes or topics that form the overall narrative of the book. The resulting juxtaposition of voices and perspectives under each heading evokes a variety of relationships: often complementary or supplementary but not always corroborative. Occasional dissonances and leaps are left to stand unresolved and exposed "as is." Among other reasons, this is done in the spirit of *iham*, the multiple layers of meaning deliberately manipulated by Persian classical poets, who thereby recognized that reality is complex, demands multiple perspectives, and is more than occasionally inconclusive. It is more honest to present the complexities of our topic with this in mind than to maintain the pretence of tidy categories, linear logic, and certitude often professed and expected by the scholarly enterprise. Indeed, the style of exposition employed here resonates with the layered, nonlinear idiom often used in Persian literature of various types. While this study was designed to be read in a linear fashion, it is also well suited to surfing and cherry-picking. From another angle, the format flows like a documentary film and presents the reader with an obligatory performance opportunity in navigating and interpreting the layered text.

Ostad Shajarian's comments were taken from several interviews with Amir and me, conducted both separately and together, in 2002 and 2008–2010. When Ostad Shajarian's comments are cited by only a date, it refers to one of these interviews. We have also drawn upon published written sources (with regular full citations) and recent television interviews (cited via footnotes with Web URLs). The latter two sources are voluminous and almost all in Persian. In addition to supporting a given point of discussion in this book, we feel that translating these interview excerpts into English is itself a useful contribution to future scholarship. Most of these translations were crafted by Mahmood Schricker, whom we sincerely thank. Readers will note that sections of Ostad Shajarian's comments are frequently comprised of quick juxtapositions of different sources of varying lengths. We generally include the specific questions asked so that readers know the context of Shajarian's statements. Occasionally his responses seemingly veer off the topic of our intended question, in which case we have usually placed such statements under the appropriate topic heading and included the original question for readers to make connections that we may have missed. In a few other instances of this kind it seemed better to place the discussion under the topic heading relevant to the question rather than the response. It is surely the bane of celebrities that they are asked the same questions over and over in interviews—some of his varied responses to standard questions have been included for the insights they offer.

Ostad Shajarian very generously and openly collaborated with us in writing the study over a period of many years, but because of his schedule our interviews were conducted sporadically and each under limited time frames. Like any good conversation, each interview spontaneously took on its own flavour and direction. They were not entirely systematic, as we balanced our prepared questions with the dialectical flow of the moment. While Ostad Shajarian responded to all of our questions, we were not able to pursue with him all of the many details contained in a study of this size; hence, questions on some matters remain and some facts are unclear, for which hypotheses or conjectures are occasionally posited. Amir Koushkani's and my sections are the result of a long process of bouncing ideas off each other, of dialectical growth and mutual revision. Most of Amir's contributions were transcribed from our recorded conversations while a few others were written in prose, which accounts for occasional differences of tone and style. While the entire text was made in collaboration with Amir, I was the arranger/editor and am hence the "teller" of the overall narrative.

Our study is not a detailed biography of Shajarian. The biographical content is painted here in very broad strokes, focusing on his musical formation and career path and not his personal life or a micro-account of his professional resume. It is rather a detailed portrait of his music-making; any micro-accounting occurs in the transcriptions and concerns his art of weaving poetry with music. Our interest is in elucidating the nature of his music, including its structure, aesthetic, and relationship to poetry; sketching the larger picture of Iranian performance genres, the tradition of Persian music and the musical culture of twentieth/twenty-first century Iran and placing his music in these wider contexts; and finally, positing Shajarian's cultural significance to Iranians and the wider world. In terms of his music, the focus is on his avaz—singing classical Persian poetry in free rhythm using the traditional modal repertoire and accompanied by solo instruments—at the expense of the integral musical work (i.e., the album or concert program), its arrangement and form, the instrumental responses to his avaz, the framing instrumental compositions, and tasnifs (metrical, strophic songs). This is lamentable in some ways but Shajarian's renowned mastery of Persian music is for his avaz, and few connoisseurs will argue against the fact that avaz constitutes the most important core, the featured climax, of any performance of Persian music.

I have taken heart in Jean During's view that "ethnomusicology is one of the least clearly defined disciplines, in which one uses all sorts of methods to treat a diverse range of subjects, providing that they touch more or less on music as an object, a practice or a symbol" (1994:24). Some of the subjects covered and theoretical bases employed in an interweaving fashion in my contribution to this study include history and political analysis; mythology and archetypes; aesthetics, rhetoric, and theories of Affekt, oral composition and narrative tradition; poetic scansion and interpretation; "old school" transcription and musical analysis; Sufism, Islamic ritual and doctrine; and philosopher Ken Wilber's integral studies. I also make occasional allegorical references to so-called "chaotics": the cultural paradigm or framework that emerged from the broader social, intellectual and artistic response to, and application of, the sciences of chaos theory and fractal geometry (see Borgo 2005:85; Hayles 1991:7, 1990). The glossary provides definitions for terminology from this field applicable to the allegory (e.g., attractor, feedback, scaling, etc.). Finally, this study also draws on the perspective of performance studies, which provide a wonderfully unifying point of reference for the wide range of themes covered in our presentation. In general, I have signposted ideas from performance theory at relevant points in the text but deliberately left the theoretical ramifications of the examples undeveloped for specialists in this area (which I am not) to pursue further, if they so wish.

All theories generalize—that is exactly what they are designed to do—and in the process of explaining and predicting, they often steamroll important subtleties, sensitive initial conditions of great potential significance. Theories are useful tools and maps, as long as they are regarded as such and not as an end in themselves or confused with "the real thing." They are vehicles that can take us to a better theory, the next station on the endless journey of exploring the cosmos. The focus of this study is Shajarian's music, its context in the tradition of avaz, and its significance to contemporary Iranian culture—not theory or methodology, which is soft-peddled throughout and can be either followed up or glossed over without losing track of the discussion at hand. In a further invoking the spirit of *iham*, theories are layers of possible meaning that can be taken or left, perceived or missed, their significance ranked according to the individual reader's sensibilities.

The primary impetus behind our study is a love of Shajarian's music as listeners (indeed fans) and recognizing it as a valuable resource for musicians—both vocalists and instrumentalists—to learn practical aspects of avaz performance. I confess that a major motivation for my dissertation at the time was to respectfully appropriate (less euphemistically, to steal) musical materials and compositional techniques from Shajarian's recordings for my own playing purposes, a practice of acquisition that he not only sanctions but emphatically prescribes. Finally, from a more exclusively scholarly perspective, it is impossible to look at Shajarian's music without examining his huge influence in contemporary Iranian culture, history, politics, media and globalization. In order to do this it has been necessary to "zoom" in and out between perspectives, alternately focussing on the specifics of Shajarian and his music, and stepping back to contemplate various gradations of the bigger picture of Iranian, musical, and global relationships.

A fundamental goal of this study is to move beyond the reductive, normative view of "Persian classical music" as it has been conventionally treated by ethnomusicologists at that time (cf. Dabashi 1999:15). While the perspective of this preliminary work was of course necessary at the time, we are left with a term that is loaded with baggage and assumptions, that Iranians do not use consistently themselves, and that denies the multicultural demographics that constitute Iran and have contributed to the formation of the music. Having seriously considered the use of various alternate emic terms—*asil* music, *dastgahi* music and the like—we decided to retain the standard epithet "Persian music" (without ironic quotation marks, which was yet another option) for reasons that: it is a default term that is generally understood by non-Iranians; it is identified as such on Shajarian's recent global releases of recordings and in his concert program notes; and the poetry, which is synonymous with the music, is indeed in Persian. We use the term Persian music throughout conscious of its distorting convenience and with the understanding that it includes the above qualifications. This study is not the appropriate place to further challenge or highlight the issue. Similarly, following contemporary convention the use of "Persia" and "Iran" is synonymous and used alternately throughout the text, although my sections tend to use Iran/Iranian more consistently in recognition of the multicultural reality of the country and its history.

Transliteration of Persian follows the simplified practices adopted in an increasing number of recent publications from various fields (including the authoritative multi-volume *History of Persian Literature* [London: I.B. Tauris, 2009]) and reflects the appropriation of the Latin script by digital-savvy Iranians in their routine use of "Finglish." It is sufficiently recognizable for anyone who reads Persian, and for those who do not, it is sufficiently accessible and unobtrusive. The only diacritical mark used is the macron "ā" (to denote the long vowel as in "father"). The transliterations of album titles are left as they appear on those publications. Neither italics nor macrons are used for Persian musical vocabulary that occurs frequently in the text and is well known by now within ethnomusicological publications (e.g., avaz, radif, gushe, tasnif, tahrir, etc.). Persian words are given the anglicized plural marker "s." Our priority is to communicate and connect readers of English to the contents of the study; the vast majority of Iranians concerned with our topic, including Ostad Shajarian, do not have a problem with these concessions. Transliteration and translation of Shajarian's album titles are given as they appear on the album covers and his English website (delawaz.com/en). All dates are given AD for the easy reference of Western readers. For various reasons, dates occasionally slip by one year due to inconsistency in sources and oral reports or arising from complications in conversion from the Iranian solar calendar.

Readers should know that we explicitly asked Shajarian what he wanted to see in the study, what he thought to be important. Among other things this affected the choice of the recordings we transcribed and analyzed in detail, along with our emphasis on the poetry and its relationship to the music. While we have included other levels of structural analysis, these were decidedly secondary in his view or less than half of the story. Upon showing him the work as it was presented in my dissertation, he immediately criticized the lack of connection between the meaning of the poetry and the music (his exact words are found on p. 203 below). We asked how we could make the project constructive from his point of view. *"Everything— including my potential, my knowledge, my experience or my creativity—is at the mercy of one thing, and that is the lives of the people of my country and the poetry that I choose, based on the life that I have lived. Ultimately, the music presents this poetry. So these all come together. Presenting just one angle of it is OK but it is not the whole work"* (2008).

The following year we explained our revisions and progress to date and asked if he was satisfied with the direction our work was taking, to which he responded: *"Yes, but only under the condition that you really develop these ideas, really develop the subject and get results. You must connect all of these subjects together so they have a flow, a continuity, and are not independent from each other, so it doesn't seem that one subject is stuck out on its own"* (2009).

This was indeed a tall order. We have done our best to fulfill the former condition of developing ideas but the latter directive regarding the smooth integration of the topics involved proved to be particularly difficult to realize given their individual complexity, vast range and intricate interrelationship. While there are a bewildering number of possibilities for organizing and presenting the material, the form of this study follows a broadly chronological and biographical narrative with lots of "sideways" linkage that follows Shajarian (and the art of avaz) through ever widening social and geographic spheres—from the provincial outback of Mashshad to national and then global stages.

Chapter 1 of this volume provides a brief introduction to Shajarian's artistic achievement and some essential features of avaz in general while presenting the central ideas and themes that are encountered throughout the study. Chapter 2 discusses roots, Shajarian's early formation as a singer in Mashshad, followed by an examination of Iran and Shi'a tradition in general. Chapter 3 focuses on Shajarian's early career in Tehran, his influences, teachers, and professional accomplishments which are contextualized by briefly sketching an overview of Persian musical culture from the late Qajar period (late-nineteenth century to 1920) through the 1970s. Chapter 4 examines the craft of avaz composition and performance as practiced by Shajarian, particularly as he established his mature style, with detailed discussions of acquisition, technique, creative processes, materials, and structures. Our companion volume (Simms and Koushkani 2012) picks up the biographical-historical trajectory from the Islamic Revolution to the present.

Despite my many ideas and words contained in this study, I have tried to bear in mind the great dangers of "fancy thinking" along with the greater wisdom of *khamush* ("silence"), of knowing when to stop. Like a fractal, the art of avaz and Shajarian's representation of it are infinite in detail, depth, and scope. A complete picture is impossible: research is never finished, only abandoned. I hope others will continue to pick up, correct, expand and explore the many aspects and dimensions both included and left unattended here.

I wish to thank sincerely Jean During, Christy de Felice, Jim Kippen, Irene Markoff, Bruno Nettl, Valorie Salimpoor, Vladimir Simosko, Mahmood Schricker, Urszula Starzec, and Shahrokh Tuisrkani and his family for their support and assistance. I also thank my many other Iranian friends and acquaintances over the years, who taught me much about generosity, beauty, humour, and good food—in a word *adab*, "the etiquette of being human." Special thanks to Shabnam Ataei for her invaluable help. Ultimate thanks to Ostad Shajarian for his great music, which reminds us of the way of depth and beauty in life, and for his generosity in contributing to this study.

Amir Koushkani wishes to thank Pari Azarm Motamedi, Mansour Motamedi, Camran Chaichian, Teymour Dowlatshahi, Ehsan Ovisi, Hossein Omoumi, Mahmood Schricker, and Homayoun Shajarian. I asked Amir to provide his own preface but he deferred to the great tar master Jalil Shahnaz and answered this ritual call very quietly with something like "Let's play and see what's going to happen."

Rob Simms

Chapter 1
Before Coming In (*Pishdaramad*)

Introduction

OS

In terms of our musical talent we Iranians stand no less than elsewhere in the world, we even excel. If there is any shortcoming in our music, it is due to the obstructions it faced in its long history and the fact that no real opportunity has been given to our artists to properly show themselves. [The authorities] have prohibited the music, otherwise it has all kinds of potential. Music in every culture is the message of that culture; it is the inspiration of those people and their culture. This inspiration is then dependent on the activities that took place in that culture, so music is dependent on the living conditions and the mentality of its people. Because the artist lives amongst his people, the music that pours out of his heart is the message of these people and their conditions. Restrictions, pressures, oppression, and the brutality of its rulers have all influenced the music of Iran. This music has always been the voice of complaint for people; it is the language of criticism and we can't escape this fact. It is like a painter who draws whatever is inside of her upon the canvas. If she creates a sad or a cheerful painting it is not because of the brush or the canvas—those are only tools in her hand. The scales, the notes, and the phrases in our hands are also reliant on our own feelings and desires. Our feelings and desires are the feelings and desires of our society and its people.

Interviewer: So I conclude from your comments that you are trying to reflect as closely as possible the state of your society.

Yes, that is completely right. (Mirian 2007)

AK

In order to analyze and appreciate the place and achievements of Mohammad Reza Shajarian in the art of Iranian avaz one needs first to define the features and attributes of this art form and study the historical role of avaz in the larger context of Persian music, art, and culture as well as the sociopolitical environment of the country over centuries.

The word avaz has many different meanings in the Persian language. In this study avaz is defined as sung classical Persian poetry characterized by unmetered, melodic modality based on the dastgah system, and improvisatory performance practice. This form offers the possibility of change, flexibility, and rich, powerful expression in varying sociopolitical and cultural circumstances. It is very closely related to language, especially the arts of diction and recitation. At its best avaz can convey to the listener the true message of the word and the poem. The non-metric flexibility of the form enables the singer to adjust and adapt the melody as needed for the best expression of the meaning and intent of the poem. The freedom of rhythm in these melodies helps the singer to bring out the full potential of the words without unnecessary rhythmic restrictions. In the context of traditional Persian music melodies and songs have various expressive functions such as "tension and release," "call and response," and rhetorical repetition, among others. Within the performance of avaz these techniques can take their true form in a close relationship with the poem. In such a performance an accomplished artist can deepen the meaning of a poem and even add a new layer of meaning to it.

Throughout the history of Persian music the art of avaz has been one of the most important ways of orally conveying of the message of the poem to the listener—declamation and recitation being other oral means. Depending on the prevailing message and purpose of the word, the techniques can change. Each technique has emerged and evolved to respond to different needs and purposes. For example, in the *rowze khāni* (a form of religious singing), *marsie khāni* (expressing grief), *masnavi khāni* (sung renderings of Rumi's *Masnavi*) or *zikr* (mantra-like invocation), the techniques change according to the meaning and circumstances of the performance. Similarly, avaz is a form of singing with deep roots in our culture, it can change with the circumstances and convey the pains and aspirations of the people, and the most accomplished, dedicated artist performing it becomes an icon for the era during which they perform and even for future generations. Mohammad Reza Shajarian has achieved this status both nationally and internationally and is regarded as the most creative and inimitable artist performing in this genre over the past century.

The relationship of music and poetry and the relative role of each in the expression of meaning has varied and changed over time according to different situations throughout Iranian history. The work of Ostad Shajarian in the art of avaz, in the marriage of music and poetry, has moved through a brilliant trajectory that culminated in the "mature style" he arrived at in the 1980s. He now took a more innovative compositional approach to avaz, interiorizing the poem and drawing out its hidden music, weaving it with the words with such sincerity and strength that the listener feels it is the poet who is singing. For many contemporary Iranians, the works of many of the most important mystics and poets of Iran become accessible and immortalized through the avaz of Shajarian. He uses the wisdom and poetry of ancient mystics and scholars to convey the messages of today. Because of current sociopolitical confusions and conflicting contemporary ideas and assertions, the timeless wisdom of mystics like Rumi or Hafez are trusted and more attractive to listeners. This wisdom and the messages contained within it are still relevant, and in the avaz of Shajarian they are revisited and conveyed in a new form. Ancient, trusted wisdom becomes the trusted and appreciated wisdom of today through his avaz.

Avaz has changed with the sociopolitical developments and upheavals throughout Iranian history, and due to its flexibility, it can adapt to the needs of both secular and sacred singing. There are, however, specific qualities and criteria that are always present in the most excellent performances of avaz, qualities that elude the majority of singers. Some of these include: a special voice quality with extensive range, sincerity, strong connection and harmony of the voice with the soul of the singer, dedication and love of the art form and a lifetime of work. The artist needs to have attained a deep understanding and knowledge of the history, the culture, poetry, art, and musical traditions of Iran. As the poem and the music are the most important tools for transferring these aspects of the culture to the listener, the artist must also have an in-depth awareness and knowledge of the mystic traditions of Persian poetry and music. The confluence of these diverse attributes and qualities in one person is very rare and it is for this reason that there have been very few artists of the caliber of Ostad Shajarian in the history of avaz in Iran. As Hafez said, "beyond beauty a thousand other attributes have to come together for one to be embraced by the wise," and without exaggeration, Shajarian demonstrates all of these attributes in his avaz.

RS

Mohammad Reza Shajarian was born in Mashhad on September 23, 1940. He grew up in a family of religious singers and became a child prodigy of Qur'an recitation, performing live before large audiences and in his later teens on local radio broadcasts. He pursued the autodidactic study of avaz while working as a school teacher in Mashhad before heading to Tehran in 1967, where he studied with a range of prominent, senior masters and became a regular artist on national radio and television programs through the 1970s. Shajarian became the top classicial artist in Iran in the period following the 1979 Revolution, developing his mature style and making a series of brilliant and highly successful cassette albums. He began touring regularly outside Iran in the late 1980s in ever widening geographical circles. Coupling his touring with the release of wide-distribution CDs on Western labels, his profile was truly global through the 1990s and 2000s, when he received prestigious awards and distinctions from various global organizations, and his audience expanded beyond that of the Iranian diaspora.

The historical and functional roots of contemporary avaz (though not its present style) lie in the great tradition of Persian classical poets, extending from Rudaki (ninth/tenth century) through Jami (fifteenth century) and continuing into modern times. Viewed crossculturally and historically, the legacy of this poetic tradition is without equal in the field of world literature in terms of both quality and quantity. The strong tradition of Sufism throughout Iranian history and the intrinsic flexibility of the Persian language are key factors in forging the remarkable poetic genius of the Iranian people. Poetry often had an exterior courtly function but has been and is still appreciated by people of all walks of life throughout the centuries, functioning simultaneously on various levels according to the multiple layers of meaning (*iham*) woven into it and an individual's subjective perception. Among other things, Persian poetry is a form of innocuous diversion or escape, an art form of aesthetic beauty and inspiration, a venue for individual artistic expression, and an emotional outlet for both the author and audience. It is a platform for social commentary, political critique, and resistance, a tool for propaganda, a means of flattery and elite patronage, a commodity for entrepreneurship and possible income. This poetry functions as a source of erotica, a conduit for narrating stories, myths and history, a promoter of moral-ethical principles, a personal oracle, a transmitter of wisdom, religious doctrine, and mystical knowledge. It is also a fertile springboard for creating music, as well as a source of shared metacultural identity amongst a diverse multicultural complex of Iranian peoples and those within their sphere of influence, which comprises the vast stretch of Eurasia wherein Persian poetry has been revered and cultivated.

The word *adab* entails a variety of things and is variously defined as: "literary humanism" (Dabashi 2007); that which is "concerned with the etiquette of being human" [1] (Sardar 2004:273); or as the "ideal refinement of thought, word, and deed" (Khaleghi-Motlagh 2010), the latter triad has deep Iranian roots, resonating with ancient Zoroastrian tenets (Chehabi 1999: 149). Dabashi maintains that as an important medium of *adab*, the tradition of Persian poetry and prose constitute a primary common denominator unifying the great diversity of cultures—from Central Asia, India, China, Afghanistan, Azerbaijan to the furthest outreaches of the Ottoman empire and sub-Saharan Africa—that make up the abstract, politically-constructed boundaries of "Persian" identity, the imagined community of Iran (2007: 18–20, 29, 286–87, n. 16.).[2] Indeed, Anderson's seminal study identifying this sense of imagined community as being integral to nationalism notes that "there is a special kind of contemporaneous community which language alone suggests—above all in the form of poetry and songs" (2006:145). The great post-Enlightenment rise of New World and later European nationalism was due in large part to the rise of vernacular languages and their mediation via print capitalism (ibid.: 9–46). But in Iran *adab*, especially in the form of poetry both memorized and in manuscript, had already been serving the purpose of linking a heterogeneous, spatially dispersed group of people for many centuries.

While Persian poetry was indeed recited, it is also likely that singing was a primary mode of performance (Hillmann 1976:149; Miller 1999:112; Lewis 1995:80ff., Pirnia and Nakjavani 2001). In Persian the same verb—*khāndan*—is used to denote reading, reciting, and singing;[3] the suffix "*khānī*" commonly seen in vocal genres such as *Shahnāme khāni, Rowze khāni, Masnavi khāni*, etc., simply means "the recitation or singing of such-and-such text" or "one who recites/sings such-and-such text." Poetry was so closely aligned with music that poets were often musicians themselves and/or wrote about music. In ancient Iran the two vocations were synonymous: the Parthian (247 BC–224 AD) vocation of the *gōsān* "minstrel" did not differentiate between poet and musician (Boyce 1957), the first clear distinction between the two was noted by Key Kavus in the mid-eleventh century (de Bruijn 2009: 20), possibly influenced by the Arab separation of the two types of artists (Lewis 1995:87–89). This dual practice applied to Rudaki, the ancestral progenitor of the great lineage of Persian poets (Farhat 1980: 292; de Bruijn 2009:20) and continued with the great masters Farrokhi, Sa'adi, Khayyam and Hafez, who frequently wrote in praise of music, while Rumi purportedly enjoyed playing the *rebab* (spike fiddle) and formulated an elaborate and profound symbolic language based on musical images, most famously that for the *ney* reed flute. Following its extemporized "composition" or perhaps more accurately, dictation, Rumi's poetry was undoubtedly sung spontaneously in the early Mevlevi *samā*[4] before becoming more formalized in ritual with its set repertoire of compositions (*ayin*) after his death (cf. Avery 2004:224). Shajarian clearly follows in this tradition and emphatically insists that virtually everything in his avaz derives from the poem.

Ostad Shajarian's career was well established in the 1970s but was propelled to the highest professional ranks in the turbulent, hyperpoliticized postrevolutionary decade of the 1980s, when he became a major public figure. His music consistently and powerfully re-presented to the Iranian public their beloved poets' most profound layer of emphasis on the interior, psycho-spiritual stability that is potentially available to human consciousness amidst the fickle, chaotic flux of daily life with its inevitable suffering and absurdity. It thereby offered inspiration and hope, along with psycho-spiritual advice for living a meaningful life in spite of everything. But reflecting the frequent upheavals of Iranian history, contemporaneous sociopolitical commentary is often implied in the poets' art as well. Davis's reading of the *Shahnāme* proposes that, while not outright seditious, Ferdowsi[5] highlighted the tension between individual conscience and the directives of unjust leadership, and in one instance (VII, 116, 54) is "strongly suggesting that all the troubles that disturb the earth are due to kings" (1992:xxix). For Davis, it is "certainly a poem at odds with itself, one that offers a paradigm which it constantly subverts and one that gives evidence of a mind perpetually alive to problems of authority and justice" (ibid.:183–84).[6] Indeed, throughout the centuries many Persian poets— including Rumi and Hafez—offered political innuendo with varying degrees of subtlety and frequency. Contrary to our conventional images, Sufis did not always shun secular life, politicians and the opportunity to influence them (Lewis 2008: 328; Dabashi 1999:118). From the deep decadence and instability of the late Qajar period (late-nineteenth century) onward many poets became increasingly politically engaged, explicit and in varying degrees, critical. Their deep-rooted, resonant medium became a potent sociopolitical force that was potentially revolutionary, embodying, as it always had throughout history, elements of both continuity and change in Iranian culture (Dabashi 2007: 94–104). The poetry of Ali Akbar Saber, Seyyed Ashraf al-Din Qazvini, Mirza Ali Akbar Dehkhoda, Taqi Raf'at, 'Aref Qazvini, Malek al-Sho'ara Bahar, Sohrab Sepehri, Mehdi Akhavan Sales, Feraydun Moshiri, and Hushang Ebtehaj are particularly noteworthy in this respect.

Likewise, and partially due to increasing European influences throughout the increasingly bankrupt (figuratively and literally) and dysfunctional Qajar dynasty, other popular public entertainment—improvised theatre (*ru-howzi*), puppet plays (*kheimeh-shab-bazi*) and eventually, in spite of the gauntlet of censorship, film—became increasingly political and critical of government, elites and class disparities (Haery 1982: 20ff., 29; Dabashi 2001). This convention had earlier precedents in the post-Safavid (i.e., 1736) improvised, public theatrical farces (traditions such as *mazhakeh, pish parde, taqlid*) that openly satirized contemporaneous nobility to the great satisfaction of their audience of commoners (Haery 1982: 20ff.). In general, Iranian musicians have functioned as subversives throughout history in that they often defied the restrictions imposed upon them; by virtue of their marginal, pariah status within the general populace they marched to their own bohemian beat and operated on their own social wavelength (Tabar 2005: 520). Youssefzadeh notes how many of the strict censures, musical and otherwise, proclaimed following the Islamic Revolution were never enforced (2000:38; see also p. 40); the authorities set up boundaries without always guarding them but nonetheless reserved the right to enforce them at their whim. Musicians were certainly not above the law but perhaps below it, operating "under the radar" much of the time. Shajarian served to act, at carefully chosen times, in a dissenting capacity while simultaneously and paradoxically raising his status as a professional musician to a prestigious level rarely occurring in Iranian culture, spectacularly transcending his predecessors and the long-standing ethic of "amateur prestige" whereby some of the greatest exponents of Persian music derived their income from other means.

Ostad Shajarian took center stage of Iranian public life as the foremost exponent of avaz, of embodying and performing *adab*, at a historical juncture of magnitude unprecedented in the modern era. Like the conventional layering of multiple meanings in the poetry he so brilliantly sings, Shajarian simultaneously employs *avaz* toward a variety of directions. As moving, superbly executed singing, it provokes a deep aesthetic experience that resonates with the poet's call for spiritual depth and transcendence but it frequently also implies a fairly obvious critique and disillusionment with contemporary Iranian political life, which carries an equally powerful resonance with most Iranians. In a sum that is even greater than these weighty parts, his music powerfully embodies a fundamental expression of the aspirations of the Iranian people—the vast history, the core values both articulated and unsayable. Perhaps more than any public figure, Shajarian embodies and personifies *adab* in contemporary Iranian culture.

This chapter introduces general topics and issues that resurface throughout the study. The thread of the chapter begins with the poetic technique of *iham* as being particularly emblematic of the entire study, wherein it is transposed to many spheres of activity and levels of observation. This leads to a discussion of narratives on various porous levels, from the mythic to that of an individual's life, and how these are activated and transmitted via performance featuring the essential components of tale, teller, and telling. A brief outline of the historical narrative of avaz follows. As the chapter toggles between Shajarian and the larger context of the tradition of avaz throughout, the topic of the relationship between the individuals and the social collective is examined, along with how this impacts continuity and change of musical style. Bumping matters up to the level of intercultural relationships, the central issues of "East and West," Westernization, and tradition and modernity in Persian music are also included. Many of these issues are contentious points of debate, in which case our task is to present the basic oppositions while clearly explicating Shajarian's and our own perspectives that inform the rest of the study.

Iham: Multiple Meaning, Uncertainty and Complexity

There ain't no answer. There ain't gonna be any answer.
There never has been an answer. That's the answer.—Gertrude Stein

Do not be certain about uncertainty.—Ray Grigg

Avaz is sung poetry and in any culture poetry is the art form par excellence of ambiguity, its *modus operandi* is to use language homeopathically to undermine the linear logic of language (a closed system trapped within itself, wherein words merely refer to other words) and point to the spaces between words and ideas, to paradoxically say what cannot be said. The basic tools of poetic discourse and semantics—symbolism, metaphor, allusion, puns, word play—are intrinsically polysemous and ambiguous. This quality is particularly cultivated and valued in Persian poetry, where it is known as *iham*. The flexibility of Persian grammar, multiple meanings of a large portion of words in Persian vocabulary, and further meanings rendered possible by slight variations in pronunciation provides for an incredible depth, richness, and nuance of semantic exploitation. One need only compare different translations of a Hafez ghazal and see the wide range of interpretation and meaning possible. Moreover, Nooshin notes that the power of music, in its broadest application, is due in large measure to its even greater intrinsic ambiguity (2009:15). Thus, with *iham* and music at its very foundation, any study of the art of avaz must squarely face the notion of intrinsic ambiguity, which is operative on a wide range of disparate levels. Indeed, in the first appearance of the word *iham*, Vavat's *Hada'eq al-sehr* (twelfth century), it is "defined as a [rhetorical] figure aimed to throw the hearer into doubt" (de Bruijn 2009:156). While *iham* is a primary tool of poetry and music it also reflects the rhetorical technique of deploying oblique references and veiled comments embedded in other areas of public and personal discourse in Iranian culture.

While no culture, of course, is free of amibiguities and paradoxes—this being so central to the human condition—they particularly abound throughout Iranian culture. Consider the demographics of Iran itself: the complex and diverse aggregate of peoples who have contributed in multifarious and inseperable ways to the poetic and musical repertoire that constitutes avaz. "Persian music" is a handy but highly essentialized category for a complex blend of cultural strands whose exact nature is ultimately unknowable. Since the revolution these diverse people have been governed by the constitution of the Islamic Republic, which is itself designed with intrinsic contradictions (discussed in Simms and Koushkani 2012); while the de facto political spectrum reflects this great diversity, the infrastructure of empowerment is exceedingly labyrinthine. "Iran has never been more a country of paradoxes and contradictions than it is today. Many people in the West continue to see Iran as a truly radical Islamic country. But the truth is that Iran is a country in a painful transition to democracy, and may be the only Muslim country where people are rapidly moving away from radical Islam" (Jahanbegloo 2004: xvii).

Furthermore, certain aspects of the Persian language seem ambiguous (especially when compared to Western languages), notably the lack of gender indicators in pronouns, which is exploited for great semantic play in poetry. The orthography of Persian does not indicate short vowels, which presents foreign students of the language with particular challenges for accurate reading.

As noted by Nettl, Iranian culture—hardly alone in the Muslim world on this count—is paradoxically predicated on the doctrine of equality of all Muslims within a society that is rigidly hierarchical; Iranians generally value individuality and surprise and yet have lived under pervasive authoritarian systems throughout history (1983:139, 1992:248). In an apt resonance of quintessentially dualistic Zoroastrian and Manichaean teachings, contemporary Iranian identity is integrally predicated on both ancient dynastic and Islamic foundations. Indeed, any political authority in Iran that does not strike some kind of acceptable balance between these poles is ensured instability and resistance (Nooshin 2005:237, Del Giudice 2008). The dualistic certainties integral to Zoroastrianism, Manichaeism, and Islam stand in sharp contrast to the ambiguities characterizing Iranian culture and identity, wherein nothing seems to be black or white (or maintain its polarized quality for very long).

Avaz presents an ambiguous meeting of the sacred and secular on various fronts. The best singers of art music often come from a background of religious singing, the genres and practices of which exist in a great variety in Iran: Qur'anic recitation, *azan* (call to prayer), *rowze khāni, nohe khāni, marsiye khāni, madih khāni, monajat, ta'ziyeh* (a theatrical genre that incorporates singing) and so on. These vocal arts were often maintained through many generations of particular families. A cursory review of great avaz singers emerging from this tradition, besides Ostad Shajarian himself, include Qorban Khān Shahi, Seyyed Ahmad Khān, Qoli Khān Shahi, Iqbal Sultan, Jenab Damavandi, Hoseyn Ali Nakisa, Seyyed Ali-Asghar Kordestani, Rajab-Ali Amiri Fallah, Adib Khānsari, Qamar, and Seyyed Javad Zabihi, among others (liner notes to the Mahoor CD set *A Century of Avaz*). Nelson (1985) similarly noted the two-way traffic of vocal artists in Egypt between the fields of Qur'an recitation and Arab art music, the paradoxically porous border of non-music and music, quintessentially sacred and suspiciously secular in terms of emic conceptions. As discussed in further detail below, many of these genres of religious singing and recitation are performed in the context of mourning rituals that are characterized by a simultaneous conflation of past and present, the mythic and historic.

From the historical standpoint of Iranian aesthetics and philosophy, commentators frequently associate the secular art forms of music, poetry and miniature painting with the hypostatic realm of *Malakut* (sometimes designated as *Hurqalya*, the name of a "city" located therein) in traditional Sufi cosmology, an "imaginal" interworld of the soul and Platonic Forms where noumena and phenomena, spirit and matter meet, where "bodies are spiritualized and spirits take on form" (Corbin in During 1977:29, Nasr 1987:177–84).[7] These art forms are both a bridge to this ambiguous dimension (or state of consciousness, depending on one's perspective) and an explicit, "earthly" representation of it. *Malakut* is also the realm of angels, who, like music itself, are immaterial yet possess form (Wilson 1980: 49), and are agents of revelation, intermediaries between the human and divine. Persian poets from the time of Sana'i (d. 1131 AD) onward engaged poetry as a medium for conveying and transmitting Sufi doctrine and, through the key influence of Ahmad Ghazali, devised an elaborate language of symbolic imagery that placed particular emphasis on "theo-erotic" love and intoxication in a provocative ambiguity of the sensual and divine: the very hallmark of classical Persian poetry.

Many facets of structure and performance practice in Persian music highlight an integral ambiguity. Rhythmically avaz is performed in a so-called "free" rhythm that purposely defies a sense of regular pulse, though one constantly shifting in tempo is usually present. The use of meter in Persian music (*zarbi* sections or pieces) is characterized by an overall approach of "roundness" that usually wavers in and out of triple and compound categories.[8] Persian music features microtonal intervals that many cultural outsiders (beyond the neighbouring and historically related modal traditions) would consider to be ambiguous in the context of their scales. During has commented on the instability of the Iranian tuning system, with its characteristic quarter tones, noting that "(h)alf of the intervals are artificial and have no rational and acoustic foundation" (1987:25). He also notes that the 3/4 tone divides the pure minor third into two equal halves and thereby "holds an intermediary position which takes both the value of the tone and that of the semitone"; the "neutral third" likewise bisects a perfect fifth (During 1987:26). This seems to suggest a correspondence to the intermediate world itself, ambiguous and "otherworldly." "One could say that they (the neutral intervals) express alterity, that which is different, but also separation, the pain of separation and a nostalgia for the other world . . . a dimension which transcends reason itself, the mark of a mysterious order which can only be apprehended by intuition" (ibid.:27–28).

In terms of modal structure, dastgah Shur—the most emblematic mode of Persian music—is characterized by a fundamental ambiguity, both in its intrinsic structure and in comparison to other modes in the radif, which generally feature modulations that are more clearly differentiated from the main scale. The radif itself is a complex labyrinth of modal connections oscillating between logical and non-linear, seemingly haphazard organization. Many gushes spawn a cluster of satellite melodies or present similar melodic identities that are subtley differentitated as they are cast in various contexts and groupings.[9] Fragments of individual gushes are recycled in new, unpredictable contexts; melodies reappear with very subtle variation. Especially in recent times, and not unrelated to Shajarian's pervasive influence, the vocal range and tone of male singers is routinely roughly the same as that of females. As with most other musics, the relationship between improvisation and composition is a fuzzy one in the performance practice of avaz. The transcription and notation of avaz, which by now has great currency amongst musicians of Persian music, is an ultimately futile exercise in constructive ambiguity, particularly with regard to rhythm and ornamentation while completely neglecting timbre. Despite this liability, transcription has many useful functions (detailed in appendix 2) and is employed extensively in our study.

Various social contexts and values regarding avaz present ambivalent, contested or porous boundaries, such as the relationship to Qur'anic recitation mentioned above, the precarious, highly-suspect vocation of being a musician in Iranian society, and the historically polemicized role of music as *samā'* (with its association of music and questionable states of consciousness; see Rouget 1985 for a good summary of the latter). Musicians must carefully situate themselves within an aesthetic continuum that expects fidelity to prescribed, preset materials—signifiers of "the tradition"—and the imperative of engaging the listeners' interest through elements of freshness, surprise, and innovation. They must tread a fine balance between their individuality and "the tradition," the precise line of which is constantly shifting, predicated on subjective taste and thus impossible to draw clearly. There is a telling lack of consensus among Iranian musicians and connoisseurs regarding the defining features or even existence of specific regional stylistic schools (*maktab*)— such as Tehran, Tabriz, Esfahan, etc.—or whether discernable stylistic consistencies are due to influential individual masters and their followers.

As we will explore in greater detail below, there is also considerable debate among culture theorists regarding the veracity of the dichotomized categories of "tradition vs. modernity" in contemporary global cultures, which according to many critics exist within much more blurred boundaries if they don't render the binary entirely anachronistic and irrelevant. Iranian culture in general presents a complex case study with respect to this debate and avaz in particular offers a perfect vantage point from which to explore the hybridized vagaries of the polarity, as it occupies a position that is seemingly suspended at the fulcrum of the poles. Shajarian himself is at the same time a high-profile, hypermediated, jetsetting celebrity and a refined contemporary embodiment of *adab* who emerged from the deeply traditional milieu of religious singing in the holy city of Mashhad. The period of the 1980s in which he made many of his greatest recordings was one of great uncertainty, ambiguity, and anxiety for Iranians—in varying, unpredictable degrees of intensity it has remained so to this day.

Despite our deep-seated craving and intense cultural conditioning in pursuit of order and certainty, the world and our place in it has always been ambiguous and uncertain. In the West, new insights from a wide range of natural and social sciences—from particle physics, environmental studies, nonlinear mathematics,[10] and dynamic systems, to global economics and geopolitics, sociology, postmodernism throughout the humanities, and so forth—all update and reaffirm the ultimate ambiguity and uncertainty of our world. From another angle, the rise in religious fundamentalism around the globe in recent decades may be partially explained as a clinging to the certainty religions offer us in the face of rapid, disorienting sociopolitical change. Indeed, traditions of all sorts, both long-standing and invented, take on a new significance in the contemporary global context, offering their adherents a vestige of purported certainty amidst the quickly shifting sands. Although far from obvious at first glance, from a Sufi perspective (along with other Asian esoteric traditions, notably Taoist) this inescapable uncertainty is potentially liberating and facilitates creativity, the perception of previously hidden subtlety, and a great depth of meaning. But for most people it remains a source of relentless anxiety.

AK

The diverse ethnic groups that have lived in Iran over dozens of centuries share many of the dominant cultural and social characteristics and values of the country. However, these groups also possess distinct cultures, languages, religions, customs, and social boundaries which have developed over centuries. There are also the spoken and unspoken expectations and restrictions that govern the life and work of individuals, and specifically artists, who work and perform in different genres and spheres of society. Changing social values and even sociopolitical developments and conflicts add a new layer of expectations and limitations as well as new possibilities. The combined effect of these parameters results in a very complex society in which the overlapping of sociocultural boundaries defines acceptable behavior, limiting the choices and freedom of expression for everyone, but especially for the artists.

Musicians, their work and life, are also governed and limited by numerous overlapping cultural and social boundaries. The "container" in which the art is performed and presented becomes very important. The artist's work becomes defined and limited by the perceptions of society, sometimes based on parameters that have little relevance to the real quality and value of the art. The art and the artist receive a label and the musician or singer is expected to perform within the boundaries of that label. For example, a musician who becomes known as one who performs Persian music would normally not perform in a venue assigned to pop music and if this happens, he or she loses some of their artistic prestige.

In 1997 Ostad Shajarian told me of an experience he had in Baku where he witnessed a completely different attitude in the audience when they faced such a situation. He spoke of an occasion when, accompanied by a very distinguished classical singer with impressive artistic and academic achievements, he goes to a restaurant for dinner. In the restaurant there is live music, being performed by a popular singer, who recognizes the Azeri master singer and courteously invites him to sing for the patrons of the restaurant. Shajarian was surprised to see the highly distinguished singer accept the invitation and sing in the restaurant to a very grateful and admiring audience. He spoke of the respect, admiration, and emotional closeness that he felt between the master singer, the popular singer and the audience in Baku and noted that such an event could not and would not occur in Tehran, or any other city in Iran, where the limitations and boundaries are strongly defined and adhered to.

There may be similar attitudes in other societies but in Iran the borders are more deeply ingrained and the judgments are stronger and harsher. Sometimes the art or music is not judged by the inherent quality of the art or the music but by external values and criteria. The freedom of the artist and his or her creativity is limited and as a result, instead of limitless and spontaneous creative work the artist has to pay attention to external limitations and somehow adapt his or her work to remain within the social boundaries.

Shajarian is interested in talking about how the words of the poetry he chooses express his opinions about today's Iran more than any metaphysical or philosophical meaning they may connote. The poetry used in the avaz is usually that of the great Persian mystics. As far as I can tell, recent interpretations of these poems seem to concentrate solely on the spiritual and little emphasis is placed on their sociopolitical meaning. Through the art of avaz Shajarian changes the emphasis of the poem to a sociopolitical meaning.[11] There can be no doubt that the original poets, in many cases, were making just such sociopolitical commentaries themselves and engaging in the art of *iham*, much as Shajarian is doing. Indeed, the only way to rebel and survive in the repressive regimes under which they almost invariably lived was to speak in this riddle-like form, where meanings are veiled. Perhaps as the relevance of the original poet's socioeconomic conditions dissipated with the passage of time, the singers of those poems leaned more towards their spiritual aspects. For his part, Shajarian is undoubtedly rejuvenating the art of *iham* by putting it to a use that is current and relevant. Thus, it may be argued, he is giving the poem new life through his vocal expression of it, breathing a new fire into it. In fact it must be noted that Shajarian's *iham* has been so masterfully implemented, that the often intensely critical sociopolitical commentary he expresses seems to have escaped the notice of the powers that be. One can safely assume this, given that the government has not prohibited (or been able to prohibit) the dissemination of his music.

Narratives and Their Performance

Myth is man's way of coming to terms with the vast uncertainties of his universe.
. . . There is no limiting the historical person's myth-making necessity, in response to the ever-changing parameters of anxiety. . . . From a Zoroastrian to a Manichaean cosmology, from Islamic theology to Persian miniature painting or coffeehouse painting, there is a relentless engagement with bringing the vast universe of shapeless and endless possibilities to metaphysical or aesthetic order. (Chelkowski and Dabashi 1999:64–65)

Most history, when it has been digested by a people, becomes a myth. Myth is an arrangement of the past, whether real or imagined, in patterns that resonate with a culture's deepest values and aspirations. Myths create and reinforce archetypes so taken for granted, so seemingly axiomatic, that they go unchallenged. Myths are so fraught with meaning that we live and die by them. They are the maps by which cultures navigate through time.—Ronald Wright[12]

RS

Human experience is conceived and conveyed through symbols and narratives, which mutually arise—they define each other and elements of one are included within the other. Many cultures are explicit in their recognition and deployment of stories in this fundamental capacity, such as in Australian and North American aboriginal or Sufi cultures. Persian poetry is lyrical but employs an integral narrative mode: besides famous works such as Rumi's *Masnavi* or Attar's *Conference of the Birds*, lyrics frequently draw upon and allude to narrative themes (often well-known ones in a "sideways/linking" fashion) or sketch out and thickly describe vaguely narrative vignettes. Narratives play out in multiple levels of human activity and consciousness, from the mythical[13] and archetypal through historical, traditional (including artistic), political, and individual biographical domains, the borders of which can be porous, with stories from one domain spilling messily into another. The meaning and significance of these narratives are highly susceptible to the "spin" applied by those telling them. Stories appearing on these various levels or scales suggest a self-similarity within the human experience, as smaller fragments of the whole bear similarity to larger ones. The essential components of narratives include characters, roles, and objects that are knitted into scenarios and plots (which include numerous subplots and episodes) by which themes are worked out toward various messages and conclusions. Different dynamic currents are simultaneously at play, as characters both traverse the plot and yet shape and direct it as well.

Thus, in Iranian mythology we have a vast cast of deities and cosmic players (e.g., Ahura Mazda), creatures (lions, dragons, Simorgh), mythical figures (Jamshid, Siavesh), some of whom seep into an ambiguous historicity (e.g., Zoroaster,

Barbad), and objects (Jamshid's cup, fire) that populate the myriad and intricate plots that teach of loyalty, treachery, leadership, kindness, love, search, integrity and wisdom among a wide array of other themes. Throughout its 5,000 years, the historical domain of Iran overlaps considerably with the mythical, particularly with the events and individuals central to the founding of Islam and Shi'ism. The historical narratives of dynasties, potentates, conquerors, religious leaders, Sufis, artists, scientists, and civilians, etc., is well documented and exceedingly complex. Furthermore, this sprawling history can be viewed on multiple levels: from the individual strands of a decade to the larger historical arcs of centuries; of a single locale or city to an empire. History is formed by many things but one of the more influential of these is politics, which at any given synchronic point in Iranian history features a complex, often tumultuous narrative of players, agendas and drama, the late-twentieth century furnishing a spectacular example that deeply impacted a global geopolitical narrative. Of course, each individual has their own story, populated with a range of characters both central and peripheral, wherein they work at the common themes of family, career, social relations, and existential issues through time, space and the activities of their lives. Traditional and artistic narratives include fables, folktales, scripture, sacred histories, epics, literature, and episodic vignettes of poetry (both oral and written). Less obvious but equally applicable in contemporary Iran, the art of traditional music also has a decidedly narrative quality, with a cast of musical structures—instruments, scales, gushes, themes, motifs, tahrirs—populating a musical unfolding of events, indeed a plot, predicated upon the radif in the form of an expected series of gushes along with rather stable and predictable musical forms: *pishdaramad, chaharmezrab, tasnif*, etc. (cf. Blum 2002: 8, 10–11).

The description thus far has given the impression that narratives are things when they are really activities, performances in various orders, of human agency (the mythical order, for Jungians, reflecting human collective subconscious). With the exception of its conventional use regarding the musical narrative, "performance" is used here in the very broad sense that it acquired in performance studies, a new scholarly discipline established in the United States during the 1970s that arose from theatre studies and anthropology. A key concept for performance theorists is "restored" or "reiterated" behaviour, wherein we repeat, redo specific things—be that singing a specific ghazal of Hafez in a specific dastgah in a concert hall, barking out orders to your subordinates in the army or making baby talk with your one-year-old daughter. The scripts in these scenarios stay the same but our performance of them is never exactly the same each time due to a number of transitory factors. We perform and reperform art and daily routines, social roles and identities (e.g., gender, class, ethnicity or nationality), ritual and politics, and so on. In this view, tradition and culture are also activities, things we do and perform. The historical past is known and recounted (already done and performed), while our present activities and performances of culture constitute the continuous unfolding of history. The reiteration of myriad patterns and scripts provide some security in the essentially unpredictable future. The maintenance of narratives through time involves the reiteration of stories so central to the culture that everyone already knows them thoroughly, there are no surprises. In view of the intrinsically pervasive redundancy, the whole point is their refreshment through skilful performance. Over time an infinite number of "variations on the theme" accumulate and feed back into the texture of the narrative, which maintains its overall shape amidst the ever changing flow of the surface. This same process (and even the technical term) of reiteration is central to chaotics, where a system feeds back into itself, cumulatively incorporating each new rendition in the manner of compounding interest. We are dealing here with deeply archetypal human behaviour: scholars note that Australian aborigines unite music, story, dance, painting, and travel in a reiteration of themes that may extend back forty thousand years.[14]

Avaz is one strand amongst a wide range of ritual and artistic practices in Iranian culture—religious solo recitation and group chanting, the *ta'ziyeh* drama, epic/bardic recitation, storytelling (*naqqali*), secular theatre, and, in many respects, film[15]—that are narrative, performative, rhetorical and in varying degrees mythical or sacred. Practices vary widely in terms of the occasion, intended audience and ritual (both sacred and secular) behaviours. The narratives are cultural knowledge that may be conveyed through language, music, body movement, and visual media, or any combination of these. Collectively these practices serve to recreate, re-animate and bring into the present moment deeply embedded cultural archetypes and memories. By doing so, they connect people on multiple levels: as a micro-community attending the particular performance, as a larger shared cultural identity of being Iranian, as a contemporary continuation of a vast historical legacy, and in some cases, ultimately to a transpersonal, spiritual state of grace. History, myth and ritual; art and craft; seriousness, play and entertainment; tradition and invention; spontaneity and fixity; personal, impersonal and interpersonal; past and present; sacred and secular; immanence and transcendence all come together in a complex, interrelated whole made of porous borders open to resignification. In a very direct manifestation of Geertz's famous formulation, they are indeed stories people tell themselves about themselves (1973:448).

What is the significance of these narratives and their performance to non-Iranians, cultural outsiders? Following deeply ingrained historical tracks (perhaps better described as ruts), the narrative performances initially provide a means for constructing Otherness, defining both themselves and Iranians in the process while projecting upon the latter a wide range of fears, fantasies, biases, and misunderstandings. Given sufficient care and effort, however, a wonderful potential opens itself whereby the outsider can feel a personal resonance with the narrative and the people performing it, transcending while including cultural differences to form an integrated, synergistic relationship on an entirely different level. Misunderstandings can still abound but they are now framed in a constructive relationship that promotes mutual growth.

The various manifestations, genres and modes of narrative performance exist through the integrated triad of "tale, teller and telling" (Scholes et al. 2006:240), wherein the tale consists of the narratives from any of the domains discussed above; the teller may be a bard, a singer, a religious reciter or a group of actors; and the act of telling occurs during a particular performance, for a specific occasion and audience, resulting in a unique rendition of the narrative with the distinct opportunity for the teller to put their individualistic spin on the contents of the story. In contemporary Iranian culture Shajarian is one such teller, his tale is classical Persian poetry and the melodic narrative of the radif, and his telling consists of large public concerts and mass-mediated broadcasts and record releases. Practical aspects of performance have a direct correspondence to narration, as we shall see throughout this study. Shajarian's full-length works are veritable musical journeys (a long journey essentially amounts to the same thing as a story) for both performer and listeners alike that reveal a mastery of pacing and dramatic unfolding on a large scale. Shajarian is a master of quickly grabbing the listener's attention to focus on the mode and mood at the beginning of a performance (like a good rhetorician's proem or exordium), of establishing musical-dramatic atmospheres, sustaining them for as long as he wishes and then shifting gears through another episodic cycle. The component episodes combine to create a powerful whole, a musical story/journey of truly symphonic sweep. All of these skills are at the service of delivering his rendition of the poetic text, with its embedded narrative layers. Berliner elucidated in compelling detail how storytelling, journey, and language were primary metaphors used by musicians in the jazz community to describe psychological, cognitive, aesthetic, and strategic elements of their craft (1994).[16] Berliner's findings have a much wider crosscultural relevance in general and, as detailed in this study, apply specifically to Shajarian's conception and practice of avaz.

AK

As an instrument of communication, avaz uses many of the tools that have been employed in Iran by mystics, writers, and poets over the centuries for the effective delivery of ideas and opinions. In many literary works, rather than directly presenting advice or suggestions for living life, allegory and allusion are used. The most significant source of such use of language goes back to an Indian manuscript from the fifth century AD, the *Panchatantra* in Sanskrit, or *Kelileh va Demneh* in Persian.[17] This is a collection of animal fables in prose and poetry originally intended for teaching social and political behavior to princes and young royals. It was translated into Middle Persian during the reign of Khosrow I and eventually into Arabic and other languages. Using the characters of animals and their behaviors in various situations and the descriptions of the outcomes of certain behaviors and actions, the wisdom of ages is conveyed without giving direct advice to the reader or the listener. This indirect communication of ideas becomes a much more effective, subtle, and nonthreatening vehicle for teaching and conveying ideas.

The same use of allegory and allusion is employed in all the different areas of artistic endeavor in Iran, as well as avaz. Instead of direct expression of a message the deeper esoteric meaning and intent is obscured within an apparent image or narrative. This form of expression is thought to have a superior aesthetic value and quality as well as a deeper, indirect, subtle effect on the person who receives the message. For the observer or the listener, discovering the beauty of the various layers, initially veiled in mystery and allusion, is a very pleasant component of the interaction with the artist and the message, and remains vivid as a picture in the memory of the recipient for a long time.

In avaz, allegory and allusion are employed in different ways. If the singer has a deep knowledge and understanding of the literary, mystical, and sociopolitical ideas of the poet and the allegories and allusions employed, the message of the poet is conveyed by the singer through an inward assimilation and presentation of the message as if the singer was the poet. But in some cases, talented artists with a deep knowledge of the social and political milieu can add their own input to the allegorical expression. Rare among singers, Ostad Shajarian is capable of such an expression.

Shajarian uses several tools and methods to express the messages in the poem and to add new layers of emphasis to the allegory through his avaz. He employs different forms of speech and expression, changes the emphasis of a word or phrase, stresses a specific part of the poem through varied repetition, and can slightly alter the poem to allude to an ongoing social or political event. Through his deep knowledge of the structure of melodies and the use of dynamics he can also deepen, change or add a new layer of experience to enrich the combined effect of the music and the message. However, Shajarian, as the most accomplished singer of the last one hundred years, has another attribute that goes beyond cognitive abilities or learned tools. If the tools are used superficially the expression seems unnatural and forced but Shajarian has an intuition and spiritual connection with the messages and the contexts of those messages that enables him to use the tools appropriately, with great sensitivity and strength. An informed, knowledgeable audience receives this message as it is conveyed and through this interaction a rare and unexplainable unity occurs between the artist and the listener. A unity that comes from a mutual understanding of the various layers and nuances of the hidden message, sung and expressed by the artist and received and appreciated by the listener.

The Occasion, Connectedness, and Appropriateness

RS

The ritual performance of retelling narratives not only transmits and communicates, but also refreshes and revitalizes through the inspired use of creative license. The roots of this dynamic run deep: "Zoroaster's originality lay not in the creation of new myths, but in the interpretation he placed on old ones" (Hinnells 1985:9–11). In Iran the tellers are expected to do nothing less and they accomplish this maintenance and reinvigoration through the process of improvisation: by improvising on archetypal "repertoires" that signify "the tradition," they effectively improvise the tradition, propelling it through time and space. Iranian culture generally privileges the dynamic oral performance of a written narrative over the text itself, retelling the epic of the *Shahnāme*, the sacred history of Karbala, the ghazal of Hafez, refreshing them according to the spirit rather than the letter.[18] Each retelling is like a fractal reiteration that endlessly rearranges the well known tale. It is more truthful to recast it in the present moment and context as a living, ever-relevant cultural landmark than to repeat it mechanically. As large groups within the Iranian population were illiterate (up to the 1960s) but nonetheless interested in the preservation of art and ancient rituals, oral tradition and performances were the most important, and sometimes the only, alternative. According to performance theorist Diana Taylor's terminology (2003), the repertoire (i.e., embodied practice, performance) took precedence in the transmission but existed alongside and in a dynamic relationship with the archive (storable objects, books).

This continuous reenactment or performative maintenance is both socially bonding and emotionally engaging, as the best tellers form an intimate rapport with their audience, whose emotions and minds they attempt to manipulate by various dramatic, formal, and psychological means. This is akin to the art of rhetoric in its original conception throughout much of Western history: the effective development and delivery of an argument in the course of a public speech in order to convince and persuade the audience. The role of the individual teller, then, is essential to the maintenance of the collective tradition. Moreover, the creative license allowed and expected in the animated retelling allows a skilled narrator, in the spirit of *iham*, to put a judicious amount of spin on the tale, which clearly elevates them to a position of influence with the potential to challenge authority.

Performance theorists use the term proto-performance to describe "the source or impulse that gives rise to a performance; a starting point. A performance can (and usually does) have more than one proto-p[erformance]" (Schechner 2006:226). In Iranian narrative performance the essential proto-performances are the layers of narratives and the occasion. The occasion (*monāsebat*) or immediate social context of the performance—the particular venue, time, audience and the reason for gathering—is itself a ritual of deep social significance in Iranian culture, rendering most performance genres as specific rituals within a metaritual. It integrally implies both connectedness and appropriateness. The nature of occasions calling for performance range enormously, from religious rites and festivals, anniversaries of historical events to civic functions, social gatherings and entertainment, both private and public. Whether it is in a teahouse, mosque, concert hall, banquet hall, living room or the street, the occasion brings people together to listen to recitation and singing. In all cases, the performer must first and foremost respond appropriately to the occasion and the expectations and needs of those in attendance, a fundamental social obligation that goes beyond the specific contractual relationship with patrons (which of course also applies).

> The term used most often describing this craft [of singing religious poetry] is *munāsib* (fit, appropriate, suitable). A performer must continually gauge what the most appropriate subject matter and style of presentation will be in terms of audience, the occasion, the time of year, his own performance specialty and his relation to the preceding or following performers. . . . The term "munāsib" is also used to describe the desirable voice quality for a performer as well as the musical line appropriate for the meaning and purpose of the text. . . . Munāsib is further used to refer to the appropriateness of the performer's combination of the poetry, prose, ethical sayings, wit, Arabic quaotations, and free elaboration on a subject to make a point clear to the audience—a point that will be effective and convincing enough to move the audience to action. (Reckord 1987: 91)

Medieval sources attest to the high value placed on musicians being responsive to their audience and performance setting (Blum 1998:29–33), attributing the same imperative to the quasi-mythical Sassanian musician Barbad (D'Erlanger 1938: 548). The anonymous seventeenth-century treatise *Bahjat al-Ruh'* prescribes specific modes to use for particular listeners and occasions (Zonis 1973:209–12). At an occasion, the telling—be it song, chant, speech or drama—must be customized for the audience in attendance, further underscoring the key role of flexibility and improvisation in performance practice. In addition to providing the forum for the re-enactment of myths and their conflation of past and present, a type of "time travel," the occasion serves to unite attendees, highlighting their collective existence and relations as they resonate together. Music is the medium par excellence for focusing and marking our awareness of this moment, the occasion for gathering, drawing upon the power of now. Like a good meal or stick of incense, it can be made and enjoyed again but it will never be exactly replicated, only remembered. Music's very transience made it more valuable. While this was especially so in the prerecording period, when music was truly ephemeral, even listening to a recording will be different each time depending on our surrounding context and state of mind—listening thereby becoming a performance for the listener. Music serves the occasion by ritualizing (in both sacred and secular contexts) time, by entraining and synchronizing the group (both audience and performers), and by enhancing the goals of commemoration and remembrance. Mounting neurological evidence suggests that music, through its engagement of emotion, rhythm, and associative capacities serves to "'tag' the memories as something important" in our neural record base (Levitin 2006: 231; see also ibid.: 166, 167, 267; and Thaut 2008: 6, 76, 138, 186). In complex systems the local interaction of "street level neighbours" taking cues from each other, spontaneously self-organizes higher levels of order. The interaction must be a two-way exchange between neighbours to effect the global ordering (Johnson

2001:75ff.), which is precisely what the occasion facilitates: the singer responds to the immediate social situation of the audience, who in turn listens to the singer, each taking cues for how to behave from the other.

Contemporary concerts of avaz bring a wide spectrum of social classes together to synchronize in an intensely meaningful but explicitly secular ritual. Following and perhaps intensifying the historical tendency evident in Persian musical culture since the early-twentieth century, the public ritual of Shajarian's concerts is virtually identical to that of a concert of Western classical music: advanced promotion and ticket sales, assigned seating, artist entrances and exits, cued bowing and applause, expectations of silence, artist dress that is formal (in an Iranian traditional aesthetic), restrained gestures while performing, intermission, and encores. A major difference is that Shajarian and his accompanists frequently sit on cushions or short risers on a carpeted stage (often decorated with flowers) rather than chairs, although chairs and even music stands were used for his 2010 world tour with the Shahnaz Ensemble. Another subtle difference is that Shajarian prefers to perform with house lights dimmed rather than black, for purposes of facilitating audience feedback.

Among his other natural assets as a singer and performer, Shajarian's character is well suited to being an effective *monāsebatkhān*, singer for the occasion. He is clearly adept at replying to his environment and society, explicitly proclaiming that his job is to mirror the social milieu and reflect public sentiment. The occasion drives and guides his performance, whether this is a concert or an interview; the social context of who is in the audience or in his personal company matters immensely. His performances are customized to fit the audience and occasion, hence his performance of the same setting of a poem to avaz will differ from night to night, audience by audience (discussed in detail in chapter 4). Similarly, being constantly asked the same questions in interviews, his answers often differ according to the company, audience, and occasion of the interview.

OS
My path and goal have never changed. I was looking for beauty in art and in voices and wanted to sing better and more beautifully for my audiences. Later on, I not only wanted to perform my best and be aesthetically beautiful but I also wanted to have a social message. I did this by keeping the beauty there but put it in service to the message. From the time after the revolution onwards, I came to the realization that "I must live for you"—"you" meaning the people, anything that was outside myself. This was a result of reading an article by [singer and philosopher] Ostad Dadbeh in which he wrote that one must efface oneself entirely, and give oneself over to the "workshop of existence" (kargah-e hasti). You must love others, rather than yourself and live for others, rather than yourself. This article had an incredibly potent impact on my life.

But you still have to be selective, attentive and maintain high standards (sakht giri) *in working in this direction; I don't work with just anyone or for any reason. From my childhood, other people's energy* (hāl) *really affected me. When they're happy, I'm happy; when they're dark, it brings me down. I resonate with them. Joy and happiness only have a meaning for me when others are feeling that way. When I met Ostad Dadbeh I realized that my nature aligned with his teaching and I knew my path was correct. I had found my true path and happiness, and art gave me the opportunity to put this into practice. (2009)*

We keep the art for the people and this is for the people that we are living among. And that is very satisfying for me. I'm living among these people, we have the same thoughts; I love them and they love me.[19]

AK

Ostad Shajarian was clearly blessed with natural musical gifts but his character also made him who he is. You can be equally gifted and still not accomplish what he has. Shajarian is a seeker: he is curious and always learning, always growing. He works hard and is a good student.[20] He pays attention to what is going on around him and has a wide range of interests. He likes consulting with people, especially those who are experts in their fields; and of course, he knows many great artists, intellectuals and masters in Iran. I've seen him sit and talk to different people about all kinds of things—carpets, cooking, business—and he blends in with people, tuning in to whatever is being discussed without saying a thing about music. You can see this flexibility in his music, where he can change his style to adapt to different situations, different audiences or relationships of poetry to melody. Whether he was working on his own or with a master, he was very diligent and meticulous about his studies. He is ambitious and keeps very high standards in everything he does. The amazing thing is that even now, with all of his achievements and cultural position, he is still interested in learning and growing. This is who he is and what seems to keep him going in life.

Dr. Hossein Omumi, the well-known ney player currently residing in California, has talked about the master vocalist Taj Esfahani (1903–1981), with whom he frequently went to the *khaneghah* (Sufi meeting place) of Sheikh Zayn El Abedin, as the best *monāsebatkhān*. These *khaneghahs* are different from mosques where everyone is supposed to be performing a certain ritual or prayer at the same time. The various dervishes in the *khaneghah* are at different levels of attainment and the atmosphere there is very spontaneous with each day having its own fluctuating cycle of energy. The atmosphere of the day may be agitated or at other times it may be very serene. When Taj was in the *khaneghah* he would spontaneously choose a poem and the music and would start to sing. The Sheikh used to say that most of the time it was the best poem and music for that moment. They were practicing this "occasional" singing all the time and Taj was called the master of *monāsebatkhāni*.

Taj was invited to perform in all the occasions that called for a suitable form of performance—for example, at a memorial or a funeral Taj was always considered as the best vocalist to perform. Other performers with less experience, empathy and feeling for the occasion may choose to perform pieces that would be totally inappropriate for the occasion. I can recall a situation in the *khaneghah* of Safi Ali Shah in which a poet was invited to perform at the funeral of Mr. Bik-chekhani, a master tar player, and started to recite a "non-poem" of some sixteen lines on the subject of motherhood. He clearly did not appreciate the occasion and the suitability of the material, which resulted in him commiting a major so-cial error.

According to Omumi, in Esfahan more so than in most regions of Iran, the concept of *monāsebat* is understood and practiced in everyday life, even in the way people relate to children and young people. The ability to understand the occa-sion and the nature of conversations and to give fast, appropriate answers is en-couraged and admired in children. They are allowed to participate in adult con-versations and those who can respond with sensitivity to the occasion are consi-dered smart. The same importance to the occasion is carried over to musical per-formances. For example, when the great tar master Jalil Shahnaz (who was very influential in the development of Ostad Shajarian's musical excellence) plays a piece and Kasa'i (the doyen of ney players) brings in a powerful response to that music, the masters listening in the audience immediately hear and feel the suita-bility of the response to the occasion and cannot refrain from vocalizing their admiration. Responding quickly, accurately and appropriately in *javab-avaz*, the accompanimental response to avaz, is very important. In every occasion, spon-taneity and speed in thinking and giving the most suitable response is important. According to Shajarian and many other authorities, Master Jalil Shahnaz, who grew up in the society of Esfahan where expressing correct, fast and spontaneous responses to every occasion is learnt from a young age, is the greatest master of *javab-avaz*.

Another tradition relevant to this discussion is the game of *Mosha'ereh*, which is played everywhere in Iran by people of all ages and social groups. In the simple version of the game, someone recites one line from a poem and the other person takes the last alphabetical letter of the last word and recites a line of a poem starting with that letter. Sometimes large groups of people sitting in a cir-cle play this game and players who are good at responding with speed get a lot of recognition and credit. The more sophisticated version focuses on the subject and the occasion. The first person sings or recites one poem and the next one responds with the same subject but a different poem. The poems are usually cho-sen from the poetry of masters of Persian classical poetry, such as Hafez, Attar, Sa'di and others. The game is an incredible challenge to your memory and know-ledge of poetry. There is an even more sophisticated version that is practiced among poets. Shahriar (1906–1988) was the master of this form of *Mosha'ereh* and would improvise an original poem in the very moment that his turn would come in the game, a poem with good structure and character relevant to the occasion and the prevalent issues and Zeitgeist of society. Poets such as Malek al-Shoara Bahar (1886–1952), 'Aref Gazvini (1882–1934), and master musicians like Abol-hassan Saba (1902–1957) all admired Shahriar for this ability.

All of these examples support the fact that in the performances of music and recitation of poetry and avaz, compatibility with the occasion, whether religious, social or political, is of the utmost importance. During the last three decades, Ostad Shajarian realized his role as a leader in his art and studied the importance of being sensitive to, and recognizing the need of, the various occasions in which he performed. In the same way as a master carpenter would use certain specific tools and methods for the construction of a commissioned piece, Shajarian would use all his talent and tools for the performance that would be most compatible with each occasion.

OS

Question: How do you define the notion of *monāsebat* and how does it relate to your work?

There are different levels of monāsebat. The first concerns the issues and themes of what is going on in contemporary society—specifically my understanding of these. The next level is the selection of an appropriate poem that is directly linked to this social context. We present this theme back to society along with our opinions regarding it. This then leads to the monāsebat of choosing an appropriate dastgah or avaz that will deliver this message of the poem and its present social significance in the best way possible. Sometimes people make such an inappropriate choice of mode for a poem that it can even sound comical. I always try to make the poetry and dastgah support each other and the poetry to be about the theme I am trying to present. So this relationship is another form of the monāsebat. And finally there is the level of engaging one's vocal technique to deliver the poetry and its message: the use of dynamics, articulation, and timbral shading. The goal is to bring out the best possible meaning of each word, to convey the best effect to the listener so that they feel an unprecedented fulfillment in my rendition of the poem, even if they knew the poem beforehand. These are all aspects of monāsebat and have the ultimate goal of realizing the central idea within the act of musical creation and performance.

Are these your thoughts or did the older Ostads think like this as well?

Actually these are mentioned by the Ostads as well but not with much precision and elaboration. They briefly talked about the relation between poetry and its subject, the poetry and music. There is even a book about it, entitled Bohur al-Alhan,[21] *but when I looked at it I realized that my taste is very different from the author's. He states, for example, that a particular poem must be sung in Chahargah and I said to myself, "this is wrong, this should not be sung in Chahargah." When I read this book I realized some of it is correct and other parts are not that precise.*

What is the best performing environment for you, the studio or live on stage?

For me the stage is something else because I am performing in person for my listeners—be it on stage or a private gathering—but the stage is more serious and that is why I prefer it.

When you have a concert like today in Holland, do you adjust yourself to this environment and to this particular occasion? What part of your performance is about this particular city and its particular atmosphere, and what part is pre-composed?

Well, I have obviously prepared a purpose for this concert that guided me to choose the poems, and in general everything moves towards that purpose. At the same time, the space and time are not autonomous from the quality of the concert. The listeners and the viewers are very important, it is very important for me as to who is sitting there. If they are people without much knowledge, my throat gets clogged, and I won't be able to sing. I can sing better if the audience is knowledgeable—I feel that I am able to express myself better and say what is inside of me. Otherwise I would feel like I am talking to strangers, and I don't like talking to strangers. So it is very important for me to know who my listeners are. This is the most important thing and it is even capable of changing the quality of my performance. The work on the whole may be the same but the form of the phrases and their construction [i.e., the specific contents of the melody] of the performance varies because one's mood changes from one day to another.

When you are performing a specific poem do you feel, for example, that you should deliver three tahrirs to set the mood and the message at one concert and perhaps at another that even one short tahrir would do the job?

Absolutely, you are right, I mean all these things are connected to one another. It is like a game of soccer: when the person who is playing in the position of forward encounters four defenders and a great goalie, and if he is a good player, he would still be able to score. [22] *This is because he puts a lot of effort in that situation—this includes his focus, his physical exercises, the speed of his delivery. And just as avaz is improvised, the soccer player also must improvise to create something valuable in the moment. Singers must be able to create something beautiful. Obviously these two fields are very different from each other but from some perspectives they are alike. The soccer player doesn't work towards the interior, psycho-spiritual human domain—instead he plays to put on a show that people will appreciate. However, I never want to try to show off my skills and make a sensational impression with my voice. I never do that because it is a lie and I don't like to lie. I direct all my efforts in service to my message and how to deliver my message. I will then try to deliver it in the most perfect way. The chief quality here is the speed of that delivery, the speed that relates to the emotions that I am encountering and those contained in the message. So both the musician and the soccer player must have speed of delivery so that, in the case of the soccer player, he can pass through the defenders and the opposing team. Speed for me relates to the musical notes and words, and I must try to deliver the message from within this field.*

The soccer player wants to score a goal, and I want to deliver my message. Singers must know the radif so that they can improvise and present a spontaneous reaction to their knowledge; this reaction is based on what they know and the situation they are in. I believe that in addition to knowledge of music and poetry, and the present situation or occasion, they must also have a speed so that they can make a decision in one tenth of a second. I mean, in that short period of time one must recognize his opponent and understand what move he has to make. Whoever has a better speed of delivery and speed of judgment is the one who always wins.

Is the concert stage the best place to deliver your art?

The stage is like the stadium in which the athlete is playing. When he is playing alone he doesn't feel much joy. If there is no one in the stadium he cannot really play, he can't play at all. So the studio is the same. Although it is true that the quality of the sound is better, I can never have the same mood and ambiance of the stage there. (2009)

How are you influenced by the things you see on the street, your daily routine, and other people?

In general you are influenced by everything you see in your surroundings. When you see happiness around you, you become happy. I personally get happy when my people are happy, I cannot have a private happiness unless I'm in a situation that I see everyone is happy. But when you are surrounded with people who are upset and angry, well, one feels the same. Everyone expresses their anger differently due to their strengths and abilities. In society we all influence and are influenced by each other. Our youngsters whose hearts are clean and want to start planning life, they want a bright future for themselves. They want to reach their ambitions and goals, so they must be in an environment that is conducive to that. Naturally, if such an environment is not available to them, they will complain. But one must be able to answer to them, because they are the ones who will be building the future. They want a path to a happy life and we must respect that.[23]

Avaz and Tasnif

RS

Strophic, metrical songs have a long history in Iran, known variously as *tarāne*, *sorud* (which predates the Islamic period), *zarbi*, and since the fourteenth century, tasnif (Caton 1983:18ff.). This study focuses on Shajarian's art as a singer of avaz and treats his composition and singing of tasnifs in passing as it relates to various discussions. The reason for this is that Shajarian's greatness as a singer is because of his mastery of avaz, which provides a much wider latitude and open format for creativity as opposed to interpreting tasnifs. Comparing a number of singers interpreting the same tasnif and then the same group performing avaz of the same poem in the same dastgah, their relative powers of musicality, invention, technical and compositional command will be much more distinguishable in their avaz performances. Indeed, the placement of avaz in the extended suite of contemporary performance practice (originating with Darvish Khan and outlined in appendix 1) suggests a dramatic buildup that frames and highlights avaz as the premiere musical element. As discussed at the end of this chapter, musical style is predicated on feedback and reception from musical peers and the general audience and varies according to their varied tastes, depth of knowledge and musical expertise. Many listeners of Persian music find it too heavy going. Like Shakespeare to many English-speakers, they do not really understand the poetry (despite the relative stability of the Persian language compared to English through the past 800 years) or its musical rendition. For them the tasnif, along with the rhythmical *reng* and *chaharmezrab*, is much more catchy and accessible.

The text of a tasnif is usually not narrative but aims to sustain a mood or an emotional reaction to an event or situation (Caton 1983:21). The tasnif and *sorud* have always been the vehicle for mass appeal and were engaged for political discourse and mobilization in the twentieth century (though towards very different agendas) by 'Aref and the Pahlavi administrations. The heaviness, sophistication and concomitant exclusivity of avaz may have led the Gholamhossein Banan (counterintuitively, as he was a great master of avaz) to call for a focused cultivation of the tasnif. Shajarian has sung and become identified with some of the most emblematic, significant and politically charged tasnifs of the past decades—*Morghe Sahar*, *Sepideh* and more recently *Zabane Atesh*—and it is quite likely that his widespread fame among the majority of Iranians is more a result of these tasnifs than his avaz.

OS

[In the late Qajar period] the singers of avaz, singing in free rhythm, wouldn't lower themselves to singing a tasnif because they were considered to be creators and worked from a basis of improvisation. On the other hand, the singer of tasnif was incapable of singing avaz. (Kasmai and Lecomte 1991:251–52)

Interviewer: Ostad Banan used to say that we should expand on tasnifs and make more of them.

Yes, that's correct because in the older days there was more avaz and it was frowned upon to sing tasnifs. For example, the avaz singers looked down on the tasnif singers and they didn't approve of them. But the tasnif eventually found its own ground. The only tasnifs that they used to sing were ghazals on a particular rhythm but then later composers started to move beyond the borders of ghazal. 'Aref and Shayda actually started this—they weren't using ghazals but created songs and set poems to them. Later on, other important composers came along [composing tasnifs], from Hossein Yahaqi to Tajvidi and more contemporary ones. Then later still, we realized that the record labels were primarily interested in tasnifs, so again there was imbalance. If avaz disappears then all of our ghaz-als lose meaning as well, so there must be a fifty-fifty relationship of avaz and tasnif. That's why in all my works I always include both of them.[24]

Histories of Avaz and Sung Poetry

We don't really have any information about the history of avaz. Because history has to either be passed from "heart to heart" [oral transmission] or it must be written down or be recorded on tape or vinyl, so we cannot trace it back to more than 150 years. History has to be recorded on something that we can literally hold in our hands if we want to talk about it. However, in their present arrangement these radifs, dastgahs, and avazes date back to the middle of the Qajar period [mid- to late-nineteenth century]. At the same time that they are potentially ancient we have to realize that they are always subject to ongoing change. This music that we are presenting today, this avaz, certainly did not exist five hundred years ago, not in this arrangement. If, however, it existed, it was surely in a different format.

Actually, Mohammad Reza Darvishi [a prominent Iranian ethnomusicologist and composer] is now researching a music that existed in Abdolqader Maraghi's time [fourteenth/fifteenth century]. Darvishi found notations in present-day Turkey of the songs that Maraghi sang and you realize that it has very little to do with the Persian music of today. What is interesting is that Maraghi notated these songs but neglected to include rests for the singer to take a breath. So that's why I told Darvishi that this cannot be right. How can Maraghi notate something and ignore putting in any rests? A singer is not like an instrumentalist who is able to play continuously; he needs to take a breath at some point. But we don't even see a half-bar of rest for the singer. Therefore this project contains an error somewhere in it: either the interpretation of these transcriptions is incorrect or the person who originally notated it did something wrong and made a mistake; in any case, there is an error. Abdolghader Maraghi was a Hafez himself—the word Hafez being a title of honour for a singer. When they said Hafez Abdol Shafi' or Hafez Abdolqader Maraghi they were referring to a singer, it is not that he only played the 'oud. So these transcriptions are not exactly accurate and are not exactly what Maraghi had composed, but in any case we see that they are very different from what we sing today. The terms that we are now accustomed to—for example, the distribution of long and short syllables in appropriate rhythmic values—none have been considered in any of Maraghi's compositions. All of a sudden a note has been sustained for no reason and there is no clear function for the poetry. Each word in the poem functions as a vehicle for the music rather than the music clarifying the intentions of the poet. So I don't think the music that we have today goes back to more than three or four hundred years.

If we look at the history, we realize that Iran was a large empire. At the same time, art always develops in a place that is surrounded with courts of patronage, noblemen or emperors. In those days both Persian and the Roman empires existed and artists from different locations were attracted to those courts

*and music would be developed. The music that currently exists in Iran was
created from the many different peoples that were connected to Iran throughout
history. Therefore, this music is a collection of pieces obtained from different
places, since musicians always ended up settling around the courts. It was a
large empire and that is the reason why this music is very old, very methodical
and has a strong foundation. (2008)*

RS

When they are asked about the origins of their music, Iranian artists generally
give two apparently contradictory responses. First, they say that the *radīf* goes
back to 'Alī Akbar Farāhānī, the father of Mīrzā 'Abdollāh, who revived art
music around 1845 to 1860; the names of the masters active between the
seventeenth and early nineteenth centuries are unknown, and there is no
evidence that they played the same music. Second, while recognizing the lack
of evidence that the *radīf* is ancient, the vast majority of musicians are
convinced that, under a broader definition, the kind of Persian music they play
is directly traceable to an ancient past: through the Safavid era (sixteenth to
seventeenth century), 'Abdolqāder Marāghī (fourteenth to fifteenth century),
Ṣafī al-Dīn Urmavī (thirteenth century), and Fārābī (tenth century) all the way
to Bārbad (sixth century), the first great name of music that was wholly
Iranian, preceding the Islamic era. (During 2002:859)

While taking care not to indulge in the Orientalist and Traditionalist tendency to
privilege and authenticate traditions by constructing an exaggerated antiquity, it is
clear that the generic tradition of sung poetry in Iran and West Asia is very
ancient, indeed archetypal. The earliest historical sources that have survived from
Mesopotamia, China and later documents from India and Greece (where music
was explicated, conceptualized and debated by philosophers in unprecedented
detail) all show the integral relationship of poetry, drama and music. The point is
not to romanticize or exaggerate this legacy but rather to be conscious of
historical layers, their balance of continuity and change through time, allowing a
broader perspective for "zooming in and out" of the larger crosscultural context
and flow of the tradition. The following discussion will zoom out considerably,
differentiating the particular musical style and concomitant structures of
contemporary avaz from the activity of singing poetry. In complex systems
attractors are any point or region in the system's cycle that attracts the system
toward it, a point of magnetic appeal within the system: water swirling around
and down a drain is a common everyday illustration. The climate of a particular
region or an individual's personality exemplifies attractors in other domains and
on varied scales. Singing poetry is a pervasive attractor feeding back with West
Asian history and culture, subject to infinite variation and change throughout
time.

Like many neighbouring West Asian classical music traditions, Iranian sung
poetry has been crystallized into its contemporary form since the late-nineteenth
century. Due to the limitations of sources we cannot say if this style was

recognizable to artists and audiences before that time. Through the evidence of recordings we know that avaz subtly changed throughout the twentieth century through the work of individual artists and as a collective conception. And while it will continue to change through the twenty-first century, it is still clearly recognizable as an extension of the late-nineteenth century art form. If the Orientalist mandate was to buttress colonial control through dividing and conquering, the following discussion reflects more recent scholarly recognition and valorization of human connection, interdependence and post-colonial "sameness." Despite the stubbornly pervasive "old school," polarized discourse, Iran is not a selfcontained nation-state with a monolithic national identity but— like any other area or culture in our contemporary world—is rather part of an integrally linked, hybridized, mutually arising interaction of human and environmental orders. Its cultural borders are fuzzy and overlapping with those of neighboring cultures, including the West. To this end, I frame the following brief but broad historical sketch of sung poetry in terms of Eurasian music history.

Avestan and Vedic chant features liturgical poetry sung in melodic proto-modes and a flowing meter; documentation of the former represents the earliest concrete historical source of the practice of sung poetry in Iran (Miller 1999:108). Rgvedic chant held the distinction of being the oldest notated melodies in world history until the deciphering in the 1970s of cuniform tablets that turned out to be Hurrian hymns dating to 1800 BC. The historical roots of nonliturgical, sung poetry lie in ancient Mesopotamia: there is evidence that suggests the Sumerians may have practiced a form of vocal improvisation based on melodic modes and skeletal melodies (Koch 1980: 549–50; Volk 1994: 186–89). Sources are quite clear that Greek music in Hellenic times was based upon setting poetry to microtonal modes and preset melodic formulae (*nomoi*); the word "lyric" originally signified poetry sung to the accompaniment of the lyre. Such practices, like so many aspects of ancient Greek culture and knowledge, were likely adopted from Eastern sources. The implications of this early manifestation of "East meets West" extend to Zonis's contentious suggestion that contemporary Iranian music may be the closest surviving remnant of the ancient Greek tradition (1973:29–30). The oldest iconographic evidence of Iranian instruments highlights the triangular harp *chang*,[25] which was a popular instrument and regularly featured throughout western and central Asia until the middle of the sixteenth century (Farmer 1954: 679). In contrast to the loud outdoor instruments of the ancient Iranians (trumpets and large drums) the *chang* had an indoor courtly function (ibid.), probably accompanying sung poetry, some distant ancestor of modern avaz. Ancient Egyptian iconography regularly shows the harp accompanying singers, both solo and in small groups (Hickmann 1961). The harp also figures very prominently in ancient Mesopotamian iconography but its connection to singing, while highly likely, is less clearly evident (Rashid 1984).

We know that the Sassanids (third to seventh centuries) maintained a vital tradition of court music, with the famous musician Barbad[26] supposedly creating a cosmological-musical system with specific modes for each day of the year. An anonymous commentary on Safi al-Din's *Kitab Al-Adwar* written circa 1375[27] mentions how Barbad would improvise melody and words in a manner that would never be the same twice and would correspond exactly to the occasion and the mood of listeners at the moment (D'Erlanger 1938: 548),[28] which aligns with conceptions of modern avaz. While the reliability of this claim is quite questionable (some eight centuries later), it illustrates the creative reperformance of cultural themes and narratives through the centuries along with the blurring of history and mythology. The Sassanid tradition was decisively broken with the arrival of Islam in the seventh century, and there must have been a rich integration of Arab singing and modal practices. While we will never know "who took what from whom" and nationalists from both sides lay claim to provenance of the emerging culture (musical or otherwise), the exchange was likely two-way. Iranian musicians, who at the time implied individuals who were simultaneously poets, singers, and instrumentalists, were highly valued, in demand, and influential in courts throughout the early Muslim empire (Miller 1999:6). The most famous example is Ziryab (claimed by many to be an Iranian) of the ninth century, who left the Abbasid court in Baghdad and, according to the quasi-mythical narrative, subsequently founded the entire Andalusian art music tradition.[29] As sung poetry avaz also shares a heritage with the various bardic traditions that are an important and ancient genre in folk traditions throughout Iran, which both overlapped with, and functioned quite outside of, court cultures. Indeed, the radif has absorbed melodies from these traditions.

As discussed further below, recitation of the Qur'an, though emphatically *not* considered singing or music by many Muslims, nonetheless displays some striking relationships to avaz in terms of both structure and performance practice. Faruqi (1985: 457ff) has suggested that this reflection of the Qur'anic archetype in art and life is an aspect of divine unity (*tawhid*), and accords a particular prestige to avaz among the tonal arts of the Muslim world. The role of sung poetry, improvised and in free meter, is also found in the *samā'* ceremonies of many Sufi orders. While *samā'* regularly includes set hymns, *zikr* practices are often characterized by spontaneous recitations of memorized and/or improvised poetry. This recitational style can be heard in the field recordings of various Sufi orders throughout Asia and Africa. A soloist or succession of soloists improvise declamatory melodic lines, often highly elaborate and ornamented, over a group ostinato of a short *zikr* pattern featuring a short phrase, syllable or rhythmic breathing motif (During 1992a:279–81; 2006a:81). While there is no evidence to confirm that these styles of Sufi singing preserve an older practice, this does not discount the possibility. In sharp contrast to the secular circles that cultivated instrumental music, professional religious singers and Sufis were the key conduit for preserving and transmitting avaz into the modern period (Tabar 2005:46, During 2009:126, Musavi 2003).

The resilience, preservation and indeed flourishing of avaz through the tumultuous events of the twentieth century stands as a testament to the survival of music through other periods of general cultural decline, such as the Safavid and Qajar periods (sixteenth to early-twentieth century). The vital transmission lines of the tradition were in fact private and outside the regulatory sphere of the authorities, among Sufi brotherhoods and a closed circle of connoisseur artists. The pendulum of various authorities alternately tolerating and proscribing music repeatedly drove the transmission underground. This unwittingly helped preserve the music with more fidelity, sheltering it from the dynamics of change that characterize musical transmission in less repressive environments. Outside the paucity of Safavid sources, Demetrius Cantemir's famous treatise on Ottoman court music (written around 1700) notes that Persian musicians of the late-sixteenth century in Istanbul sang poetry in an nonmetrical fashion (known as *taksim* in Turkish) according to melodic formulae (*terkibs*) learned from their teachers (Feldman 1996: 285–87, 298), which bears interesting comparison to the contemporary practice of avaz based on the radif.

While recognizing the deep historical and archetypal roots of avaz as belonging to the generic category of sung poetry, we follow Ostad Shajarian's comments above that sources only allow us to objectively examine its musical style and structure with any accuracy from the mid-nineteenth century or perhaps even the early-twentieth century, when the first sound recordings were made.

Individuals and Groups

In the middle of no street in Baghdad, Konya, Esfahan or Tus can we seek, shake hands with, or have a cup of tea and a half-decent conversation with a chimerical construction, a figment of the essentialist Orientalist imagination, called "The Persian," "The Arab," "The Turk," "The Muslim." Individuals, individuals, i-n-d-i-v-i-d-u-a-l-s—these are the autonomous subjectivities that people and animate history. (Dabashi 1999:9)

OS
I am a singer, my instrument requires words. I have to choose words that say the same things that the composer is trying to achieve with his music. So I go and search in my poetry books and present the poems according to the way I have been influenced by them. The poems that I sing no longer belong to Hafez, or Sa'di or Mowlana! They are my words and my idea. I have borrowed them to say what I want to say; I speak the minds of the people with them. (Shajarian et al. 2004: 229)[30]

RS
Borrowing the neologism from the polymath writer Arthur Koestler,[31] philosopher Ken Wilber uses the terms "holon" and "holarchy" to describe how everything in the cosmos functions simultaneously as both a whole and a part, where wholes transcend but include parts in an endless series of nests: "contexts within contexts forever" (Wilber 1997:78). Any holon consists of individual and collective qualities in

addition to interior and exterior dimensions. Where hierarchy implies power from top down, wholes and parts mutually arise in a holarchy wherein both are equally honored and valued. Atoms are parts of molecules, which are parts of cells, which are parts of organs, which are parts of individual humans, who are part of families, clans, communities, and endless other larger groupings—the larger groupings are predicated upon the smaller parts but also transcend them, functioning as different entities. Each entity at a particular holonic level is a complex system in and of itself that entrains with other entities at the same level to constitute the larger holon. Chaotics teaches us that small things, small beginnings can have an immense impact in a complex system and the nonlinear reality we inhabit.

Musicians are individuals who function within a local community of musicians, who form a larger subculture of musicians within a tradition, who are in turn part of a larger society that constitutes their audience. Individual musicians feed back with their peers by listening to them play in concerts and on recordings, studying and socializing with them, and performing together. This is the most immediate "street level" of two-way communication between "neighbors" that spontaneously drives through a culture, initiating a web of links that self-organizes into order on its global levels. These performances feed back with the wider audience of the larger society, be that on an intimately local level or wider. When first learning, musicians take from others with more experience, but with sufficient effort and talent, they may eventually have something to offer others in the endless rhythms of complex feedback that make up a musical culture (cf., During 1994:73). Shajarian went through this very process and took an exceptionally wide swath of influences and programming from the tradition of twentieth-century Persian music, brilliantly crafting these into a personal style that is paradoxically original and yet deeply encoded with the "artistic DNA" of his predecessors, whose stylings he includes but transcends. His music can be viewed fruitfully from the perspective as both an individual and as a representative of the avaz tradition; the tradition is not some anthropological abstraction but the group of individual singers who preceded him and who caught his interest. From this perspective, tradition equates to individuals and groups of individuals.

In spite of our common physiology and DNA, individual humans are unique, unrepeatable, and endlessly varied; even identical twins are different. Among other domains of life, individual personalities play a key role in the maintenance and enrichment of a musical (or any other artistic) tradition, which is not a monolithic, unanimous entity but rather a sum of these multiple points of view. Aside from the natural gifts we may or may not receive and how this feeds back into our personal musical identities, once basic competence has been attained musicians must position themselves in relation to the tradition they have inherited and from which they emerged. In a great number of musical cultures there exists a continuum of personal aesthetic orientations ranging from being a conservative and preserving the tradition on one extreme, to a middle position of being more progressive and renovating[32] the tradition to varying degrees, to a polar extreme of being a radical and transgressing the boundaries of the tradition (cf. Markoff 1986: 158–162). Where musicians situate themselves depends a great deal upon their individual personalities, dispositions, taste and their particular musical gifts (or lack thereof). Positioning is dynamic and some musicians shift to different locations throughout their creative lives. As we will discuss shortly below, social feedback between the individual and the group—of both other musicians and the audience at large—also plays a significant role in shaping the individual's positioning on the continuum. Indeed, bumping matters up a holonic level, groups of musicians collectively make similar decisions based on shared values, self-organizing into cliques and subgenres within the tradition. Simultaneous activity and subgenres existing simultaneously across the entire aesthetic continuum, with its inherently fuzzy borders and gradations, is a sign of the tradition's vitality. Despite the inherent tension in this, we need activity in all quarters, on all wavelengths as the tradition spontaneously updates itself to new historical conditions. While the following discussion tends to emphasize the individual quadrant of the music culture holon, it does not deny the significance of the collective: indeed, it is their mutually arising nature that is underscored throughout.

Tellers: The Power of Individuals as Mythmakers and Myths

Tehranian (2004: 200) notes that Iranians are collectively characterized by a "rugged individualism" along with a negative attitude toward compromise (*sazesh*) that harkens back to the archetypal figure of the *rend*—the spiritually enlightened, fearless, unpredictable nonconformist who follows their own path as opposed to those of the traditional Sufi *tariqah*s. The *rend* can be viewed as representing the archetype of the trickster, the ambiguous purveyor of both chaos and deep insight, or the closely related vocation and function of the shaman. The most emblematic *rend* figures endeared within Iranian collective consciousness include the lowbrow mythical figure of Mullah Nasreddin and the highbrow Hafez. Shajarian frequently chooses poems that contain references to the *rend* and entitled his 2009 album *Rendan e Mast/Drunken Rends*. Discussed further in chapter 2 regarding Sufism, the point here is their independent, nonaligned source of enlightenment, analogous to the notion of *jiriki* ("self power") in Zen attainment. Zonis observed during the height of Mohammad Reza Shah's rule that for Iranians "values of individuality are prized over and above collective thinking and . . . artistic independence is the chief merit of artistic performance" (1973:63). Nettl similarly characterized performance aesthetics of the period as hinging on a tasteful balance of surprise and expectation, the assertion of individual expression within the canonical language of the radif (1992[33]:241–42, 248ff.; 1974:411), also noting the paradox of Iranian authoritarianism in view of this valorisation of individuality and surprise, which may signify or assert high social standing (ibid.: 252, 1983: 139).

Despite the best efforts of Western media to spin us images of monolithic "Muslim masses," it is indeed gifted individuals who hold the greatest potential for social change, artistic influence, and political power. This is particularly true for the role of the tellers in the various narrative performative genres outlined above, who are given the social responsibility to retell myths with all the spin they see fit to impart. In Iran and elsewhere certain gifted tellers have gained renown and fame throughout history whereby they become very much larger than themselves, ascending from their local circle of activity and influence to a massively extended audience and sociohistorical impact. Powerfully entraining a large audience, their works become central points of reference, obtaining massive social cache and legendary status, canonic attractors that feed back into society spawning myriad variants by others. Their role as individual messengers itself becomes mythologized by their mass of devotees, who rightly or wrongly project their dreams, ideals, and desires upon these new heroes—their Barbads, Rumis, Beethovens and Coltranes, Um Kulthums and Shajarians—resulting from both a sincere appreciation of the hero's work and an unconscious effort to assuage their own existential fears and insecurities. These heroes are mythmakers in a dual sense: they create legendary works of art and then their very lives as individuals slip into legendary status, often fulfilling an archetypal role from the mythological realm (Apollonian, *rendi*, tragic, triumphant, etc).

The sacred history of the martyrdom of the Prophet Mohammad's grandson Hussein has long been the central narrative of Iranian culture (discussed further in chapter 2), but it now must compete with the relatively recent influx of Western icons and their narratives via the electronic media of globalization: the neobardic[34] tradition of Hollywood and New York with its culture (cult?) of crass celebrity. These media comprise a potent force for constructing contemporary mythologies that seem to take on a quasi-religious function for voracious global consumers. Perhaps these tendencies are simply the contemporary manifestation and devaluation of the archetype of the hero in wealthy, hypermediated consumer cultures rife with narcissism, existential angst, and alienation (Niedzviecki 2006, 2009: 266ff.; Postman 1986; Hedges 2009, Becker 1973). Until fairly recent times one had to actually accomplish something significant—conquer a good portion of a continent or create a large body of brilliant work—in order to be accorded fame (Braudy 1986).

Of course, amidst the vacuity of contemporary celebrity culture (wherein people can simply "be famous for being famous") there are talented individuals who unquestionably accomplish truly great things, artists and activists who inspire us by demonstrating the loftiest, noblest potential of humanity. Most of these individuals are not members of the show biz pantheon, dodging paparazzi as they strut around Los Angeles performing their celebrity. In the world of music, many are only renowned within a narrower regional or national demographic. Among these famed musicians, it is inevitably their unique individuality that empowers them artistically and socially. Indeed, as an index of their individuality we may note that they are frequently, to varying degrees, autodidacts. Shajarian's autodidactic tendencies clearly emerge in the following chapters. Some of these influential artists are restless iconoclasts or border-stretchers who face severe criticism before being recognized as brilliant innovators or even geniuses (while often remaining reviled by purists), such as Ornette Coleman or Paco de Lucia. Some are renovators who crystallize, update and reinvigorate the spirit of a tradition—Charlie Parker, Nusrat Fateh Ali Khān,[35] and Mohammad Gubanchi come to mind. Still others follow this latter path but orbit closer to the border of preservation within the aesthetic continuum, bringing an unmatched state of focus, inspiration and perfection to their art. Ostad Shajarian fits this latter description, as would Um Kulthum and Ali Akbar Khān in his prime years.

In all of the cases of this random sampling, it is the powerful individual vision, expression and talent of the artist (along with a requisite measure of personal ambition and good luck) that account for their rise through the professional ranks to achieving iconic status in their respective fields. Both their work and their public persona become legendary. Ostad Shajarian is a celebrity in Iran and the diaspora, his standing is predicated on his prodigious musical gifts and a range of other highly refined and admirable associations, including courageously confronting the injustice of the government of the Islamic Republic.[36] As a living legend he is also uncontrollably subject to the concomitant projections of the collective hopes and ideals of Iranians.

Schools/*Maktab*s of Avaz and Influential Individuals

Traditions are comprised of individuals and groups of individuals, and as we noted above, one layer of groupings is based on a shared personal aesthetic orientation. Many musicians and connoisseurs speak about the existence of four or five separate schools (*maktab*) of avaz in the twentieth century based on style, transmission and repertoire. Considerable debate surrounds the defining features, affiliated masters, and even the existence of these schools. While calling for a systematic and objective study to counter the vague and partisan discourse fueling these contentions, record producer Mohammad Musavi notes that three schools are generally posited: the Esfahan *maktab*, supposedly the most prestigious with its own brand of tahrirs, concern for the appropriate alignment of poetry and music, and clear articulation of the text; the Tehran *maktab* with its emphasis on the radif; and the Tabriz *maktab* with its elaborate melismatic style (Musavi 2003). Massoudieh lists the existence of four *maktab*s without elaborating on their definitve features: Qazvin, Shiraz, Esfahan, and Tehran (1985: 16).

OS
What is left of those *maktab*s, for example in Tehran, Esfahan, etc.?
There is no basis for them. People want to judge out of thin air and prove it, as if they know something, and often they know nothing about anything. So they have said that there is a Khorasan maktab, *an Esfahan* maktab *and a Tabriz* maktab. *Tabriz has no* maktab *in our avaz. They want to link Tabriz to Eqbal Sultan but he was from Qazvin, which is located near Tehran. He was a student of Jenab*

Qazvini, the style that he followed and sang very well was the style of Ahmad Khān Saberi—therefore Tabriz has no school of its own in our music. There isn't a trace left of the Khorasan maktab. *The Esfahan* maktab *on the other hand has something of its own but it is only a style, not a school.*[37]
Question: So is it individualistic?
Yes, of course. You see, wherever the dynasty and the courts of men were located, that was the place that music subsisted. When it was in Khorasan, everyone was in Khorasan. When it was in Baghdad everyone was in Baghdad, when it was in Shiraz everyone was around Shiraz. Then in the Safavid period [1501–1779] the court was positioned in Esfahan. Now, the reason they say there is a school of Esfahan is because Esfahan was the final place that the court was situated before it was relocated to Tehran. Esfahan was the capital and the place that the king stayed. It still has that grandeur attached to it, not because of the city of Esfahan itself but rather because of the people from diverse places who went to Esfahan. (2008)

RS

Whereas Iranian instrumental music showed increasing influence of Western aesthetics and techniques leading up to the revolution, avaz remained remarkably insulated from the same, presumably due to its integral relationship with classical poetry. And while all musicians are subject to their individual taste and placement within the personal aesthetic continuum, the best vocalists tended to come from the subculture of religious singers who naturally had conservative orientations. The following discussion offers some brief comments regarding the styles of some important public exponents of avaz, notably those who left recordings. Shajarian made a thorough study of the recordings of most of these masters, took what he liked from each of them and integrated them into his own style (we will review some of his specific influences in more detail in chapter 3), which is at once both original and a brilliant consolidation of this rich and diverse legacy.

A distinction should also be made between private and public contexts of performing avaz. There are many low-profile masters who remain amateurs in the sense that they do not derive their livelihood from public performance but are nonetheless gifted artists and integral to the tradition (see During 1996 for a detailed view of one such "alternative scene"). In contrast to Western sensibilities, such musical expertise devoid of professional accomplishment and standing is considered prestigious among Iranians. Although all singers share a style that is unmistakably Iranian due to the transpersonal quality of the radif, one marvels at the range and variety of their personal characteristics and preferences as representatives of the art. It is interesting to note that students studying under the same master could have quite different styles, such as the case with Taj Esfahan and Adib Khansari, who were both students of Seyyed Rahim. The three-CD set *A Century of Avaz*[38] presents an excellent chronological survey of representative recordings from thirty-two important twentieth-century masters, ending with Shajarian. Shajarian is a great collector and connoisseur of avaz recordings and was consulted by the producers of this anthology, which they in turn dedicate to him.

The main criteria for describing the style of these masters—which generally corresponds to qualities attributed to various *maktab*s—are vocal tone, delivery and evocation of text, approach to tahrirs, quality of *tekye* (a glottal appoggiatura ornament), and approach to the radif. Musavi (2003) notes that singers in the first two decades of the twentieth century had a style that differed greatly from those who followed, associating the latter style with radio broadcasting. These differences are at least partially the result of the corresponding technologies of acoustic recording versus the introduction of the electronic microphone. The older style featured a brighter vocal tone in a high tessitura,[39] a wide variety of tahrirs and an approach that supposedly regarded the voice to function more like a musical instrument. The "radio style" is marked by a softer vocal tone in a lower tessitura, a preference for melismata to occur in this lower register, a decrease in the diversity of tahrirs, and the inclusion of more lines of poetry. Liner notes to the CD *Flowers of Persian Song and Music: The Gulha Programmes*[40] differentiate these two styles as Qajar and Pahlavi respectively, which, however labeled, reflect a larger dynamic of tradition and modernism in Iranian culture (discussed below).

If one accepts Musavi's view, it is ironic that while instrumental music took on more stylistic features of Western music throughout the century, changes in avaz, in part due to Western technology, were a move away from previous instrumental approaches to one more idiomatically vocal and logocentric. The relationship between avaz and instrumental music is one of chicken and egg. As the radif was transmitted largely through the tar and setar lineage of the Farahanis, it is not unreasonable to assume, based on the evidence of the extant recordings, that singers were following the plucked-lute idiom that was responsible for defining and consolidating the style of Persian music in the early-twentieth century. We have no way of knowing what avaz sounded like before this time but it is equally likely that instruments were following vocal idioms in early periods, as is common in modal traditions throughout Asia.

The earliest recordings of avaz were made in Tblisi, Georgia in the first decade of the twentieth century. The following comments are based solely on the recordings they left, which may not have necessarily reflected all aspects of their style. The dates of birth and death of many of the earliest singers are unknown. Mirza Seyyed Ahmad Khān was an outstanding singer from this period; his singing featured a wide range in terms of tessitura and tone quality, a variety of tahrirs, and extensive use of vocables (syllables devoid of semantic content). Qorban Khān had an extroverted style with intense, penetrating tone, and executed lengthy tahrirs, while Qoli Khān was more restrained and stately, featuring a relaxed tone with relatively brief tahrirs. Aqa Hossein Ta'ziyeh Khān recorded tasnifs that were prefaced by short sections of avaz; he sang in a very high tessitura with a bright tone, biting *tekye*, and characteristically short phrases.

Shajarian was introduced to a recording of Seyyed Rahim over the phone by Hossein Omumi Sr., and was immediately impressed and obsessed with obtaining a copy (Hossein Omumi Sr., personal communication, 1995). Seyyed Rahim was the master of several important singers, including Seyyed Zia Rasa'i, Hossein Taherzadeh (1882–1955), Taj Esfahani (1903–1981) and Adib Khansari (1901–1982). Taherzadeh, considered by many to be the most important singer of the twentieth century, sang in a high tessitura with flawless technique and employed a light *tekye* in concise tahrirs. His style was refined, dignified, somewhat conservative and emotionally reserved compared to other great vocalists. Taj Esfahani had an extroverted style, featuring a broad, powerful tone and brilliant, aggressive tahrirs; as mentioned above, he was a renowned *monāsebat khan* whose spontaneous choices of poetry and music were greatly appreciated at Sufi *khanegah*s. Adib Khānsari sang in a comparatively lower register with a full but loose and relaxed tone, and preferred a light *tekye*.

Iqbal Sultan (a.k.a. Eqbal Azar [1866–1971]), whose early formation included singing in *ta'ziyeh*, was renowned for his knowledge of the radif and a highly emotional style. His voice had an attractive roughness (a quality appreciated in blues and flamenco singing), particularly evident in his assertive execution of *tekye*. He coupled with this a vigorous, exciting style of delivery that was still evident in recordings made after reaching 100 years of age. Iqbal's star pupil was Reza Qoli Mirza Zelli (1906–1945), who shared his teacher's emotional intensity in addition to possessing considerable natural gifts in terms of technical precision, a powerful, bright tone, and brilliant, flowing tahrirs. Of all previous singers, an important facet of Shajarian's wide-ranging style reflects Zelli's vocal tone and tahrirs.

There are many significant singers from what may be considered the second generation of the recording era, i.e., artists born in the first decade of the twentieth century. Abdollah Davami's student Gholamhossein Banan (1911–1985) stands out for his gentle, warm elegance and sensitivity, and the great care he took in the pronunciation and musical evocation of the text; while frequently mellow and understated on the surface, there is always an emotional intensity bubbling underneath his singing. Hossein Qavami (1909–1988), whose recordings were included on well-known anthologies of Persian music available in the West during the 1960s and 70s, likewise featured an attractive understated style with a relaxed, warm tone and fastidiously clear pronunciation. His tahrirs were judiciously placed and restrained, and he made a dramatic use of pauses in his phrasing and pacing.

The most influential female singer from this period was Qamarolmoluk Vaziri (1905–1959), whose penetrating vocal tone, electrifying tahrirs, and emotional engagement combine to make a style unrivalled in its unrelenting intensity. Ruh Angiz (1904–1984) is another fine female singer from this generation whose voice is characterized by a penetrating tone, agile tahrirs, and occasional exploration of her low register. The role of female singers, musicians and poets in Persian music will be discussed in chapter 3.

Musical Tradition

A tradition may be viewed as an aggregate of characteristic qualities and tendencies, an attractor transposed to the level of the culture holon, a larger scaling of what a personality is to an individual. While personalities can be divided, this analogy is exponentially complicated by the great number and variety of individuals who maintain and perform the tradition in the present and through history (retained in the collective memory). Depending on the cultural domain of the particular tradition and the orientation of those involved in it, a tradition can have a predominantly "top-down" dynamic, functioning as an archetypal, quasi-Platonic Form that directs activity below it with regard to local practices, materials, and behaviors. Religious traditions are usually based on a revelation that is scrupulously followed and, while its manifestations will vary in maintenance and interpretation, the tradition itself is resistant to change. Conservatives frequently adhere to this dynamic across other cultural domains, including the artistic. But art is more often characterized by a strong "bottom-up" dynamic where individual and local activity self-organizes order on a higher collective level. Musical traditions are a whole resulting from the dialectic synergy of these opposing dynamics, a feedback loop of programming from above and propelling and updating from below. "The oral singer illustrates the extremest form of the individual talent at the service of the tradition, also perhaps the extremest form of the tradition at the service of the individual talent. The two are simply aspects of the same entity. Without songs [*or individuals performing and re-animating avaz*] the tradition would die; without the tradition, there would be no songs" (Scholes et al. 2006:24, insertion mine).

Reflecting a Taoist perspective, the philosopher Alan Watts often described the general situation in terms of spontaneously organic and emergent human behavior (nature in general) interacting with a superimposed "grid" of culture, institutions and tradition[41]—of seeming chaos and an attempt at imposing order, a mechanism over-laying an organism. One refers to what people say things are and the other to what they really are. The resulting dance between the two results in ever shifting borders, (laws, customs, controls and ideology) to contain and direct spontaneous human and environmental activity. The grid denies the quirks, ambiguities, and changing of the "growth," ironing out its wrinkles and wiggles with straight lines. The growth is thus greatly influenced by the grid, as a plant is to its container and surroundings, but over the long haul, the former drives and ultimately outlasts the latter: it leads the dance. *Iham* functions as a lubricant to the inherent friction involved in the dance. Any view of tradition must take into account both the growth and the grids. One needs to look no further than the plethora of musical categories, subcategories and genre fragmen-tation that arose in Iran (see During 1994:37–52) and guided censorship for a clear illustration. Here, as elsewhere in the world, such categorization usually has "more to do with ideology, politics and economic power than with the formal qualities of the music" (Schechner 2006:38).

In European languages the word tradition derives from a root that means "to deliver, to hand down," implying both an activity and an object. Persian designations for tradition are Arab-derived words that carry more decidedly narrative and performative implications: *rivāyat* ("narrative"), *asar* ("an effect, trace, mark"), *khabar* ("news, information, to announce"), *hadith* ("discourse"), *naql* ("to transfer, narrate"). Tradition is the tale along with the protocols and routines for telling it on the level of the culture holon. In artistic traditions the tale can be understood as a script but it is more often, more accurately like a scenario (Diana Taylor 2003:28ff.), designed for flexibile, varied engagement, a platform for performance. Layers of performance follow from the scenario: performing one's general personal aesthetic, one's rank among peers, performing for the occasion, or performing one's artistic personality through the reiteration of specific traditional materials (narratives, motifs, theatrical roles, etc.). While there is always "something" being done, the emphasis is on the doing.

In Persian music the radif functions as the principle attractor or fulcrum of the tradition. Based on individual and subgroup attitudes, it may be reified into a static, closed, top-down artifact or regarded as simply something you do and redo, involving essential bottom-up contributions. When performed it can be approached as a set script or an open, flexible scenario, a vehicle for creative activity; both in his work and his interviews, Shajarian clearly identifies with the latter position.[42]

Signifying at once *adab*, Persian music and the radif, avaz is regarded by contemporary Iranians as a prestigious emblem of tradition and identity. As a globetrotting, hypermediated, top-selling celebrity whose fame is based on singing medieval Persian poetry in the conservative musical style and language of the radif, Shajarian aptly embodies the tensions and paradox emanating from the superimposition of tradition and modernity in contemporary Iranian culture. Growing up in a very traditional and religious milieu during a period of government-engineered modernization, Shajarian's life, work and subsequent fame offer a richly informative case study illustrating the complex interrelationship of these conceptual poles, which permeate virtually all aspects of Iranian culture in the twentieth century and figure prominently throughout the present study. This is an immensely important and complex topic, the myriad strands of which run throughout a large portion of During's encyclopedic writings on Persian music (especially 1988, 1989a, 1994, 2005, 2009), including a major monograph devoted exclusively to it (1994); Nettl also devotes considerable attention to this issue (e.g., 1970, 1978, 1985, 1992). Readers interested in obtaining a more complete and nuanced treatment of this central theme should consult these works.[43]

The Constructions of Cultural Purity, East-West, and Tradition-Modernity

(T)he world of humankind constitutes a manifold, a totality of interconnected processes, and inquiries that disassemble this totality into bits and then fail to reassemble it falsify reality. Concepts like "nation," "society," and "culture" name bits and threaten to turn names into things. Only by understanding these names as bundles of relationships, and by placing them back into the field from which they were abstracted, can we hope to avoid misleading inferences and increase our share of understanding. (Wolf 1997:3)

All cultural practices everywhere—from religion and the arts to cooking, dress, and language—are hybrids. Cultural purity is a dangerous fiction because it leads to a kind of policing that results in apparent monoculture and actual racism, jingoism, and xenophobia. The "natural" proclivity of humankind is promiscuity—which results in an always changing, if sometimes unsettling, diversity. (Schechner 2006:322)

There is only one history: world history. There is only one story: the human story. (Weatherford 2010:ix)

Cultural purity is an oxymoron. (Appiah 2006:112–13).

The above quotes are representative of a large contingent of contemporary scholars from a wide range of fields that emerged with a concerted critique of the deep-seated binary oppositions of "East and West" and "tradition and modernity." They regard these oppositions as false though still highly operational constructions that function to implement and sustain imperialist power and ideology. Anyone who makes the effort to connect objectively the historical dots will see that the "East" (or any cultural Other) and the "West" mutually arose and are not the self-contained, independent entities promulgated through various scholarly and cultural discourses that we have inherited and comfortably accept.[44] From the Eastern side of the mutually arising relationship, the impetus toward modernization was understandably predicated on the challenge posed by Western military superiority, which by the nineteenth century was consistently and unequivocally demonstrated.

Despite the realization of several late-nineteenth century Iranian reformers that modernization did not equate to Westernization, that an "indigenous solution" engendering "progress" while retaining cultural traditions was both possible and necessary (Ringer 2000), the vast majority of stakeholders viewed the categories as an either/or dualism. Like most cultures, however, the reality of contemporary Iran flies in the face of this false dichotomy to reveal a complex, ever-emergent hybridization. But Western global dominance is such that many of "the Rest" were successfully co-opted to reinforce these binary categories from the "other side,"[45] declaring their own local brands of the same. In late-twentieth century Iran this "internal colonialism" manifests, among other things, as the construction of Western linear materialism versus Eastern nonlinear spirituality (Mohaved 2003:107) or as a fundamentalist anti-modernism/anti-Westernism, a position further entrenched in the aftermath of the Islamic Revolution. In response to the relentless onslaughts of colonial intervention—candidly named "The Great Game" in the nineteenth century—and postcolonial globalization over the past two centuries, many Iranians have naturally taken refuge in an idealized past and various invented traditions surrounding it.[46] Indeed, the radif itself may well be a prime example of such an invention, which among other things furthered the modernist agenda of nationalism. Tradition and modernity are here enfolded upon one another in an integral, inseparable relationship—it is not either/or but both, not a binary opposition but a dyad. Working in tandem with the constructed accumulation of invented tradition is the selective exclusion of facts and histories that might challenge these status quo constructions, as identified and acknowledged by the poet Mehdi Akhavan Salis's "stories vanished from memory" (*qesse-hā-ye rafte az yād*) (Tavakoli-Targhi 2004: 136).

To further complicate matters, in accepting the Traditional-Modern opposition, Iranians were often unclear or very selective as to what modernity meant (Ringer 2000; Behnam 2004:5–11; During 1994:13). Likewise, calls for a "return to tradition" (paradoxically reflecting the modernist stance being protested) were equally unclear as to what exactly constituted tradition but often centered on some form of cultural romanticism, such as an impossibile "returning to the village" and concomitant "technophobia" (Jahanbegloo 2004: xi; Behnam 2004:6). For many artists of Persian music, the "heart of the tradition" is clearly defined by the radif, oral transmission, and the presence of *hāl* with its concomitant dependency on the correct intonation of definitively Iranian intervals (During 2002:854ff.).[47] Even in the restricted domain of Persian music, exactly how an undeniably new musical style and canon arising in the late-nineteenth century is connected to earlier historical practices is quite problematic (During 2002:853, 859), and one senses a nationalistic urgency and constructed purity attached to the notion of Iranian intervals as conceived by some musicians.[48]

Among these and other confusions, adoption of the pervasive dichotomization gave rise to the volatile love-hate relationship with the "West/Modernity" that characterizes Iranian culture through the late-nineteenth century to the present. A yearning and long-thwarted struggle toward democracy, a sincere admiration of Western art of all sorts, and an enthusiastic embracing of popular technology (especially the Internet in recent years) exists alongside a deep—and historically well-founded— suspicion of Western imperialist agendas, and contempt for its social decadence, both real and perceived. The negative pole of the equation received support from various quarters of society in the latter half of the twentieth century, from intellectuals decrying "Westoxification" throughout the 1960s and 1970s to the fundamentalist, radical policies of the postrevolutionary government. The complex history of public music education in Iran outlined in chapter 3 becomes more intelligible when viewed as a tug-of-war between three factions: those who wanted Westernization, those who wanted to preserve traditional music, and those who didn't want music at all.

The Shiraz Arts Festival was a recurring, tangible embodiment and lightning rod of polarized traditional-modern/East-West values in Iran. Harkening back to the great World Expositions of the late-ninteenth and early-twentieth century (and almost twenty years before Peter Gabriel's WOMAD), the programming between 1967 and 1970 included Indian sitarist Ustad Vilayat Khan, American violinist Yehudi Menuhin, numerous Persian classical musicians and artists, a Balinese gamelan ensemble, the Senegalese National Ballet, and performances of the Persian passion play *ta'ziyeh*. Shajarian performed regularly at the festival and recorded two of his live albums there.[49]

A more accurate view of the dilemma is promulgated by many contemporary Iranian intellectuals whereby the false dichotomies of East-West and tradition-modernity are reassessed, their debilitating either/or straitjackets rejected,[50] and their integral hybridity acknowledged (Jahanbegloo 2004:xiii). Accordingly, echoing late-nineteenth century critics such as Abd al-Rahim Talebof, Behnam states that for Iranians the challenge and "aim is to become competent to live in the contemporary world, and live with contemporary peoples, while maintaining cultural identity" (2004:14)—a view consistent with Shajarian's life work. Clearly, the definitions and dynamics surrounding the dichotomization are unstable and shift considerably throughout the period, as detailed in the chronological discussion throughout this study. Nooshin describes the constructed binaries in terms of a broader dynamic of "belonging," with an inward-looking disposition in contrast to "not belonging," with an outward orientation, but which has now collapsed and become exponentially complicated through global integration (2009:13, 19–21). Of course, one can have a strong sense of belonging to a culture and be both inward and outward looking, as Shajarian and many others have elegantly illustrated. Likewise, outward-looking non-Iranians may now identify and "belong" to the culture of avaz in a limited way, though there is a significant language barrier, resulting in a major qualitative difference.

Tradition and Change, Peer Review and Feedback, Art and Craft

> "Everyone who has come here has built a new structure; each departed,
>   turning over his dwelling to another;
> And that one also had desires and whims, but no one has completed this structure."
> —Sa'di (prologue to *Golestan*)

OS
Question: What motivates you to do traditional music and at the same time innovate new ways of approaching the same material?

We must first differentiate between two facts: one is the traditional music, which is not capable of change. Tradition is always stable and it does not change. When they talk about tradition, they talk about a certain habit that was shaped at a certain time for everyone and people have accepted it, and they will always repeat it. You cannot change it in a big way because then it would be damaging your tradition and, logically, you should never damage any tradition.

The other is the authentic (asil) *music of Iran. I have tried to follow a music that had a true connection to the roots* (nezhadehgi va esalat)—*in other words it was purely Iranian with all its characteristics and potential for development— and avoided following just one strand of the tradition. For example, Mr. Lotfi only likes to perform the traditional music of the Qajar period, or Majid Kiani, who is more dogmatic and only wants to perform the traditional music—that doesn't really have any followers. I am strongly opposed to this approach. I believe that music transforms with the needs of society; when society changes, its tradition also changes and evolves into a new tradition. Then after another fifteen or twenty years, when society changes again, the music also changes and all its traditions change with it. These traditions all exist but they all belong to a certain time, just like history. This is the way I look at traditional music. I know the traditional music and sometimes only perform that, but in general I like to create something new in each work that is in sync with the needs of society and to some extent with the needs of the youth—but not in a way that completely changes the shape of our music.*

Do you have more plans regarding further innovation in avaz?

I don't have a specific plan that, for example, I must create a specific music by a certain time. However, since I am always dealing and working with this music and have my eyes open to the needs of people, and am at the same time listening to other kinds of music and forms of technique and recognize that my listeners have also heard those kinds of music, I have accepted those expressions. These are the reasons why I use whatever forms I can to mix with the music while at the same time being careful to not hurt its fundamental roots. (2008)

(In response to observations regarding the Persian-Canadian genres of fusion music flourishing in Vancouver):

It's important to mix music—provided you do it in the right way—because it brings people together. (Ditmars 2009:65)

Human beings in this era have no desire to be bound by the impediments of tradition. We are eager to leave the cage. A free soul wants to fly out of this cage. We are prisoners of these boundaries of tradition, and this impedes our ability to fly. I believe we should break free of this cage and fly towards completion and fulfillment. Tradition isn't complete or perfect (kāmel). *It's like attempting to climb Mount Everest. On the way, there are rest shelters* (panāh gah). *Traditions resemble the stations on the path. If we stop at these stations indefinitely, we won't be able to reach the mountain summit. We must progressively leave each station for another until we reach the final goal, the mountain summit. The same challenge will be true of artistic endeavor. Most teachers believe in traditions, and students are constantly trying to break those traditions. But we also realize that these breaks in tradition don't always take a positive direction. It's possible that these go in a negative direction and make things worse. Not all breaks are good. Sometimes they're destructive and not the right approach for making good music* (Shajarian et al. 2004:263).

Be rooted (asil), *not traditional* (sonnati).[51]

RS

Some instructive interpolations follow from Shajarian's wonderful alpine simile. These camps function for rest but, more importantly, for the climbers to acclimatize to the rarified atmosphere of the altitude, signifying that periods of organic adjustment, evolutionary gradations, are required and one cannot just blast up to the top—change must proceed at a natural, gradual pace. Cultures likewise need time to digest and assimilate. Change often requires growth in some capacity, and in the imagery under consideration here cultural and artistic pioneers lead the way beyond usual limits. Clearly, the number of people able to realistically fulfill this function is quite limited. While initially only few have what it takes to be able to push these boundaries, their very accomplishment inspires others to follow and set a standard whereby the higher altitude can be regarded collectively as being less daunting. Climbing Everest was a major achievement in 1953 but is now routinized into a consumer-driven, "adventure tourism" niche market wherein dozens of people summit (and resummit) every year. Anyone with the interest and sixty thousand dollars can get guided to the top. Everest base camp is apparently a busy, crowded tourist trap in its own unique way. And there are always detractors, notably the local Buddhist monks in this case, who maintain that people are not meant to go that high, that we must accept natural limits and that mountaineering endeavours are symptomatic of an unnatural and unhealthy inflation of the ego. Likewise, for musical conservatives the radical innovation of traditional forms is an unnecessary, negative extension of egotistical ingenuity. Why the restless push onward and upward when the point of the music is to find inner balance and integration? In addition to this division some climbers acclimatize quickly and want to move on while others have simply not adjusted to the new altitude and need more time, creating another schism in the group. We will look at concrete illustrations of these points throughout twentieth-century Iranian history throughout this study.

A pervasive characteristic projected upon our default concept of tradition is that it is static, stubbornly unchanging, a view shared by Ostad Shajarian. However, scholars from various disciplines—including anthropologists and international development advocates working directly with traditional communities in the field—note to the contrary that these cultures are also in a flux, constantly updating to accommodate changing social and environmental conditions (e.g., Tucker 1996, 1999; Norberg-Hodge 1992; Sardar 2004). Postmodern critical and historical insights presented their own challenges to the concept of tradition, most significantly that there is no "authentic," "original" or "pure" tradition to begin with but rather imagined ideals along with their concomitant constructions and inventions. The advent of recording technology, and the recent accessibility of a vast range of digitally restored early twentieth-century recordings from around the globe provide objective historical evidence of stylistic change in the vast majority of cases over a relative short, albeit unprecedentedly tumultuous, period of time. Shajarian is Iran's premiere recording artist and we will discuss the profound and paradoxical effects of recording technology on Persian music in chapter 3.

Traditions are comprised of individuals, regardless of whether or not their names are remembered: one line of thinking only half-jokingly maintains that "traditional" is simply the default designation when the names of composers for particular pieces are forgotten. With regard to their agency for change in tradition, the contributions of individual musicians—who may be provoked by changes in the environment or institutional support—add a nonlinear, chaotic element that implements change in a tradition. Periods of stasis, even atrophy, alternate with those of dynamic change; as During notes, large changes are often the cumulative effect of a long series of small changes (1994:80). A major change in the state of a complex system is known as a phase transition, such as water freezing at zero degrees Celsius and boiling at 100 degrees. The formulation of the radif represents such a phase transition in Persian music. We have no idea regarding the back story of the formulation of the radif, what incremental changes led it to the tipping point, but we know that it was accomplished by a few individuals reacting to their surrounding environment and interacting with other musicians and their audience.

Particularly in oral traditions, the medium itself inherently provides performers with constant opportunity for updating "on the fly," to edit outmoded, ineffectual materials that may no longer hold contemporary relevance or interest to their audience—a principle with a rather long history among ethnomusicologists and folklorists (Nettl 1983:188). Both continuity and change are ensured here, as most oral traditions are conservative (which mitigates abrupt and drastic alterations) yet also elastic and dynamic in their delivery, the reiteration and system feedback of the tradition through continued performance and transmission.[52]

Musical tradition exists as a function of the balance between the individual and the consensus of peers and listeners; it is therefore fragmented or refracted according to individual and shared tastes and aesthetic positionings.[53] Calibration varies with regard to the acceptable bandwidth of change tolerated before exceeding the threshold of what may still be considered to lie within the fuzzy boundaries of the tradition (cf., During 2002:854). A critical mass of acceptance by upper-level stakeholders— Ostads and connoisseurs—must be obtained for individual styles and pieces of repertoire to be absorbed into the tradition (During 1994:77ff.).[54] This elite body of musicians acts like a thermostat, a form of negative feedback, in defining and maintaining the tradition's centre of gravity: blowing cold on performers who may be playing too hot, and vice versa. This specific bandwidth of acceptance remained fluid and temporary, and as there were until relatively recently no objective means for comparing historical styles (i.e., recordings or accurate notations), gradual change could stand without protest from the old guard as they naturally passed on (During 2002: 859–60). Furthermore, the definitions of both tradition and change are significantly problematized in considering the common scenario whereby exterior forms and structures may change while their underlying conceptual, intentional, and aesthetic foundations remain intact (ibid.: 860). Taking these vagaries into consideration, the distribution of musicians across the personal aesthetic continuum at a given time is likely, if not definitively, a rough bell curve centering on the thermostat setting of the Ostads.

Traditional consensus is also conferred by the general audience for whom the musicians perform, whose less-technically informed responses are more liable to a self-organizing swarm of popular support. A serious complication to the feedback mechanism arose in Persian music in the twentieth century (detailed in chapter 3) when the constituent stakeholders, formerly a small and artistically elite subculture, were expanded to include the public at large via mass mediation and education. As every musician knows, the quality of an audience has a tremendous impact on musical performance. So-called "golden eras" of music throughout history and across cultures refer to periods characterized by both great performers and knowledgeable, discriminating audiences that had high expectations interacting over an extended period. Performers and listeners entrain into a larger transpersonal entity. But by their very nature, musical peaks are based on a fragile balance that usually cannot be sustained for long, whether in the time frame of an individual performance or in the history of a culture. We call them golden moments and golden eras precisely because they are rare and stand out from the ordinary. While lamenting what many connoisseurs of Persian music regard as contemporary decadence of both taste and musical activity, During notes that it was ever thus, with contemporaneous commentators issuing similar complaints throughout past centuries. Indeed, the pendular cycle of boom and bust is inherent in all tradition as it propels through history (During 1994:331–338).

> (T)he history of Persian music doesn't appear as a continuity . . . but as a succession of ruptures and renewals. . . . The continuity of the Iranian genius perhaps resides precisely in its capacity for renewing itself, and further still, to overturn the flow of ideas, to produce new ideologies and to recreate traditions, affecting religion (with a propensity for heterodoxy and schism), culture and political movements." (ibid.:17)

Through the complex interaction of individuals, their grouping in various configurations and the continuous reiteration of music through performance, a pattern self-organizes in the form of a tradition—fluid, emergent, unpredictable and sensitive to subtle changes from both above and below, and yet stable and orderly enough to be easily recognizable. As far as it is possible to identify previous styles, practices and conceptualizations, we might suggest that over the long haul, tradition can be considered as the proverbial "unchanging in the changing." Ostad Shajarian subscribes to the notion that unchanging tradition indeed exists but he clearly holds the aesthetic approach of a moderate renovator and views tradition as a springboard for creative growth of the individual, which in turn—and particularly in his high-profile case—powerfully feeds back into the tradition.

Without the naturally transforming feedback of individual renovators to update and reinvigorate a tradition, the latter runs the risk of becoming ossified and devolving from art to mere craft, an issue that comes increasingly to head in the postrevolutionary period.[55] Traditional Iranian literary values clearly differentiate the inspired poet (*sha'er*) from the technically competent versifier (*nazim*): the key difference being that the former "says something," something profound, substantial and moving, whereas the latter does not. This ability moves the focus from tradition as a collective vehicle, an operating system that allows for communication and comprehension, to the message of the individual. Like the celebrated archetypal *rend*, this individuality is assessed on the truth value thereby expressed, which can and often does depart from conventional practice. Most artists are consciously aware of the paradox that the more an artistic expression sincerely reflects one's subjective self, the more it likely resonates with the subjective sensibilities of others. Some performance theorists see the restored behavior of craft as the hallmark of a performance tradition; particularly in Western classical music, the whole point of hearing another performance of Beethoven's Ninth symphony for the n-th time is precisely the performance, not "the piece" (Godlovitch 1998:4–5; Cook 2001). But slavish imitation (*taqlid*) has a decidedly pejorative connotation of conformity in Iranian culture (Nettl 1992:212, 241, 249). In the prerecording era, some masters were regarded as such strictly because of their extensive and faithful memory of repertoire for ensuring its accurate transmission rather than for being inspired performers—they represented the letter rather than the spirit of the tradition (During 1994:50, 59, 72).

Real artists must "appropriate the music" and imprint upon it both their personal stamp and the spirit of the times (ibid.:73–74). An artist must start the creative process and not resist the natural impulse to change things in the practice of their craft; but they also have to know when to stop, to listen to the natural pace of change. This becomes a problem in the face of technology that hyper-accelerates time, collapses space, and intensifies system feedback in an unprecedented way—there is a lot more chaos and noise now than in previous eras. There are various degrees of renovation, but the very word implies innovation *with* continuity; iconoclasts, the avant garde, and the hybridizers go too far and break continuity. Persian musicians will share the reaction of jazz musicians in these cases, and complain that their music is "lacking roots or lacking history" (Berliner 1994: 249). Like Shajarian's alpine metaphor, acceptance of a particular renovation hinges upon altitude and speed: how far has it departed from previous practice and how fast has this distance been covered?

Viewed comparatively with singers other instrumentalists, ney players—particularly as exemplified by Ostad Kasa'i, the doyen of ney players in the second half of the twentieth century—tend to improvise more freely and with minimal reliance on radif materials or display of reportorial prowess.[56] While this individuality and freedom is generally admired regarding ney players, Ahmad Ebadi's similarly freewheeling style of improvising on the setar, much loved by a broad audience through his radio broadcasts during the Pahlavi period, is regarded by many musicians as extending beyond the acceptable aesthetic boundaries of the traditional models. One wonders if stricter criteria may be applied to performers of setar and tar, the key instruments of radif transmission within the Farahani line, of which Ebadi was a direct descendant (and whose canonical nonchalance may appear all the more offensive to disapproving connoisseurs for this very reason). Ebadi's position clearly illustrates subjective fuzziness and potential for a rift along the range of constituents in the peer review process, based on individual taste, familiarity with music, and social network or subcultural affiliations, which likely reflect a shared collective aesthetic. Ebadi, who was one of Shajarian's principal mentors, was highly creative: each time he played the same dastgah it would be quite different ("I'm not a gramophone machine," he unapologetically declared) and was often performed in novel, idiosyncratic scordatura tunings (*chap kūk*). For Ebadi, creative exploration was essential: "Creativity in music is a difficult thing but for me, all real artists should possess their own style," he declared (During 1994:73–74). But for some, he went too far, departing from the tradition and flirting with a lightweight and overly individualistic style. For many other listeners and musicians, however, his playing was undoubtedly liberal and yet exhibited the traditional qualifying marker of *hāl*, an inspired, spiritual depth (discussed further in chapter 2). As is often the case in Iranian culture, we enter a disorienting hall of mirrors here, rich in *iham*:

> Though some object to the ideology of the *hāl*, this objection is intended to purify it of its sensuality or elicit other kinds of emotion. The *hāl*, implicitly opposed to technique or reason, remains the public's primary criterion. Beyond the formalism of classical tradition, the music refers to personal experience, insofar as the *hāl* alone guarantees authenticity. Perhaps this is why the progress of Iranian artists, although "modern," remains "traditional" insofar as the *hāl* is transpersonal, not individualized, permitting one to communicate by opening an intersubjective space while retaining one's own experience. (During 1994:863)

Differentiating spiritualized, transpersonal *hāl* from individualized emotion is not always easy, of course, and is clearly open to subjective criteria and experiences. Ebadi was the heir to the Farahani tradition. What if his chosen direction was a fulfilment and successful realization rather than denial of their lineage? What if the ultimate priority was to keep making new music, to keep it fresh?

From Wilber's integral perspective, spirit bids individuals, groups, and their traditions to evolve through a balance of transcending (via individual innovation) what is inherited while simultaneously including it (through collective consensus) in what you pass on to others, especially young people. As another expression of the personal aesthetic continuum: too much including without a modicum of transcending leads to atrophy, and transcending without including leads to dissociation and dissolution of the tradition.

AK

One of the reasons for the reiteration of cultural art forms over many years in Iran was due to the perceived notion that the only way to preserve the tradition was to continue maintaining its inherited, historical form as much as possible. Many artists spent entire lifetimes trying to excel at repeating such traditional forms for the purpose of oral preservation. Unstable sociopolitical situations drove artists to preserve those features of the past that they knew and appreciated but were in danger of being forgotten. It is a kind of recovery or a first step towards creating foundational stability for future developments, which, of course, do not always happen. Shafiee Kadkani, a contemporary Persian poet, speaks about this in the following poem:

The Wheel of the Well[57]
Suspended in the groan of the wheel and the rope
from the depth of the well, the pail is on a voyage upwards.
As soon as it reaches daylight and the sun
it is turned over headlong down to the depth of the cold wet well.

The story of the pail is a bitter, dark experience:
reaching the threshold of daylight,
travelling the arduous distance with hope,
and then once again being thrown to the heart of darkness.

Music in Iran is not divided or categorized properly. The way that people look at the music is different. Some people like what we could call "early music," music presented by the old masters—they're looking for those materials and if you tell them it is ancient, they like that. Others prefer creativity, spontaneity, especially as it exists in a good improvisation, and this is more reflective of contemporary artists; they're looking for beauty regardless of its source. All of these people have been working together at the same time without having had the opportunity to classify, divide, and demarcate these different types of music. Sometimes they don't know that they're talking about different things, for example, the music of Ostad Ebadi and Mr. Madjid Kiani. Kiani likes to preserve, he wants to present something from the past. This type of musician likes to pursue the idea "I've found the actual music that Maraghi used to play." How they establish this, nobody knows, but the idea is very nice because it's like finding an old coin in the Alborz mountains that belongs to some ancient dynasty, maybe to Cyrus, and it's therefore very expensive. People like that. Those musicians with the idea of preserving and cultivating old material, such as Kiani, have to prove the historical basis of their work, that's their homework.

When Ostad Jalil Shahnaz played tar it was the same sound, the same frame-work, even the same dastgah most of the time but he doesn't believe in repetition, so he always looked for new ways to present the material, new gestures. Basically, if you know how to listen to these different kinds of material and approaches to it, you find the music that you like. Unfortunately, in Iran people don't make this division and they sometimes compare someone who is actually singing folk music to a singer of pop music—like comparing Sima Bina to Googoosh or comparing so and so to Mr. Shajarian. They are doing so many things like this. But the purposes and func-tions of these musics are quite different. Even in Persian music, singing avaz and singing a tasnif is a different thing. It's very important to take the time and make the effort to learn how to listen to these different types of music. If you don't know how to listen to Beethoven, you may not like his music. You may really love and understand Bach but he's a totally different composer who, among other things, looks at the process of musical variation quite differently from Beethoven. You can't listen to Palestrina in the same way you listen to Stravinsky; it takes an effort to acquire the ability to hear what they are saying. At any rate, if we're going to di-vide music we should try to do so without judging it.

Avaz is a complex art in which all of one's knowledge of Persian music can be presented effectively and with flexibility, it is a set of tools that can be adjusted to the poem to express whatever it is you want to say. All of the gestures can be changed in a way to influence the reaction of those listening. You can adjust avaz. But you have to have permission to do that, and this permission comes from understanding the goals and effects of a particular dastgah or the progression of a melody in a certain gushe. Then when you read a line of poetry you see right away that "this is Bidad or such and such a gushe is an appropriate musical vehicle here." The best avaz should clearly articulate the words and yet play on the potential *iham* for multiple interpretation of meaning. It should be an additive process, one that adds to, that enhances the impact of the poem, not decreases it. Sometimes, however, when listening to avaz you don't hear the poem and then you hear some melodies treated flexibly but you really don't derive the quintessential meaning of the poem from the performance itself. A considerable part of the impact obtained from avaz is the meaning of the poem combined with an appropriate dastgah and melodic treatment.

I think that avaz is designed the way it is because it was the primary means for presenting the poetry of these masters—Hafez, Attar, Mowlana, 'Iraqi, and Sa'di. These great souls were carrying a culture, they were fighting to keep this culture with a language and an idea of how we should live. There is an ideology; if we pay attention, we realize that they're following the same ideas. There is also an element of providing a survival kit contained in their art, with the tacit understanding among Iranians that they can trust these masters. Especially right now in Iran with this situation we have, people don't trust each other. Someone can write a poem now and you may like it but you don't know who this person is or if they can be trusted. But you can trust Hafez, you can trust Sa'di. That's why, at the beginning of the revolution, people started to really turn to this poetry. In the prerevolutionary era, Banan and Marzieh were singing poetry written by contemporaneous poets—in fact the poet was often directly involved in the production process of the music. It was nice but they were mostly talking about love in a personal relationship, dealing with interpersonal feelings. It was generally secular in outlook and intention but devoid of any political dimension. Some pop artists addressed political issues but they used local, contemporaneous poets; I can only think of two examples when they used a classical poet: one was a setting of Hafez by Mr. Faramarz Aslani, and I believe Darioush Eghbali also used couplets from Mowlana. The fact remains that the multidimensional meanings of classical Persian poetry (as realized through the device of *iham*) cannot be easily achieved by means of pop music. And in any case, the superficial domain of pop music would never need to deploy such deep levels of meaning, even if sometimes this pop music had political messages to convey.[58]

The tools of avaz were designed in order to present the art of poetry. It's the best way to present poetry; it's better than just reading it by yourself. The art of poetry is a framework for intellectual, inspired, spiritual people, spiritual and cultural leaders. And they proved through the centuries that what they were saying was true. "Whenever you listened to us, you could move forward. Whenever you didn't listen, you'll see what will happen. Please listen to us. Please try to empty yourself, try to understand unity." And when someone with a good voice and deep understanding becomes their voice, and their words create trust and unity, it brings people together, if people will listen and actually understand what these masters were saying. As long as we can remember the books of Hafez, Sa'di, Attar, and Mowlana have been published and circulated. They are presenting the same teachings in many different ways—poetic forms, words, expressions, images, and approaches. It's just like dastgah Afshari: if you really understand it, there are so many ways it can be presented. It really depends who you are. And each person should have their own style. And if you have more tools, use them. Nobody should make accusations like "this music is bad, it's *motrebi* ("minstrel," with clear derogatory connotations), that one is *shirin navazi* ("sweet, light playing," generally used derogatorily)." I think these judgments tell us more about the critic than about the music. I personally don't think that a restaurant is a good environment for playing my music but that guy playing in the restaurant might be playing good music; you have to listen and shouldn't jump to preset conclusions or associations. Recently the concert violinist Joshua Bell agreed to do an experiment and busk in the Washington subway for an hour; no one paid attention to him and yet he could have played in Carnegie Hall to a full house the night before.

The idea of traditional music versus *shirin navazi* comes from Mr. Kiani; everyone knows that. The situation is somewhat like early sacred music in the West. If you go back to the time when the church was controlling everything in Europe, you see that they didn't like emotion in music. They wanted to be detached and anything that created emotion was to be omitted. Mr. Kiani says, "The reason I play these melodies so dry is because they're authentic." What does this mean, authentic? Something is going on here. Performance is something individual, everyone has their own taste. Some people like glissando, others don't. Some like to exaggerate the vibrato and bending notes, while others dislike this. But being a successful performer is based on the material you play and the relationship between you and your instrument. We can't accuse someone like Ostad Shahnaz of being "untraditional" because he plays a lot of intricate ornamentation, subtle and precise glissando and vibrato, bringing a lot of delicate feeling into his music, and he manipulates the rhythm, slowing down and varying the pace in a conversational mood. All the creative potential that he has gained through concentration and practice and by bringing love to his instrument is now being deployed in full force. So we're criticizing him because he's talented and is utilizing the tools he has fashioned in this highly dynamic and creative way? This is very wrong.

Since the Islamic Revolution of 1979 there has been considerable controversy over what is considered to be "traditional music." Mr. Madjid Kiani accused Ostad Faramarz Payvar of being European, of espousing a European idea of what Persian music is. Yet Payvar had the approval of Saba and many great musicians. Kiani says that he is the continuation of Habib Somai's *maktab*, but he never met Somai (who died in 1945); the only person who saw Somai was Saba. Payvar was Saba's student and the only one of whom Saba would take in to the radio to play with and introduce to everyone as his student and friend. No one needs to ask who Payvar was: he was a great master. He had an amazing understanding of this music. More than *anybody*—this is a huge statement! He had an immense library and was very erudite. He wrote a massive amount of music. So this man's ideas come from European music? No. When I listen to Payvar play Chahargah, I hear Chahargah very clearly. I think Kiani's division of *shirin navazi* and *sonnati* ("classical") and European style or new music is wrong.

There are personal ways to play this music and this is what Persian music demands. The radif is a pedagogical system, it's a way of transmitting musical knowledge between people—in fact it's the only way you can teach and learn Persian music. But it's not the way that you should perform. The radif shapes the mind but the next step is improvisation, being creative.

We have to learn from masters such as Ostad Ebadi. He was the son of the great master Mirza Abdollah. Even if he didn't learn his art directly from his father, he inherited the family's tradition through his sister. He knows the tradition and knows the radif, but one shouldn't *play* like that. The radif is not for presentation—you must play where your creativity transports you. For example, we have one short piece recorded by another great master, Aqa Hossein-qoli (brother of Mirza Abodollah). If Mr. Madjid Kiani is right in saying that the tradition should be preserved at all costs, why didn't Ostad Aqa Hossein-qoli confine himself to radif on this recording, instead of improvising creatively? He simply "plays tar"; and very beautifully at that! We even have recordings left by Ostad Darvish Khan, but does he play radif? No, he plays "beautiful tar," featuring the best of his understanding of timbre, instrumental technique, melodies, and phrases, not forgetting that all these reverberate from the soil of Iran, the depths of the Iranian soul. But he's limited by the three-minute recording format of the time, so the music is densely packed. What does that mean? It implies that Darvish Khan and the musicians of the cylinder and 78-format era were flexible because the music allowed them to be so. It allowed them to bring all of their knowledge and all of their creativity together and make their best presentation of it, even under this severe time constraint. Ostad Ebadi liked to play with a tape delay/echo machine. He adjusted his style to interact with the machine. He understood the purpose of *riz* (tremolo)—to sustain a note—but this isn't always necessary when playing through this machine, so he made the appropriate adjustments and proceeded to play the most expressive Afshari imaginable.

Notes

1. Ekmeleddin Ihsanoglu also identifies *adab* as the source of the liberal humanism cultivated later in Renaissance Europe (Sardar 2004:273).

2. Under the heading of "Decolonizing Historical Imagination" in a critical, alternative reading of the historical construction of tradition and modernity in Iran, Tavakoli-Targhi adds the following nuance to this assertion:

> The conventional Persian literary histories, moreover, regard poetry as a characteristically Iranian mode of self-expression. With the privileged position of poetry in the invented national *mentalite,* the prose texts of the humanities are devalued and scholarly efforts are infrequently spent on editing and publishing nonpoetic texts. Thus a large body of historically significant prose texts of modernity have remained unpublished. This willful marginalization of prose is often masked as a sign of the prominence of poetry as an intrinsically Iranian mode of expression. (2004:146).

3. The same semantic clustering is found in the closely related tradition of Iraqi maqam, where singers are designated as reciters (*qari'*), which also alludes to the prestigious art of Qur'anic recitation.

4. *Samā'* ("audition," or "deep listening" [after Becker 2004]) is the traditional use of music for spiritual development practiced by many Sufi lineages; it is discussed further below in chapter 2.

5. Ferdowsi's (940–1020 AD) *Shahnāme* was the central expression of pre-Islamic mythology in Persian culture for future transmission and played a major role in reinforcing the Persian language in face of the Arabization that accompanied the adoption of Islam.

6. Davis was consulted by Del Giudice for her article on the ancient foundations of contemporary Iranian identity (2008), which asserts that the *Shahnāme* "is haunted by the idea that those most ethically fitted to rule are precisely the ones most reluctant to rule, preferring instead to devote themselves to humankind's chief concerns: the nature of wisdom, the fate of the human soul, and the incomprehensibility of God's purpose" (ibid.:63).

7. The complex nature of this cosmic plane is further discussed in chapter 2.

8. E.g., six beat units irregularly and ambiguously flowing between two groups of three and three groups of two.

9. E.g., Hijaz, Beyate Kurd and Dashti, or Rohab, Shah Khatai, and Takhte Taqdis.

10. The recent BBC documentary *High Anxieties—The Mathematics of Chaos*, (available at http://www.youtube.com/watch?v=VRT0c4qT3LI) presents an interesting view of the profound historical and psychological consequences of the revolutionary mathematical insights initiated by Henri Poincaré.

11. For numerous examples of this see Simms and Koushkani 2012.

12. Ronald Wright, *Stolen Continents: Conquest and Resistance in the Americas* (New York: Penguin, 1992), 4.

13. I use the term "myth" here in its widest and nonderogating application to encompass the sacred and secular, historical and contemporary, factual and fictional, collective and individual. According Joseph Campbell's renowned interpretation, myths arise spontaneously from both individual and collective consciousness but are also deliberately sought out, constructed and diffused, with archetypes being constantly updated and endlessly varied.

14. BBC documentary *How Art Made the World* (BBC Worldwide Programs, 2006), program #4, "Once Upon a Time."

15. In 1966 Scholes, Phelan & Kellog declared film to be the preeminent narrative medium of our time, effectively displacing literature and live performance arts, noting a decisive shift that had been well under way for several decades (2006:280-81). The post-revolutionary decade saw the remarkable rise of Iranian cinema to global prominence, providing a poetic, sympathetic view of Iranian culture and a welcome foil to the austere radicalism of Ayatollah Khomeini, who donned the archetypal role of the Oriental despot in Western consciousness and played it to the hilt. While essentially narrative, the creative process and "performance" of film is by definition monological, completely detached from the live audience and the micro-occasion of individual screenings. The direct rapport, interaction and adjustments necessitated by this that characterize the performative narrative arts do not apply. In this sense, the process and statement is analogous to a studio album; the playback of a recording, whether a studio or live recording, is essentially the same, though cassettes and CDs are generally listened to alone or in small groups (like a film DVD or video cassette) as opposed to the collective viewing of a film in a theatre. The performative action and evolution of the work here resides with the viewer/listener, who recreates the work each time it is experienced.

16. This has been recently corroborated by two great jazz pianists. Abdullah Ibrahim notes in his CD *Senzo* (2008), "This recording and live-concerts are based on the original concept of story-telling." While the first thing Randy Weston declares in his autobiography is: "I come to be a storyteller: I'm not a jazz musician, I'm really a storyteller through music." (*African Rhythms*, Durnham: Duke University Press, 2010, p. 1). Weston's latest CD release (2010) is entitled *The Story Teller*.

17. This famous work is another excellent historical example of Iran's multicultural constitution.

18. The Qur'an presents a unique exception in that the text itself, even its manifestation as a bound book sitting on a shelf, is regarded as sacred. As discussed below, its recitation is integral rather than supplemental and while it is ideally recited to a different melodic setting each time, there is absolutely no question of altering or varying the text.

19. From Australian television May 2010, Youtube.com/watch?v=bnoGhSCA-kQ.

20. "The traditional artist should always consider himself a student" (Majid Kiani quoted in During 2002:857).

21. "Meters of Melodies", written by Sayyed Mirza Mohammad-Nasir Forsat Shirazi's (1855–1920) in 1914; discussed in chapter 3.

22. It is noteworthy regarding the following discussion that Shajarian was a talented athlete as a child and young man, especially in playing soccer and volleyball.

23. Interview in Persian, broadcasted June 19, 2010; http://www.youtube.com/ watch?v=wHiPVsJIJIY.

24. Interview in Persian, broadcasted June 19, 2010; http://www.youtube.com/ watch?v=wHiPVsJIJIY.

25. The name is a cognate of similarly prestigious stringed instruments in ancient India and China: the *vina* and *chin.*

26. He is commonly known by this Arabized form of the ancient Persian name (variously rendered as Pahlbod or Fahlidh).

27. Entitled *Sharh-e Mowlana Mobarak Shah bar Adwar* and attributed to Jorjani (During 1988: 209).

28. As we will see below, these traits are coincidentally operative in Qur'an recitation.

29. This spectacular accomplishment was not lost on the renowned flamenco guitarist Paco de Lucia, whose 1990 album entitled *Zyryab* alludes to his own legacy of single-handedly establishing the modern tradition of flamenco guitar playing—an interesting contemporary reperformance of this mythic-historical "script."

30. This useful book, which is frequently cited as a source throughout the present study, is partly an anthology of interview excerpts taken from various Persian sources—books, magazines, journals, television programs, public addresses, etc., most of which date from the 1990s and are difficult or impossible to obtain at present. As I don't have access to most of the original sources, I will simply cite their occurrence in Shajarian et al. (2004), which is reasonably accessible through Persian book sellers at the time of writing.

31. From his book *Ghost in the Machine* (1967).

32. I have taken this term from the late Uzbeki master Turgun Alimatov. When asked about his uniquely creative style of playing and repertoire he responded:

> I didn't create music. I took what existed, ready-made, and I played it. I listened, I played, I listened, I played…[The music is not new]. One person builds a house and leaves that house. I come to that house and remodel it. And that remodeling will be valued for a long time. And then a still better master will come along and do another remodeling. He'll take down certain parts and build them again in his own way. It will be still better. That's how I understand it. I'm not the one who built the house, I just did the remodeling. I can't say that it's mine. Whoever sees this house says the workman gave it a good paint job. He doesn't say that the workman built it. (Levin 1996: 66)

Alimatov's metaphor may be an expansion, consciously or unconsciously, of an image from Sa'di's *Golestan* (see p. 43 below; also, cf. Stravinsky's quote below in note 42).

33. The pagination for Nettl 1992 is taken from the digital copy available at www .scribd.com, which likely differs from the printed version.

34. For an interesting interpretation of how media and popular culture assume the bardic function of transmitting America's influential postmodern "epic," see Neal Gabler, "Pop Culture Passes on the Ties That Bind," *Albany Times Union*, February 2, 1997, 1(E). http://www.highbeam.com/doc/1G1-156965893.html.

35. Of course, these categories are not airtight and individual musicians often function in different categories simultaneously or at different stages of their creative lives. Most of Nusrat's voluminous collaborative "Fusion" work with Western popular musicians is clearly iconoclastic by traditional standards. The same applies, though to a lesser extent, to some of Toumani Diabate's work.

36. See Simms and Koushkani 2012.

37. We were unable to clarify Shajarian's distinction between a school and style, though the former seems to connote a lineage, the latter structural features of the music.

38. M.CD—133–135, Tehran: Mahoor Institute of Culture and Art, 2003.

39. These qualities continued to characterize neighboring Azerbaijani music, a close cousin of Iranian Persian music, throughout the twentieth century. In this tradition, men, women and children sing in virtually the same register.

40. SOASIS20, London: SOAS, 2009.

41. Ken Wilber later utilized this image in expounding his integral philosophy (e.g., 1996:273ff.) while Nederveen Pietrse (2004) fully develops it in an application that is particularly relevant to the present context.

42. Along with Stravinsky, among others, who freely roamed the personal aesthetic continuum throughout his career: "A real tradition is not the relic of a past that is irretrievably gone; it is a living force that animates and informs the present...Far from implying the repetition of what has been, tradition presupposes the reality of what endures. It appears as an heirloom, a heritage that one receives on condition of making it bear fruit before passing it on to one's descendants" (Stravinsky 1970:57).

43. As well as Markoff (1986: 143ff.), who provides an interesting comparative case study of how questions of the individual and tradition apply to contemporary Turkish folk musicians.

44. "We have been taught, inside the classroom and outside of it, that there exists an entity called the West, and that one can think of this West as a society and civilization independent of and in opposition to other societies and civilizations...By endowing nations, societies, or cultures with the qualities of internally homogeneous and externally distinctive and bounded objects, we create a model of the world as a global pool hall in which the entities spin off each other like so many billiard balls" (Wolf 1997:5–6).

45. "The very order of the world seems to have been seriously questioned [in Iran] following contact with the West. After the fifteenth century, musical treatises were no longer regulated by the laws of mathematics. Three centuries later, the great tables analyzing the symbolic connection between music and the cosmic or natural order were no longer of concern to musicologists. In the nineteeth century, Iran produced few musical texts and left theory to scholars trained in Europe. When the Persian and Azerbaijani repertoires were reconstituted in the nineteenth century, the number twelve was maintained, but it had no connection with other orders of reality. At most, the twelve modes were distinguished by their expressive character, but even this is debatable, since here we enter the sphere of the relative and subjective" (During 2002:862).

46. Though differing in immediate causes, this very same reaction and dynamic is evident in European "second-generation" nationalism of the early to mid-nineteenth century (Anderson 2006:195).

47. During expands this to an objective sixfold typology of parameters definitive of musical tradition: form and content of musical structures; process of transmission; means of production (instruments and type of ensemble); performance and listening conditions/environment/approach; social and cultural context; meaning and values (2002:854–55).

48. "According to the musicians [consulted in 1990], intervals define authenticity in two ways: by the purity of the form's ethnic origins (which encompass the whole Iranian nation-state) and by the intensity and nature of its aesthetic experience. In other words, authenticity is a "pure" product of national genius, unsullied by anything taken—borrowed or imitated—from beyond the border" (During 2002:856).

49. Through the 1970s the festival's self-conscious "East meets West" theme grew increasingly contentious through the top-billings of Xenakis, Stockhausen, Cage, Peter Brook, Jerzy Grotowski and Merce Cunningham. The splashy, ostentatious setting at Persopolis ruins, the royal patronage of Empress Farah Diba (along with the allocation of tax money through the sponsorship of the state's radio and television) soon became "exhibit A" for those critical of the Shah, his self-aggrandizement, rampant modernist-Western proclivities, and, amounting to the same thing, his deluded disconnection with the cultural sensibilities of his subjects.

50. Like his entire legacy, G.W. Bush's absurd marshalling of "You're either with the terrorists or you're with us" after 9/11 laid bare the profoundly unsound basis of these classic techniques of manipulation, which were usually engaged throughout history with much more finesse and craft (or "higher production values," as an Iraqi friend once phrased it) by more competent imperialists.

51. The latter term implying "closed or dogmatic" by Shajarian; quoted by Shabnam Ataei (personal communication, 2010).

52. In literate traditions there eventually arises a disconnect between actual worlds of the author and future readers.

> In an oral culture this problem does not exist. Singers and listeners share the same world and see it the same way. Those elements in a traditional tale which in the course of time might become irrelevant or confusing to the singers and their audiences are, in the course of time, eliminated or accommodated in new ways; and, conversely, the oral tales themselves act as a conservative element in culture, tending to curb new ways of living or of perceiving the cosmos. In a culture of written letters, however, such as our Western civilization has become, a fixed text will tend to survive its native milieu and be forced to make its way in alien surroundings. Not only will its language become archaic and obsolete, but the assumptions about man and nature and about the proper way to tell a story . . . will also recede farther and farther from the assumptions of living men. (Scholes et al. 2006:82–83)

These dynamics of transmission and change resonate with notions of selection in memetic theory (see Blackmore 1999), whereby songs and tales either successfully adapt to new environments or perish, and individual performers function as agents of "mutation."

53. Storr cites a psychological study that concluded that a sample of architects divided into three main groups according to their creative approach and capabilities: "the most creative group were primarily concerned with meeting an inner artistic standard of excellence which they discovered within themselves; the least creative group with conforming to the standards of the architectural profession" (Storr 1991:235). While the study was conducted in the 1960s, I suspect that things like this don't change that much over time.

54. This musical judgment is functionally analogous to both Western academic peer review and the *ijtihad* ("exertion") of Shi'i Jafari jurisprudence, where qualified clerics reinterpret and update Islamic law to fit "exigencies of changing circumstances" (Tehranian 2004:193).

55. "As the years pass, [art] worlds settle down and begin to experience their own segmentations, differentiations, and splits. An already developed world commonly defined by insiders and outsiders alike as an art world, complete with appropriate ideologies, aesthetics, and forms of social organization, often (in another characteristic sequence) changes in the opposite direction. The originally expressive art works and styles become increasingly more organized, constrained, and ritualized; organizational forms subordinate the artist increasingly to partially or entirely extraneous sources of control; and the world

and its activities begin to resemble conventional craft worlds. In this sense, an art turns into a craft" (H. Becker 1982: 288).

56. Though nonetheless exuding what Dariush Safvat describes as the "soul of the radif," discussed in chapter 2.

57. Translated by Pari Azarm Motamedi.

58. As in the music of Fereidun Foroughi during the reign of the Shah, and Darioush Eghbali during the reign of the Shah (and even more recently), along with a host of younger artists born after the revolution.

Chapter 2
Mashhad Roots

Shajarian's Early Musical Formation and Activities

This chapter focuses on roots: of traditional Iranian culture, both sacred and secular—the key narratives, related performance genres, and those who maintain them—and of Ostad Shajarian, who grew up in this milieu in Mashshad. Mashshad is regarded as the most sacred space in Iran and has been, and continues to be, a bastion of traditional Iranian values and culture, incredibly rich in sacred and secular narrative performance traditions. While the cultural scene in contemporary Mashshad is much more complex, we use the city here as a symbolic rubric for examining these Iranian traditions and values in general in order to contextualize avaz as a branch within this larger performance tradition, and Shajarian's approach to avaz as it unfolds throughout the study. After briefly outlining Shajarian's youth in Mashshad, we sketch out the role of clerics, the range of narratives and concomitant performance traditions, along with their practioners and approaches. We then examine the role and implications of the performers' interpretive spin, so often central to these practices, and the interactive relationship of the performers and audience in general. This overview of traditional values and practices is rounded off with a look at Sufi conceptions regarding music, which have shaped and continue to have a major influence on Persian music, its performers and audience.

A shrine city and the resting place of Imam Reza, Mashhad receives millions of pilgrims a year, far exceeding the local population: Curtis and Hooglund cite four million in the early 2000s (other estimates are far higher) and note that "(s)ince the nineteenth century, it has been customary among the bazaar class and members of the lower classes to recognize those who have made a pilgrimage to Mashhad by prefixing their names with the title *mashti* [i.e., Mashhadi]" (2008: 124).

61

Complementing this core Iranian identity, the city is also associated with Ferdowsi in nearby Tus. It is a center of both religious and secular education, sciences and arts, and a magnet for a diverse range of performers and artisans cultivating Khorasani traditions. A major hub in the general urbanization of Iran in the twentieth century, the population of Mashshad was 75,000 in 1900, leaping to 242,000 in 1956, then 410,000 in 1966 (Bharier 1972:54), and over 2.4 million in the 2006 census. It is the second largest Iranian city after Tehran.

OS

My father, Mehdi Shajarian, was born in 1911 in Mashhad. Hajj Aqa Seyyed Ali Akbar Tabasi, my grandfather, was a generous and famous landlord in Tabas.[1] He had an excellent voice and was an able singer but wouldn't sing except among his intimate friends and lovers of music. My grandfather died when my father was only twelve but my father, who had inherited his musical voice, fell in love with singing from his early youth but my grandfather's death had deprived him of a good teacher of song. However, my father's friends introduced him to the Qur'an recitation classes which were managed by Aqa Seyyed Mohammad Arab, a clergyman, and after several years of practice he emerged as the best singer and teacher of Qur'an recitation in Mashhad.

I remember well one Friday morning when I was three or four years old and the Qur'an recitation session was held in our house. My mother deposited me with Mohammad Shater, our servant, who put me on my father's lap. I was so shy of the audience that I repeatedly concealed myself behind my father. On that day I saw Aga Seyyed Mohammad Arab for the first time. He was an old man who was wearing a green turban and a cleric's cloak. Since that time my father occasionally took me to Qur'an recitation sessions.

From six to nineteen years of age I regularly accompanied my father to the Qur'an classes. When I reached puberty my father awakened me early in the morning and told me to recite the Qur'an with a loud voice in order to overcome the difficulty of change in my voice. In fact, my father's continued care and teaching laid the foundation of my future success. My father used to hold Qur'an teaching lessons in his house three nights a week with a wonderful faith in religion, which continued into late hours. He was a skillful master of his art and trained well-known Qur'an reciters and commentators. He continued these classes until he was eighty-two. From then on, due to the chronic illness of bronchitis, he was unable to leave the house—instead he was constantly praying for people and these prayers continued until his last moments. What I remember from my father was his simplicity, honesty and compassion. I love him dearly and I am proud of him.[2]

When I was ten years old the whole city knew me as "the kid who recites the Qur'an well." At twelve years, I sang before twelve thousand people and it was beginning at this age that I became interested in the tradition of Iranian singing—that is to say classical singing. But my family was devout and the radio was forbidden in our home, music in general was prohibited and my study wasn't successful. However, I made great progress in the practice of religious singing and began to be regarded as a prodigy. When I was around fourteen years of age, after being introduced to people who knew music, I learned some gushes. The first one I learned was Gham Angiz in dastgah Dashti.

Question: Could one say that the training in religious singing that you underwent in your adolescence helped when you approached classical music later?

Certainly. I think that my voice had been formed in my childhood, I should say the basis of my voice, and then I got accustomed to singing . . . singing in front of crowds. (Kasmai and Lecomte 1991:247–48; 250)

AK

Mashhad is to Iran what the Vatican is to Italy and the Roman Catholic world; it's the holiest city for Iranians and the followers of Twelver Shia Islam. It's an important center of pilgrimage, so it's part of a kind of travel industry with a strong tourist attraction and many people in Mashhad work in facilitating this. Millions of pilgrims arrive who need accommodation, food, transport, guiding, and so on. The people are religious but there is also a quasi- "show business" quality to life in the city, a sacred show business that involves all kinds of performances. Much thought and decision-making has gone into how they are going to present this sacred place to pilgrims from all over Iran and the Shi'a world. For me, as an Iranian who has visited there, Mashhad is a place of presenting Shi'ism. The Imam Reza mosque is the most beautiful building—a palace, really—I've ever seen. There is a lot of ceramic art in one room, mirror art in another: these are the contributions of masters from around the Shia world who came and left their amazing work. It's overwhelming to see all of this incredible art in this magnificent building that goes on forever. So apart from his family of religious reciters, Ostad Shajarian grew up surrounded by this excellence in various fine arts. And there are local people standing around wearing particular hats known as "servants of Imam Reza"[3] who help visitors and show them around the shrine; they have been doing this traditionally, as volunteers, for generations. Some of them are doctors or engineers who know three different languages.

Because of the favourable circumstances that Mashhad has as a centre of spiritual tourism, it provides the opportunity for art to flourish. Tourists come there not only to savour the spiritual atmosphere, but also to appreciate the artistic excellence that is ubiquitous in Mashhad. The inhabitants of Mashhad are therefore, as a matter of course, highly attuned to anything artistic, aesthetically agreeable and inspiring. It is a town full of artistic merit and vision, a major hub for artisans and dealers in jewelry, engraving, and calligraphy. The bazaar is filled with an unusually high proportion of these arts because visitors want a special souvenir from their pilgrimage.

RS
Shajarian was a child prodigy of Qur'an recitation who went on to a spectacular career as a virtuoso classical singer. It is interesting to note that, quite counterintuitively, the majority of child prodigies do *not* go on to become adult virtuosos
and assume high professional standing. One estimate from the 1970s in the realm of
Western classical music posited that only about 10 percent did so (Storr 1991: 50). In
addition to his remarkable talent at singing and gifts in the visual arts,[4] Shajarian
excelled in sports as a boy and through high school. He entered teachers college in
1957, where his studies included music education with a Mr. Javan (Abdollahi
2003:2068). He had already gained considerable experience performing for large
audiences by 1959 when he began working for Radio Khorasan—his debut with the
mass medium that would be the primary means by which he later established a national profile—singing Sufi poetry unaccompanied and reciting the Qur'an or chanting in other religious genres. The following year Shajarian received his teacher's
diploma and began working as a primary school teacher in Mashhad. Having struck
out on his own, he began to study avaz and radif in earnest, though without a teacher
he pursued this on his own through "lifting" melodies off the radio and records (discussed in detail in chapter 4), occasionally asking the names of these melodies from
others who might know. It was also during this time that he was introduced to playing the santur by a colleague in his school, which led to taking lessons on the instrument with Jalal Akhbari in 1961. Shajarian built his own instrument in 1963 and was
already interested in improving its sonic potential. He married Farkhande Golafshan
in 1962 and was transferred to different teaching positions in the Mashhad area over
the next four years, while his family grew with the arrival of his daughters Raheleh
and Afsaneh. His radio broadcasts continued throughout this period but out of respect for his father, he continued to sing unaccompanied. Of this early phase of his
adult life Shajarian recalls, *"My environment was very closed, my family circle prohibited me from performing freely, from singing classical music: at the time Mashhad was a religious, provincial city where a young singer didn't have a lot of possibilities"* (Kasmai and Lecomte 1991:248).

Tradition and Its Guardians

The Clerical Subculture

Given the almost complete lack of credibility and legitimacy currently attached to
the government of the Islamic Republic of Iran and its concomitant network of
clergy (*ulema*), as a high-profile, influential public figure, Ostad Shajarian has very
good reasons for downplaying his connections to the clerical scene around which he
grew up. His dissociation with the subculture of Shi'i clerics became even more
pronounced since the so-called election crisis of June 2009, about which he was a

vocal critic of the government.[5] While he has regularly discussed his upbringing in previous interviews, he was not interested in following up our questions with regard to the larger context of avaz in relation to religious genres of singing and recitation. His only recording of sacred recitation officially released for wide distribution, Qur'anic recitation on the album *Yad-e Pedar* ("In Memory of Father"), was explicitly dedicated for the occasion of his father's passing, which provided legitimate and much needed cover for his carefully maintained nonclerical stance and image. He prefers to leave his roots in sacred recitiation—which carry a bona fide social prestige as being rooted in tradition, unsullied by postrevolutionary events—understated, as they can be easily conflated with the highly compromised status of the clergy and religion at present. The role of the Shi'i clergy has become synonymous with the Islamic Revolution and the government, and indeed has strong political affiliations in Iran since the founding of the Safavid dynasty in the sixteenth century. Aside from the often uncomfortable tension between secular and sacred authority, the clerical subculture was a primary bastion defining and maintaining tradition in Iran. The *ulema* and their guardianship of tradition may be found all over Iran but naturally come into even stronger focus in the shrine cities, such as Qom and Mashhad. Thus, despite growing up in a religious, traditional milieu and gaining his early vocal skills among the clerical subculture, Shajarian presents an adamantly secular persona as a public figure.

In the clerical context tradition is ideally conceived as being archetypal, its source is divine revelation originating outside of time. Time is calibrated by sacred events in the Islamic calendar and space sacralized by the presence of shrines and mosques. The narrative of this tradition is governed by the historical-"mythical" narrative of the Qur'an and sacred texts of Shi'i Islam as well as oral traditions and ritual practices held by the *ulema* and the faithful. Traditional life centers on prescribed ritual—in addition to the standard Islamic rituals contained in the "five pillars" and following the *shariah*, this includes practices such as *rowze khāni*, *ta'ziyeh* (both detailed below), processions, festivals, local pilgrimage, and other acts that build up spiritual merit (*sawāb*). Following these patterns of ritual aligns believers with the archetypes and myths with which, through ritual reenactment, they seek to synchronize and ultimately unite. This ideal of tradition is a continuous spiritual practice or yoga.

Social assemblies ranging from a dozen to several hundred members known as *hay'ats*—described by Reckord as the most influential unit of social organization in Iran after the family (1987:33)—facilitate the transmission and cultivation of religious practice, arts, and skills as well as dealing with various community affairs. *Hay'ats* are often organized along certain age groups (youth, elders) or interest groups (guilds, professions, clergy) and centre on activities such as studying the Qur'an, religious chanting, and other religious arts, often but not always with the help of clerical expertise. The *ulema* and their extended community of adherents are by definition conservative, particularly those in the shrine cities. The most conservative among these even disagree with some of the popular religious ceremonies, which they feel misrepresent Islam or even blaspheme it, as in the case of *ta'ziyeh* where imams are represented by actors. Not surprisingly, music is often subject to the age-old dynamic of the *samā'* polemic (debate surrounding the legality and appropriateness of listening to music, discussed below), ranging from outright proscription to tightly guarded regulation. Shajarian notes that radios were not allowed in his house while growing up in Mashhad, and that his only opportunity to learn to sing was through the study of Qur'an recitation and religious chanting. Despite the intrinsic conservatism of the *ulema*, it is interesting to recall here that the Jafari school of Shi'i jurisprudence includes an explicit mechanism for updating and revision: clerics at the rank of *mudjtahid* (just below that of the preeminent *ayatollahs*) are charged with the function updating the traditional interpretation of the Qur'an and *hadith* according to changing circumstances and the acquisition of new knowledge (Reckord 1987:29). This theoretically acknowledges that tradition needs to flow with change but how this has been translated into practice at present and throughout history is, of course, another matter.

Traditional Narratives, Performance Genres and Performers: Sacred and Secular Scripts

As one mode among a wide range of Iranian narratives and concomitant performance genres, avaz is an expressive performance based on the scripts of classical poetry and the radif. This section briefly reviews key Iranian narratives, practices and practioners in order to place avaz within this larger context.

In an apt resonance of quintessentially dualistic Zoroastrian and Manichaean teachings, contemporary Iranian identity is integrally predicated upon both ancient dynastic and Islamic foundations. A fascinating chapter of Miller's dissertation (1995:35–54) that was excluded from the published version of the work (1999) connects dots emanating from theories expounded in James Frazer's classic *The Golden Bough* to suggest the crosscultural mythological heritage of Shi'i mourning rituals, and by extension the valorization of martyrdom, which thereby emerge as vital, surviving manifestations of a truly ancient archetype. Fear of death is the deepest mystery and anxiety of the human condition, driving all aspects of individual psychology, collective culture and history (Becker 1973, 1975). In the mythic consciousness, micro- and macrocosmic phenomena correspond in the manner of fractal scaling and self-similarity: as above, so below. The polarity of life and death is applied through the ontological planes of the gods, humans, the seasons, vegetation, and so on. Decay of the growing season transposes to the death of the god responsible for this cycle, who humans attempt to resurrect through ritual mourning and sacrifice, thereby ensuring the return of life-sustaining crops. In addition to the ubiquitous imprint of this archetype on world mythologies, archaeological evidence from around the globe attests to the widespread practice of ritual sacrifice and regicide. As noted above regarding the "slippage" and fluidity of actors and the set roles in the historical transmission of narratives, this archetype spawned a vast range of manifestations. Among many other portrayals, the cosmic drama unfolded in Mesopotamia with Dumuzi (known as Tammuz in Syria) and Ishtar, in Egypt through Osiris, and Greece via Adonis and Attis. These myths feature the premature and violent death of the protagonist, who frequently has foreknowledge of his[6] martyrdom, undergoes a descent to the underworld and, like the vernal sun itself, subsequently resurrects. The rituals accompanying these cults typically included mourning, weeping, loud music, "frenzied" dance, offerings of flowers and cakes, self-mortification, bloodletting, and varied forms of sacrifice. Bull sacrifice was central to the Persian cult of Mithraism that spread widely throughout West Asia and Europe, surviving in our times in the form of the bullfight.

While not explicitly linked to agricultural renewal, the martyrdom of divine or righteous individuals figure prominently in ancient Iranian mythology, usually as a result of intrigue surrounding succession of power, as exemplified by Zarer and Siavesh. Before he was successful and secure enough to perform under his own name Ostad Shajarian performed under the stage name Siavesh, the upholder of righteousness and truth. According to the tenth-century account of Narshakhi, a tradition of mourning was still practiced at that time, featuring mourning songs known as *kin-e Siavesh* or *geristan-e mughan* ("weeping of the Magi") (Miller 1995:42).

> Although the Zarer story is of Zoroastrian origin, the Siyavesh martyr concept is said to predate Zoroastrianism, having its roots in Eastern Persian pagan traditions related to the Tammuz or Adonis cults of Mesopotamia, Anatolia and Egypt . . . . The martyrdom of Hosein at the hands of the evil Yazid at the battle of Karbala . . . for Iranian Moslems was reminiscent of their pre-Islamic martyr heroes. For this reason, the Tammuz, Adonis and/or Siyavesh cults seemed to find continued expression in the rites of mourning for Hosein and the martyrs at Karbala. (ibid.:43)

Furthermore, Miller notes the correspondence of this mythic archetype to Sufi doctrines of annihilation of the ego (*fanā'*) and death of the lower self (*nafs*), after which the initiate's consciousness is "resurrected" at a higher level (ibid.:49, 51). Fakirist displays of extreme self-mortification practiced by a small minority of Sufi orders[7] figure into this as well. Whether the Shi'i rituals (and Sufi symbolism) stand in a continuous, atavistic or merely coincidental relationship to this ancient mythological heritage, the correspondence is evident and provocative.

With only an estimated 35,000–60,000 Zoroastrians currently living discreetly in Iran[8] (of the 200,000 worldwide) and having endured centuries of sporadic persecution, their ability and force in maintaining the collective identity of pre-Islamic legacy of Iran—despite their direct lineage to it—has been minimal. This legacy was of course brilliantly consolidated by Ferdowsi in his secular epic *Shahnāme,* which became the primary vehicle for transmitting and sustaining ancient Iranian mythology, history and cultural identity among Iranians throughout the

Islamic period to the present.[9] Up until the 1970s, with the widespread establishment of radio and television broadcasting, the *Shahnāme* was recited in well-attended coffee houses throughout Iran[10] and its stories were the staple of both bardic and *naqqali* repertories (performative modes that will be described in more detail below), contemporary representatives of the pre-Islamic bardic legacy of the *gōsān*.

> *Shahnameh* is not only a text written in a particular year by a particular man but also a collection of stories dealing generally with the history and great heroes of Iran. It seems that for both storyteller and audience, Ferdowsi's work represents only one rescension of a *Shahnameh* which storytellers today also tell. The storyteller does not recreate someone else's work but rather creates his own interpretive version in the process of telling the story. Through the use of such devices as analogies, the storyteller imbues the familiar material with meaning relevant to his audience and puts his own particular stamp on the stories... It is the process of the actual telling before an audience that forces the storyteller to shape and continually to reshape his material. (Page 1979: 212–13)

Performing Islam; Islamic Narratives

Qur'an Recitation

Qur'an recitation or cantillation is the central focal point and performative rite of all branches of Islam, standing beyond its Five Pillars while simultaneously constituting their foundation.[11] The imperative issued to the Prophet Mohammad to "Recite!" (Qur'an 96:1) was both an historical event and an archetypal one with a spiritual resonance that projected outside of time and space. It marks the beginning of a sacred mandate of prophecy, the founding of a colossal spiritual and sociohistorical movement presently followed by one-fifth of humanity, and is an archetypal act wherein Muslims directly partake and participate in the word of God. For Muslims, reciting or listening to the Qur'an is the ritual reenactment of the Prophet Mohammad's archetypal act of "reciting" the word of Allah, roughly analogous to the rite of the Eucharist for Christians, who thereby partake in the Word/Logos of the very same God. In terms of its narrative content, a good portion of the Qur'an is devoted to storytelling. Other types of discourse and content include esoteric and exoteric doctrine, legal injunctions, practical matters concerning daily life, and ritual prescriptions, among other matters—all expressed in a miraculously poetic beauty of impeccable Arabic. The Qur'an is the means by which Muslims conduct their lives; they "perform" the Qur'an as way of living. And they perform it, in a more immediate sense, through recitation.

Qur'an recitation occurs in a great variety of contexts, from private individual practice,[12] through small intimate groups of modestly-skilled believers, to large public recitals by highly specialized and masterfully-skilled professionals. As we have seen, Shajarian was born into a family of religious singers and his principal formation and subsequent activity through his childhood and teens was as a prodigy of Qur'an recitation. While the art of Qur'anic recitation requires extreme precision according to the intricate rules of *tajwid* with regard to pronounciation, the rhythmic distribution and flow of the text, the placement of pauses and silences, the reciter has great freedom in terms of melody, including the selection of mode,[13] melodic line, ornamentation, and "dramatic" expression (the latter, providing one stays within dignified boundaries reflecting the sacred nature of the text). Upon mastery of proper *tajwid*, qualities of good recitation include cultivating an appropriate vocal tone and the ability to evoke the spirit of the text with an appropriate melodic setting and engaging expression. The delivery should be beautiful, powerful, and inspire those who hear it. This setting is improvised and ideally never the same for reciting the same verse; unlike the Christian practice of setting religious texts to repeatable compositions, Islam regards the Qur'an as the direct words of God, which transcends the relativity of any human utterance. These features of Qur'an recitation are clearly transferable to the art of avaz.[14] Faruqi (1985:457ff.) proposes a hierarchy whereby various sonic art forms are "more or less Islamic," and thereby legitimate, depending upon the degree to which they are structured upon the Qur'anic archetype. In many of its definitive characteristics, avaz is clearly and closely influenced by, and related to, Qur'anic recitation and indeed carries the most prestigious position amongst the Iranian musical arts. That said, as a secular art form it is immeasurably subordinate to Qur'an recitation and, despite the apparent similarities and relationship, many Muslims regard the latter as conceptually and doctrinally neither singing nor even music.

Performance Example 1: Rabbana

While Shajarian was familiar to many Iranians through radio broadcasts and concert performances, many more knew his voice through his famous recording of the Rabbana.[15] Broadcast widely across the country, especially during the month of Ramadan and key dates of the religious calendar, it reached an audience that may not have paid attention to art music. Whereas his cassette album *Bidad* (recorded in 1982) is probably Shajarian's most famous recording of avaz, his rendition of Rabbana may well be his most well-known recording, period (even if many listeners didn't know who the singer was by name). Shajarian included this spectacular recitation on his 1999 album *Be Yad e Pedar*. Recorded at the end of his early period in 1979, I have transcribed it here as an outstanding example of his abilities in the sacred idiom with which he began his vocal training and performance career. In terms of his vocal skill and public exposure, the recording indeed represents a culminating point of his work in the genre of sacred chant.

The back story to the rise of this iconic recording is marked by revolutionary intrigue. Among the first hapless souls to be executed in the chaos following the Islamic Revolution was Seyyed Javad Zabihi, a singer of religious music who kept close ties to the Pahlavi regime and was featured prominently on national radio broadcasts. Acting as an advisor to the radio, Shajarian was preparing singers to record chants that would replace Zabihi's for future broadcasting. Shajarian left his study materials with the radio and was surprised to hear it broadcasted instead of the composite recording of the singers he had prepared (BBC Persian 2010).

> *I didn't sing Rabbana for broadcast: I sang it as a lesson for a few singers (students), which we took to the studio to record. One day before the month of Ramazan I gave the tape to the radio. Later I hear that they are broadcasting my recording of Rabbana. I phoned them and asked why they broadcasted it and they said "The arrow has left the bow" [i.e., it's too late now and out of your control]. I sang it in the month of Tir 1358/June–July 1979. Before then, Zabihi had sung the Rabbana [for broadcast]. They said that because of the revolution, the program for the month of Ramazan should now be commensurate with the revolution and have the same dignity. For three or four months I was teaching the class of singers and singing all of the du'as (prayers). I went inside the studio and I sang. Afterwards I said to the students: now you sing based on these models and then I'll edit your performances into a composite final version. I did a lot of work. (Shajarian et al. 2004:130)*

Rabbana consists of verses in the Qur'an beginning with the word *Rabbana* ("Our Lord") that are supplications (*du'a*) made to Allah by angels, prophets (including Jesus), along with other prominent figures and righteous believers. Shajarian links four such verses together, each from a different *surah* (chapter), to form a short, unified recitation. Some lines of each verse are repeated rhetorically in effective variations. Translations of the four verses are given below, the verses indicated in the transcription through corresponding Roman numerals:

I.
Our Lord! (they say), Let not our hearts deviate now after Thou hast guided us,
But grant us mercy from Thine own Presence;
for Thou art the Grantor of bounties without measure
[Qur'an 3:8]

II.
Our Lord! We believe; then do Thou forgive us, and have mercy upon us:
For Thou art the Best of those who show mercy
[23: 109]

III.
Our Lord! Bestow on us Mercy from Thyself,
and dispose of our affair for us in the right way!
[18:10]

IV.
Our Lord! Bestow on us endurance, make our foothold sure,
and give us help against the disbelieving folk
[2:250]

Ostad Shajarian was curious as to whether we would attempt transcribing his version of Rabbana. When affirmed that the work was in progress but very tough going, he responded with considerable understatement, *"Everything in Rabbana is completely different from avaz—the language, the rhythm, even the singing technique differs"* (2010). Indeed. Despite the massive amount of time, energy and care put into transcribing this four-minute recording—very much more than required for transcribing his avaz—the resulting accuracy is humblingly limited. Interpreting and denotating the rhythm presents enormous difficulties. It has a slippery, polymetric quality that is a rhythmical equivalent of *iham*. This quality brings to my mind microtiming involved in Mande (West Africa) jembe drumming that both alternates and falls between the cracks of a triple/compound and quadruple division of pulse. It is a very explicit musical illustration of the organic, spontaneous "growth" of Shajarian's singing defying containment in the linear grid of rhythmic notation. It is very beautiful and shows Shajarian to be a great master of musical time, among other qualities. The transcription offers some insights into its nature while conceding (no contest) that the music breathes, moves, and grows in its own mysterious way. As one's perspective is constantly shifting when "microlistening," the security of a given grouping or subdivision of the pulse never lasts long, it seemed fair to try different evocations of this in the transcription and let it stand as is, limited and subjective though this may be. Other parameters bring about difficulties—ghost notes, vowel shifts, abrupt stops or microrests, articulation, ornaments, shifts in vocal tone (e.g., the brief moment of strident rasp at 3:52), brief shifts to the head voice, use of consonantal noise, etc. A truly amazing degree of fractal detail is contained in this performance for those who listen to it repeatedly and carefully.[16]

Rabbana is set to the Arab maqam Rast, which does not exist as such in Persian music (though there are moments in Oj of Esfahan, Rohab, and even Afshari itself that evoke it). Shajarian's mastery of Qur'an recitation included the perfect command of this and other non-Iranian maqams, notably Saba, as demonstrated on his recording *Be Yad e Pedar*. (The transcription here is transposed up a perfect 5th in order to conform to the Arab convention of notating Rast with a tonic of C.) The effect of his powerful, bright tone and rapid ornamentation at the beginning is arresting, immediately commanding the listener's attention. Modally, it begins somewhat ambiguously by stressing the fourth degree of the maqam, and then the fifth, although the tonic is reasonably clear by the end of the line. The rest of the performance evokes Rast in a clear and powerful fashion. The second verse includes brief "weeping" ornaments on the word *faghfir* ("forgive") at 1:39 and 2:07 that engage *taswir al ma'na* "word-painting" techniques of evoking the text used by Egyptian reciters (Nelson 1985:63-65), along with the crosscultural signifier of heightened emotional intensity by deploying this vocal ornament. In this case the implication is sincere regret and remorse for one's errors in the process of the petition. The third verse particularly conveys an inexplicable, gut-level sense of supplication, indeed pleading, through his articulation and shifts in vocal colouring (especially at 3:02ff.). After this evocation of submission, the final verse shifts dramatically through a range of contrasting "postures" (this is admittedly subjective and complicated by crosscultural factors but seems strikingly clear to me nonetheless) of reestablishing individual power, strength, dignity and nobility. The huge prestige, influence, and cultural cachet associated with Shajarian's Rabbana over the past three decades made a decisive shift from embodying deep-seated spiritual values to including an explicit element of political resistance in the summer of 2010, discussed in Simms and Koushkani (2012).

Rabbana

(transposed up a perfect 5th)

Rab-ba-na

lâ tu-zigh qu-lu - - - ba - na Rab-ba-na

la tu-zigh qu-lu - ba - na

ba' - da 'idh ha-da a - ta-na

wa ha-ba la-na min - la dun - ka rah - ma-tan

'in - na - ka 'an - (ta al)wah-hab

II: 1:23

Rab-ba - na

a - man - na   fagh - fir la - na

war - ham - na

Rab - ba-na   a' - - -

(2:07)

- man - na   fagh - fir   la - na   war - ham - na

wa 'an - ta kha - y - ru   ar - ra - him-in

III: 2:37

Rab - ba - na

'a - ti-na   mi(n) - la - dun - ka ra - h - ma - tan

Rab ba na

'a - ti - na mi(n) - la-dun - ka rah - ma-tan

wa hay - yi' la - na min 'am - ri - na

IV: 3:28 5

ra-sha-dan Rab - ba-na a - frigh 'a -

la - y - na sa - b-ran Rab-ba-na

(3:52)

a - frigh 'a-a-la ' y - na sa-bran wa thab-bit

3

'a(q) - da - ma - na (wan) sur - na 'a -

la al - qaw - mi (al)-ka - fi - rin

Karbala, *Rowze khāni, Ta'ziyeh*

If the Qur'an is the central archetype of all Muslims, the martyrdom of the Prophet Mohammad's grandson Hussein at Karbala in 680 AD while en route to Damascus to assume leadership of the Muslim community is the defining historical moment of Shi'i Islam, one that subsequently transmuted into archetypal, "mythic" significance. In this transformation—which, as mentioned above, resonates with extremely old martyrdom mythologies—the Umayad Caliph Yezid is the archetypal usurper, a tyrant who ruthlessly arranges for the murder of Hussein, who is not only the direct lineage with the Prophet Mohammad but through these events becomes the symbolic embodiment of righteousness, revolution, and personal sacrifice. The seventy-two followers of Hussein who were martyred by his side on the tenth day of the month of Muharram became the archetype of loyal, uncompromising revolutionaries. The historical martyrdom of Imams Ali, Hasan, and Reza are similarly transformed into quasi-"mythical" symbols combining justice, resistance, martyrdom, outrage, and sadness. "The Karbala event, as a defining master narrative, has remained at the heart of Shi'i collective consciousness, to be reinvented for any number of political ends" (Chelkowski and Dabashi 1999:46).[17] Dabashi extrapolates on the Karbala narrative to identify a fundamental paradox intrinsic to the doctrine of Shi'ism, which as "a historically combative and intransigent religion of protest must always be in a position of defiance and rebellion and thus can never come to power without immediately discrediting itself" (2007:190).

The central role of martyrdom and sacrifice in Shi'ism is roughly parallel to the role of the passion of Christ in Christianity and the ennobling act of early Christians "becoming Christ" through martyrdom—like the proto-historical mythological and ritual roots described above, the archetypal event invites believers to follow suit and "participate." In the Shi'i tradition this "vicarious suffering" (Reckord 1987:19–20) meant upholding conviction, endurance and a willingness to sacrifice in the face of hardship and injustice (Chelkowski and Dabashi 1999:78) and that the righteous may suffer but will prevail, just as the forces of light triumph over darkness in Zoroastrian dualism. The events of Karbala initiated the subsequent tradition of performing martyrdom and its concomitant grieving on various planes of Iranian culture, from literally dying in battle to various symbolic and ritual activations.

Beginning in the Buyid rule (932–1055) a range of mourning rituals evolved to commemorate the anniversary of the quintessential Shi'i sacro-historical events in Iran and other Shi'i communities, particularly during the months of Muharram and Safar, which are marked by collective sadness, public emotional catharsis, and social solidarity. These rites and practices are numerous, diverse and are highly localized. While some existed beforehand, these mourning rituals were not central to Iranian public life until the sixteenth-century ascension of the Safavids, who were keen to differentiate themselves from the neighbouring Sunni Uzbeks and Ottomans (Chelkowski and Dabashi 1999:77).[18] One of the most prominent and emblematic of these public rites is the *dasta-gardani*, large processions of male devotees who self-flagellate or beat their chests as they march en masse through streets lined with observers, some of whom join the procession.

Dated in 1501, Kafeshi's *Rawzat al Shuhada* (Garden of Martyrs), describing the martyrdom story of Karbala, is the first collection of martyrdom stories (*maqtal*) written in Persian and gave rise to the "stationary Karbala ritual" of *rowze khāni*: the recitation and chanting of elegies indoors in a venue known as *takiyeh* where the audience encircles the seated *rowze khān*, who "runs the show" of the ritual and "becomes the effective truth teller" (Chelkowski and Dabashi 1999:54). The explicit goal of the *rowze khāni* is to play on the emotions of audience and make them weep (Chelkowski 1979:102). Clearly, a strong rapport between the *rowze khān* and his audience during a performance is integral—success of a performance may be judged by how intensely people cry. Blum paradoxically notes, however, that while *rowze khāns* are in demand and popular, they are also frequently regarded with some ambivalence for these same definitive abilities to manipulate and for charging a fee to do so (2002a:826–27). Unlike the separation of class in public ceremonies in past centuries, *rowze khāni* was inclusive, "the only devotion participated in by the elite and more orthodox" (Chelkowski 1979: 67), by comparison it was largely the common people who constituted the street processions and *ta'ziyeh*. Haery (1982: 26–27) describes two types of *rowze khāni* specializations: the *wā'zin*, who comments on the Qur'an, various sacred discourses, appealing to intellect, and the *zākerin* who recites the religious incidents of Muharram, for which a high-quality voice is advantageous. Reckord notes that the *wa'iz* are more erudite, are authorized to preach and recite in their own words and include exegesis of doctrine in their performances while the *mollahs* (defined as those who dropped out of seminaries before the completion of their programs) are restricted to memorized text without offering exegesis. The latter group, however, "often extemporize freely in their own words during ceremonies for reasons of heightening the emotions of the audience, enhancing their own prestige, or pleasing the masses and thereby gaining a better income for their services. Some informants suggested that those with good voices and quick wit dropped out of their studies early, while those more prosaic continued" (1987: 28).

Modern avaz performance, especially as practiced by Shajarian, effectively unites these functions of appealing to both the intellect (based on the poem selected and his evocation of specific layers of *iham*) as well as the emotions, showcasing a beautiful and powerfully expressive voice. Avaz presents a clear secular parallel to *rowze khāni* as a venue for uniting social classes in the act of listening. Singers of avaz frequently emerged from the milieu of *rowze khān*s: Mirza Lofollah Esfahani, Sheikh Ali Zargar, Jenab Damavandi, and the more widely known Qamar (Nakjavani 2008) and Parisa (Safvat and Caron 1966:203; Miller 1999: 41). Both the *rowze khān*s and audience perform their scripted roles in these rituals, the former by singing and provoking and the latter through the expected response of weeping. Given their large, diverse audience and their mandate for emotional manipulation, *rowze khān*s had great potential for political influence in their act of telling.

Using the language and metaphors of *The Garden of Martyrs*, he (the *rowze khān*) might also make allusions to the contemporary situation, emphasizing the suffering of the deprived and the wrongdoing of current rulers and administrators. *Rowze-khāni* thus became a historical vehicle of renarrating the events of Karbala to conform with the actual exigencies of the time . . . (and) served to mobilize the crowd, to provoke marches, sit-ins and the chanting of slogans. Converted to religious political action, these meetings could prepare the crowd to go out into the streets to express its discontent and anger over grievances. (Chelkowski and Dabashi 1999:78–79)

The *ta'ziyeh* ritual drama—the only indigenous Islamic dramatic tradition—arose in the mid-eighth century as a fusion of processional and stationary Karbala rituals and evolved to include over one hundred plays concerning some two hundred to two hundred-and-fifty story plots that provide a detailed, provocative narration of the martyrdom of Hussein and other Imams (Chelkowski and Dabashi 1999:54ff.). *Ta'ziyeh* employs both spoken and sung conventionalized voice stylings to characterize roles within the narrative—especially differentiating good guys from bad—which are readily understood by the audience. Sung portions assign a conventionalized vocal register, tone, and melodic mode (which generally correspond to those of Persian music) to specific characters. A tight, intimate rapport is established between the actors and the audience, with the latter often plunging into the audience or addressing individual audience members in the course of the performance (ibid.: 80). While scripts were and are still written, they play a secondary role to performers' improvised elaboration and animation, a performance practice common to the contemporaneously arising secular theatric traditions of improvised farce (*ru-howzi*) and puppetry (*kheimeh-shab-bazi*).[19] Dabashi describes *ta'ziyeh* as a theatre of protest, a performative function of Shi'ism as a religion of protest wherein

> reality and fiction are counternarrated, bringing the tragedy of Hussein home to bear on the moment of its actual performance. . . . In ta'ziyeh, acting is not mimetic; it is entirely suggestive—with a full contractual agreement, dramatically articulated, between the actors and the audience that they are *just* acting. Actors hold their script in their hands, not because they don't know the lines but because they want to demonstrate distance and suggest a dissimilitude. . . . The stage never loses sight of its not-being-the-stage. Non-actors have easy access to the stage area; actors move in and out of character at will. There is fluidity between reality and acting because the actors are performing no act of fiction. . . . The characters of ta'ziyeh drama are not just metaphorical, they are metamorphic—they easily mutate into contemporary historical figures. (Dabashi 2005:94–95)

The performative art of *parde dāri*, commonly performed in coffee houses, shares features of both *rowze khāni* and *ta'ziyeh*. Here a large painting illustrating the events of Karbala is animated by a solo narrator, who points to the corresponding scenes with a cane and through both speech and song improvises a dramatic description of successive scenes in an attempt to engage and manipulate the emotions of the audience (Chelkowski and Dabashi 1999:56ff.).

AK

Ta'ziyeh is a good example for what we are trying to elucidate regarding avaz: first, the occasion; second, Persian classical music in relation to the poem and the subject. In ta'ziyeh different characters sing their parts in different dastgahs. For example, the character of Abbas, the cousin of Hussein, always sings in Chahargah and Mahur, nothing else: that is his character and these modes will support the character. There are other characters, like Zeinab and her offspring and each of them have their own music that corresponds to their personalities. The music can be changed or ornamented differently and performed in different styles, depending on the abilities of the people singing the part. They have their own character and their body language and individual voice expresses that character. Many good singers and teachers were originally ta'ziyeh singers such as Malik Al-Zakerin and Iqbal Sultan.

Ta'ziyeh has its own rules. There are specific musical instruments used for ta'zieh: especially after the Qajar era they brought in instruments such as the trumpet, the side drum, bass drum, and woodwind instruments, like clarinet. Mostly brass instruments are used although the brass never plays with the singer. The role of instrumentalists and singers are not same as their roles in Persian classical music—for example, there is no jawab avaz (instrumental responses between sung verses). They perform their sections separately. Once in a while when someone wanted to be creative they used flutes. It was difficult to be really creative at these kinds of events because they had to be approved by mullahs, who didn't want music, voices, poetry, and religious recitations performed together. Particular musical expressions hold associations for people and this adds a layer of meaning when employed by characters in the drama. This could lead to problems with the mullahs: for example, they don't want Shemr, the killer of Hussein, to sing beautifully and capture people's hearts. So he usually recites in a declamatory style called rajaz. This kind of poem has been written exactly for this recitation. It's interesting to note that we also have the gushe Rajaz in the radif, in Chahargah.

Stylistically, rajaz is a kind of musical declamation involving a simple intoning of a few pitches. Rajazkhāne comes from an old protocol or ritual of military engagement. Instead of attacking each other (or before they engage in armed combat), opposing sides would meet and the leaders of would step forward and introduce themselves in a defiant and boastful way: "I am so-and-so, son of so-and-so, I have conquered x and y, I am stronger than a and b, I can split a tree in half with a single blow of an axe," and so on, in this manner. The way they are presenting this is very important because everyone surrounding them, from both sides, is listening to them and this sets up how the combat is going to proceed. Leaders also employ rajaz when they are rallying their troops—you know, the classic Hollywood scene where the general is on horseback saying, "We are fight-ing the good fight, we are right, if you die today you die with honour." This is *rajaz*. There are many expanded applications of this. In the ceremony of Ashura, someone addresses the public about who the brother of Imam Hussein was; it is done musically, with *rajaz*. In reciting the sacred histories of Karbala it was for-bidden to sing at certain points, so *rajaz* was the perfect compromise. It's very effective and you can deliver anything with it, prose, poetry, even conversation.

Ta'ziyeh is not just about the tragedy of Hussein; it carries many older tradi-tions from Zoroastrians and others who wanted to preserve their culture and their arts. They had an elemental need to do this and founded *ta'ziyeh* as a venue for preserving all kinds of genres—*madahi, marsiye, nowhe khāni*, and so on. All of the sections of the *ta'ziyeh* have their own character, subject, and relationship to previous art forms. At the end of a *ta'ziyeh* performance there is the ritual of the march, which is a ceremony common to many religions in Iran. While marching, people beat themselves with *zanjir*, which is a sort of chain, or beat their chests and sing in call and response. The tempo gets faster and the meter changes from two to six beats, reminiscent of other forms of music and ritual like *samā'*, where the rhythm is coordinated with the breathing of the performers. They end with a kind of *marsiye rowze*—people start to cry or just listen. At this point the group is indoors and usually the lights are turned off while the singer performs the *mar-siye*.

In the *ta'ziyeh*, as in all other forms of avaz, the poetry is chosen in relation to the occasion and in most parts of Iran Persian classical melodies are employed. But in the *ta'ziyeh*s of Shiraz, Esfahan, and Lorestan, you sometimes hear the in-fluence of their respective folk music. *Ta'ziyeh* was discouraged in Reza Shah's era, as he wanted to make the country more secular. It's still practiced now but not as much as previous decades.

OS
Question: There are other styles of traditional Iranian singing like *ta'ziyeh, rowze, maddahi*. What do you think of them?
Yes, I have heard them all but don't hear anything there that grabs my artistic attention.
Why not?
There is no particular artist in these genres that attracts my attention. There is no real technique involved and no particular tone that appeals to me. But I can easi-ly sing like Pavarotti or that method of singing because I have worked on it, and even when I sing today I use some of their techniques. (2008)
What is the relationship between religious a cappella chant and classical singing with the dastgah system?
It is very close…You know, the genre of religious song is interpreted on the basis of modulations (morakab-khani). For example, in chanting the Qur'an, one always

begins in dastgah Shur (Salmak-Eragh),[20] *the Oj of Shur, one octave above, and then after Ashirin, which is an Arab maqam, one starts to modulate to Bayat-Esfahan or Mahur and one ends in Shur. (Kasmai and Lecomte 1991:250)*

RS
Ostad Shajarian's unequivocal disconnect with religious singing in our 2008 interview runs against one of the fundamental assertions of this study: that avaz is one bandwidth within the wide spectrum of Iranian narrative vocal arts, a bandwidth very close to that of religious song. Given the circumstances of this interview we chose to not pursue the topic further at the time but his remarks require some comment here. Firstly, he is clearly focussing on the musical styles versus the performance processes and social functions involved. Of course, Shajarian also distances himself from the regime of the Islamic Republic and likewise from being in any way associated with, or sympathetic to, the *ulema* culture, which surely colours his response. It's interesting to compare his reaction to a similar question when it was posed to him in 1990, a few years after embarking on international tours and a time he had to be more careful, less openly opposed to the regime. The context of the latter interview was of course very different and the question was also phrased in a different manner from that of our interview. Many more things are likely involved in both of these replies.

Secular Narratives

Iran possesses an incredibly rich array of diverse, long-standing, multicultural bardic traditions known by various local titles such as *bakhshi, ashiq, avesta, luti, shā'er, pahlawān, beytbij*, etc. Khorasan is particularly rich in this respect and Mashshad is a major center of diverse performance activity (See Youssefzadeh 2002, Blum 1972). While it is somewhat useful to regard these vocations as the secular guardians of tradition, there is often a liberal inclusion of sacred references included in their performance, not to mention the very strong possibility of links to ancient, archetypal shamanistic traditions (During 1994:183ff., 1996:335, 370ff.; During and Khudoberdiev 2007; Zeranska-Kominek 1990). Bardic traditions around the world have been effectively replaced with radio and television media: in some areas they disappear entirely (e.g., the Balkans), while others are updated through high-tech syncretism (e.g., popular strands of Mande *jaliya* in West Africa). As with other areas in Asia, a wide range of Iranian bardic traditions remain surprisingly resilient and vital in the rural outback. The same mediating technology that marginalized them in the first place has also served to transmit them both within and outside their original locales. The bards of northern Khorasan especially embody and reflect the pluralistic reality of Iran, their art and audience demanding a working knowledge of Persian, Turkmen, and Kurdish languages, memory of a range of the concomitant epic literatures both written and oral, along with a solid command of their corresponding musical idioms, repertoires and techniques (see Blum 1972, 1972a; Youssefzadeh 2002).

Westerners need to recalibrate their definitions of literacy and illiteracy—specifically, softening their simplistic binary categorization—when considering these traditions and the larger demographic they grew from. Illiteracy in oral cultures does not necessarily entail the modern associations with deprivation and ignorance (Scholes et al. 2006: 18ff.). Dabashi recounts the highly refined and cultured sensibilities cultivated through the memorization of poetry and other means throughout Iranian history, and more recently the diffusion of newspapers (read aloud to groups of people) and radio, cassettes, etc., as naturally extending the traditional means by which people may acquire oral knowledge (Dabashi 2005: 92, 142–44).

Like their counterparts who were until relatively recent times found in most cultures around the world, the Iranian bards are performing epic history and mythology, retelling well-known stories that both inform and entertain ("infotainment" in contemporary media-speak), and provide a sense of cultural identity, of belonging to an in-group with shared values and history.[21] As with the emblematic Westerner bards Shakespeare and Wagner, the stories narrated are not of their own invention but rather taken from the public domain and reworked for pitching to a contemporaneous audience. Along with an epic, narrative repertoire Iranian bards also perform purely poetic genres based on well-known poets from various periods of history belonging to the immediate locale or with a wider claim to fame. As the audience is already familiar with the narrative or poetry, the bard's success is contingent on their inspired delivery and ability to engage the audience through a fresh, dynamic combination of narration, singing, dramatic expression, instrumental accompaniment and solos, that tastefully balances expectation with wit and surprise. The performances are constructed by weaving the text, whose rhythmic delivery is subject to flexible variation that nonetheless maintains the integrity of the original scansion, with preset melodic formulae, themes, formal schemata and developmental strategies. Options abound in the talented bard's toolkit for rearranging, including, deleting, alluding to or developing particular episodes in the narrative both textually and musically. The primary function of the bard and epic as a focal point for reaffirming community (local, often ethnic) identity is similar to avaz but becomes classicized and nationalized in the latter.

Traditional storytelling (*naqqali*) was also popular in coffee houses throughout Iran before its rapid decline in the 1970s. The art of the *naqqal* had much in common with that of the bards, particularly requiring a good memory to command a large repertoire of epic literature, written plot summaries (*tumar*) and lyric poetry, along with the ability to form a close rapport with the audience and captivate them with fresh retellings of stories they were intimately familiar with. A strong, expressive voice was required along with appropriate gesturing to effectively illustrate and propel the narrative. The best *naqqal*s were "always aware of their environment and in touch with their listeners (to) create an atmosphere of excitement, vehemence, and even, at times, of frenzy" (Haery 1982: 26). In other words, they were aware of the occasion and used a wide range of tools to respond appropriately to it. The *naqqal* had considerable freedom to vary and embellish the plot which was largely delivered in prose with occasional interjections of poetry—almost invariably Ferdowsi—as well as incorporating various digressions in the form of episodes from Karbala, proverbs, anecdotes, and comparisons to contemporary events. A short page or two of *tumar* may be expanded into a ninety-minute performance (Page 1977: 201). While a particular performance of a story can differ substantially from its epic source text, *naqqal*s interviewed by Page believed that they were still faithful to it. As the texts were old, they felt it their job to refresh them and indeed audiences demanded as much—a balance of surprise along with what they expected of the plot—and that their invention was further justified in that it followed the practice of *rowze khān*s, who do the same with what is supposed to be sacred historical fact (Page 1979: 208). Moreover, they felt that retelling stories meant "interpreting" them, which included the responsibility of "teaching values" to the audience (ibid.: 209)—an activity at the junction of narration and rhetoric.

Performing Truth: Truth-Telling and Authority

A well-educated speaker of advanced years thinks and then speaks his words.
Do not expend your breath in speaking without reflection. Speak well,
    and if it takes you a long time to speak, what of it?
Reflect and then speak, and be done with it before everybody shouts, "Enough!"
By speech is a human better than the beasts; but beasts are better than
    you if you do not speak the truth.
                      —Sa'di (trans. Thackston 2008:9)

. . . the Sunjata story
Is very strange and wonderful.
You see one griot,
And he gives you an account of it one way,
And you will find that that is the way he heard it;
You see another griot,
And he gives you an account of it in another way,
And you will find that what he has heard has determined his version.
                      —Banna Kanute[22]

OS
Question: Mystical poetry is integral to avaz; did you have any formal training in mysticism?
This training is partly due to the great people that I have met in my life, not the ones in the field of avaz but those in the fields of the humanities. They showed me how to interpret the truth, because I was always interested to find the truth. Fortunately I was able to find many of my answers, but I can't tell them because

some people are unable to tolerate hearing them. If a person wants to find the truth, she can, only if she is not fanatical towards a certain belief. She should be able to correct herself and realize that she may be wrong in some instances. She shouldn't think that everything she knows is true. She must think that she also can be wrong and allow herself the possibility that the truth may be other than what she thinks and it is always like this. There are always some other truths in the world that we do not know about: you must really go after the truth as perpetual seekers to find it. This on its own creates a special feeling in a person and therefore his breath becomes different than someone who does not have this knowledge. This knowledge is like a fragrance that is sprayed on something and will change it completely.

Humanity is pure thought; our whole being as humans consists of thought. I do not believe in faith because thinking and faith are on the opposite sides of each other. All the problems facing the societies of the world, especially the ones that are based on "conviction," are due to their faith and that's why they are in conflict with each other. It is faith based on the beliefs of others, a blind faith that does not utilize their own thoughts and consciousness. It therefore turns into fanaticism, which results in killing themselves and others. This is because of faith: if it was due to thinking it would not make them act like that. The weaker the thinking gets, the stronger the faith grows. If one wants to have faith, one has to think about it with one's own consciousness and then realize that two plus two is four. Once our consciousness accepts the logic of an idea and has tested it numerous times, then that faith becomes true.

I want my work to be for people and in service to people and through people. The greatest joy is when people are happy and people can easily understand whether you are honest with them or whether or not you are lying to them. This means that you have to be very honest with yourself and your beliefs so that you don't lie in your day-to-day life because that will reflect in your art. Of course, at times we all tell white lies when confronted with certain situations. But lying is never part of my moral fibre because when I lie, it is dishonesty to my own being and I am not keen on being dishonest with myself. Now, people have a very great sense for how honest you are and how deceitful you have been in your life. Sometimes, however, a small group of people may believe a dishonest person; but that never lasts long and at some point people will usually realize their own mistake. The opposite can also happen, and out of jealousy some people will call you dishonest. But if you always remain honest, they also realize what a big mistake they had made and will come to know the true you. Once they know that you are honest, nothing can ever change it because human beings always want honesty and truth. Even when a thief steals something from someone, that thief gives it to someone else who is "honest" and he can trust! So you see, even a thief wants to be around honest people and not dishonest and disloyal people. So it is in the essence of human beings to appreciate loyalty and honesty. People who lie are in the first place disloyal to themselves, and secondly, they put them-

selves in jeopardy. So a person must be a service to people and be honest so that people can trust him or her.

When I sing, I always focus on my message and delivering that message, that idea. When my listeners are present, I know that even if they don't understand the message right away, they will definitely understand it later on. I sing based on the fact that my audience may only understand my message afterward. Sometimes, however, I only sing from my own heart and I want everyone to hear what's inside it and, in a sense, the message travels into space, because I pour out everything that is in my heart.

What is your ambition and goal?

My ambition is to be able to put forth my art in the most beautiful way in the service of social issues and compassionate messages, for the benefit of people, and to be standing in solidarity with the people (2009).

How is it that two or three different generations really appreciate your music and are so moved by you?

One reason is to really know one's potential, what one is capable of, and also to know one's own society, the history of one's own craft and to be honest with one's listeners. It is with honesty that you can exert the most influence upon people so that they start believing in you and trusting you. If people lose trust in an artist, he is done for. This is about anything in life, from art to business. If there is honesty in the work, that work is successful. If people feel that what the artist is saying is true and it is in accordance with their own thoughts, then people will start paying attention.[23]

RS

The broad array of Iranian narrative performance genres discussed above serve multiple functions: to foster a sense of collective identity and facilitate socialization; as an economic field; as focal points of aesthetic cultivation and artistic craft; as conveyors of information and beliefs; and as a means of spiritual contemplation or simple diversion, among others. But what is ultimately at stake in many of these performances is nothing less than the truth, or perhaps more accurately, "the truth." While all religions, philosophies and cultures are concerned with truth, it is particularly explicit and foregrounded in Zoroastrianism, with the cosmic struggle between Ahura Mazda, embodying truth (*asha*) versus Ahriman-Angra Mainyu and the forces of falsehood and disorder (*drug*). Over eight hundred years ago, the brilliant, prescient Iranian writer 'Ayn al-Quzat realized that the medium is the message, that truth is contingent on its telling, which is in turn contingent on language (a closed system trapped within itself wherein words simply refer to other words), narrative devices and interpretative spin that in effect render it uncertain and untellable: it is impossible to tell the truth, only "truths" (Dabashi 1999). The paradox that words cannot convey the truth, yet we have no choice but to use them (as "no words" or silent contemplation alone cannot fully convey it either) was noted by Taoists since the opening chapter of the Tao Te Ching.[24] We therefore need both words and "no words," silence—or perhaps even better, words, silence and music—in our ultimately futile attempts at telling the truth. The great rub in this conception of truth-telling is that the individual teller is in the powerful position of being able to put a spin on the telling: indeed such spin, whether conscious or not, is quite inescapable. Telling the truth is a performance. We are then left with the delicate question of the authority and legitimacy of the teller.

> "Truth-Telling" thus became the most unexamined metaphysics, the unquestionable question, upon which "Islam" was imagined narratively. Successive generations of dynasties and sultanates, revolutions and resurgencies, orthodoxies and heterodoxies ever more deeply routinized and de-questioned the strange claim of the narrativity of *truth*, the unexamined assumption of the possibility of *telling* it. 'Ayn al–Qudat's writings effectively challenged that claim and that assumption and thus subverted the very possibility of truth, by demonstrating the constructed narrativity of it. (Dabashi 1999: 609)

Alas, things are not so freewheeling in the real world of human affairs, where various social institutions are in place to regulate consistency among the tellers and maintain the status quo (which of course changes with the natural flow of history) by any means necessary. While individual tellers hold a crucial, influential position, there are rigid (if temporary) collective borders superimposed upon the amorphous spontaneity and infinite complexity of the truth. 'Ayn al-Qudat spoke his truth, which brazenly subverted authority and slammed into a particularly well-fortified border that, not surprisingly for his times, resulted in his brutal torture and execution. Outside of one's subjective consciousness and its relationship with nature, in the world of collective humanity truth must be authorized through institutionalization—this is self-evident from both historical and contemporary vantage points. In a koan-like exercise of circularity, can we really trust D.H. Lawrence's famous injunction to "trust the tale, not the teller"? There is never a "single story" and when authorities insist upon enforcing one, the truth is flattened and incomplete.[25]

"Truth sits in narrativity as being in time. . . . Narrativity can thus be identified as the temporal space of all truth-claims" (Dabashi 1999: 644). This sounds like another good way of describing the occasion/*monāsebat*, as discussed above. Based on the particular requirements of the occasion, which are always different, Ostad Shajarian retells and reanimates poems in a new, contemporary context, and his audience bounces the archetypal images and narratives contained in the poetry off the current state of affairs, the present moment, according to their individual consciousness. In doing so, both performer and audience individualize, customize and perhaps even renovate the truth to its full polysemic complexity. Regardless of what Shajarian's original rationale or intentions may have been, it is interesting to note in connection with this discussion that his choice of stage name in the 1960s, Siavesh, signifies the martyred upholder of righteousness and truth from the *Shahnāme*. "Truth" is forever shifting,[26] dependent on context, occasion and consciousness. In perusing interviews and in Amir Koushkani's personal contact,

Ostad Shajarian displays sensitivity to this in often answering in different ways the same question posed at different times, in different contexts and among different company—as most of us do. Despite our deep social conditioning, many branches of scientific enquiry[27]—our contemporary quasi-religious constructor and gatekeeper of "truth"—suggest that reality may not be "out there" awaiting discovery but is rather a function of embodied consciousness.

> Any reconfiguration of colours and shapes, memories and melodies, signs and symbols, rhythms and meters, can claim a measure of belief and obedience in a reactivated collective consciousness. The ideological bent of all acts of signification begin to gain their momentous power from the properly manufactured framing they receive from their individual or collective constructions. "Truth" or "lie" is irrelevant. What matters is the power of convincing that links the signifier, the sign, and the signified together, and with them locks the targeted audience into the grip of the manipulator of the whole act of signification. . . . A revolution . . . is the opening of the deepest and hardest wounds of a people's historical endurance. A revolution also reveals how utterly arbitrary the collective construction of reality, of truth, of trust, of significance, is. The semiotic manipulation of shapes and colours, of memories and fantasies, is at the heart of (the revolutionary) man's conception of his being self-consciously in the world. The historical borderlines between truth and falsehood, reality and fantasy, begin to lose their received authority the moment the brutal artificiality of conviction makes itself apparent. (Chelkowski & Dabashi 1999:306–07)

Inventing tradition is fairly common in Shi'a Islam, where the present hierarchy of the clergy dates only from the nineteenth century (Curtis and Hooglund 2008:125). Khomeini went further and invented the doctrine of *velayat-e faqih*, whereby the guardianship of religious jurisprudence and clergy over all aspects of Iranian public administration institutes a divine order: as a theocracy, "God/Truth" now guided and ran the country. This doctrine did not exist previously in Shi'ism. It follows that the art and performance of persuasion is of outmost importance in public discourse, including the performance of avaz.

The Art and Performance of Rhetoric

Shajarian himself has used the metaphor of the *khānande* as an orator (Ocora liner notes, 1991: 4).[28] Focussing on musical processes, During suggests that rhetoric—the art of persuasion in public speaking—provides a useful model for conceptualizing improvisatory practice in Persian music based on the traditional categories of invention, disposition, elocution, action, and memory (1987:138), an approach to structure and process that we will expand upon in chapter 4. These applications follow on Powers' theoretical discussion that musical improvisation in West Asian and South classical traditions is more specifically akin to rhetorical oratory on a given traditional theme than to language processes in general (1980: 42–43). Noting the relationship between music and rhetoric is indeed ubiquitous since antiquity, with a flourishing among Baroque *Figurenlehre* and *musica poetica* theorists (Bartel 1997) that particularly resonates with Shajarian's conceptions detailed in chapter 4. In avaz the rhetorical analogy goes beyond analytical and generative processes in the music to elucidate its social function: its intention, purpose, and influence. Throughout these discussions my use of the metaphor of rhetoric is illustrative and suggests a wider view and interpretation of the art. I am not suggesting that Shajarian or other musicians make a conscious connection with it, nor am I interested in unearthing historical linkages of the arts of rhetoric and avaz beyond the brief discussion that follows, as this highly specialized area lies well outside my expertise. Rather my interest lies in explicating the relationship, showing its manifold usefulness and suggesting that it is a manifestation of some larger historical-cultural pattern that is perhaps collectively subconscious. There are too many correspondences between avaz (especially as it is conceived and practiced by Shajarian) and rhetoric to be merely coincidental.

While most societies throughout history have featured occasions for public speaking, it comes as no surprise that the philosophical investigation of rhetoric and an accompanying literature arose among the ancient Greeks, as effective persuasion was crucial to the founding of democratic governance. Aristotle's *Rhetoric* emerged as the most influential text on the art in the classical world, which along with the works of Cicero, occupied a central position in its cultivation through medieval and subsequent periods. There are various scholarly opinions regarding the transmission of classical rhetoric in Iran and the existence of indigenous practices. Parsinejad notes that pre-Islamic Iranian elites were likely familiar with Greek rhetoric (2003:13), while During observes in passing that

> (a)ll study of musical discourse in the traditions of the Middle East must be considered in these [five-fold rhetorical] categories, not only for the convenience of analysis but also in concern for epistemological coherence, for in these cultures the art of discourse, poetry and prosody have been largely cultivated and have integrated the concepts of Greek rhetoric. (1987:138)

Aristotle's *Rhetoric* was translated into Arabic in the early Abbasid period and soon followed with commentaries by Farabi, Averroes, and many others that emerged as a local school of rhetoric in Baghdad that in turn spread to Iran. The Abbasid school divided the rhetorical arts into eloquence/elocution (*balāgha*) and persuasive oratory (*khatāba*), with far greater emphasis placed on the former by scholars (both Eastern and Western). This resulted in the paradoxical conflation of persuasive oratory with Greek (i.e., non-Muslim) rhetoric on the one hand, whereas its main sphere of activity appears to have been among those preaching in the mosque, following a tradition extending back to the Prophet, Caliphs and early Muslim community (Hallden 2005: 20–24).

There is considerable (and rather typical, in view of similar issues concerning music) debate among scholars as to "who contributed what" in West Asian rhetoric, which components are foreign and which are authentically indigenous. Until recently Western scholarship of these questions has tended to marginalize Eastern contributions (Ezzaher 2003). As a typical illustrative example of the complexities involved, the *badi'* "new style" of literary embellishment, a major branch of medieval West Asian rhetoric, was indeed passed on to Iran via Arab sources, but it was to a large extent originally based on poetic and musical traditions of the Sassanid court (Chalisnova 2009a:140–41). Once again our deeply ingrained sense of insular, autonomous "turf" and yearning for illusive cultural purity, be it East/West or more specifically nationalist, can obscure the myriad connections and ultimately shared heritage that emerges with an impartial view of the evidence.

Beginning in the eleventh century with Raduyani's influential *Tarjoman al-balāgha*, Persian theoretical treatises on rhetoric appear continously through to the early twentieth century. This tradition focuses on the systematization of devices and figures, on elocution as opposed to persusive discourse; it is unclear what influence it had on the compositional practices of the great poets. According to van Ruymbeke, the Greek legacy of translations and commentaries of the Abbasid school stayed within the confines of philosophical circles and probably had little influence on Persian poetical and rhetorical theories (2009:362–63). Practicing poets were cognizant of the rhetorical arts, however, as among the many skills deemed necessary in order to be a successful poet, Nezami-Aruz (twelfth century) in his *Chahar maqale* advocates knowledge of *aruz* (prosody) and rhetoric (de Bruijn 2009:19).

Until relatively recent times the main social venue for public speech in Iran was outside the court and in the mosque, in the form of the homily. Hallden (2005) draws attention to this vibrant arena of rhetorical practice in the "Arab Islamic" context that has been unjustly neglected by scholars. Alongside vibrant contemporary practices, the tradition has deep historical roots in the founding of Islam, and fans out into parallel traditions, both contemporary and throughout history, in the *khānegah* with the extemporized sermonizing by Sufi sheikh speeches (Pourjavady 2009:292), and to some extent, the exegetical discourses of the *wa'zin rowze khāns*. Nooshin (1999: 62) denotes the art of "emotive oratory" in Iran as *rajazkhāni*, which also seems to have been overlooked by scholars of rhetoric. Rhetoric is part of the *muqadamat,* the introductory four-year phase of curriculum studied at Qom by all the young boys aspiring to be clerics (Reckord 1987: 26–27; see ibid. 94ff. for a brief discussion of the rhetorical techniques of religious singers). Shajarian grew up precisely in this milieu and would have assimilated, if only unconscjously, these oratorical traditions of *khatāba* and *rajazkhāni*; and through his deep study of Persian poetry he also has a firm inductive grasp of their elocutionary rhetoric (*balāgha*).

While Aristotle's legacy may have had little influence on the technical aspects of Persian rhetorical theory, it

> had a major impact on the thought of the Persian world about the condition
> and mission of poets and writers. There is, for example, a possible affiliation
> between Aristotle's definition of rhetoric and that of poetry by Nizami-Aruzi
> (12th c.). Both authors insist for the poet or rhetoritician to be of an "honest
> nature." However, they also recognize that good rhetoric is little concerned
> with truth when one tries to convince an audience of either a fact or its oppo-
> site. In his *Poetics*, Aristotle also mentions, as does Nezami Aruzi, the poet's
> power to arouse the emotions of his audience. (van Ruymbeke 2009: 362–63)

The aforementioned separation of elocution and persuasive oratory (*balāgha* and *khatāba*) of the Abbasid school has an interesting parallel in later European rhetoric. The influential sixteenth-century theorists Ramus and Talon instituted epistemological reforms whereby "students of rhetoric were to restrict themselves to matters of style and delivery, as *inventio* and *dispositio* were more properly handled by philosophers . . . "rhetoric" was increasingly conceived of as an art concerned with how to communicate and, if needed, to embellish a Truth, which was to be found and established outside the rhetorical domain" (Hallden 2005:26–27). This is the ubiquitous technique of spin noted above that characterizes many of the narrative performance traditions in Iran.

Cicero declared that "(t)he eloquent speaker is he who in the forum and in the courts will speak in such a way as to achieve proof, delight and influence" (*Orator*, 75). For him influence is "the single most thing responsible for advocatorial success, and just as the orator must be subtle in proof and moderate in charm, so he must be vehement in exerting influence" (Lawson-Tancred 2004:55). There is no shortage of examples in Iranian history of the influence that poets and musicians exerted on their ruling patrons: Barbad's lute playing and sung poetry famously, even mythologically, held sway over Khosrow Parvez just as Rudaki's influenced the Samanid ruler (de Bruijn 2009:20). Shajarian is remarkable in that his considerable influence is with a mass audience, which may include the ruling elite but his power is not predicated upon them. In Iran this democratic appeal and influence is much more volatile and dangerous to the latter than in former times, when the swaying of individual elites alone could maintain or upset the status quo of power in society.

Shajarian's recordings of the 1980s were commenting upon and "documenting" Iranians' view of their recent history.

> In the works on rhetoric (or literary theory) of Cicero and Quintillian history
> is seen as an art: an art which owes a debt to truthfulness and impartiality and
> also a debt to ornamentation and heightened emotional effect. . . . As had
> happened in the ancient world, narrative artists [in the West] began, at the
> close of the Middle Ages, to substitute for the authority of traditional narrative
> the authority of the eye-witness, the *histor*, or the creator. . . . The *histor* is the

narrator as enquirer, constructing a narrative on the basis of such evidence as
he has been able to accumulate. (Scholes et al. 2006: 64, 251, 265)

Very fine lines separate rhetoric as persuasion, influence, spin, propaganda and—
especially in Iran—sedition. With regard to style and social function, avaz may
be very cautiously viewed as a secular transposition of Qur'an recitation (or by
extension *roze, ta'ziyeh* chanting) in the same vein that Rumi's *Masnavi* is colloquially and endearingly regarded as the "Persian Qur'an." It assumes the function
of a surrogate spirituality, a "secular spirituality" in the sense that the Sufi poetry
upon which it is based is Iranian, nominally Muslim and yet outside the purview of
exoteric and fundamentalist Islam. This was and is especially the case with Iranians
in the wake of postrevolutionary disillusionment with the clergy. Shajarian emerged
as a secular preacher offering the integrity, freedom, moderation, and spiritual
inspiration that the majority of *mollahs* clearly lacked. He occupies this role that
presents constant dangers of religious and political sedition, challenging authority
by offering an attractive alternate to the *mollahs'* increasingly fragile status quo
agenda.

While I have been toggling between various traditions of rhetoric, my point
is that these traditions have an interrelated history, a shared heritage (though I do
not claim to conclusively connect the individual strands used as examples), spirit
and function, and that viewed as a macrotradition, Shajarian's deployment of
avaz is characterized by many key features of rhetoric. As a specific example, his
technique of "word painting" in avaz (described in chapter 4) is a rhetorical skill
achieved through the synergy of language and music and used to great effect in
his most famous recordings.[29] More generally he unites, or perhaps reunites, the
rhetorical functions of elocution through the masterly craft and brilliant artistry of
his singing, and persuasion, through his intelligent and often shrewd deployment
of *inventio*, in the construction of his "argument," of Cicero's ideal of *controver-
sia*: the substantive disputing of differences of opinion, "parliamentarian" discourse or public debate. These dimensions must be included because, while
rhetoric and avaz are on the surface monological activities, Shajarian's conception of avaz after the revolution became very much dialogical, a function of the
occasion, social interaction, and his perceptions regarding the views of the mass
audience who so devotedly listened to him.

Affekt

Affekt—the emotional impact of music, the atmosphere and mood it instills, the
affect it has on us—must be viewed from the perspective of both the individual and
the collective. While individuals perceive and construct their own experiences, much
of this, including the intentions of those delivering the music (the tellers), is
predicated on the group. In addition to physiological and psychological factors,

emotion is culturally/socially programmed with expected behaviour, reiterated behaviour and hence performance (Becker 2001, 2004).

Response and Manipulation

The main function and priority of the occasion is to highlight being "here and now": time, space, the particular people in the audience, the context or reason for the assembly are coordinated and embodied in the music to create a sense of immediate togetherness, group solidarity. The emotional atmosphere may be joyful or sad but it is experienced in the moment, with the support of the group, and is predicated on the interaction of the audience with the performers and their subsequent entrainment. Once the tenor of the occasion is ascertained, the performers clearly lead the accumulative construction of this collective synchronicity. As in English usage, Iranian religious singers use the term *garm* ("warm") to describe the goal of gaining the audience's attention so that they will truly listen (Reckord 1987: 92)—the first order of business at any performance. Through the skillful use of gesture and modulation of their voice, the best *naqqali* were "always aware of their environment and in touch with their listeners . . . (to) create an atmosphere of excitement, vehemence, and even, at times, of frenzy," in a clear emphasis on emotion rather than intellect (Haery 1982: 14, 26). The same may be said of *ta'ziyeh* and *ru-howzi* actors, the *pardi-dari* narrator and the *rowze khān*, whose performances frequently include the seating arranged so that the audience more or less encircles the performers, facilitating the establishment of this close rapport. Concerning singers of religious occasions in general,

> (a)ll the performer's skill in the various aspects of *munāsib khwani* (appropriate singing) are (*sic*) focused on one central goal: to move the audience to respond, usually with tears and expressions of grief, by a controlled manipulation of ever-increasing emotion in an effective and convincing presentation. (Reckord 1987: 91–92)

Indeed, in some of the earliest conceptions of the poet's vocation both Aristotle and Nezami-Aruzi mention his "power to arouse the emotions of his audience" (de Bruijn 2009:363). Knowing the character of your audience and making the appropriate adjustments in one's delivery maximizes one's ability to persuade and is thus a fundamental concern of rhetoric. Ostad Shajarian routinely requests that the house lights remain on, slightly dimmed, while he performs, so that he can see the faces and reaction of individuals.

Beginning with the Ikhwan al-Safa in the eighth century, medieval accounts of the role of music in West Asian court life frequently mention anecdotes where a musician induces the audience to cry, then to laugh, then to fall asleep, then wake up, and so on, explicating the manipulative powers of the performer (Godwin 1987:71). Indeed, the ability of music to manipulate emotions and behaviour, to bypass rational faculties and trigger altered states of consciousness, was a primary issue in the extensive *samā'* polemic that occupied philosophers and jurists from the Middle Ages through to the present. Some of the states induced by music were uncomfortably uncontrollable and chaotic for those who relied on rational and predictable behaviour—it induced a freedom, a temporary letting go of social order and was therefore potentially dangerous. As noted above, many Iranians are wary of *rowze khān*s for their unabashedly manipulative skills (who, ironically, do nothing beyond fulfilling their job description). Other cultures have a similar ambivalence toward musicians for similar reasons, the bards of the West African Mande *jaliya* tradition being a particularly famous example in this regard.[30] Whether accorded high or low status in a given culture, this type of manipulative power through music ultimately rests on a shamanistic archetype, such as famously embodied by Orpheus in Western culture.

In contrast to manipulative dynamics, the interaction between performer and audience in Arab culture is more predicated upon the generation of positive feedback between the two in a quest for achieving *sultana*, the psycho-spiritual state of grace that translates into secular Western culture variously as "flow," a "peak experience," or being "in the Zone" (Racy 1991, 2003). But whereas the experience with classical Arab music is ecstatic, the feedback process between the performer and audience in Persian music is decidedly "enstatic"—interiorized, without visual display, "sober," disembodied and silent, a correlate to the serene, blank, emotionless masks characteristic of the faces in traditional miniature painting. This aesthetic of minimalist gesturing is discussed further in chapter 4 but the point for the present discussion is that it explicitly illustrates how expectations govern reaction: performers and audience have their scripts and know the roles to be assumed and behaviour to be expected.

Shajarian's 2004 album *Faryad* was recorded in California before a bicultural audience of American-Iranians that clearly understood the rules of engagement and followed their scripted part. Wild, rock concert-style applause greets the musicians and ends the performance but as the musicians sit down to play, this quickly drops to a dead silence. Another very fast and disciplined shift from Dionysian to Apollonian response occurs between movements at the end of track 7 between 8:08–8:20. In reacting to a musical climax, the large crowd spontaneously erupts for twelve seconds of raucous rapture and retreats to back to Zen-like silence just as quickly (the track sounds unedited, though one never knows). Of course, the occasion and venue of a performance greatly influences expectations and responses to music—our response to music in a large hall with hundreds of strangers is different, and one's outward reaction is expected to be different, from sitting in someone's living room with a dozen other people, all of whom know each other well, listening between rounds of tea.[31]

OS

[There is a] sincere common feeling between the audience and me. When I hear their silence and feel the powerful and beautiful waves of energy from their faces, this gives me power and strength. (Shajarian 1993:43)

Question: When you are on stage, how do you see the audience, how do you see people in general?

It is amazing the kind of effect I feel when I am in front of my audience. I can never perform in the studio the way I can on stage—because it is hard to sing for the door and the wall—unless I really focus and remind myself that I am singing this for my people and they will listen to it. But when I am on stage there is a direct contact with the audience and I have always asked the hall manager not to dim the hall, so I can feel their presence. I don't need to recognize their faces, but the fact that I can feel them sitting there and listening to me is astonishing. [32]

We have read that you like to see the faces of the audience in order to get feedback from them, but they are not usually vocal in their appreciation, so how do you then get this feedback?

We get this feedback through their silence. [Laughs all around, then Shajarian quotes a line of poetry] "Bi khabar sho ke khabr-ha-st dar in bi khabari" *("Become empty, as there is much information in this uninformed state").*

My work is completely classical and my audiences are classical music enthusiasts as well. I mean when they come to our concerts, they stay in absolute silence the whole time. They do not even shake any part of their bodies and stay in total silence the whole time as if they are listening to Western classical music. (2008)

Sometimes in my concerts I have only intended to sing the radif and speak of nothing else—for example, to only introduce the dastgah of Rast Panjgah and sing it with a nice poem about love. But not all concerts follow the same direction. In some concerts I like to express my views of society and make social statements because, as an individual living in society, I have the right to judge it, in my own way. So I sing "Dusti key akhar amad, dustdaran ra che shod" *("When did friendship end, what happened to our friends?").* [33] *I have to add that poets usually write their poetry under the influence of their society and as singers we must also sing it back to society by following its influence. I mean, the composer writes the piece but I sing it—it is all dependent on what society wants. (Shajarian et al. 2004: 222).*

What I do can be compared to a showman who stands all by himself on a stage and talks about the politics and the events of a particular day that everyone is aware of, saying words that make everybody laugh. Now if something unexpected happens during this event he must be so aware that he can instantly reference that matter to something else—that is the point that he really gets a big laugh and people applaud him. This is something that he has to sense. (2009)

(A singer) has to learn how to improvise with talent and stamina, in a spontaneous way so that, like a seasoned orator, he can express what he feels without

losing his breath and without referring to notation or a composed melody before him. He is at the same time the composer and the performer and accomplishes these two tasks simultaneously. He must choose the poems he sings with taste and talent, for the most appreciated singers are those who choose the most beautiful lines, expressing profound thoughts.[34]

Music should be in response to the needs of today. The avaz that is being sung should answer the needs of my listener and myself (the singer), and our living environment must be recognized. Therefore at any given time, the concert that is being presented has that particular social or cultural quality. It is natural that I am highly influenced by my people, my society and I do indeed receive a message and an idea from them. I then deliver this message, which already contains society's signature, back to them in a form of poetry...Unfortunately, at the present, we do not have artists such as 'Aref, Sheyda or Morteza Mahjoubi or songwriters and poets such as Darvish Khan and Malek al-Shoara Bahar to write music that is appropriate for our own time. So this is part of the reason that my hands are tied and therefore I put most of the pressures and the load of work on the avaz [as opposed to tasnifs and other forms of composition]. (Shajarian et al. 2004:223, 225)

If I didn't have anything to say I couldn't even sing. I always have to have something [to say]. I mean, an artist is like a pregnant woman that's giving birth. On the stage I have a similar feeling. When I come on the stage, whatever is bottled up inside me, I throw it out. Whatever is in me, it's related to the environment and the society that I'm living in.[35]

AK

Another Iranian tradition that involves manipulating the feelings of listeners' emotions occurs at funerals. Funeral ceremonies in Iran are very important, even for people who aren't really religious. It's important that you take care of this properly for someone in your family; and you'll probably be criticized by others if you don't. It's a very chaotic ritual, beginning with a procession through the street, carrying the bier. Especially if the person was well known, this can get very chaotic and intensely emotional, with people loudly crying and reciting sacred formulae. The scene at the cemetery is also chaotic—usually lots of dust everywhere with an increase in the energy that was building up in the procession. There are singers working in the cemetery and you have to book them well in advance because they're very busy. They are amazing singers of a kind of avaz; some of them speak several different languages. The organization administering these singers will ask you where the family of the deceased comes from and they will choose the singer accordingly. Based on the makeup of the group attending the funeral, the singer will choose the appropriate language or languages and then choose a poem that is fitting for the age and situation of the deceased. There are different ceremonies—seven days, forty days, and then one year after the death—where people come back to the cemetery and perhaps later the mosque, it depends on the family. Like the *rowze khān*, his goal is to manipulate people through his singing and make them cry intensely. He knows exactly when to shift to Abu Ata and burst the built-up bubble of emotions. He's an actor, too. He shifts between languages. If appropriate, especially if the deceased is a young person, he'll do *rajaz* or some *naqqali* in relation to one story. He knows the poem he chose to perform inside out and he'll write down the names of people of the family and improvise those names into the story or poem he's narrating. In the middle of the narrative he'll address the chief mourners with something like "I understand your feeling!" or will find out details of the deceased's life and knit those into the proceedings. This usually creates a chaotic, cathartic reaction. They really connect with the people attending the ceremony.

These singers play with your mind: they create a sense of honour for the deceased and then they break it. They make you feel proud of the person and then they slip in from behind to hit you with the loss. The background of this picture is loss, which the singer maintains all of the time but to intensify this, he takes you out of that feeling—he can't go as far as joy or make people laugh, but he contrasts this loss with honour, power, and beauty—and then, with devastating timing, he brings it back to the loss. I find these singers to be very artistic, creative and masters of occasion and manipulation. Nobody knows them in the way we know great singers in the music world but some of them are amazing singers with great voices. They get paid very well—much more than any musician in the town. Everyone will think the singer is good if he can get the whole assembly to cry intensely. I assume they have training because their singing is in tune and quite refined.

Blurred Boundaries of Sadness and Weeping

RS

The question of why sadness and pain is desirable, even pleasurable in art is an old one, receiving formal investigation by Aristotle in his *Poetics*. Iranian Persian music is renowned by cultural insiders[36] and outsiders alike for its pervasive sadness (e.g., Nettl 1969:189; Zonis 1973:17; Farhat 1980:296; During 1984:210–11; During et al. 1991); for many Iranians, this sadness is a fairly common reason for their dislike of the music. While various explanations are put forth for this melancholic quality—Iran's troubled history (a view held by Shajarian[37]) to its desert landscape—the music's relation to the wider matrix of narrative performance arts, particularly those associated with Shi'i mourning rituals, would seem to play a central and rather obvious role. These rituals, in turn, may well reflect a much deeper archetypal and mythical substratum wherein the entire point is to cultivate sadness and weeping. This is precisely the mandate of the *rowze khān*, the success of whose performance is largely gauged by how intensely he induces the audience to cry, entrained in grief. *Rowze khāni* melodies are generally set to the more plaintive dastgahs: primarily Shur and its satellites, followed in frequency by Segah and Homayun.

Reckord reports that the five most common adjectives to describe a good voice for religious singing all invoke sadness (1987:103–04). The radif is replete with gushes whose names signify sadness, weeping or exhaustion and pain: *Hazin, Hozan, Mure, Muye, Delkash, Ghamangiz, Koshte, Khaste, Bidad,* etc. Collective weeping is also common among the audiences of *ta'ziyeh,* which embodies many things but specifically laments political oppression, injustice and tyranny. Of course, social conditioning plays a prominent role in our emotional responses (J. Becker 2001), particularly for men, who in many cultures, including the West, rigidly separate and regulate their public display of emotion (e.g., at funerals) and reserve the act of "letting it all hang out" for private moments. In the Shi'i mourning rituals there is no such reserve, the juxtaposition of large groups of men weeping in public at a *rowze khāni* performance or in the *dasta-gardani* processions of self-flagellants (which among other things signify a certain degree of machismo) is a remarkable, paradoxical display of strength and "weakness." From another angle this deeply archetypal sadness reflects the human tragedy of unattained ideals, of not realizing our ideal selves and ultimate human (i.e., spiritual) potential (Reckord 1987:107–14). For many social psychologists, it is an obvious expression of existential angst, fear of one's own inevitable death (E. Becker 1973). Facing this universal human fear requires heroism: in traditional Iranian culture this took its most potent form in the martyr. While most Westerners find this doctrine and its related rituals to be utterly alien, every culture has its means of dealing with death anxiety. While the Passion of Christ is central to Christianity and entails an elaborate theology of blood sacrifice, Western consumerism, celebrity culture, and military expansion function as secular surrogates for dealing with this primal fear (E. Becker 1975).

Traditional Iranian culture by no means holds a monopoly on such a fixation on sadness. Among many other examples, Feld's famous work describing Kaluli musical conceptions and aesthetics—which is also anchored to one of their key myths (centering on the insecurities of food supply) and the integral role of weeping—comes to mind and is of comparative interest to these Shi'i practices,[38] as does the traditional Korea concept of *han,*[39] among others. The famous category of *wabi-sabi* in Japanese aesthetics—focusing on impermanence in general and the fleetingness of beauty—does not explicitly include weeping but evokes sadness. While triggered and propelled by the myth, the expression of grief in such practices, whether they are in Iran, New Guinea, Korea or elsewhere, of course resonates with contemporaneous collective and individual anxieties of the participants:[40] mythic and immediate grief is coupled in a collective emotional catharsis. As a further function of such rituals, contemporary grief and anxiety is projected onto the mythic in the course of the performance, thus serving as a release valve of repressed feelings both individual and collective, a heightened sense of group identity and solidarity, and sense of continuity with the archetypal past. In either case we have a conflation of collective myth and self, past and present.

It is one of the great psychosomatic paradoxes of humanity that uncontrollable tears are triggered by intense grief, pain, and fear as well as intense laughter, joy, and relief (from some previous trauma). In this state we have no choice but to "let the moment happen," lower our social watchguard and be overwhelmed by its ambush. In reaction to opposing stimuli, weeping signifies surrender to an overwhelming experience, to deep-seated emotional and often irrational forces, resulting in a massive shift in our neurochemistry, a purging catharsis and a heightened state of consciousness. [41] This paradoxical relationship is explicitly manipulated in the ta'ziyeh play "The Marriage of Qasem" from Iran's Northern provinces, featuring the cathartic narrative collision of a wedding and funeral:

> On one side of the stage, funeral rites are performed with interludes of mournful music. The spectators dishevel their hair and beat their breasts. On the other side of the stage the wedding ceremony continues accompanied by jubilant music. There is a cacophony of sound, the audience turning from side to side changing from weeping to laughter. (Chelkowski 1979:5–6)

Likewise the secular ru-howzi improvised theatre at once served "to express and reflect upon the pent-up emotions of an oppressed people" through satire and music that was "jovial, comic and festive" (Haery 1982: 51, 104–05). Iranians continue to develop this admixture in cyberspace, where a YouTube search under "rozi khane" draws numerous hits that are comical and satirical.

In the famous opening of his *Masnavi* Rumi noted that the wailing lament of the ney[42] is in good company with both those who are miserable and those who are in a happy state—each one thought they were the ney's friend. And so it is, the ney is simultaneously a "poison and a cure." The allegory of separation from the reed bed illustrates the longing of our souls for something larger than ourselves, for a heightened awareness of and contact with our spiritual depth and source.[43] With Rumi the ney also refers to *nīsti*, "non-existence," or being empty of one's ego, conveying his belief in the necessity of purifying oneself from the ego as a means for becoming fully human. Inayat Khān (1882–1927)—the first Sufi master to actively propagate teachings in the West did so in tandem with Hindustani music—maintained that sad music was the best means to help us look inward and deep, to psycho-spiritually implode.[44] Even on the less lofty level of the sentiments, there is something comforting about listening to sad music when we are feeling down, the quasi-homeopathy of the blues and songs that are "sad and sweet." Surely this has something to do with the fact that we feel the solidarity that we're not alone in our black dog days, that proverbially, misery loves company. Even on a strictly empirical level, Judith Becker cites evidence from clinical and neurological studies suggesting that sad music may create more arousal than happy music (2004:53).

The landmark recordings that Ostad Shajarian made in the 1980s[45] provided a mass-mediated focal point for the collective mourning, suffering and anxiety explicitly caused by the ongoing Iran-Iraq war and implicitly by the revolution. In a manner reminiscent of 'Aref's sociopolitical engagement in the early-twentieth century, Shajarian transposed the traditional Iranian Shi'i function of public mourning to the realm of national art music culture, the concert hall, and the market place by producing top-selling cassettes.

AK
The famous poet Akhavan Saless (1928-1990) wrote a wonderful poem entitled "*Avaz-e Cheghur*," which means "The Song of the *Cheghur*." *Cheghur* is another name for the *dotar* (a long-necked, two-stringed lute) in Khorasan. He says at the end of it: "Oh, now I understand, your screams, your melodies. It is a pain in my heart that you're singing, that's why I don't want to go there." This is referring to the history of music, especially the position of musicians and their situation in society. Also, we Iranians have always been involved with war through invasion by other peoples like the Mongols and the Arabs and also fighting between two different groups within our own country—Turks against Kurds and so on.

Music is a deep reflection of what's going on in the country. And of course not only music, but poetry also. Most classical Persian poetry is not very joyful, it is often about something sad, about separation. While Sufi poetry is often about separation from the Beloved, it also refers to what is going on in society. Hafez's *Saqiname* is a very famous example, where he gives a lot of advice to musicians, and is complaining about so many things. In the middle of it he just keeps repeating "Oh one day, Khezr,[46] my only hope is Khezr will come and solve these problems." Then he says: *Mara ba adu aghabat forsat ast*. This is a very important line for our conversation because it means: "The time for a reckoning with my enemy will come in the end." So this quest for destiny is always happening in our culture.

Another poem by Akhavan, entitled "*Mirās*" ("Heritage"), gives us great insight into answering the question of sadness in our music. "I have one *pustin* ("sheepskin"), a very old one." He is referring to our culture. He says, "I tried to change it once and then something happened." It is a long poem that describes why we are like this, why we are always waiting, and why we want to change this culture and then how most of our problems come because we want these changes. But all of this sadness comes from the dissatisfaction of people living in any time, in any period. There is really no historical period in Iran where people are happy, gracious, and settled but they are nonetheless saying that this is what they want.

As a performer, I believe that the content of the music, the material, is designed to evoke this kind of sadness—it is installed in the music. Even in Iranian movies and theatre productions, the primary target is "how can we make the audience sad"? If you look at most of the movies from Iran, they are sad. It's exactly like the *rowze khāni*. The target is to make you cry. Filmakers have to imitate the techniques and styles from other counties to create comedies. The most successful comedies are imitations, exact copies of a particular movie from outside of Iran. If you listen to *naqqali* or other traditional art forms, all of those refer to sadness.

The sadness of dastgah Chahargah, for example, is very different from the sadness of Shur. Iranian Chahargah is in general heroic, and performs the function of a herald or town-crier bringing news, making an announcement. Chahargah is used for the oldest songs of *Nowruz* and for weddings, and in old days people used it a lot in music performed with *dohol* (drum) and *zurna* (double reed), to announce that something is happening. More often than not, though, the announcement was of news that was not good. Also, the intervals of Chahargah are very poignant and attention-grabbing. As a performer, my target is intentionally (and from the other side the material is helping me) to "scratch the heart." Different gushes in Chahargah have varying effects. *Hesar* evokes an imaginary sense of hope, a mirage, but then moving to the forud, I feel like there is no hope for me. The gushe *Muyeh* means "crying." Particularly the old *Muyeh*, as played by Ostad Ali Akbar Shahnazi and others, added even more microtonal spice and tragic intensity to it.

Each dastgah has a character, has a specific feeling, but there is a margin, there are options the performer can push in various directions, and he would know in which direction to go to add appropriately to the depth of feeling. And then the opposite, he or she can also make the music lighter. Sometimes when performers play during spiritual occasions or events such as Sufi ceremonies, they may be asked to play some happy songs. Some people believe Mahur is happy but this is not totally true. One might say that all of the dastgahs have a feeling of sadness and melancholy. It's there in all of them, if you play them right. The only thing the performer can do to make the music joyful is with regard to rhythm. He can create this through certain rhythmic patterns, and by not referring to many gushes, by staying within one gushe, which results in some kind of minimalist texture, he can concentrate on working with the rhythm. Certain rhythmic combinations can therefore evoke joy.

I think sadness comes from what happens to the people. But for me, this sadness is not making me a depressed person because in this culture, in the depth of sadness there is a joy, and that joy will come to you if you don't run away from that sadness. If I play Chahargah it makes me free to speak, and then it makes me empty of all this sadness. There is a joy at the end and the joy is so different from other means of attaining happiness. These people who are listening to *rowze khāni* and to sad music, Persian classical music, I don't see them as being depressed—they're not. In our culture there are so many poems that say "I find joy of the Beloved in the sadness of separation." A ghazal by Rumi says that "the reason you don't have peace is because you are always looking for peace. You have to attack the chaos and then you will find the peace." [47]

So this is something working through opposites but in a paradoxical way. The Sufi masters were so deep and connected to the truth. They're telling us this is how music should be—it's so real, it connects with what's really going on. It's addressing your wailing, your needs, but if you're playing or listening to it, it's not going to make you sad. Some musicians and artists maintain that this music is not sad. But no, it is sad, it's very sad. It depends on how you connect to and deal with the sadness. Is it good or bad? If you're going to "play positive and negative," in this culture it's not bad, it's positive. If you want to find deep joy, the path is in this direction. You have to confront your problems, you have to touch them. You have to face them, instead of running from them and trying to make yourself happy with something unrelated, a diversion.

Modes and Moods

RS
Following Aristotle, classical rhetoric hinged on the essential pillars of logic, character (i.e., knowing your audience), and emotion. While an orator has some means of manipulating the latter, the singer is much better equipped, as music adds a most penetrating, nonverbal medium that directly appeals to the emotions.

In an ancient conception of musical Affekt that had a very wide distribution in the ancient world and survives to this day in many Asian modal systems, mode and mood are integrally related. The vibrational patterns of the music couple with the listener's soul, which vibrates in sympathy and thereby activates a specific emotional response. Indian raga theory codifies the corresponding emotional affect of a mode through the conventionalized aesthetic categories of *rasa*, designated through the theoretical-historical authentication of treatises and oral tradition, and resulting in a fairly strong consensus among musicians. Like the notions of Affekt in European Baroque music, and particularly their codification with musical gestures and structures by German theorists of the period, the vital role of social programming in suggesting (even dictating) how we should feel is clearly evident in India. The mode-mood affinities of West Asian modal traditions are less codified and vary more with the subjective feelings of individual musicians. Aside from an overall consensus on the "sad" quality of most modes, with a few exceptions noted below, more subtle nuances of modal affect are generally subjective in the case of the Iranian dastgahs, which were arranged or reconfigured from earlier maqam practices only in the late-nineteenth century. Indeed, the relationship between mode and mood belongs to the realm of *iham*, dependant on context and subjective perception, whereby we often project our own interior states and consciousness onto the music—there is no linear relationship or certainty here. In the context of various conversations (i.e., occasions) Shajarian speaks of both the intrinsic subjectivity and what may be described as the affective tendencies of certain modes, or at least his conception of them. Shajarian reset the tasnif *"Zaban-e Atash,"* which became the unofficial anthem of the Green Movement following the election crisis in 2009, from Mahur to Dashti in order to better reflect and provoke sentiments of that occasion.[48]

OS
In dastgahi music Mahur has a happier mood, Shur is sadder; Segah and Abu Ata, for example have different moods. Some people who use these maqams can

consciously convey these effects very well. Each of these maqams expresses a different human feeling and then again, some maqams are similar to each other. It's possible that Shushtari will have an effect and Abu Ata or Dashti can make the very same impression, but it's also possible for you to not feel this way—it depends on your openness, perception, memory and sensory experience.

Dastgahi music is subject to the influence of its surroundings. Under various conditions, dastgahs can create different emotional effects. No one can say that Shushtari only really expresses such and such an effect. Depending on the time and place, the listener will have a particular sensory experience with the same music each time. Of course, the sentiments of dastgahs really can't be solely attributed to the listener. I'll explicate further. For example, you see that the late Khaleqi composed the sorud *[anthem]"Aye Iran, Marze Pargavha/Oh Iran, Bejeweled Land" which is a heroic* sorud *in Dashti, a maqam that evokes sadness—this is exactly what he did! He didn't make it in Chahargah, on the contrary he used Dashti, which always possesses a crying quality. With a rhythm and melody in maqam Dashti, a* sorud *is produced that is heroic.*

Sometimes there are also compositions set in Chahargah that are very sorrowful. Chahargah speaks of separation and remoteness. Since childhood I listened to the wedding song "Aya Yar Mobarak Bad (Ah, Friend, Congratulations)" that evoked in me a feeling of separation and sadness. At that time I had not yet become a father or gained the knowledge of my child when he/she gets married—that the night of the marriage is a night of my separation and differentiation. This Chahargah is sung in the wedding ceremony. Instead of being happy, people are sad! This depends on the rhythm and melody or particular composition that we set in Chahargah. The conditions of the performance depend on what time and place it occurs and how receptive the listeners are to the piece. In any event, this expression of feeling or mood taken from the piece depends more on the musicians and listeners than the prescription that, for example, "dastgah Nava produces a mood of reflection."

Rast Panjgah is like Mahur, it doesn't present difficulties. Nava is similar to Afshari: they don't present complexities. With regard to tar performance and fingering they are more difficult. The epic, heroic mood of Chahargah is rather more difficult than these. In an epic work it's used often, people have a practice of expressing epic situations with Chahargah[49] but this isn't the only mood it produces or carries. Chahargah is difficult to sing and few musicians are able to perform it well. However, you see that Chahargah is also performed a lot relative to the other modes. But there are other dastgahs that aren't complex—like Nava and Rast Panjgah. Rast Panjgah is a Magian (Zoroastrian) term, it's the dastgah for a very high place where glory and loftiness are featured—the glory and pomp of the court or glory and magnificence of places where everyone is seeking the truth. It's used in situations where you want to deploy the loftiest speech. (Shajarian et al. 2004:305–06)

[Abu Ata] "speaks of the feelings manifested in love. . . . (A) lover reveals the secret of his love and his need to the beloved and expresses to her the purity of his love. At times he begs and pleads and at times he complains and asks for her tenderness and attention. In the melody of Hejaz, the lover speaks to God of the truths in love and life. At times he dares and challenges the rival, and at times he warns the beloved. These feelings and motifs are so clearly articulated in Abu Ata that there is no need for poetry, or any words. The music expresses them all.[50]

If you want to sing something that is regretful and sorrowful, about something that you have lost, for example if someone has lost his or her country, this must be done in Bayate Esfahan, because Bayate Esfahan can produce that regretful and sorrowful feelings that you get when you lose something. Hence I will never sing this kind of lyric in Bayate Tork, because that has a different expressive power. (2008)

Dashti is appropriate for hardships, pain, and being away from the beloved. (2009) [Afshari has a] sad, sorrowful nature . . . which expresses the desperation of the separated lover who can do nothing but wail the loss. At times, in the height of his suffering, he lets out a cry which deeply distresses the listener. But in Rohab, which we play at the end, weeping and wailing are over: this piece brings hope and soothes broken hearts.[51]

Sufism and Music

What ensures the symbolic continuity and cohesion of Persian culture over the long term (that is, before and after Islam) is not so much language, which has evolved considerably; or geographic area, which has shrunk; or race, which has become mixed, but mysticism, and with it ethics and a certain spirit of dualism and aesthetic sense. While many structural analogies can be drawn between religious and musical traditions, the musicians almost without exception used the analogy of the mystical domain and the *ḥāl* as a privileged means of access to that domain. (During 2002:858–59)

RS
Above and beyond the effects of music on the emotions and morals of listeners, most musicians and connoisseurs speak of a deeper, ultimately spiritual function and significance of music. This is certainly the case among Sufis, who have played and continue to play a vital role in the transmission and cultivation of both mystical poetry and Persian music. If the concepts discussed in this section are not always in the forefront of the minds of those involved in musicking—including Ostad Shajarian—they unquestionably form an important part of the collective historical-cultural conceptual backdrop of both Persian poetic and musical traditions. Many musicians are spiritual in this context without being explicitly religious or officially aligned to institutional Sufism (During 1994:157). This "basic Sufi doctrine" is a widely accepted canon of principles established over the past millennium by various

Iranian and West Asian writers associated with Sufism in various capacities, as well as the dialectical, transcultural shaping of Orientalist scholars over the past two centuries.

Critics like Dabashi (e.g., 1999:34ff.) note the homogenizing, essentializing and depersonalizing distortions of institutionalized Sufism and its Orientalist authorizers, especially pinpointing and lamenting Ibn Arabi's thirteenth-century "systemization" of Sufi thinking as a descent into rigid dogmatization that marked its death-knell as a dynamic, spontaneous, living path of free inquiry and authentic spiritual growth. Indeed, already in the eleventh century Abu al Hasan Fushanja complained, according to the first Persian treatise on Sufism, Hujwiri's *Kafsh al Mahjub*: "Today Sufism is a name without a reality, but formerly it was a reality without a name" (Nicholson 1976:44). Sardar notes problematic authoritarian and blindly uncritical tendencies in contemporary practice that similarly stunt spiritual growth and inhibit genuine questing (2004: 339). These criticisms do not derogate or invalidate the musical concepts under discussion nor the sincere belief in the same held by many musicians and music enthusiasts. They rather soften them into a larger, more complex context of multiple individual experiences and collective possibilities, denying them absolute, airtight authority by insisting that they breathe with sincerity through living, often untidy and imperfect, three dimensional humans. The following discussion distills some of the main concepts related to music as they are presented in the scholarly literature.[52]

Music was not publically encouraged nor practiced by many of the traditional Sufi orders, possibly in order to detract attention from exoteric religious authorities during repressive times (During 1975:131, 133; 1989:534). However, much of the Iranian *samā'* polemic (debate on the legality of music) was levelled at organized Sufi practices, and likewise defended by Sufis (e.g., al-Ghazali, Ahmad al-Tusi, and Ruzbahan Baqli). Persian music was largely maintained in the royal courts and in the private gatherings (*majles*) of connoisseurs. Despite the overall lack of official sponsorship by most Iranian Sufi orders, many influential musicians of the late-nineteenth century musical reform that resulted in the establishment of contemporary performance practice and repertoire were affiliated with the order of Safi 'Ali Shah (During 1975:131). This order detached from the more traditional Ne'matollahi order, and was particularly successful among nobility and musicians attached to the court (During 1989:535). The order rejected most religious obligations in favour of concentration on mystical experiences unconstrained by traditional initiatory doctrine. If official initiation in the conventional sense is downplayed, it is replaced with an interesting form of social initiation amongst the musicians themselves, based on a shared gnostic orientation.

Many Iranian musicians, past and present, have also been known to behave in ways that are at odds with the moral and ethical codes of traditional Sufism— not following the exoteric tenets of Islam, using drugs, having questionable personality traits, etc.—but who nonetheless seek and attain elevation to a mystical plane through their music. During describes these anomalous "mystical attitudes" in terms of the traditional typology of *rend, kharabi, malamati,* and *qalandar,* denoting varying degrees of conformity (1989: 536). Lewis includes the category of *ovaysis* among these "Sufi Bohemians," independent gnostics unconnected to traditional Sufi orders and their spiritual transmission lines (*silsila*) who were inspired by the mythical figure Khezr[53] (2008:33ff.). The tendency toward nonsectarian esotericism amongst Iranian musicians is perhaps best symbolized in the poet Hafez, whose expressions of mysticism (*'erfan*) are both the spiritual and formal stuff of Iranian music, but who does not appear to have been initiated into a particular order. Of course, the intimate spiritual and formal connection between mystical poetry and Iranian music clearly testifies to the essential influence of Sufism, whether directly through bona fide Sufis (e.g., Rumi) or individual *'arefs* such as Hafez. The musical situation reflects the wide variation of Muslim esotericism itself—from the anomalous, transgressive *qalandars* to the "drunken" *tariqahs* (such as the 'Aissawiyas with their fakirist practices), to the "sober"/conservative branches (such as the Naqshbandis) (Nasr 1987:107). It is unclear but seems unlikely that Ostad Shajarian has been officially initiated into a Sufi tariqah or his connections with the same, though we note the importance of his long-standing relationship with the "unity philosopher" Ostad Dadbeh in chapter 4, exploring it in greater detail in Simms and Koushkani (2012). As a widely recognized "child of Hafez," however, it is appropriate that Shajarian holds Hafez's nonaligned position of an *'aref.* Sa'di, Shajarian's second most frequently selected poet after Hafez (see chapter 4), kept a similarly detached relationship with mainstream Sufi *tariqahs.*

The traditional transmission process of Persian music was itself often marked by an initiatory tenure resembling that of a *murid* to a *sheikh,* a spiritual as well as an artistic apprenticeship (During 1989:545). Likewise, after the successful completion of the apprenticeship, selected students were given permission from the ostad to teach his beginning students, analogous to the initiatory practices of classical Sufism.[54] Many Iranian musicians regard the radif with great veneration, believing it to be perfect and unalterable (though we will see in chapter 4 that Shajarian does not share this view). It is *the* fundamental canonical prototype of Persian music, studied and memorized in scrupulous detail. Through the process of this absorption the student is transformed into an artist who gains the "soul of the radif," as described by Safvat: the spiritual element inherent in the radif itself, whereby, once attained, "whatever we play is 'pure radif' and 'nothing but the radif'" (During 1991:246). This process corresponds to the Sufi doctrine of the Prophet Mohammad as the Perfect Man (*al-insan al-kāmel*) and the sacred status and function of the *sunnah* ("actions" of the Prophet) (Bakhtiar 1976:10–11; Nasr 1966:67–92). The latter comprise a huge literature that include detailed descriptions of the Prophet's personal habits and mannerisms, right down to the most mundane of trivialities (e.g., how he would put on his shoes or the manner in which he would fall asleep). Certain

Sufis and pious exoteric Muslims alike copy and integrate these details, along with the obligatory *shariah*, into their daily life—copying the Perfect Man so that they may become the Perfect Man through a process of spiritual alchemy.

Sound plays an important role in Islamic cosmology[55] and music has a further role beyond that of elemental sound *per se*. Sufi cosmology, particularly as expounded by Suhrawardi's twelfth-century Illuminationist school (*maktab al-ishraqi*), holds that reality is comprised of five cosmic planes, known as the five divine presences (*al-hadrat al-ilahiyyah*) or what are known in "perennial philosophy" as ontological levels or links in the "Great Chain of Being," which are rather better envisioned as nested circles or holons. As mentioned in chapter 1, an intermediary world, a *barzakh* ("isthmus") serves as both a buffer and link between the realms of gross forms, sensory perception, and that of subtle archetypes, Plato's Ideas known as *Malakut* ("Royalty")[56] or alternatively, by the "mystical city" within this realm, *Hurqalya*.

> *Malakut* . . . possesses forms but not matter in the ordinary Peripatetic sense. That is why in fact this world is also called the world of "hanging forms" (*suwar al-mu'allaqah*). . . . But from another point of view this world possesses its own matter (*jism-i latif*), which in fact is the 'body of resurrection', for in this world is located both paradise in its formal aspect and the inferno. This world also possesses, likewise, its own space, time, and movement, its own bodies, shapes and colours. In its negative aspect this world is the cosmic labyrinth of veils which separate man from the Divine, but in its positive aspect it is the state of paradise wherein are contained the original forms, colours, smells and tastes. (Nasr 1987:181)

To which we may add sounds, particularly those emanating from the turning of the celestial spheres, constituting a celestial music. "Thus, it is conceivable that there are sounds and melodies in the celestial Spheres which are not conditioned by the air nor by a vibratory disturbance. And one cannot imagine that there could be melodies more delightful than theirs" (Suhrawardi in Godwin 1987:86).[57] This celestial music is the archetypal source of which Persian music is a terrestrial resonance (During 1977; 1989:576–86; 1991:177–81). Suhrawardi's intermediary, "imaginal" world is the meeting place of spirit and matter, where "bodies are spiritualized and spirits take on form" (ibid. 1977:29), and where aesthetic and mystical experience both flourish. It is also this dimension that is depicted and symbolized in Iranian miniature painting (Nasr 1987:177–84). The two art forms are both a bridge to the imaginal world and an earthly representation of it.

One of the most striking Muslim myths regarding music, presumably drawn from the oral tradition of Sufism, clearly reveals its imaginal nature (During 1991:169; Jargy 1971:11). The soul of Adam refused to enter into the material body that God created for him. God had a group of angels descend into the body and sing a *samā'*, whereupon Adam's soul became entranced with the sound and entered the body as well. After the concert the angels departed, leaving the soul of Adam captive in the body. *Malakut* is the realm of the soul, where forms become spiritualized and spirits take on forms; it is also the realm of music, and of angels—the archetype par excellence of mediation between the physical and the spiritual realm.

Souls making a spiritual ascent are met in *Malakut* by angels sent descending from higher realms, just as descending angels met Jacob halfway up his ascent of the cosmic ladder. The archetype of angels, found across cultures in various cognate forms, are almost invariably associated with birds (or at least wings), ambiguous good or bad ("trickster") characters, and with music, both vocal and instrumental, the latter most often trumpets and stringed instruments (Wilson 1980:16, 38, 100). Birds—and particularly the nightingale—are a central symbol of Persian music, while understanding the "language of the birds," as Solomon was credited with in the Qur'an (27:15), referred to mystical contact with higher levels of consciousness. Furthermore, Guenon (1972) noted that this language corresponds with "rhythmic language" and the "science of rhythm" in the human domain. Revelation is accomplished through the agency of angels in Islam, as it is in many traditions (Wilson 1980:62–63). As noted in chapter 1, angels, like music itself, are immaterial and yet possess form (ibid.:49), which situates the positions of both in the imaginal world particularly clearly. In consequence of its mediating function, music has the potential for both good and bad. Belief in angels and *jinn*, "tricksters," is an article of faith incumbent on all Muslims. The Muslim emphasis on the polarity of angel and *jinn* directly symbolizes the equally ambiguous position of *samā'*, as we will soon see. If music belongs to the angelic realm, then it can partake of both positive and negative aspects,[58] which is essentially the Sufi interpretation of *samā'*. Angels ultimately function to unite knowledge and love (ibid.:159–60), which is precisely the purpose of the *samā'* (During 1988:32).

The primary terms used by Iranian musicians and connoisseurs to describe the subjective experience of listening to and performing music are *'eshq* ("love") and *hāl*, a spiritual "state" of peak experience. Of the three great modalities of humankind's spiritual experience—the paths of action, love, and knowledge—Iranian Sufism is primarily a path of love. While this is not meant to minimize the great Iranian gnostics (Ibn Sina, Suhrwardi, Molla Sadra, etc.) nor imply that the modalities are mutually exclusive, it is the way of love—which in Islam reached its highest form of expression in Rumi—that is most relevant to Iranian musical expression and activity. *'Eshq*/love is an attribute of God that ultimately exists independently of man and creation. From a more limited perspective, however, it is also a primary cause of creation, the principle by which it is maintained and by which all activity occurs (Chittick 1983:194–231). Love, need, and desire exist on various planes and, likewise, set the human sphere in motion on various levels. All lower forms of love (*'eshq-i majazi*) are transpositions of the transcendent universal principle of love (*'eshq-i haqiqi*). It is the goal of humans to realize this by penetrating the veils of multiplicity in order to focus their love upon this higher principle. A concomitant of this quest is the complementary pair of separation from, and union with, the Beloved (the Absolute or God). Movement toward union is characterized by a progression through various evolutionary levels of consciousness or spiritual stations (*maqāmāt*). It is precisely the sense of separation, a longing for spiritual union, that characterizes Iranian music, the sadness or nostalgia for union, a return to whence we came, as immortalized by Rumi's famous allegory of the ney.

This state of union is an experience of bliss wherein one's individuality is annihilated; in Rumi's imagery, the foam of the wave realizes it is nothing but the ocean itself. The brief and transitory but intense psycho-spiritual state of ecstasy known as *hāl* ("state"), first described by Hujwiri in the eleventh century and subsequently integrated into Sufi discourse (Blum 1998:32), is a fleeting reflection of this eternal bliss and therefore analogous to mystical experience itself. *Hāl* is the ultimate aesthetic goal of Iranian music (During 1975:137; 1984:211; and a particularly detailed treatment in 1994). According to interviews conducted with a range of musicians by During in 1990, it is largely induced through the accurate intonation of the distinctively Iranian intervals and is at once a primary signifier of tradition, authenticity, a specific ethos, and inspiration (During 2002:854–56). From a Sufi perspective, like a genuine mystical experience true *hāl* transports one "outside" of time; it is a state of grace and a "moment" (*vaqt*) in the discontinuous flow of temporal atoms in the "perpetual renewal of creation"[59] (During 1987:92; 1989:574–75; see also Burckhardt 1967:65–69). The moment is experienced in its full vertical depth, in full consciousness of its creative source. *Hāl* is frequently described in terms that allude to a "harmonizing" archetype characteristic of Islamic music: "a supernatural balance between the moving and the immovable, between the hidden and the manifested, between the one and the multiple" (During 1982:84; see also During 1989:565–69).

Hāl is closely associated with various types of sacred trance states (Rouget 1985:281). Sufis differentiated sensuous, profane states from genuine spiritual states on the basis of moral qualities, e.g., taste (*zowq*) and love (Safvat 1984:103). *Hāl* can therefore be either human or angelic (ibid.:105). The true state of spiritual *hāl* is a glimpse of the bliss of the universal principle of love (*'eshq-i haqiqi*), expressed in mystical poetry through an elaborate symbolism of drunkenness (*masti, sukr*) and wine (Chittick 1983:311–33).[60] It is primarily through techniques employing the privileged medium of sound—*zikr* invocation and music—that, upon completing the prerequisite spiritual contraction, an adept may move into spiritual expansion and ascent. As *zikr* and *samā'* are huge subjects unto themselves, each comprising a voluminous literature, this discussion can only present a cursory introduction.[61]

The spiritual experiences of "drunkenness," immersion in being, attained through exploiting the spiritual efficacy of sound and various other means, belong to the expansive stages of spiritual ascent. Like many esoteric traditions, Sufism categorizes the path to realization in terms of a spiritual alchemy that transmutes the substance of the initiate's soul through a progression of contraction-expansion-union. In Sufi terminology this progression is known as *qabd'-bast-fanā'/baqa* (Nasr 1987:167). Contraction in this microcosmic sense implies asceticism, emptying oneself of the ego (*nafs*), individuality, desires, and attachment to the immediate phenomenal world. Once emptied of the lower self, one may begin to seek transpersonal states of consciousness, which fill or expand one's being. Of the many existing formulations, Sufis often refer to the means by which forms are connected with their true spiritual nature as the "Breath of the Compassionate" (the Compassionate being one of the foremost names of Allah, *Rahim*), in which case expansion refers to being filled with this divine breath (Bakhtiar 1976:12-17).[62] As in the Old Testament, the universe was created through the word of God in Islamic cosmogony,[63] which entails the divine Breath; our own breath is synonymous with life itself and carries important spiritual implications for singers.[64]

The technique of *zikr*[65] ("remembrance," "invocation") is universally employed by all Sufi orders (though often in quite different ways) as *the* primary spiritual tool or method. It is essentially the controlled repetition of a formula[66]—an act that integrates word, sound, breath and rhythm.[67] An enormous variety of techniques are found amongst the various orders and indeed amongst individual *sheikhs* within a given order: collective practice, solitary, silent, loud, spoken, sung, with and without body movements, slow and sustained, fast and successively accelerated, etc. It is a potent means of focussing one's attention and reintegrating oneself through sympathetic vibration with the "Breath of the Compassionate."

Samā' is an immensely complex topic, even in comparison to *zikr*, to which it is closely related but unquestionably subordinate (ibid.:104). *Samā'* is variously defined as "audition," "spiritual concert"[68] (see Rouget 1985:255–58; Lewisohn 1997) and generally refers to Sufi gatherings centred on the ritual performance of Qur'an recitation, Sufi hymns and musical repertoire and frequently dance. *Samā'* ceremonies frequently incorporate *zikr* as well.[69] While our discussion focuses on its Sufistic context, During (2006a) examines *samā'* in relation to shamanistic practices, of which (like the bard) it may be a functional, if not historical extension and survival. The expressed purpose of *samā'*, which has been the subject of a bitter polemic since the early period of Islam, is to bathe in or fill oneself with artistic rhythm and archetypal beauty, through which one experiences the ecstasy of cosmic rhythm and beauty itself. *Samā'* is a venue for ecstatic, visionary contact with the imaginal world (During 1982:78; 1986:477). All those who attend the *samā'*—which, again, take on a seemingly infinite variety of forms (During 1992)—participate in it as well, as either performers or listeners (Nasr 1987:80).

From one perspective, the spiritual principle behind *samā'* is that of invocation and focussed concentration, similar to that of *zikr*.[70] As elucidated by During, *samā'* is, even more than the practice of *zikr*, an explicit expression of sacrifice (1982).[71] *Samā'* gatherings were traditionally lavish events incorporating multi-media art forms, perfumes, and expensive gastronomical offerings, often involving animal sacrifice (During 1982:76, 82 note 10). It is not surprising that such overt displays of seeking ecstasy could degenerate into profane revelry (due to lack of the prerequisite spiritual contraction), and that even in the cases of legitimate practice they would be denounced by the exoterics. Sufis clearly distinguished the legitimate from the illegitimate and insisted on the strict supervision of a *sheikh* in conducting *samā'*. He alone could decide whether an initiate had passed the necessary stage of contraction. Sufis maintained that the legitimacy of *samā'* was totally contingent on how it was used, which depended on the individual. Sa'di cautioned, "I will not say, my brother, what *samā'* is before I know who the listener is" (*Bustan*, line 1970). We saw earlier how music, belonging to the ambiguous, angelic (and *jinnic*) interworld (containing both heaven and hell) is essentially neutral or ambiguous, conducive to both spiritual ascent and corruption.[72] It is therefore like "fanning a fire . . . (a) person's substance, whatever it might be, would be strengthened by the music" (Chittick 1983:325).[73]

To practice Sufism, to live according to its "way," entails performance. These performance activities include attending gatherings, practicing *zikr*, meditating, writing poetry, delivering discourses, among other things. Arguably more so than many of these, *samā'* is a primary means and marker of performing Sufism, displaying one's specific ideology in a manner that holds specific significance for those both inside and outside the subculture of Sufi orders.

OS

[There is a] sincere common feeling between the audience and myself. When I hear their silence and feel the powerful and beautiful waves of energy from their faces, this gives me power and strength. It creates a common unity between us in such a way that sometimes I feel like I've levitated and am transformed into an infinite number of tiny particles spread throughout the room. Certainly in most concerts I experience this wonderful state, which I can only call "visionary" (ruya'i) . . . and in those conditions the music feels like the sound of being (sedā-ye hasti). Sometimes in these situations my heart feels like it is palpitating or stopping. Unfortunately, these states last a very short time and I return to my ordinary state . . . one should pay attention and respect this link with the people, who persuade one to do one's best and be sincere in accomplishing one's work. Alas, various difficulties and obstacles prevail to break this powerful link. (Shajarian 1993:43)

Question: What are your thoughts about *hāl* in Persian music at this stage of your life?

In general, every one of us, as a private individual, has a special state in our private moments. We all take pleasure in certain things, can feel elevated and inspired by something and experience a feeling of satisfaction. One can even cry in that state, I mean literally produce tears. One can get so high, in an emotional level that one can even cry. This is the climax of hāl, *to reach a point where one sheds tears. Nevertheless, these tears are not the tears of sadness but tears of something else, some other kind of state. Humans have always already lost a beloved somewhere. Therefore we always want to find something in this regard: some people call it "God" and some chose various other "idols." There is something that humans are always in search of—from the person who has a religion through to those who do not—there is something that they want to achieve through their emotional states. I have sensed that everyone has this thing in them, Iranians particularly have it, and I sense that other people in other places in the world have it too.*

I like to understand people and society and sense their feelings, to understand their culture and realize their emotional needs. Then I will adjust myself to their emotional needs. If my needs and theirs turn out to be the same, then a type of sympathetic relationship occurs between us, and I can very easily start singing that which is inside of me. I usually pick a poem that is related to that particular time and place or to that environment and region, and then I start to sing. I will influence my listeners in this way and sometimes they get so excited that they even cry. This is a relationship that has always existed between people. The only thing that we have to know about this relationship is that it exists. We have to understand this relationship and understand the situation and speak at the right moment. In my case, instead of speaking, I will be singing. So I really have a good sense for this feeling, this two-way relationship—perhaps this is why I have become successful. I mean, you cannot talk thoughtlessly; I believe that you have to speak at the right moment. Sometimes you must keep a thought to yourself until you find a right moment to speak it, and when you find that right moment, you really hit the bull's eye. The artist's job is to recognize this moment and I have always recognized it when I have been with the people.

Have you ever been surprised by yourself by having such a state or *hāl* that you perform something that even amazes yourself?

Yes, this has happened to me many times. Sometimes when I sing, it becomes like a car that is going at a very high speed but has wings as well. At some point it will eventually lift off the ground for a minute or two and then it will land back. But in any case, this does not happen too often. It all depends on the conditions of the environment and whether they align in a powerful combination. First of all, I have to be in the right mood myself and the instrumentalist has to be in the same mood as well—that's very important. If the person who is playing with me gives me energy, this state takes place. But if he gets behind a little bit this lift doesn't occur. It is very important for the instrumentalist to be in touch with me and move me with his feelings and his technique. In that state I can fly. But I only fly for a

few moments, it is not long lasting. I have never experienced this elevation for more than three minutes but a lot of great things happen in those minutes and every time I hear that recording I remind myself of what a great state I was in to make this happen. In any case, it happens—but it's very rare. (2008)
What do you feel is the best avaz you have ever performed?
That I cannot say, but in some performances I have given some phrases their best possible presentation and in those situations I have felt like I have been lifted up from the ground. I sing one or two phrases in this state and then I come back. It depends who my listeners are and what mood or state I am in personally. If the instrumentalist is not highly trained that also pulls me down. But Lotfi, for example, gives me this spiritual state.
There is a deep essence, a profound aura, within your voice. Can you elaborate on this?
(Shajarian recites a *beyt* from Hafez):
Latife-ist nahāni ke 'eshq az ān khizad
ke nām-e ān na labe lālo khat-e zangārist

*"An attraction is hidden inside us from whence love arises
And its name is neither ruby lips nor copper that rusts"*

These latife-ye nahāni *or "secret attractions" are inside each and every one of us. They are the perfume* (attr) *of being. Have you ever seen the narcissus flower? You may perhaps see four different types of narcissus but the narcissus of Shiraz has an intoxicating scent. This scent is not because of its colour or shape or its size: this is the fragrance of its existence, its inner being, it is the essence of that flower. Perhaps another flower may be even more beautiful but it would not have the same powerful scent. It is like this wind that is blowing* [the conversation is taking place outdoors]*—if it is coming from a swamp it will then have that character, and if it is coming from a meadow of wildflowers we will say to ourselves "what a refreshing breeze." These two winds are not different from each other but because they are blowing from different places they each have a different significance. One is blowing from a marsh and another from a flower, even from a particular flower. This is the key element: the perspective of human beings and their voices come out of this essence.*

This inner being is very important and all the techniques and tools must be available for that, for the "that" of being which is already part of the being. This esoteric being belongs only to that particular individual and she cannot pass it on to another being. It belongs only to that individual. You can learn a lot of things from others but this essence of being only exists for one individual. It is partly derived from the genes and family and other things that make his or her shape and essence. It is all summed up in the pain of sympathy, the pain for human beings, the need for seeing others happy, to share our being with others, and many other things. All these make the essence of being. The ones who are too selfish, only thinking of themselves, can never see their own essence and inner being. The inner being of humans is traced back to their emotional needs and consciousness and the way they think about the cosmos and life. The sum of all of this is what I mean by the perfume of being and it really comes to life in art. The essence of being becomes transparent in art.

You have been the voice of many of Iran's mystics, people like Araqi and Attar, but they are more than just poets. Have you worked on the philosophy of the mystics?

Yes, of course. When I read a poem I also analyze it from the poet's perspective and what he has done with the words, what he intended to say and how he has delivered his subject. These poets don't just write words. (2009)

In order to find the unique treasure of humanity that is inside of us all we should live in peace, concentration and thoughtful reflection. The artist should look at life with a view that is full of love and forgiveness, and avoid dishonesty and cruelty. An exceptional being [artist] would not stoop to cruelty. Therefore, the artist must look at music from this angle and talk about love and the beloved and occasionally talk about the deprivations of society. Society isn't ready for the "Superhuman" (insan-e nāb), so you wait for society to accept that to acquire respectful "manners," whereby everyone lives peacefully beside each other— from the most common person of society to the most important political figure. And they find that "promised heaven" right here in this place. (Shajarian et al. 2004: 220–21)

Why did you start singing, what was your ambition behind it all?

Well, beauty is within us. It is part of us, it is within the embryo and it continues as one grows up. Ever since I was little, I enjoyed and could recognize a beautiful voice. Ever since I was two years old, when I went along with my father to those Qur'an recitation gatherings, I could recognize this. From then on I have lived with the voice and singing and it has continued to this day. It is the force of beauty that has taken me this far. Beauty has taken different shapes for me: from singing avaz to designing and making instruments, my life has been the path around this beauty.

Where do you see the roots of this beauty? Is it in Iranian literature, mysticism or culture?

Art creates beauty and beauty creates love and love is the vehicle that enables humans to reach their greatest values. Love shows itself in different forms and in music it is the sound or voice [seda] that takes one somewhere else. Then one has to understand the meaning behind the sound, and what message it has and to which direction it is taking them. It is then that you realize why you chose to listen to a particular music and where that music is taking you.

So is this part of our nature or is it just technique?

Well, it is part of our nature in the beginning but then it turns into technique and one must learn that, in order to control it. I mean, if one wants to make use of the voice, one has to learn how to control it. But you must have a voice to begin with, then an ostad, then a good environment, and then you must work hard. The voice also needs love, so that it can reach its potential. Love is congenital, it is born with human beings and it dies with them. One's appreciation of beauty is the same, it is born within us and it dies with us. If one wants to reach the absolute of one's art, one must go and learn it and practice it, you cannot just depend on your talent.

Is art a vehicle for cultivating purity?

The best art is the art that can describe, in the best possible way, that which is in the artist. An artist should be capable of describing that which is inside of him, in a matter that no one else can. This art must then create sympathy and bring people together and teach them their own uniqueness and oneness and show them that God is inside every one of us—to think of oneself as nothing less than a god—and to start loving each other and showing love to one another. Life is nothing but a gathering; it is these gatherings that have value and one remembers—like what we said and did with a particular person on a particular day, and so on. You see? No one really remembers the lonely parts of life.[74]

Notes

1. A town located 950 km southeast of Tehran.
2. Notes to the Delawaz album *Be Yad e Pedar*, "To the Memory of Father," 1999.
3. Imam Reza, martyred in 818 AD, was the eighth Imam of Shi'a Islam.
4. See Simms and Koushkani (2012).
5. See Simms and Koushkani (2012).
6. The mythologies concerned all feature male protagonist/gods.
7. Various orders are noted for this (particularly in Morocco). See the video documentary Aryana Farshad (dir.), *Mystic Iran: the Unseen World* (New York: Wellspring Media, 2004).
8. Thirty-two thousand in 2005 according to official Iranian statistics cited in Curtis and Hoogland 2008:295.
9. See Zaehner 1965 for preservations of Zoroastrianism in other areas of Iranian folklore.
10. While most sources corroborate this timeline, Del Giudice reports that its recitation still occurs in teahouses in South Tehran (2008:63).
11. The primacy of sacred recitation, which has an almost universal distribution in world cultures and history, is partially due to the interior nature of singing itself. The abstract nature of music makes singing "heightened language," a mode of elevated discourse differentiated from normal language when addressing the spiritual dimension.
12. While the Qur'an is also read silently, this is a subordinate practice to recitation as it was initially memorized and transmitted orally and only recorded and transmitted in written form after the death of the Prophet Mohammad, who was illiterate.
13. As mentioned above, in Iran this includes Arab maqams not used in *dastgahi* music, notably Rast and Saba.
14. Cf. Feldman 1996: 283–85, regarding the relationships to the Ottoman taksim.

15. This famous recording is available on a number of internet sites, including several postings on YouTube, e.g. http://www.youtube.com/watch?v=H35tR9VCrPQ.

16. According to Shabnam Ataei, after Shajarian won the standoff with the national media prohibiting them to play his music following the election crisis of 2009 (discussed in Simms and Koushkani 2012), the government sought out reciters to replicate his iconic Rabbana for future broadcasts but no one was able to copy it (personal communication, 2010).

17. The coalition of parties and groups that initially assumed leadership in the aftermath of the Islamic Revolution included significant secular and democratic players, but in the chaotic months that followed, some observers believe the Karbala narrative was engaged in rallying Iranians, wherein support for the Islamic Republic was effectively support for Imam Hussein and his seventy-two uncompromising revolutionaries (Chelkowski and Dabashi 1999:70–77). As noted above, while roles are fixed the actors in the narrative are fleeting and transient, so that the archetypal tyranny of Yezid was easily channeled into slogans of "Death to the Shah!" to "Death to America!" to "Death to Saddam!" and in the post-election crisis of June 2009, the thinly veiled sedition toward the leaders of the Islamic Republic: "Death to the tyrant!" There are precedents for this throughout the twentieth century, notably the insertion of Reza Shah into this role during the deadly Imam Reza shrine uprising of 1935.

18. See Blum 2002a:826–27 for a description of music in contemporary rites.

19. For a brief introductory illustration and overview of *ta'ziyeh* see the short YouTube documentary video: http://www.youtube.com/watch?v=8aKAPL9Fkz4&feature=related.

20. This is an interesting description, as Qur'an recitation is usually set in Arabic *maqam*s.

21. This "folk music" was engaged by the postrevolutionary authorities to promote nationalism in the Islamic Republic (During 1992; Youssefzadeh 2000).

22. From Gordon Innes and Bakari Sidibe, trans., *Sunjata: Gambian Version of the Mande Epic by Bamba Suo and Banna Kanute* (revised ed.) (New York: Penguin, 1999).

23. Interview on VOA Persian, broadcasted June 19 2010; http://www.youtube.com/watch?v=wHiPVsJIJIY.

24. And more recently treated with exceptional lucidity by Ray Grigg (1994).

25. See Chimamanda Adiechie's address "The Danger of a Single Story," wherein she poigniantly discusses the issue and, following Chinua Achebe, calls for a "balance of stories." http://www.ted.com/talks/chimamanda_adichie_the_danger_of_a_single_story.html.

26. Though the ancient Chinese allude to an inexplicable, illusive unchanging in the constant change, inadequately described as the Tao.

27. E.g., particle physics, neurology; see also J. Becker 2001: 109ff.

28. In a very interesting twist, he has also used the metaphor of *khānande* as a showman or comedian (p.102 below).

29. The performance examples of Simms and Koushkani (2012) provide many concrete illustrations.

30. While traditionally accorded a high social value for their skills, services and function as oral historians, *jalis* had a low status in traditional Mande society, as they are believed to be able to manipulate their listeners' spiritual energy (*nyama*); blacksmiths fall into a similar category for their supposed alchemical powers.

31. For more this traditional context/ritual of performing avaz, see During 1989: 205 ff.

32. Interview in Persian, broadcasted June 19, 2010; http://www.youtube.com/watch?v=wHiPVsJIJIY.

33. From his famous 1984 recording *Bidad*, discussed in Simms and Koushkani (2012).

34. Liner notes to Ocora 559097, 1990:4.

35. From an interview on Australian television, posted at www.YouTube.com/watch?v=bnoGhSCA-kQ.

36. Complaining of the inadequacy of traditional Persian music, Vaziri wrote in 1929: " [Our music] is a reservoir of sad feelings, of memories of pain, suffering, imprisonment, and condemnation, of the influence of continued attacks by savage tribes, of mourning songs. Our legitimate songs are those that . . . were used to make one weep, and all others were banned" (quoted in Chehabi 1999:147).

37. In the film *The Voice of Iran* (2003) Shajarian explicitly states that the sadness of Persian music especially reflects Iran's long, lamentable legacy of tyranny.

38. According to Feld:

> The purpose of the songs is to make the hosts nostalgic, reflective, and sentimental. During the performance the sadness evoked by both textual imagery and the pathos of the performer moves members of the audience to tears...People weep this melody [D C A G] while shedding tears, sometimes adding text. This style of weeping is also heard at funerary events where women improvise wept-sung laments using this same melodic form. The importance of this weeping, as response to song for men and leading to song for women, is articulated in a Kaluli myth in which a child is denied food by his older sister. The profound sadness from this rupture of the normal course of social events leaves the child lost and abandoned, at which point he turns into a muni bird. (Feld 1981: 27, 28).

39. *Han* is a "national sentiment" of sadness, pain, and suffering felt as a result of violence, oppression or injustice. The vocal genre *shushimga* or "songs of sorrow," usually sung by women, embody and express this deep-seated, codified, and collective feeling of sadness (see Willoughby 2000).

40. The nineteenth-century pianist and composer Louis Gottschalk wrote in his diary (*Notes of a Pianist*, London: Knopf, 1962, p.107): "Play a melancholy passage to an exile thinking of his distant country, to an abandoned lover, to a mother mourning for her child, to a conquered warrior, and be assured that each one of these various griefs will appropriate the plaintive harmonies to itself and will recognize in them the voice of its own suffering."

41. Judith Becker associates the act of weeping to music with bona fide trancing (2004:2).

42. While Rumi is famously and justifiably associated with the allegory of the ney, it did not originate with him: he inherited it from Sufi tradition and gave it his own brilliant and expansive stamp. Ahmad Ghazali's less developed allegory from the early-twelfth century (Godwin 1987:78) predates Rumi by more than a century.

43. For further discussion of this sense of "nostalgia" in Persian music, see During (1982:80, 84; 1984:210; 1989:531; 1991:171–74).

44. While the connection seems distant at first glance, it is perfectly reasonable to view Shajarian as an exponent of Inayat Khan's "lineage" in terms of the globalization of Sufi poetry and music.

45. Examined in detail in Simms and Koushkani (2012).

46. "Khezr is a mythical figure sometimes associated with the Biblical Elijah, believed to have initiated Moses in the ways of esoteric knowledge and guided Alexander through the realms of darkness to the fount of life" (Lewis 2008:34). Showing archetypal

correspondence with the story of Utnapishtim in the epic of Gilgamesh (Attar 1984: 231), Khezr is particularly associated with good fortune in Iranian culture.

47. The opening line is: "Breathe, you are with yourself, Breathe, you are with the beloved." Ghazal number 323 in *Kulliyat-e Shams Tabrizi (vol.1)*, ed. Badi al-Zaman Foruzanfar, 119, Tehran: Tala'i, 1386 AH/2007.

48. This tasnif and the context surrounding it are discussed further in Simms and Koushkani (2012).

49. Recitation of the *Shahnāme* is conventionally delivered in Chahargah.

50. Liner notes to KCD-107, 1997:3. On one informal interview occasion (2002), Ostad Shajarian mentioned that Abu Ata was his favourite mode, by which, in the course of inspired performances, he can enter altered states of consciousness.

51. Liner notes to Ocora C559097, 1989:20.

52. Especially the many excellent works of Jean During on this topic, notably During 1975, 1982, 1984, 1987, 1988, 1989 and 1991.

53. See note 46.

54. For additional aspects of the initiatory structure of Iranian musical life, including a response to the question of using the mystical association of music as merely a means for social legitimization, see During's penetrating discussion (1989:544–48).

55. It is through the agency of the word (*Kun!* "Be!") that Allah's will instantaneously transposed all archetypes into phenomenal existence (Qur'an 16:40). This of course corresponds to Genesis 1:3, and therefore to Judeo-Christian cosmogony as well.

56. Cf. with dastgah Homayun ("Royalty") for which Shajarian shows a clear affinity, given its frequent appearance in his large ouevre of recordings, not to mention the fact that this is the name he gave his son, born in 1975.

57. This clearly corresponds to *anahata nada*, "unstruck sounds" of Indian philosophy.

58. Cf., the positive and negative aspects of the interworld.

59. This cosmogonic formulation of Ibn Arabi has a somewhat Buddhist flavour. As Nasr expounds:

> (I)n the same manner that the human breath goes through the cycle of contraction and expansion, the Universe undergoes the two complementary phases of the same cycle. It is annihilated at every moment and recreated at the next, without there being a temporal separation between the two phases. It returns back to the Divine Essence at every moment while in the phase of contraction and is remanifested and externalized in that of expansion. (Nasr 1964:112)

60. Due to the explicit surface content (*batin*) self-evident in the poetry, such literature was naturally a target for exoteric polemics against the Sufis.

61. Interested readers should see Lewisohn 1997 and consult the detailed work of During 1988 and 1989, along with relevant works included in his copious bibliographies.

62. This formulation elucidates an aspect of the symbolism of the ney reed flute, the instrument most valued by the Sufis. The flute must be hollow in order to sound and the sound is produced by the breath; the resulting music is joyful and ecstatic (see During 1988:202–05).

63. See note 55.

64. Breath, our most vital and primary energy is the medium of singing, an integral relationship that leads to concepts of sacrifice (Schneider 1982), magic (ibid.: 1957:8–12, 41ff., 1968) and spiritual alchemy, the most well known of which are probably the Indian practices of *prana*, *sabda* and *mantra yoga*, which are parallel to Sufi *zikr* techniques and which indeed exist as cognate practices in many other cultures.

65. This transliteration reflects the Persian pronunciation; the original Arabic word is translated as *dhikr*.

66. Most often a name of Allah or the *shahadah*, the Muslim declaration of faith *La Illaha Illa Allah* ("There is no god but Allah" or "There is no divinity but The Divinity").

67. *Zikr* is the Islamic cognate of esoteric practices found in various traditions around the world: Hindu *japa/mantra yoga*, Christian rosary prayer, various Buddhist practices, etc.

68. Or, more colloquially yet effectively, as Becker's qualified usage of Oliveros's "deep listening" (Becker 2004).

69. See During 1982 and 1988 for the relationship between the two practices.

70. *Samā'* corresponds in many ways to the Hindu practice of *kritan/bhajan* sessions.

71. Cf., Schneider's interpretation of Christian and Hindu views of music as sacrifice (1982; 1986).

72. Of course, this ambivalence is by no means restricted to the Muslim or Iranian world. Note the ambiguous role of the Hindu *ghandarvas*, musical commentaries in the Chinese (especially Confucian) classics, the role of music in Greek mythology, Plato's treatment of music and the ambiguous social position that musicians hold in many cultures, including Western.

73. Ruzbahan Baqli, a Persian Sufi master of the twelfth century, noted that "Spiritual music is of three kinds: one for the common people, one for the elite and one for the elite of the elite. The common people listen through nature (i.e., the imperfect nature of most men dominated by the passions) and that is destitution. The elite listen with the heart, and that is being in quest. The elite among the elite listen with the soul, and that is being in love" (cited in Nasr 1987:159).

74. Interview on VOA Persian, broadcasted June 19 2010; http://www.youtube.com/watch?v=wHiPVsJIJlY.

Chapter 3
To Tehran

Ostad Shajarian held various teaching and administrative posts in public schools in the Mashhad area throughout the first half of the 1960s while continuing to broadcast programs on Radio Khorasan. Out of respect for his father's wishes, these were exclusively programs of sacred genres and mystical poetry, sung solo without instrumental accompaniment. Shajarian was transferred to teach high school in Tehran in 1966, a decisive move for him and his young family that paved the way to a major transformation of his musical career, setting him on the path to becoming a national star through his work on national radio. At the time of his move the population of Tehran was 2.7 million, more than five times bigger than that of Mashhad (Bharier 1972:54).

This chapter traces Shajarian's expanding musical network, training, and the development of his career working in Tehran up to the 1979 Islamic Revolution, while simultaneously treating the city as a symbol of the secular tradition of Persian music, urban Iranian musical culture and Iranian modernity in general. Although Shiraz, with its prestigious though controversial annual festival, was a symbol of artistic modernity in late-Pahlavi Iran, Tehran was indeed the undisputed center of Iranian musical activity in the country since the beginning of the Qajar period and has served as the nerve center of Iranian musical media since their inception in the early-twentieth century. It is necessary to briefly sketch the broad outlines of Iranian musical culture in the twentieth century in order to properly contextualize Shajarian and his work throughout the rest of this study. Iran underwent tumultuous upheaval and rapid change in political, social, and cultural domains throughout the last century. As these conditions are typical and key variables for spawning Hobsbawm's now-famous theory of the "invention of tradition," it is prudent to remain on the lookout for Iranian manifestations here. While it is of course beyond the scope of this study to delineate a detailed history of twentieth-century Iranian musical culture, the work of During (e.g., 1984, 1988, 1992, 1994, 2001, 2002, 2005), Nettl (1970, 1978), Blum (2002a), Movahed (2003), Nooshin (1996), Miller (1999),

Youssefzadeh (2000) and Wright (2009), among other scholars, offer the interested reader further insights and precision to the necessarily cursory overview that follows. The topics of this discussion include patronage, transmission, various forms of mediation, scholarly discourse, the role of women and key individuals who made a significant impact on the overall musical culture.

In any historical outline of Iran it is essential to bear in mind the immense diversity and complexity of Iranian culture. This is particularly the case for Western readers, who are subjected to a long-standing barrage of systemic propaganda that entrenches an insidiously manipulative, monolithic view of "Iran," "Iranians," and especially "the Middle East"—the latter constituting an entirely unhidden Western imperialist construction for those who care to look at the amply documented historical facts of the twentieth century. Dabashi emphasizes that Iranian culture is "syncretic and hybrid to the very bone of its character" (2007: 16), its integral plurality is such that "'Iran' is a state of mind, systematically set to contradict itself" (ibid.:6).[1]

There is great diversity and numerous variables to be considered: ethnicities, languages, and environments; social and economic milieus; political agendas; religious and spiritual modalities; musical styles, aesthetics, and tastes. Tehran was the primary hub attracting and concentrating this diversity in the rapid urbanization that characterized the twentieth century. Shajarian is particularly skilled at understanding and replying to this plurality, and in a single mass-mediated performance centering on the crucial common denominator of Persian poetry, he attempts to communicate with, and fulfil the expectations of, an immensely diverse audience. Another theme underlying the twentieth century and running as a set of illustrative variations throughout is the complex, dynamic relationship of tradition and modernity (as introduced in chapter 1). This takes a polemic form—paralleling widespread pre-revolutionary sentiments in the political realm regarding Iranian culture in general—in which musicians and connoisseurs grew increasingly concerned that essential features of Persian music were being undermined. It is a complicated historical narrative, which unfolds largely in chronological order here (and is continued in Simms and Koushkani [2012]), with occasional exceptions made in an effort to preserve a coherent bird's-eye view of issues, spheres of activity, and historical perspective—to make neat, tidy, and linear a real story that is anything but. We begin with this contextual sketch by tracing the main historical strands of the musical scene Shajarian entered in 1966 and then turn to his formative, professional and creative activities within it.

Innovators and Modernizers of the
Early-Twentieth Century

[Art world] revolutions differ from the gradual shifts in interest, attention, and convention. . . . They attack, ideologically and organizationally, the standard activities of that art world at that time. The ideological attack takes the form of manifestos, critical essays, aesthetic and philosophical reformulations and a revisionist history of the medium, denouncing old idols and exemplars and celebrating new work as the embodiment of universal aesthetic values. The organizational attack aims to take over the sources of support, audiences, and distribution facilities. (H. Becker 1982:304)

In their very different ways Mirza Abdollah (1843–1918), 'Aref Qazvini (1882–1934), and Colonel Ali Naqi Vaziri (1887–1979) may be regarded as revolutionaries in the early-twentieth century art world of Persian music. Vaziri embodies most fully Becker's description above, while 'Aref may be regarded as the most revolutionary in the ordinary political usage of the word. Mirza Abdollah emerged as the most influential exponent of the Farahani lineage, and it is perhaps more accurate to credit his father Ali Akbar (1810–1855) with the revolutionary changes in the modal system of Persian music that Mirza Abdollah rather consolidated, perfected, and efficaciously propogated: the radif. The art world of *dastgahi* music was freshly defined yet firmly established by Mirza Abdollah and his brother Aqa Hossein-qoli (1853–1915) by the first decade of the twentieth century.

We noted at the beginning of chapter 1 how many Persian poets throughout history quite regularly included a layer of contemporary political critique embedded within their *iham*, and that other performance genres of the Qajar period often included more overt political overtones, a trend that continued among a small but influential group of twentieth century poets. 'Aref was foremost among this latter group but was also a singer and composer of tasnifs that were "impeccably suited for the popular and revolutionary purposes to which they were put during the Constitutional period" (Dabashi 2005: 102). He toured Iranian towns singing his tasnifs in the early 1920s, each song encapsulating his stance on specific political issues of the day and calling upon people to act. The "occasion" of 'Aref's work was exclusively political, and he considered himself to be a "nationalist singer," not an entertainer (Tabar 2005: 91). A staunch and literally vocal supporter of the reforms of the Constitutional Revolution of 1905–1911 (commonly reffered to as the *Mashrute*), he spent a period in exile in Istanbul beginning in 1916 and lived his final years in internal exile in Hamadan. The renowned singer Qamar took up 'Aref's cause and became the voice for his nationalist tasnifs from 1925–31 in both live performances and recordings. She recorded his tasnif "*Jomhuri*/The Republic"—which was banned by Reza Shah and those possessing it faced prison—for free, on the condition that the discs would be sold at cost (Tabar 2005: 92, 98). Of course, not all musicians wished to be associated with political activism, which could be dangerous and detracted from the more aesthetic or

transcendental dimensions of Persian music. At a recording session in Tiblisi during the spring of 1914, 'Aref asked Abdollah Davami (1891–1980) to sing his
tasnif "*Nang ān khāna*/Disgraceful that House."[2] Accompanist Darvish Khan
(1872–1926) felt that it was inappropriately political and sabotaged the session by
deliberately breaking the skin on his tar (ibid.:85–86). 'Aref stands as an unpre-
cedently innovative and revolutionary figure in Persian music history, engaging
his music to explicitly political ends through public performance and the mass
medium of recordings. It is tragic, though not surprising, that such a bold soul
would die in poverty, obscurity and neglect yet remain an inspiring symbol of
resistance throughout the century. Shajarian would resume his noble function
seven decades later in an entirely new way that reverberates around the world—
'Aref's legacy burns brighter than ever a century after his first efforts of musical
activism.

The stifling, pervasive pressure exerted by the reinvigorated colonialism and
nationalism emerging after World War I resulted in modernization programs
throughout West Asia, each locale taking on its own flavor. The sweeping musical reforms of Vaziri of the 1930s followed this larger dynamic in the wake of
Reza Khan Pahlavi's authoritarian agenda of modernization. Having acquired
proficiency in the Persian tradition through the conventional oral means, Vaziri
studied Western music in Germany and returned to Iran to institute sweeping
changes in all areas of Persian music. He advocated for: a twenty-four-tone equal-
tempered scale; the use of notation; the standardization of theory; conservatory-
style education and Western-style concert formats; and compositional practice
incorporating Western harmonic idioms, musical forms, instrumental techniques,
and creative processes. His renovations were ostensibly "retaining essentials
while modernizing format and infrastructure" (Wright 2009:11). The reforms
were contentious throughout the prerevolutionary period, a lightning rod for debate concerning tradition and modernization, polarizing the Persian musical
community between supporters and detractors. While his reforms never quite
held sway in the ongoing debate and changes in musical practices, he certainly
promoted a more open, fluid approach to the Persian tradition among many influential musicians (ibid.:12). Simultaneous with the challenges posed by Vaziri,
Iranians were increasingly exposed to Western chamber and symphonic music
with its concomitant conventions of concert presentation such as stage attire, cued
applause, ticketed seating, etc.[3] Various hybridizations of Western and Persian
musical styles, instrumentation and performance conventions occurred throughout the 1940s and became more intensified and commonplace in the 1960s and
70s under the Reza Pahlavi's more aggressive drive to explicitly Westernize in
his modernization program (Nettl 1978).

The effects of Vaziri's reformation were still played out in this latter period
but Vaziri himself was less of a driving force in the musical scene, his torch
passed to a younger generation. Farhat (2004a) notes that, due to his more tactful
and affable personal disposition, Ruhallah Khaleqi (1906–65) was ultimately
more influential and effective than the abrasive Vaziri in implementing the latter's agenda through his work in the 1950s. Still younger musicians, while per-

haps not adopting the letter of Vaziri's innovations, certainly carried forward their spirit. Faramarz Payvar (1932–2009), oxymoronically though not inaccurately described as a "progressive traditionalist" by Wright (2009:16), was foremost among these musicians in public visibility during the 1960s and 70s, serving as the director of music for the Ministry of Culture throughout the latter decade (Miller 1999:36). A gifted student of Abolhasan Saba, he developed his own style of solo santur playing featuring an exhibitionistic virtuosity and deployment of arpeggios, while composing large ensemble pieces that highlighted tightly controlled unisons, harmonic colorings, shifts of texture, and approach to arrangement taken from the techniques of Western orchestration. Shajarian performed regularly with Payvar throughout the 1970s in both large and chamber ensembles wherein his personal taste and preferences for presenting avaz were often subordinate to Payvar's dictates. Enjoying favour from both the Ministry of Arts and Culture and the public at large, Payvar became a central figure (among the legions of lesser proponents active at the time) cited in a vigorous debate among musicians and music critics alike in the 1970s regarding the imminent, possibly irreversible loss of essential elements of Persian music through his type of trademark stylistic innovations, which were deemed by many as uncategorically decadent (e.g., Miller 1999:35–36).[4]

The musical scene in Tehran during the 1960s–1970s reflected a remarkable complexity and pluralism (Nettl 1970, 1978), as this conservatively hybridized style coexisted with Western classical music in the public mainstream, various "lowbrow" manifestations of hybridized popular music—from *asil*-tinged *motrebi* to Western-influenced popular styles, such as jazz and rock—with conservative Persian music enjoying limited media exposure but increasingly retreating underground. While many prophesied the apocalyptic demise of Persian music in the 1960s, it indeed seems clear that Iranian musical culture was at the very least undergoing a veritable "identity crisis" (Nettl 1978:179) that would be addressed in part by the establishment of the Center for the Preservation and Propagation of Iranian Music in 1968 (discussed below).

Women in Persian Music and Avaz

The roster of influential singers outlined in chapter 1 highlights the dominance of male performers that continued through the twentieth century to the present, a situation that is even more exclusive in the realm of insturmentalists. Indeed, During notes that "(i)t is necessary to note that singing was fundamentally a man's business. Women were not trained in the radif and were limited to the classical tasnif and some gushehs" (1996:346n.22). Similar conditions prevailed in the neighbouring and related tradition of *Iraqi maqam*. This was apparently not the case in the second half of the nineteenth century in Iran, however, as small ensembles patronized by the court known as *daste* were frequently all-female, including both instrumentalists and singers. Often formed around a single family, *daste* ensembles could also be mixed or exclusively male but the female ensembles were more versatile in that they were allowed to play for both segregated male and female audiences in the court, whereas the male ensembles could only perform for male audiences (Tabar 2005: 49–51; Mashhun 1994: 374, 379; Chehabi 2000:156). While there were no public concerts at this time and little evidence regarding the activity of women in private performance contexts outside the court, women were undoubtedly active in the latter. Musical prowess, cultivation and display was considered socially suspect for men at this time as well. Women were included in the musical transmission of the Farahani line, directly from Ali Akbar himself (Mashhun 1994:392) and, perhaps most significantly, Mirza Abdollah's son and reviver/populizer of the setar, Ahmad Ebadi, received most of his formative setar instruction from his sisters Mawlud and Moluk Kanom (During 1996a). Iranian women were in fact highly visible and politically active in the Constitutional period in the early-twentieth century and remain a driving grassroots political force in the continuing struggles today (Dabashi 2007). Under the formative influence his mother, a well-educated activist for women's liberation, Vaziri boldly initiated among his wide-ranging reforms the inclusion of women in all aspects of Iranian public musical life and education (Chehabi 2000:157). While there was initial resistance to this, it became increasingly routine to see women perform alongside men in public concerts through the 1960s and 1970s.[5] Debano claims that this visibility during the period was largely a facade that wallpapered over *de facto* limitation and contempt among Iranians for female musicians (2009: 239).

The passing mention of Qamar in the roster of important singers listed in chapter 1 downplays the fact that she was hugely influential on a scale that was quite unprecedented in Iranian music at the time. Raised by her grandmother, a *rowze khān* whose performances she regularly attended and eventually performed in, Qamar cultivated the meditative, elegiac genre of *marsie*[6] that brought an engaging and deeply moving quality to all of her singing (Nakjavani 2008). As her abilities and career in classical music quickly developed, she became in 1924, at nineteen years of age, the first woman to perform in public without a veil and later the first to be recorded (1927) and featured on radio broadcasts (regularly beginning in 1941). Concertizing extensively throughout her prime years and supporting various charitable and political causes through her music (ibid.; Chehabi 2000:159–60), she was both loved by a mass audience and greatly respected by musicians. Her generosity earned her the *de facto* status of a female *luti*, the archetypal ideal character in Iran of a man who is "generous, ever helpful to his friends, down-to-earth, unimpressed by status distinctions, and supports widows and orphans when he can" (Chehabi 2000:165). In 1927 she legally changed her last name to Vaziri in honor of the great reformer.

To a significant extent Qamar paralleled for Iranians what the contemporaneous Um Kulthum embodied for Arabs: a voice of "the people" symbolizing deep cultural identity, values and ideals that translated into feelings of nationalism. It is likely that Um Kulthum's enormous prestige and success story in the massmedia served in some measure as a close crosscultural precedent that helped facilitate Qamar's stardom. Shajarian considers Qamar to be a major influence on his singing, and indeed her penetrating tone, spectacular tahrirs and sheer intensity of expression are evident in his eclectic style. And yet Qamar's appalling demise perhaps reveals more about the position of women in Iranian musical culture of the time than her unlikely rise to fame and brilliant career. After suffering a debilitating stroke in 1956, she retired and, despite her unprecedented achievements and popularity, was forced to live on a meagre pension from the national radio, dying in isolation and poverty in 1959. Ruh Angiz, Delkash, Parvane Khatareh, and Parisa (as well as folk singers such as Sima Bina) followed in Qamar's sweeping wake whereby female *khānande*s achieved significant public recognition as exponents of avaz, even if they were numerically outnumbered by men and had to work under much more socially restricted conditions. Professional ground gained by these women, enhanced by the Shah's proactive policies toward women in general, including musical education and employment, crumbled in the period immediately following the revolution, their voices silenced in public and their careers essentially aborted.

The classical poetry featured in avaz is exclusively dominated by male poets. Similar to the case in many cultures, including European, women were of course active as poets but not recognized within the exclusively male preserve of the public sphere, and were therefore sidelined in the historical narrative. Also paralleling conditions in Europe throughout history, women were much less likely than men to acquire literacy. Since the tenth century, the poetry of women such as Rabe'eh Balkhi, Mahsati, Padeshah Khatun, Jahan Khatun, Tahereh Ghorrat ol Ein, Jaleh Ghaaem Maghami, and Parvin Etesami survives but remains on the extreme periphery of the tradition. Forough Farrokhzad (1936–1967), on the other hand, is widely acknowledged among both connoisseurs and the general public, and particulary influenced many contemporary female poets. National radio producer Davud Pirnia broadcasted a program profiling twenty-five female poets as part of the *Golhā* series.[7]

Given the patriarchal dominance of Persian poetry, it is not surprising that Shajarian's recorded output reflects this exclusivity. The only example of him singing avaz to the text of a female poet that I am aware of is Ghorrat ol Ein on his 2003 recording *Faryad*, where a traditional tasnif on her text, featured on Shajarian's 1977 recording *Chehre be Chehre*, is given a freer, paraphrased treatment that resembles avaz. Special mention of Ghorrat ol Ein is made in the liner notes of the international release of the CD on World Village Music.[8] Shajarian's affiliation with Derakhshani's Shahnaz ensemble features talented young female instrumentalists, including Shajarian's youngest daughter Mojgan on setar and vocals. In a seemingly confrontational gesture, the program of his 2010 world tour included short sections where Mojgan sang solo before mixed-gendered audiences, which is presently illegal in Iran. A concert in Tabriz by Homayun Shajarian in February 2010 was shut down by provincial authorities because two female musicians were included in his ensemble for the sold out event.[9]

Any struggle for freedom—and Iranians are engaged in a particularly oppressive, protracted and desperate one—begins with recognizing and removing the fundamental bondage of patriarchy, working towards a just and dignified balance of power between men and women in society. Iranian women have a long-standing tradition of organizing and calling for this equality, a fact that was clearly and heroically evident in the June 2009 election crisis.[10] Despite all efforts to deny them, they will not step down or be silenced. It is incumbent on men inside and outside of Iran to push forward with them for this historic change and overdue justice.

OS
Question: You have more than thirty female students, why is that?
Well, everyone likes music and this is not confined to males. I have a different approach to teach girls and women. I have transposed my own voice two notes higher [electronically, on digital recording examples used for study] *so that female singers can sing in a range they are more comfortable with. I have around seventy-four students and they are all very good—they have taken all my worries away regarding the future of avaz.*
My question is why do women tend to like this music more these days as opposed to the older days?
In general, music started to have some credibility among Iranian families. Ever since after the revolution, my generation brought back some credit and respectability to music, and showed that an artist can be someone that is loved by everyone. It was a group of us, and this thankfully had a good influence on families, easing their worries that their children might become motrebs *and drug users. We showed that this is not the reality. So the person who plays an instrument does not necessarily have problems. Another reason is that this [musical] culture was dying away and people started to protect it. The third factor was that, after the revolution, the radio and the television needed music for their program, so they supported traditional music. Nobody would touch the dial on the radio if music wasn't being played. So the authentic music of Iran replaced the pop music of the Shah's time. All of these factors together made it possible that more and more families allowed their children to learn music.*[11]

Transmission, Patronage, Mediation, and Institutionalization

In sketching out the social processes and mechanisms by which avaz functioned in the twentieth century we encounter the mutually arising, interlocking complex of topics listed in this heading. It is quite impossible to discuss one without discussing them all, and somehow keeping all of them in mind when focusing on any one component. While outlining the general context we examine how Ostad Shajarian's career and reflections fit into this larger picture.

Patronage

RS

In viewing the types of patronage under which musicians worked it bears repeating that many functioned with little or none at all: amateur prestige still held sway in grassroots musicking throughout the twentieth century to today. Many important musicians held "day jobs" throughout their careers,[12] and many big-name performers such as Ahmad Ebadi and Gholamhossein Banan secured their incomes outside musical circles early in their careers. While he always had his sight set on wider musical horizons than Mashhad, Shajarian moved to Tehran in 1966 as a result of a job transfer, working as a high school teacher for the Ministry of Education and Training; he was transfered again in 1968 to the Ministry of Natural Resources. He vigorously pursued the myriad musical opportunities that Tehran had to offer during his early years there, deepening his knowledge of Persian music under various masters while making significant professional inroads (discussed below). He performed under the stage name "Siavash Bidkani" until 1971, hedging his bets on a musical career by protecting his personal reputation and salaried position as a civil servant in a society where being a professioinal musician was held in great suspicion, if not outright contempt. Other influential musicians, such as Saba, Boroumand and Kasa'i, were independently wealthy: they had public profiles through radio exposure and printed publications and taught numerous students privately, for which they received some remuneration but this was quite beside the point for their activities. Avaz continued to be performed and transmitted through the traditional Sufi channels, both among private individuals and through the *khanegah*s, as it always has throughout history; again remuneration in cash or kind may occasionally occur here but is not an integral aspect of this activity.

Prior to the early twentieth century the only real patronage opportunities for Persian musicians were at the court, an institutional function that collapsed with the Qajar dynasty and was in some ways replaced by public broadcasting after 1940, wherein a small pool of artists had regular employment in radio and, later, television programs. Another avenue of government patronage arose in the form of educational institutions such as the national conservatory *Honarestan* ("Place of Art"), and later the University of Tehran and the *Markaz* ("Center").[13] A great number of influential musicians taught at these institutions before the revolution. The *Honarestan* and, following the inception of public broadcasting in the 1940s, national radio and television studios, also maintained large orchestras of Iranian and Western instruments that provided work of musicians.

While some musicians found stable long-term employment with these government institutions, many more had only occasional work and also had to freelance in the new fledgling private sector of various musical enterprises that arose in the twentieth century. Such freelance work held decidedly low socioeconomic connotations in Iranian society, existing as it did in venues that were on the cusp of *motreb* activity, which was considered unquestionably decadent. Darvish Khan is considered

among the first of Persian musicians to earn a decent full-time income by freelanc-
ing, simultaneously bringing the latter activity an unprecedented degree of respectability in the public's view. This work could include teaching at private conservatories but also performing in theatrical productions, nightclubs and private house parties (the latter exclusively for remuneration); later on, some musicians also engaged
in music publishing.

Public concerts were initiated by Darvish Khan and a cultural assocation (the
Zahir al-Dawla) in 1906, riding the intial wave of liberalism that followed from the
Mashrute, grew in prominence through throughout the century and became a regular
feature of social life, especially in Tehran where Darvish Khan gave concerts in the
hall of the Grand Hotel (Caton 1994) and Vaziri established a regular concert series
in his *Kolub-e musiqi* ("Music Club"). This activity increased steadily through the
1960s and 70s. During notes that the impulse for the development of public concerts
derived from models in the West via nineteenth century "modernizing" trends in
Tiblisi and later in Baku; likewise and understandably, the secular ritual and protocols surrounding the Western concert were transplanted in the process (During
1989:205ff.). Many of the earliest concerts, especially those organized by groups
such as the *Anjoman-e Okhavvat* ("The Society of Brotherhood"), were benefits
towards charity (Anwar 1985; During 1989:206), a practice furthered by artists
like 'Aref and Qamar. Some senior Ostads only very rarely played in public, but
did so for charity concerts. While the motivation for these concerts was a compassionate and sincere support for the particular causes, they also provided a legitimate occasion for playing music in public at a time when this was socially stig-
matized. In tandem with the appropriation of the public concert for showcasing Persian music, concerts of Western classical music increased in frequency, quality and
professional networking outside Iran, especially through the 1960s and 70s.

Foreign private record companies began cultivating a market among wealthy
Iranians in the first decades of the twentieth century, offering musicians a new
avenue for employment; significant domestic Iranian companies would not emerge
until the 1960s. Associated by means of technology with government media,
recording artists were also regarded with a higher degree of prestige relative to other
freelance activities. As is generally the case in many cultures, a synergy developed
between recording, broadcasting and concert production, featuring a small group of
popular artists who monopolized the scene. Beginning in the late 1970s and growing
through the 1980s an even smaller contingent of these musicians began to expand
their freelance recording and concertizing activities toward an international audience
of expatriates and connoisseurs in the West. Shajarian played a prominent role in this
latter capacity and, indeed, has functioned within virtually all of the patronage
scenarios listed here.

Reflecting on the situation in the late 1960s/early 1970s, Nettl tentatively felt a
sense of continuity rather than rupture with regard to patronage in Iranian musical
culture:

> Patronage of music has changed, but perhaps not as much as one might expect.
> The patrons of music of the past—imperial court, private aristocrats—are still

active, but they have been augmented by various agencies of the national government, such as radio and television, the Ministry of Arts and Culture, and, most recently, record companies. There has not been a sudden radical change in patronage. . . . One transformation that appears to have taken place is the way that music is ranked within the context of Iranian cultural activities. Once viewed as having a very close alliance with the literary arts and with philosophy, music now seems to be regarded as more of a craft, with technical vocabulary and paraphernalia. Music as a private and individual activity has been overshadowed in a musical life governed by ensembles and by corporate sponsoring agencies. (Nettl 1978:154)

In observing the institutional shift of the period Zonis also noted its stifling and debilitating effects, especially the Ministry of Arts and Culture, that functioned as the engineers and gatekeepers of public musicking toward the implementation of the state's ideology: sterile standardization, bureaucratization and micromanagement of what was hitherto a more spontaneous and organic cultural growth (1973:197ff.). Musicians had to fit into the Ministry's policies and clique or starve.

But making a living and having an opportunity to hear music in public was not the only problem according to a contingent of stakeholders. Due to its hitherto exclusive cultivation among a small group of elite patrons and qualified musicians, Persian music faced an intrinsic dilemma when it was opened up to the public at large in the twentieth century through educational institutions and media accessibility and active government promotion: many observers close to the music felt that it was being fatally watered down in the process.

OS
Various friends who knew I loved music advised me to go to Tehran and try to get into working with the national radio. That was 1965. I had to pass the vetting process of the radio. I was examined by a jury who observed me and were astonished: I was nothing but a simple provincial guy and yet I wanted to present myself on national radio! They asked me a lot of theoretical questions about the radif to which I responded as best as I could, given that at the time I hadn't yet gained a deep knowledge of that repertoire. Two days later I received the observations of the jury: "Pretty good but too soon for the radio."
On the advice of a friend who was a technician, I presented producer Davud Pirnia with a cassette of my singing accompanied by Cyrus Haddadi, the ney-player for the Golhā orchestra. Pirnia agreed to listen to it. He was in the middle of writing something but when my singing began he stopped, raised his head and started to listen more attentively. After the ghazal, he lifted his eyes toward me and asked: "Is that really you who sang that?" He forwarded the tape in search of Mokhalef and Owj and then announced: "I'll take it. Yes, I'll take it, let's make a broadcast." A year later I left Khorasan for Tehran. Pirnia was no longer at the radio and I had to deal with many obstacles until I met Ostad Ebadi, whom I always regard as a relationship of father to son or master to disciple. Up to that time I never had a master for learning radif. I worked on my own and from time to time would ask the name of gushes from others." (Kasmai and Lecomte 1991:248–50)

Transmission

RS

Until the twentieth century avaz operated within Iranian culture exclusively through oral transmission and live performance, its main source of patronage was the court. Avaz was also performed in private homes and Sufi *khanegah*s, where there was usually a cultivated, appreciative audience but remuneration was not an issue. Classical Persian poetry followed a similar path—poetry and avaz being definitively joined at the hip—with the important difference that it employed written transmission, which thus ensured a stability and continuity of the "repertoire." Oral and written modes of transmission exist in a dynamic relationship with regard to poetry in Iran, especially among the bardic traditions of the *bakhshi*. But even within the realm of classical poetry several important qualifications are in order. In terms of composition, much of Rumi's poetry is believed to have been recited spontaneously and recorded by scribes, whom he occasionally refers to in the course of his voluminous improvised verse. And Rumi was of course literate, before his transformation into an ecstatic poet he was a highly educated religious scholar. Conversely, while literacy rates in Iran have vastly increased in the past few decades (82% in 2009),[14] until the 1960s the majority of Iranians were technically illiterate and yet functionally fully literate in knowing vast amounts of poetry from memory, possessing an indepth knowledge of literary history, an advanced command of language, and being highly articulate in oral composition (Dabashi 2005: 92, 142–44). In addition to private lines of transmission within the home, this was facilitated by the practice of literate readers reading aloud—poetry, literature and, beginning in the late nineteenth century, newspapers—in public venues such as coffeehouses. This functional bridging of the literate and "illiterate" was transposed exponentially through the mediation of radio and cassettes.

While there were no alternate means for Iranian musicians before the twentieth century, oral transmission in the tradition of Persian music included much more than the mechanical transfer of repertoire. The *sine be sine* "heart to heart" process of copying the musical utterances of the teacher involved the resonance or sympathetic vibration of subtle human energies, similar to the transfer of spiritual grace and blessing (*baraka*) that ideally occurs between a spiritual master and initiates, a transmission that extends quite beyond that imparted by verbal communication alone. These values are consciously preserved by many musicians, especially singers, even though they now have recourse to transcriptions and recordings (During 2002:857). The latter means are used both privately and institutionally by the majority of musicians and among other things reflect new aspects of patronage, mediation and commoditizing music that emerged in the twentieth century.

The age-old, essentially small-scale and intimate methods of traditional instruction were the exclusive means of transmission until the arrival in the 1860s of foreign Western military band music and its equally foreign concomitant vehicle of

French conservatory-style music education (itself a recently minted institution in Europe) for training neophyte Iranian military band musicians. Starting as a department within the *Dār al-Fonun*, a French-modelled military school established in 1851 to facilitate the modernization of Persia, the conservatory became an independant institution in 1918 under the name *Madrasa-ye Musik* (Farhat 2004b; Nooshin 1996: 108), retaining its government funding. The cultural, conceptual and technical challenges facing the first generation of Iranian military band musicians was formidable: an entirely foreign musical language and aesthetic; encountering harmony as an entirely new dimension of musical structure; a wide range of new brass a woodwind instruments only remotely related to indigenous cognates; and the completely alien medium of symbolic notation. The impact of this new music and the approach to learning it was profound but restricted to a relative small number of musicians, and Persian music continued to be transmitted as it always had, although there were a significant number of musicians who functioned in both worlds. Darvish Khan attended the *Dār al-Fonun* as a boy and later became an important performer, composer and significant teacher in the transmission lines of early-twentieth century Persian music. In the early 1910s he established large and long-standing classes of private students, many of whom in turn became influential performers and teachers. His methods were traditional but formatted into a three-levelled, graded curriculum of radif studies, with group instruction held twice a week, geared to each of the three levels of difficulty, perhaps reflecting the influence of conservatory-style education; as he did not read notation, his radif instruction was oral.[15]

While serving in the army, Vaziri diligently (if unsystematically) pursued multi-instrumental studies in Persian music with a wide range of masters from the late Qajar period (including Mirza Abdollah) along with Western music from French musicians stationed in Tehran to oversee the functioning of the military band education at the *Madrasa-ye Musik*. At the conclusion of World War I Vaziri left Iran to study music in Paris and later Berlin, returning to Tehran in 1923 with a clear vision of reforming Persian music education on the lines of the conservatory model, including an unprecedented focus on notation, Western-derived theoretical grounding and graded pedagogy. The timing of his agenda coinciding with the modernizing policies of Reza Shah; he enjoyed government support for implementing his initiatives, opening a private school, *Madrasa-ye ʿāli-e musiqi* ("Superior School of Music," locally known as *Ecole Superior de Musique*) in 1924. In the same year he also established the *Kolub-e musiqi*, an association that functioned as a venue for concerts and lectures that attracted Tehran's intellectuals, provided performance opportunities for students in his school, and generally cultivated public musicking.

His private school set the precedent, along with Darvish Khan's more traditionally-oriented classes, for the proliferation of such private conservatories throughout the twentieth century to the present day. Many among the first wave of these schools were established by the students of Vaziri—including Eshmail Mehrtash, whose private classes Shajarian would later attend—and Darvish Khan. Taking on the directorship of *Madrasa-ye Musik* in 1928 while simultaneously running his private school, the two institutes merged in 1934 under the name *Madrasa-ye musiqi dowlati* (Farhat 2004b), which was eventually to become the *Honarestan*. While sharing an identical social function of promoting Persian musical instruction in the private sector, Vaziri's pedagogical approach initiated the contentious "modernist-traditionalist" polemic played out by musicians in the following decades. This was particularly in reaction to Vaziri's use of notation and insistence on explicating a systematic theoretical grounding as part of the acquisition process. To this end he published a number of theoretical books, method books of exercises, and graded pieces for tar and violin between 1922 and 1936. Speaking almost seven decades after the onset of the polemic, Majid Kiani, the official and most outspoken contemporary proponent of the conservative end of the personal aesthetic spectrum in Persian music, distills the rebuttal to Vaziri's pedagogical reforms thus:

> Why talk? We learn very well without it. . . . It is in Western music that everything is explained. . . . But in our era, and especially after the "renewal" that came about with Vazīrī (around 1930), we are obliged to discuss and argue, for example with students, so that they accept [what we are saying]. . . . In fact, the master says everything without ever speaking; it is with the other senses that one teaches. (Quoted in During 2002:857)

Vaziri was offered the position of Chair in aesthetics at the University of Tehran in 1936, which eventually transformed into the Faculty of Fine Arts and the subsequent founding of the Department of Music in early 1969 (Zonis 1973:200; Nooshin 1996: 109). Like similar conservatory-derived institutions established across West Asia, both the *Honarestan* and university's Department of Music offered separate divisions and curriculae of indigenous "Eastern" and Western classic musics. Vaziri was also the chief administrator and architect of a short-lived, aborted attempt by the Ministry of Education to establish a general music curriculum in public schools in the early 1940s. In the midst of the rollercoaster political turmoil, Vaziri fell out of favour with the various powers that be after World War II and largely withdrew from public life in the late 1940s, though he retained his University of Tehran position until his retirement in 1965. While sidelined, his vigorous, omnipresent work in the second quarter of the twentieth century put in motion processes that were taken up by others and pervaded Iranian musical culture throughout the rest of the century. In what appears to be a salute (or at least a nod) to the great reformer, Shajarian included an instrumental composition of Vaziri's on his landmark recording *Dastan* in 1987.

The state-sponsored *Honarestan* conservatory, the oldest surviving musical education institution in Iran, had an unstable and checkered profile throughout its history, reflecting the transient policies and ideologies of the turbulent political sphere. Instruction in Persian music was introduced by Vaziri and then rescinded when he fell out of favour with Reza Shah in late 1934, only to be reintroduced (by Vaziri) in 1941 with the arrival of Mohammad Reza Shah.[16] By the 1960s, and following Mohammad Reza Shah's robust policies of Westernization, many observers felt that the *Honarestan*, in conjunction with the Ministry of Arts and Culture, were largely responsible for the pervasive propagation of a popularized, Westernized styling of Persian music that threatened the latter's very existence. A vigorous polemical debate burst forth from private to public discourse (Miller 1999:29–36), which in many ways culminated in the founding of the *Markaz* "Center for the Propagation and Preservation of Iranian Music" in 1968 under the sponsorship of the National Iranian Radio and Television (NIRT) by Reza Qotbi in close consultation with Dariush Safvat. The *Markaz* was dedicated to the collection of recordings and written documents of the Persian tradition, the oral transmission of Persian music under the tutelage of bona fide Ostads, as well as production and instruction in the craft of making Persian musical instruments. At once a music and trade school, an archive, publishing house, recording studio and concert presenter, the *Markaz* represented a serious government intervention and commitment to the tradition of Persian music while continuing its policies of modernization and cultural plurality. Ostad Shajarian met Nur Ali Boroumand through the *Markaz*, and got to know musicians associated with it, some of whom he would work with in the future—Mohammad Reza Lotfi, Nasir Farhangfar, Hossein Alizadeh—as well as Jalal Zolfonun and others.[17]

Eager to buttress his prodigious natural vocal talent with the requisite knowledge to master avaz, immediately upon his arrival Shajarian dug deep into the rich human resources of Tehran's musical subculture. Hitherto a gifted autodidact, his formal training in Persian music was a combination of institutional and "old school" discipleship formats, though leaning toward the latter, quite accurately reflecting the hybridized, pluralistic nature of musical transmission of the time. Shajarian had the very good fortune of meeting Ahmed Ebadi—a well-connected senior musician, boldly creative individualist, direct heir of the Farahani tradition, and by all accounts a very generous, kind, and gracious soul—soon after he arrived in Tehran. Ebadi took the brilliant young singer under his wing in the manner of traditional mentorship. Ebadi instructed Shajarian on matters of radif, technique, phrase construction and performance practice. Ebadi accompanied Shajarian and provided him with invaluable professional contacts and opportunities in radio, television, concert and private *majles* venues. Shortly after meeting Ebadi, Shajarian entered Ishmael Mehrtash's singing classes in his private "school" in the back room of an old theater; Mehrtash worked in the varied circles of Persian music, radio, and music theatre. Shajarian studied under Mehrtash for a relatively short period until the teacher is reported to have declared that Shajarian knew more than he did about the art of avaz (Siamak Shajarian, personal communication, 1995).

Shajarian was a great fan and later a colleague of Jalil Shahnaz and Gholamhossein Banan, whom he met in Tehran. In all of his interviews, he never fails to mention the profound effect Shahnaz's playing had on his own musicality. As we will see below, one of Shajarian's major innovations in avaz style was his use of instrumental idioms in his singing, which went quite beyond the original instrumental orientations evident in the earliest recordings of avaz. The influence of Banan's recordings was so strong upon Shajarian that it could move him to tears and inspired him to work intensely on copying Banan's style (Sabur 1992:213). Shajarian would later meet (and likely receive some informal mentoring from) the master, who was the most popular singer of the 1950s and 60s, propelled to fame by his talent, taste and the crucial professional support of Khaleqi. In a very interesting comparison to Shajarian's personality and public profile, Banan preferred performing live, but to a small private audience; he therefore did not concertize extensively but was known widely through his radio and records (Caton 1988). Problems and complications of viewing Persian music with a reductionist "traditionalist/modernist" dichotomy are quite evident in tracing Banan's influences and his subsequent personal influence on later singers like Shajarian. Many of the definitive features of Banan's approach to avaz characterize Shajarian's mature style as it emerged in the 1980s.

> It was [Banan's] acquaintance with the works of Wazīrī and the association with Ḵāleqī which impressed upon him the importance of clarity of singing, expressive rendering of the lyrics, and careful matching of the meaning of classical lyrics with appropriate melodic materials (*gūšas*) of traditional modes (*dastgāh*s). . . . Banān had knowledge of both Persian music and poetry. In selecting music for a poem, he was careful to choose the *gūšas* that fit the meaning of the poetry. He was also careful to match the melody and ornaments to the poetry and was attentive to poetic interpretation. . . . He had great control and musical skill and was able to express whatever meaning or feeling was in the poetry, varying vocal quality, intensity, and timing. (Ibid.)

Although he had established a name for himself as a singer with a national profile in the early 1970s, Shajarian continued his natural leanings toward "life-long learning." He met Payvar in 1971 and worked with him both professionally and as a mentor for santur performance and the radif of Abolhasan Saba throughout the 1970s; in some ways Payvar paralleled the traditional mentoring relationship he had with Ebadi. Further reflecting his varied venues of acquisition, he then met and began working with Abdollah Davami and Nour Ali Boroumand in 1973 through the *Markaz*. He distanced himself from this institute in 1975 for unspecified reasons, continuing his work with Boroumand at the latter's home, where he focused his studies on the vocal style of Taherzadeh. However, the *Markaz* asked Shajarian to supervise the recording of Davami's prodigious repertoire of old tasnifs in 1977–1978 in which 140 were recorded and eventually transcribed and published by Payvar along with Davami's radif (Payvar 1996). Shajarian's study with philosopher and vocalist Gholamreza "Jahansuz" Dadbeh beginning in 1979, discussed in chapter 4, was of any entirely different order from any other apprenticeship or discipleship, having transformative effect on his music and entire being.

OS

I'm deeply indebted to all of the many Ostads I've had who contributed to my knowledge of music, radif and gushes, and singing techniques. The ostads I tried to learn from via their recordings include Iqbal Sultan, Taherzade, Qamar ol

Moluk Vaziri, Zelli, Banan, and Taj Esfahan . . . all of them have left their mark and influence in my work. But the Ostads whose direct presence I had the great fortune of experiencing were Esmail Mehrtash, Ahmad Ebadi, Nur Ali Khan Boroumand, Abdollah Davami and Farmarz Payvar. The motifs, melodic construction, the selection and linking of motifs and phrases I mostly use were taken from the tar of Ostad Jalil Shanaz. The expression of words, poetry and declamation I've used most were taken from Taherzade and Banan. But I'm not able to forget the sole ostad under whose continuous formation and influence I spent many years: Ostad Dadbeh. (Shajarian et al. 2004:150)

There have been different people who have influenced me artistically. I have had many teachers but not all of them were singers; I just learned how to construct phrases from them—like Mehrtash or Payvar or the way Ebadi put musical sentences together. The only singer that I worked with was Davami, who taught me tasnifs and also radif. But I never use his technique, I only learned phrase construction and radif from him and the way to sing older tasnifs in their own unique manner. My other teachers, like Boroumand, didn't even have a good voice: he could just talk and give me advice, such as the methods of tahrir and what characteristics my voice has so that I can sing in Taherzadeh's style, for example. He guided me in these areas and he also sang himself, but his voice was not something that I wanted to imitate. So he taught me the forms and phrases and he kept pushing me to get it exactly right. (2009)

I became acquainted with Ahmad Ebadi when I had started to work in the radio. At one time the Golhā program was directed by Mir Naqibi and was managed by Habibollah Bada'i. Mir Naqibi was a native of Mashhad, one day he introduced me to Ebadi and he agreed to teach me. He used to advise me like his own son. He said the theatre and radio were polluted with impurities and artists were drug addicts and warned me to be careful. Since then I became intimate with Ebadi and we conducted musical programs. He taught me how to sing and warned when I was out of tune or raised my voice [unnecessarily high]. But I profited very much from his musical instrument and learnt sentence composition [i.e., phrasing] from him. I used to work with him day and night and we worked in the radio and I profited from his advice and teaching.

Mehrtash's classroom was crowded with many students and he taught music. One day I said: "Why don't you separate the musicians from others. As soon as a student asks permission you allow him to sit in the class though he doesn't know music [and can't] sing correctly." He replied: "Mr. Shajarian, if they fail to become a singer they will learn to be a good [listener] of music." We all loved our master and did not quarrel with the good teacher but we had difficulty to learn music in the crowded class. . . . Mehrtash was trying to drag me to the theatre. . . . I always evaded the theatre but at times I was obliged to submit to his command. He used to say that a singer should be an artist in theatre and be a master of dialogue [i.e., singing in a declamatory style]. Mehrtash used to build musical tableaux and was a master in that field. He composed songs for the theatre. Many artists learned dialogue from Mehrtash. He had produced the Musical Tableau, Pir-e Changi *and many other pieces for the stage. Since I was in love with Mehrtash I joined one or two plays conducted by him. He displayed the* Chaharshanbesuri *tradition with music and I was one of the players who had a main role in the show. We used to sing on the stage with makeup in order not to be identified. In other words I didn't like to play in the theatre and only acted on the stage in order not to dissatisfy my teacher. Besides the theatre, I worked in the radio with Ebadi and Mehrtash. (Manateqe Azad 2001:3)*

I live with the music of Shahnaz. In my car, there is nothing but the music of Shahnaz. His music has mesmerized me for many years. What is there in his music which has carried me away all these times? The music of Shahnaz is the only [instrumental] music that has the feel of singing. . . . Shahnaz could make his instrument sing. . . . I enjoy listening to his music. I am a vocalist who considers [an instrumentalist] his master. I owe him a lot (Payvand 2006). Probably nothing has influenced me more than hearing the sound of Jalil Shahnaz's instrument. Nothing has influenced me in avaz improvisation more than Shahnaz and I am indebted to him and the other ostads that I studied with.[18]

AK

I can only speak about what I find so beautiful about Ostad Jalil Shahnaz's playing. In Persian music we have a term phrase, it is like a sentence (*jomle*). These melodic phrases are very complete and very satisfying, in a way that is novel each time. We've heard Abu Ata before but not with his phrasing and sentence construction—it's so beautiful. He plays differently all the time; that is to say in the same environment he's telling different stories. Shahnaz's tar is different from others because it's like he's talking to you. He will play a melody that you might feel you have heard before, but in actual fact you haven't. He has the capacity to generate new material from extant, older material, as if it has been harvested in a radical way. This demonstrates the depth and penetration of his grasp of Persian classical music. The manner in which he negotiates rhythm complements the message he is aiming to convey.

Furthermore, what is novel about this artist is that it reflects the "music of the moment," it has an immediate presence. The performer is absent, only the music is prominent. The performer effaces himself completely, in total humility. The music of Shahnaz, when absorbed and grasped appropriately, can make you very joyful. Even if he plays a sad mode such as Abu Ata, it makes one happy. He never stays in one place, he's always pushing forward in his playing. He'll make a great, focused statement, and then he moves on—he never goes back to that. Culturally it really makes sense; it's a kind of Sufi music that conveys the message: live in the moment. Mr. Shahnaz's work shows us to live in the moment and move on. He plays something amazing, he finds a jewel but he's not going to repeat it. I like that. When you listen to Shahnaz you start a beautiful conversation with the man but without a word. This is a remarkable achievement, a very high art. The man is talking to me without saying a word, with only music, only his tar.

I also believe the tone he gets from his tar is the best; he cares about timbre. If you play tar and understand the instrument, you know that the way he strikes the strings is totally unique, it can't be compared to most players' right-hand technique. He plays from various positions in relation to the bridge, sometimes he plays without the mezrab, with left-hand hammers and pulls. It's a totally different kind of sound. He's a master of that. He's a chaser of sound, new sounds. He usually plays within the standard meters, he's not too adventurous in that sense, but within those structures he is extremely inventive in his melodies. I've never heard anyone create melodies like him. He's a melody creator: his melodies are better than the source melodies (such as from the radif or other previous composers or performers). He's a major creator.

Ostad Shajarian noticed this extraordinary talent, where this pure music comes directly from a master's heart. It reaches a profound level of communication. I'm sure that Ostad Shahnaz plays constantly, whether he's performing or is with friends or is by himself. You can hear that he loves the tar. The only way you can get to his level of artistry is through lots of practice, but not practice in the sense we usually conceive of it—rather through *playing*, and without the goal of being better but on the level of communication with his soul. I think that this may be the reason why Shajarian appreciates Shahnaz's music.

When reel-to-reel tape recorders first came to Iran, masters would gather for a *majles* and play for each other and record these gatherings in order to remember that particular night. Mr. Kasa'i, Mr. Shahnaz and various other people were at these gatherings. It became a tradition that they would begin the recording by introducing what night it was, who was there, why they were gathered and various other comments. And these opening comments would sometimes turn into ten-minute speeches! I heard these recordings and anytime they went around the room asking for comments and asked Mr. Shahnaz to say something, he would only say, in a very low, quiet voice, "Let's play and see what's going to happen." And no more words. When I was a kid I loved his playing and always wanted to hear his voice but then I realized that his attitude here was the best. He's saying: "I don't want to talk, I'm talking with my instrument."

RS
Diligent, curious and ambitious, Shajarian supplemented his formal lessons and informal professional mentoring with masters throughout the 1960s and early 1970s by continuing the autodidactic practice of "lifting" from recordings that he had cultivated since his earliest efforts in Mashhad—a practice that had never stopped and in many ways was his most important means of acquisition (discussed further in chapter 4). As mentioned repeatedly in his interviews for the past two decades, he studied the recordings of many important vocal masters, notably Taherzadeh, Iqbal Sultan, Taj Esfahani, Zelli, Adib Khansari, Hossein Qavami, Banan, and Qamarolmoluk Vaziri (Nasirifar 1990:402; Kasmai 1990:13; Shajarian et al. 2004:150). The late Dr. Hossein Omumi Sr. (uncle of the well-known ney-player Hossein Omumi), a personal friend of Shajarian's and great connoisseur of avaz, introduced Shajarian to recordings of Seyyed Rahim, the master of Taherzadeh and Taj Esfahani, which he admired and studied with particular enthusiasm. According to Dr. Omumi, his interest in Zelli was early, and only later did he study the re-

cordings of Taherzadeh; his interest in Seyyed Rahim came after his work on Taherzadeh (personal communication, 1995). We noted above Shajarian's enthusiasm for
Banan, whose style he acquired through recordings. Shajarian's bright vocal tone
and high register is reminiscent of Taj and Zelli; his frequent exploration of a relaxed, loose tone in his lower register seems influenced by Banan and Ostad Dabeh.
Many of Shajarian's main influences were singers from the previous generation or
two. Table 3.1 provides a composite view of his main influences and sources of
learning the art of avaz through his multipronged approach of formal instruction,
traditional mentoring through professional work, and selfstudy through recordings.

Table 3.1. Shajarian's Principle Mentors and Influences

Qur'an recitation, vocal technique:
Mehdi Shajarian (1911–1996)

Avaz vocal sources (radif, tasnif repertoire and sabk), direct instruction:
Ishmael Mehrtash (1904–1980)
Abdollah Davami (1891–1980) ——Gholamhossein Banan (1911–1985)
Gholam Reza Dadbeh (1920–2002), *Dashtestani* genre

Instrumentalists, direct instruction:
Ahmad Ebadi (1906–1992), studied radif, phrasing and setar
Farmarz Payvar (1933–2009), studied santur and radif of Abolhasan Saba
Nur Ali Boroumand (1906–1976), studied vocal style of Taherzadeh

Singers studied through recordings:
Seyyed Abdol Rahim ————————Hossein Taherzadeh (1882–1955)
(fl. early 20th c.)
                                   Taj Esfahani (1903–1981)

Iqbal Sultani ——————————Reza Gholi Mirza Zeli
(1866–1971)   (1906–1945)
Gholamhossein Banan   Adib Khānsari   Hossein Qavami
(1911–1985)   (1901–1982)   (1909–1988)
Qamarolmoluk Vaziri
(1905–1959)

Instrumentalist influences:
Jalil Shahnaz (b. 1921)

(Lines indicate master/student relationships).

Mediation

RS

Like everywhere else in the world, media technology played a major, self-organizing role in reshaping Iranian musical culture in the twentieth century. Not only is the media the message but it manipulates the message: the media is able to put spin on the teller, just as the teller can spin the tale. According to McLuhan and subsequent literacy-orality theories, it also impacts our consciousness as musicians and audiences. Recording and radio constitute a fascinating extension of oral tradition, a spectacular hybrid of tradition and modernity—the oral process is largely the same and yet it is accelerated, storable, and vicarious, effectively transcending time and space while enabling a new form of literacy among illiterates. Together with film, these mass media gradually took over the function of the bard as a disembodied transmitter of "infotainment." The impact on musical style, acquisition, and transmission is incalculable. Even if the music was set as a text via recording, the reception and context of listening to the identical text was always changing and different, performed uniquely by the same listener with each listening. The evolution of music media was an early exponent and facilitator of twentieth-century globalization, propelled by Western innovation and following the succession from cylinder phonograph and phonogram to radio, television, cassette, CD/DVD, and Internet. We will briefly review the Iranian unfolding of this virtually universal template as a crucial historical development, while keeping in mind that Shajarian's status as a celebrity and cultural icon was achieved and continues to be maintained through the mass media. Recordings, radio and eventually television and film took over the function of the local bard but transposed it to a disembodied, virtual and national level. While rural bardic traditions have survived comparatively well in Iran, in most cultures radio and television was the death knell of these long-standing oral traditions.[19]

While the first recordings and broadcasts of music clearly began with the live performance, it didn't take long for the complementary relationship of mediated and live musicking to collapse into a chicken-and-egg dynamic of feedback. Particularly with recordings, live performances are stored and reiterated by listeners where they are experienced as if once again "live." These documents in turn become the sources by which musicians acquire musical ideas and inspiration to create new music and new live performances, which they may then record, and so on. These dynamics constitute an intense form of feedback that collapses the two domains of mediated and live performance (à la Baudrillard 1983).[20] Musical transcriptions also function as a facilitator of feedback, an oral-literary hybrid invigoration of the tradition of stealthily acquiring music by listening from "behind the door or curtain" (known in Persian culture as *poshte dar* or *poshte parde*).

Before discussing the electronic media that so powerfully shaped musical culture in Iran and around the globe, and that propelled Shajarian to global success, we must look at the first form of mediation introduced into the hitherto oral culture of Persian music that had equally transformative effects, especially with regard to transmission and acquisition: musical notation.[21] Western notation played a central role in the conservatory approach to music education for military band musicians since its inception in the mid-nineteenth century, with Vaziri acting as the crucial pivot for engaging and propogating it institutionally in the transmission of Persian music from the 1920s onward. While his publications in the following decades presented graded etudes and "modernized" concert pieces, he was also the first to attempt transcription of the radif, which was accomplished through the patient dictation of Mirza Abdollah himself. This transcription, which was mysteriously lost among a host of other documents after Vaziri fell out of favour with Reza Shah, was the only direct, contemporaneous documentation of the former's seminal radif (Farhat 2004b).[22] As noted above, many of Vaziri's students became key figures in the subsequent transmission of Persian music and represent the first generation of musicians to be proficiently literate in notation, while simultaneously retaining and utilizing the traditional oral means. Abolhasan Saba made important early contributions to integrating notation into Persian transmission with his series of radif publications arranged for tar, setar, santur and violin in the 1950s, both indicating and promoting the increasing presence of notationally literate Iranian musicians. Mousa Ma'rufi's massive radif,[23] lavishly published in 1963 through the Ministry of Culture, marks a milestone in the promulgation of the radif in the form of notation and its (not unrelated) canonization as a national monument. Nooshin reports the mere fact that Persian music could be represented in Western notation was in and of itself a point of pride among Iranians (1996:157), quite transparently inferring a prestige and "awe" with which Iranians regarded Western notation as well as an inferiority complex surrounding their traditional means of oral transmission.

The main constituency of literacy among Iranian musicians was overwhelmingly that of instrumentalists and the transmission of avaz continued to be almost exclusively oral. While the radif of Abdollah Davami (discussed in chapter 4) was not transcribed and published until 1996 (by Payvar), the version of his student Mahmud Karimi was published in a detailed descriptive notation by Massoudieh on the eve of the revolution in 1978. These two versions of the same radif were important in the transmission of avaz in the latter third of the twentieth century through to today. Both masters had a large number of students who learned exclusively orally, but their published radifs were accompanied with cassettes, which facilitated a new technologically hybrid form of oral transmission examined shortly below. Jean During's transcription of Boroumand's rendition of Mirza Abdollah's radif, published in 1991 but circulated widely in pirated versions, played a crucial role in this radif, acquiring unprecedented canonical status among musicians in the late-twentieth century. Appearing in an expanded and revised edition in 2006, in its various incarnations it is likely the most widely distributed transcription of the radif. Tala'i's transcription of the same radif (1995), published with recordings of his own performance, is significant for setting a precedent of the performer transcribing his own performance and also for introducing a highly original format that is at once analytical, prescriptive, descriptive, and ingeniously reveals how performing musicians "process" and think about the music.

As literacy and dependence on notation continued under a large sector of musicians during the decades following the revolution—although traditional oral instruction continues today—there is now a very high rate of notational literacy among musicians of all generations. Notation is now an important means of transmission in private instruction, music schools and among autodidacts; the past decade has seen an exponential increase in the proliferation of radif transcriptions (including simplified, instructional versions such as Jalal Zolfonun's for setar) and method books, especially arrangements for various instruments of the canonical versions of Boroumand and Karimi. A more recent arrival on the notational front is the transcription of several complete improvisations of Ahmad Ebadi;[24] I don't know how widespread this new dimension of visual archiving is or if there are other similar transcriptions published. Nettl noted that in the 1970s the proliferation of notation contributed to an increasing standardization of Persian music (1978:163). The business of music publishing in Iran of genres lying outside of Persian music—e.g., Western classical and Iranian "light-classical" and folk-influenced—represents a comparatively modest market, mostly targeted at piano and guitar arrangements.

Like most singers, Shajarian's acquisition process is largely based on the traditional oral methods of transmission, from his early formation as a religious singer in the conservative circles of Mashhad through to his instruction with a range of Ostads described in chapter 4. As we have seen, he did partake in the group lessons in Ismail Mehrtash's private classes in his early twenties, a quasi-institutionalized format that was a typical manifestation of the broader sphere of private music schools initiated by Vaziri and is still a driving force in Persian transmission today. Unique to the acquisition of twentieth-century khanades, Shajarian invested a great deal of time and developed key facets of his style by copying the recordings of a wide range of important singers, a subject we will examine in the next section. Like most singers, he does not read notation nor does he need to. Among his musical gifts are included a "great ear"—quick, analytical and precise—and a prodigious memory. Composer Hasan Yusufzamani worked extensively with Shajarian in the 1970s and reported that he would sing or play a newly composed tasnif seven or eight times and Shajarian had it memorized and ready for recording (personal communication, 1995). Despite the fact that Shajarian never uses notation himself, he feels there is a value in transcribing his avaz, as presented in this study (see appendix 2).

A recording purporting to be Shajarian teaching at the University of Tehran circulated among some Iranian-Canadian musicians in the late 2000s wherein he demonstrated the radif of dastgah Homayun by first singing each gushe in solfege, followed by the same melody with vocables and/or poetry. While it turned out that the attribution to Shajarian was spurious (the singer is likely his long-time student Mohsen Keramati) it is nonetheless significant that his vocal quality is quite evident on a surface level and that solfege is used among some teachers—not surprisingly, conservatory settings such as the aforementioned recording are clearly a likely venue.[25]

OS

Transcriptions are indeed useful for certain things: they can tell you what to perform, which is important. But they can't tell you how to perform it [i.e., execute, realize the music in performance]. *(2002)*
Question: Do you use solfege?
No, I have not practiced solfege in a methodical way. But I have practiced the Persian intervals in relation to each mode a lot so I can land on notes accurately. We can even say that solfege exists within the dastgahs that we sing, that is, by practicing dastgahs one practices solfege [i.e., correct intonation and awareness of scale degrees]. *(2008)*

Early Recording in Iran

RS

Tabar (2005:71ff) posits four periods of early recording history in Iran preceding the founding of the national radio in 1940. As another indicator of globalization, these recordings were variously made in Tehran, neighbouring countries (Georgia, Azerbaijan, India and Afghanistan), and Europe (Paris and Berlin). The first period (1898–1906) marks the earliest recordings, the consumption of which was restricted to a small circle of political and social elites. Important masters recorded in this period include Aqa Hossein-qoli and Neyab Assadollah.

> Dust-ʿAli Khan Moʿyyer-al-Mamālek [a retired Qajar official who had spent many years in Paris] made the first recordings of Āqā Ḥosaynqoli's music on a phonograph (*dastgāh-e ḥāfeẓ al-aṣwāt*) during the friendly gatherings in his house, before there were any commercial gramophone records in Iran. These are among the earliest works of the master, and they seem to have been made during the late 1890s [Sepantā, pp. 50, 54]. (Youssefzadeh 2004a)

Tabar's second period (1906–1914) follows from Mozaffar od-Din Shah issuing a *farman* authorizing foreign companies to engage in commercial recording, particularly favouring Emile Berliner's Gramophone Company of Washington, DC (2005: 79). It was in fact common to grant Britain monopolies in all sectors at this time. This period was marked by a shift from cylinders to 78s of various sizes that allowed recording times of two-four minutes. Mirza Abdollah, Darvish Khan, and Taherzadeh recorded during this period. Indicative of Iranian tendencies throughout the rest of the century, piracy was already reported in 1908, perhaps executed via pressing facilities in Istanbul. And while financial transactions of the foreign recording companies of the period are documented, there is no evidence of payment to musicians (ibid.: 83). A third period (1915–1925) is marked by a total moratorium on recording due to World War I and the ensuing political-economic strife in Iran, when Reza Shah placed heavy restrictions on foreign companies. Tabar notes that many recordings were lost during the years of the war (ibid.:90).

The resumption of recording activities kicks off the fourth period (1925–1940), featuring a more competitive market for foreign companies such as HMV, Columbia, Polyphone, and later in the 1930s, Odeon and Sodova. Electric recording technology was introduced in 1927 that enabled a wider dynamic range and the inclusion of quieter instruments and singing styles. Qamar was a big recording star of this period. Javad Badi'zadeh (1902–1979) was also a popular recording artist but represented modernist/Westernized strains in Iranian culture by presenting waltzes, tangos, foxtrots featuring Western-hybrid instrumentation; likewise, Vaziri recorded many of his compositions during this time. Some musicians quickly realized the unprecedented potential that recordings offered as a tool for musical acquisition, assessment and improvement. In the 1930s Taherzade was among the first to utilize the new technology in this capacity, evaluating his recordings to adjust and improve his performances. In contrast to previous periods, there was a much wider public exposure to recordings, as companies in a marketing blitz installed gramophones for free in cafes, which reportedly played nonstop (Tabar 2005:98). Newspaper and magazine advertisements in the late 1920s show companies pitching both records and gramophones to ever widening markets, often in tandem with selling carpets and fabrics (ibid.: 95–96).[26] While recording technology was enthusiastically embraced in Iran from the outset of the late-nineteenth century, by the late 1920s some were complaining it encouraged "debauchery and laziness," and traditionalist-modernist polemics began to appear in the press (ibid.: 97–98), growing increasingly throughout the century, lamenting the erosion of the elite connoisseurship so integral to Persian music through its very mass mediation.

Domestic record companies emerged relatively late in Iran and the radio was the vital means of propagating Persian music but the singer Delkash (stage name of Esmat Bāqerpur Panbaforush [1924–2004]) rose to prominence largely through her domestic recordings, such as those on Caspian Records, in the 1960s. Shajarian would later play a major role in blowing wide open the domestic recording market of Persian music through the medium of the cassette in the 1980s.

OS

Question: What is the impact of recording on Persian music, radif and its transmission?

Recording is very significant; I mean, it makes the work a hundred times easier. By repeating a phrase over and over again on tape, one can very quickly learn a particular phrase. This helps a lot and I have done it myself many times. Learning a whole school of avaz usually takes a lot of time for students because they need to hear one phrase numerous times, but with this method the work becomes easier. At the same time, I cannot repeat the same phrase over and over again for them, because it becomes too tedious for me. In this way recording helps very much; for example, it allows the students to record a piece ten times in a row and through listening to those many, many times, they will eventually correct themselves and learn it. (2008)

Radio and Television

In the twentieth century national radio broadcasting throughout the world took over the nineteenth-century function of the vernacular press as the essential means of constructing and maintaining a sense of imagined community, and therefore national identity. It was, of course, even more efficacious than the press in countries with high rates of illiteracy, which meant the majority of the world through to the 1970s. To this day the crucial tipping point of both strategy and symbolism in a *coup d'etat* is to seize the national radio (and television) station in order to decisively consolidate the new order.

National radio broadcasting in Iran was established in 1940 and late in the following year the omnipresent Vaziri, recently back in favour with government offices after the exile of Reza Shah, was appointed as head of the music department of Radio Tehran in 1941, a postion he retained until 1946. Iranians quickly developed of "strong tradition of listening to radio" (Nooshin 2005:254), which expontentially increased the range of people regularly listening to Persian music. The radio is absolutely central to Shajarian's musical life: it provided his formative encounters with classical music and avaz at his uncle's house in Mashhad (as he couldn't listen to it in his own home) and it was the primary means by which he established his national profile later in Tehran. The unprecedentedly large audience that emerged across the country highlighted the vicarious listening experience as lacking and distorting the traditional value of *monāsebat*/occasion so essential to Persian music, i.e., live music tailored to the needs of a specific group of people at a specific time and place. What is the occasion here and how does an artist approach and interact with this abstract audience, invisible in the studio? The context is so enlarged, pluralistic and indeterminant, the audience so impersonal and unknowable that any sense of occasion becomes abstracted to the verge of meaninglessness by older criteria. A new sensiblity was required in this regard and Shajarian adapted most successfully. Radio also brought the brewing polemic regarding the dilution of core values of Persian music to a head (and in the following anecdote, to a face):

> Ḥabīb Somā'ī (1905–1946), heir to a prestigious lineage of musicians, slapped the director of the national radio station to protest against the station's policy of directing its programming to a large public. Somā'ī's violent reaction symbolically marks the last phase of a process of democratization. Henceforth art music would be accessible to all, not only on records but on radio and cassettes, whose popularity grew much more quickly in the East than in the West. Now everyone could hear the finest artists and, even more often, artists who were not the finest. The experts' circle was broken, the music spread throughout consumer society, and everyone felt competent to evaluate it: ordinary people could decide which artists were talented, contradicting the opinion of the experts. The great masters retired from the scene, though they returned briefly during the 1970s, a period marked by a strong though short-lived return to traditional values. (During 2000: 861–62)

It was a decade following this anecdote that producer Davud Pirnia debuted the *Golhā* ("Flowers") series of programs,[27] eventually amounting to some 1,400 programs (around 886 hours) nationally broadcasted between 1956 and 1979 and becoming the most influential force—indeed, a veritable institution—in the public propogation of Persian music (Lewisohn 2008:79). "There was an 80% illiteracy rate in Iran during the 1950s and 1960s and there were only two types of mass media—the printed page and radio—the latter being the only form of mass communication that the majority of the general public could take advantage of. With the introduction of the transistor radio, the *Golhā* programs quickly penetrated into every village and hamlet throughout Iran" (ibid.: 93–94).

Modeled on the ages-old tradition of connoisseurs meeting in private homes (*majles*), the programs featured a judiciously balanced combination of mystical poetry (read and sung) and music, both solo and variously sized ensembles. In short, it cultivated the deep-seated Iranian values of *adab* and mysticism (*'erfan*). As noted by the striking anecdote of Somā'i, there was a paradox in popularizing through mass mediation art forms that were for many intrinsically attached to an exclusive subculture. On the one hand the gesture was democratizing and nourishing, on the other its lack of meaningful occasion and prerequisite knowledge on the part of listeners was uprooting. This probably applies more to the musical than the poetic components of the programs, as we have previously noted that classical poetry is widely known by Iranians.[28] Whether this amounted to a net gain for society or a loss for Persian music depended on one's perspective and values. Pirnia and Nakjavani note several important contributions that the programs made to Iranian culture:

> First, they popularized Persian classical poetry and made a vogue of it, partic-
> ularly among the middle class and the affluent social elite. They boosted ap-
> preciation of Persian poetry at a popular level to a degree never before
> achieved. Second, they brought masters of traditional music to public notice
> and bestowed on them the dignity that they deserved as artists. This should be
> seen against the background of earlier times, when musical performers were
> considered mere "entertainers" with a lowly rank in the social hierarchy (they
> were referred to as *motrebs*, often with a pejorative connotation). The *Golhā*
> programs not only made most of them household names, but also provided
> them with a fairly secure basis of income through remuneration or regular ap-
> pointment. Third, they drew wide attention to and popularized the traditional
> corpus (*radif*) of Persian music. Fourth, they introduced variations in the hi-
> therto somewhat rigid arrangement of the different sections of musical per-
> formances...An indirect influence of the *Golhā* programs was the encourage-
> ment they afforded many people to learn to play musical instruments, now
> that the profession's stigma had been removed. More importantly, the pro-
> grams revived and revitalized the long-standing fusion of Persian poetry and
> music. (Pirnia and Nakjavani 2001)

Reflecting on the situation at the time, from the distance of four decades and an intervening revolution, Ostad Shajarian's estimation of the program is unequivocal:

> *It is my belief that Persian music owes a huge debt to Dāvud Pirniā, since at a crucial moment in the history of Iran he effectively rescued our music from perdition. If it wasn't for his efforts, Arab music, Turkish music, or Western pop music would have all but drowned out and obliterated Persian music. In establishing the Golhā programs, Mr. Pirniā created a sanctuary where Persian music could survive and flourish amongst all these conflicting and corrupting influences, so that even today the Golhā programs are still cherished among the populace at large.* (Lewisohn 2008:95)

As impled by Pirnia and Nakjavani above, one of the important effects of radio broadcasting in general was an increasing standardization and shortening of performances, "the imposition of the requirements of studio conditions upon performers, and the confluence of many different styles of music—Western, Persian classical and Iranian folk traditions" (Nettl 1978: 154–56). Furthermore, the introduction of electronic microphone technology led to a "radio style" of crooning (Musavi 2003), as noted in chapter 1.[29] Banan, who appeared regularly on *Golhā* programs, was one of the most famous singers for exploiting this style. Shajarian was also regularly featured on these programs but sang with a full, powerful force that few could match during this period of his career. This was in fact a trademark quality that accounted for his early success and it was only later in the 1980s that he would regularly explore a softer dynamic with the rich tonal quality of his lower register, which was a definitive feature of Banan and Dadbeh. Likewise, amplification expanded musical possibilities by allowing the inclusion of quiet instruments such as the ney or setar in large ensembles, while enhancing the dynamic range of others in such ensembles, such as the santur (Nettl 1978:155).

Having gotten his foot in the door with his "cold call" cassette demonstration to Davud Pirnia the previous year (and who had since retired), Shajarian made his national radio debut on *Barg-e Sabz*, program number 216, broadcasted on December 6, 1967, singing a ghazal by Hafez in dastgah Afshari to the accompaniment of the veteran santur master Reza Varzande (Abdollahi 2003:2069).[30] Varzande plays an introduction and lengthy jawabs throughout the course of the fifteen and a half minute *saz o avaz* portion of the program, occupying over half of the total time. Shajarian's singing is remarkably mature for this early date, before any of his training in Tehran. His diction is clear, intonation impeccable, the pacing leisurely (though somewhat tentative) yet with an overall sense of growth and progression, including shifts of well-placed register and some impressively athletic tahrirs. Indeed, it already includes many of the characteristics of his mature style. Over the course of the next decade he would perform in one hundred *Golhā* and approximately two hundred-and-fifty other radio programs (Nasirifar 1990:401), working with the top musicians and producers in the business.[31] In 1969 Shajarian was among the first artists in Iran to broadcast on

FM radio in stereo, singing Segah with the accompaniment of Ebadi and tarist Lot-follah Majd.

There were many fine singers working for the national radio during the time of Shajarian's tenure there; establishing and then distinguishing himself among artists of this caliber was a formidable task. These colleagues were variously mentors, models, peers and competition. Among the older generation were Banan, Qavami, and Abdulwahab Shahidi (b. 1914). Shajarian was younger than the other male singers of his generation working on the radio. Akbar Golpayegani (b. 1933), Iraj (born Hossein Khaje Amiri, b. 1932) had considerably more professional experience by the time Shajarian arrived on the scene, and both worked in *asil* as well as pop music genres. Iraj was especially popular due to his work in film music, particularly his voice-over singing for the hugely popular movie star Mohammad-Ali Fardin. Mahmud Khansari (1934–1987) was also regularly broadcasted at the time; Wright (2009) provides a description of the career of another contemporary singer, Touraj Kiaras. There were also prominent female singers broadcasting regularly and very popular at the time, who were on average fifteen years older than Shajarian: Marzieh (Ashraf os-Sadat Morteza'i, b. 1926) occasionally sang avaz; Elah and Pooran were featured regularly on broadcasts but generally sang tasnifs. Delkash sang avaz but never appeared on *Golhā*, she was nonetheless very well known and loved through other broadcasts and public avenues, particularly recordings, as noted above; she was also an actress and songwriter (see Nakjavani 2005). With the possible exception of Golpayegani, who increasingly shifted his focus toward pop music in the mid 1970s, none of the careers of these singers survived in the postrevolutionary period.[32]

Alongside the radio, television became an increasingly important medium of public musicking. In addition to their pleasurable, inspirational quality and enter-tainment value, the *Golhā* programs had a clearly educational function; Nettl felt that television of the Pahlavi era was even more geared toward instruction and music appreciation (1978:155). Shajarian began to appear on the national TV show *Haft Shahr-e 'Eshq* in 1970 but had already performed on Iraqi national television with Ebadi in the fall of 1968. According to Nooshin (2001), he ap-peared regularly on national television in the period 1971–1976.

AK

The introduction of radio in Iran, over sixty years ago, was a catalyst for the col-laboration of numerous musicians and artists. However, such collaboration was usually intermittent, never consistent and continuous. This undesirable situation was due to the social, political, and ideological environment, where the beliefs and ideas of the artists concerned were different, and also where government censorship was always in place to varying degrees of intensity. If the ideas and beliefs of the artists and musicians coincided, and the political and social atmos-phere was conducive to creative artistic endeavour, then the artists and musi-cians were able to work together. While I did not live through these earlier his-torical periods to personally experience what these relationships truly were, dur-ing the post-revolutionary period I worked with a number of artists who had worked in radio earlier in their careers, knew the scene and shared their insight with me, such as Ostad Abdul-Vahab Shahidi, and others.

The best musical movements in radio were realized through the intercession of artists such as Davud Pirnia, who founded the musical radio program *Golhā*, and later the famous poet Hushang Ebtehaj, who had more direct collaboration with later programs. It was during this period that the voice of exceptional artists, such as Shajarian, came to be heard on the radio. In this productive environment, and through the encouragement and direction of Davud Pirnia, it was possible to witness considerable expansion in musical activity on the radio. Among the most prominent cultural endeavours in the area of musical activity were the programs in the *Golhā* series. It was here that the best composers had the most favourable opportunity to create songs for the best singers. Famous singers from this period were Marzieh, Delkash, Banan, Badizadeh, Shahidi, Shajarian, among others.

It must also be stressed that during this same period, as with previous and later periods, the environment was not free for establishing a direct and unhindered connection between the artist and the people. Consequently, artistic activity was greatly curtailed in the sense that there were limits as to what could be done. The art of avaz never had its rightful or suitable place on the radio—the time allocated to it on the radio was normally very short. I remember that Ostad Shahidi was himself one of the singers of avaz on the radio. But the artists who were avaz specialists were few and far between, and in the performance of the tasnif only a short portion of avaz would be performed in between as an incidental activity. We are also reminded of the fact that the impressionable and influential presence of such artist-musicians as Davud Pirnia and Hushang Ebtehaj were very instrumental in establishing quality and excellence for radio musical programs as a whole. As a result, the presence of radio for musical artistic endeavour was very positive, especially as the phenomenon of radio represented the fruitful encounter of contrasting views and perspectives within the context of modernity on the one hand, and traditionalism on the other.

OS

In 1977, I had an argument with the radio. One reason for this was that the radio did not value healthy artists. The cancer of "culturelessness" [bi-farhangi] had spread throughout the institution of the radio. That environment was not my kind of environment. Ebtehaj, Lotfi and I used to work together and were constantly being humiliated, they constantly harassed us. Only [administrator Reza] Qotbi and his wife supported us—we could only carry on because of their support. In 1977 they asked me and Ebtehaj to gather the Sheyda Ensemble and perform on the night of 'Eid. But I said no, because that environment was not appreciative of us and I didn't want to perform in such an environment. Ninety-eight percent of it was for their own benefit and we felt that this was not our place. They used to mock us and make remarks like "Who are these people who are following tradition?" They called themselves modern and claimed that they were supporting the modern era and thought that their knowledge and wisdom was higher than any-

*body else's. My last performance on television was performing Abu Ata with Lotfi
on March 17, 1977. After that, I came back in 1985, on the night of 'Eid, to confirm that I am not part of the television and it has been seventeen years now that I
have avoided them. I don't approve of the policies of the Radio and the Television. But since they constantly played my music, people were under the impression that I am working with them.* (Qaneeifard 2003:141–42)

Question: What's the role of record companies and media like television and radio in the contemporary art of avaz?

*They have an influence. Since they are located in all parts of the country, people
will obviously hear them and sometimes they can be a good influence on music
and other times they can be a bad influence. For example, our folk musicians
listen to what the radio and the television play and little by little these media can
persuade them to change, and their music can eventually lose its colour. This is
the negative influence: that folk music loses its essence and people only follow
the radio and the television. In a sense, television and radio have replaced the
patronage of the courts and the homes of the noble men. At the same time it is
much more powerful than the courts, but back in the days when the courts existed, folk music had its own place. For example, Kurdish music, Baluchi music,
Azeri music, and the music of Khorasan all had their own place and would not be
influenced by anything. Sometimes, however, they would migrate like a small
watercourse to the lake of the cities. Their artists would come to the court or the
places near it and gradually their music turned into a classical system, so the
riverbank of the classical music is the village. It is because of the different villagers that came to the city and made this classical music—for example, the Farahani family who were in the courts of Nasser-al-din Shah. (2008)*

How did musicians [in the early-twentieth century] deal with [society's negative
view of music] and break taboos?

*Well musicians were always scattered and they "played the music silently." They
were always present in small gatherings and in families, who in return protected
them, in a sense. But musicians couldn't present themselves to society at large.
We are indebted to our villagers who have safeguarded this music. After they
protected it, it gradually started to turn into gushes and dastgahs, and then it
went to the court and was protected by the court, and now it is showing itself in
different forms all over.*

So it was religion that was in its way until seventy or eighty years ago, correct?

*Yes it was mainly religion that was against it. It was from Reza Shah onward that
religion was a little less prevalent and music could show itself better. It really
started even before, from 'Aref and Shayda, and gradually moved forward. It is
only in the last fifty or sixty years that it has really been part of society, largely
because the radio and the television adopted this music and made it "epidemic."*

*After some time, the radio and TV felt the need for pop music and they
started playing pop music on their programs, a pop music that was stolen from
the West. I think this was a political act more than anything else, but pop music
should be available and I am not against it. I am not against any kind of music:
every kind of music must exist within a society. Human beings require respect*

*more than anything else—for their thoughts and their needs, they need to be res-
pected. They need others to listen to them and give them answers. If you ignore
them and don't answer to their needs, they get upset. So this is apparent in any
society, that people need their freedom and want their issues resolved and require the means to achieve their goals.*[33]

Performance Example 2: Golhā-ye Tāze #37
RS
The prominent contemporary poet Hushang Ebtehaj (pen name/*takhallus* Sayeh
"Shadow," b. 1928) became the producer for the *Golhā-ye Tāze* series in 1972, a
position he held until the revolution and the summary dissolution of Pahlavi-era
media programming. Shajarian met Ebtehaj the previous year and subsequently
collaborated on many programs, often singing the latter's poetry through the mid
1970s. Of the one hundred *Golhā* programs Shajarian recorded and had broadcasted,
fifty-three were *Golhā-ye Tāze* (compared to nineteen *Barg-e Sabz*, twelve *Golhā-
ye Rangārang*, thirteen *Yek Shakhi Gol*, and one *Golhā-ye Sahra'i*). Shajarian's
performance in program #37 from 1974, singing a poem by Ebtehaj in dastgah
Homayun and accompanied by the tar of Farhang Sharif, is representative of his
style of avaz from his period of radio work.[34]

Translation of the complete performance;[35] *beyts* included in the transcription
are in italics:
*The discord in your eye, so sought to oppress
that my patient heart appealed to the cry*

The one who broke morning's mirror and the tulip's cup
Freed the night's dust from the mouth of the wildflower

*It was from the jest in your eyes that the world
saw this manner of people-killing and learned of it*

*I remain and the burnt-out candle of heart, Oh Creator give help
For again, the night became chaos and caught the wind*

*My song is sadder than the lovers' sigh
Ah, that wound, taken from another road to oppression*

*Sayeh, we are love's quarry, for this mild-mannered one
In expedience, sought guidance from Farhad's blade*

Interlinear translation of transcribed excerpts:
Fetne -ye   chashm -e   to   chandān pa-ye   bidad   gereft
Sedition of   eye   of you   so   foot-of no-justice took
The discord in your eye, so sought to oppress

ke   shakib -e   del-e   man dāmane faryād   gereft
that patience-of heart-of me   extent   cry   took
that my patient heart appealed to the cry

az   shukhe-ye   chashme   to   ke khun   riz-e   falak
from impudence-of eye   you   that blood poured heavens
It was from the jest in your eyes that the world

did   in   shive - ye   mardom koshi   yād   gereft
saw   this method - of   people killed memory took
saw this manner of people-killing and learned of it

manam   u   sham'-e   del   sukhte   yārab   madadi
I   am s/he candle-of heart burnt   oh Lord help
I remain and the burnt-out candle of heart, Oh Creator give help

ke   digar   bāre shab āshofte   shud   o   bād   gereft
that other   time night distressed became and wind   took
For again, the night became chaos and caught the wind

she'ram   az   nale 'ushāq qam angiztar
poem-my from   wail lover distressing (-more)
My song is sadder than the lovers' sigh

dad az   an   zokheme ke   digar   rah-e   bidād   gereft
gave from that wound   that other   road-of no-justice took
Ah, that wound, taken from another road to oppression

Sāyeh mā   koshte 'eshqim   ke   in   shirin kār
Sayeh we   killed love-are   that this sweet   work
Sayeh, we are love's quarry, for this mild-mannered one

maslahat   -ra[36] *madad az   tishe-ye Farhad gereft*
good policy   *   help   from   axe-of Farhad took
In expedience, sought guidance from Farhad's blade

The poem by Ebtehaj is full of powerful images, including a recurring motif of violence (which is more pronounced in the literal, interlinear translation). Its tone is one of distress and vulnerability; the reference to the guidance from Farhad's axe[37] suggests that we maintain our focus—in life, love, and spiritual development—with such obsession and sacrifice that we become oblivious to, or transcend, our daily strife. Shajarian develops the Daramad quite extensively in the first three sections, creating an aura of gravity and a sense of foreboding in his interpretation of the dramatic imagery of the opening two *beyts*. While the Daramad of Homayun has a comparatively wide range, Shajarian does not venture above F# until the tahrir at the end of section 2. Chakavak follows predictably in the next two sections, with the characteristic repetition and sustaining of G. This static melodic draws attention to the text of the third beyt, Shajarian's insistence of the reciting tone underscores the intensity of the murderous image (Shajarian omits the second *misra*).

Shajarian turns to Bidad and its satellite gushe Raje for the following two beyts in sections 6 to 11. The gushe, with its definitive "sobbing" portamento between Bb-A, is particularly cathartic and lamenting, evoking the distress, urgency, and supplication of beyts 4 and 5. His rendition of Bidad in this performance is remarkably similar to Karimi's radif. Previewing the centonic analysis of chapter 4, his tahrirs display multiple repeats, extended sequencing, and compounding of basic building-block units. The tahrirs of section 7 are good examples of regularity and symmetry—balanced arching contours that transpose the same centonic unit and its variants. The *forud* at section 11 is also similar to Karimi's; it leads to a brief allusion to Shushtari before returning to Homayun for the last phrase of the performance. This release of musical tension and sense of resolution coincides with the poet's prescription of Farhad's guidance.

Shajarian's vocal timbre following the Daramad centers on his bright, laser-beam tone and stays in his middle to upper register throughout, highlighting the intensity and edginess of the text. Compared to his later work, this performance has an almost metronomic steadiness of pulse based on the fastest note relationship (density referent), which was very welcome in terms of the transcription process. There is considerable rhythmic play throughout the performance: varying the length of repeated notes in section 5, repeating a motif in varied rhythmic configurations, and lots of long-held notes that suspend the melodic flow. His tahrirs are consistently fast (notated here in sixteenth-notes but subjectively "faster") and feature crisp, biting *tekyes* in great profusion. The dramatic contrast and juxtaposition of stasis and fast, sometimes machine-like staccato tahrirs evoke the general instability of the text, of not being sure where you stand or if you are coming or going. There is a very physical, athletic quality on display here that is both exciting and impressive (the tahrir in section 9 features five repetitions of the same seven note compound unit). The performance is a good example of Shajarian's focus at the time on singing technique, while evoking the overall sense of exasperation in the poem. The following transcription includes key sections (numbered) from this great performance.

With regard to musical form, the performance in general is characterized by neat sectionalization. With the exception of the brief allusion to Shushtari in the last section, the gushes are all clearly separated, each introduced with a tahrir, and they receive fairly equal treatment. While this kind of clear differentiation may be a definitive feature of the dastgah itself (just as it is with Chahargah, for example), Shajarian seems to make a concentrated effort towards a balance and clear juxtaposition of gushes. This general emphasis on formal balance boldly and effectively contrasts the poetic atmosphere of instability, a poignancy that Shajarian reinforces in this intense and passionate setting.

Golhâ-ye Tâze #37

Scholarly Discourse

To round out the present chapter's sketch of Iranian musical culture leading up to and including Shajarian's entrance in the music scene of Teheran in the late 1960s, this section provides a brief overview of the scholarly discourse of Persian music. While musical practice and cultivation had its various peaks and valleys since ancient times, including long periods when it had to retreat underground, Iranian music scholarship had even more extensive dry spells. The golden age of scholarship that ended with Maraghi (fourteenth/fifteenth century) was followed by the deprivations of the Safavid dynasty, while the late Qajar period was marked by debilitating political, intellectual, and literary decadence. The Farahani family struggled to salvage the music of the second half of the nineteenth century by reformatting it as the radif and dastgah system but this undertaking was entirely practical and the theory remained implied in the music and its oral transmission. There was likewise a dearth of any form of writing on musical history or culture that could be characterized as scholarly.

Just as Iranian musical culture of the period was radically altered by the presence and cultivation of Western military music, along with its institutions and personel, the earliest impetus for revitalizing music scholarship came from the West via Colonel Vaziri's writings and public lectures delivered at his Club in Tehran in the 1920s. The twentieth century, particularly its second half, ushered in an era of vigorous music scholarship on various fronts, [38] most of it linked in some way to Western musicology and ethnomusicology. This was propelled by four main groups: Iranians studying in the West and either staying or returning to Iran to teach and publish scholarly works; Westerners trained in ethnomusicology and active in both Iran and the West; Iranians born outside Iran and educated in the West; and scholars born and trained in Iran but familiar with the now voluminous international literature.[39] From an admittedly artificial (even hypocritical) angle verging on the notion of "cultural purity" criticized in various contexts above, the present discussion centers on indigenous Iranian scholarship that, while acutely aware of Western scholarly approaches to Persian music and influenced by it to varying degrees, represents a more "emic," local and ostensibly insulated scholarly perspective.

Despite being essentially a compilation of earlier (and usually uncredited) theoretical sources and an anthology of poetry, Sayyed Mirza Mohammad-Nasir Forsat Shirazi's (1855–1920) *Bohur al-Alhan,* written in 1914, was an influential early-twentieth century treatise. Not unlike Western Orientalists, a large portion of the work presents an historical overview of musical theory that had little connection to contemporaneous musicking and lacked much of the precision and rigour that figured into the sources it drew upon, such as Maraghi and Qotboddin. Mirza Mohammad eventually does provide a cursory description of the dastgah system, which is a significant contribution in being an early attempt (perhaps the first?) at documenting the new system that was established and existed within the oral tradition of a relatively small circle of musicians. An anthology of poetry occupies the larger part of the work, indicating the appropriate time, venue, and dastgah or gushe for which each poem was suited. This prescription of specific modes for particular poems is evident in the influential vocal radif tradition of Davami and Karimi, though Shajarian specifically states that he disagrees with this approach.[40] During notes that Mirza Mohammad's correspondences are too subjective, vague and "imprecise to be useful in practice, and this section of the text must for the moment be regarded as merely a collection of poems, though a careful examination of its contents may someday reveal closer esthetic and expressive links between poetry and music" (During 1989b).

'Aref wrote some critical articles on the contemporary music scene (published in his *Diwan* of collected works), although these were often of a polemic nature. It is a rather refreshing surprise to note that Iran's Prime Minister from 1927–1933, Mehdiqoli Khan Hedayat (1864–1955), was also a musicologist and music theorist. His *Majma 'al-adwār*, published in 1938 but probably written in 1911, contains a discussion of classic treatises, intervals, and tuning theory, modality, a description of the dastgah system, as well as the theories of Helmholtz. Another short work deals with the alphabetic musical notation found in old treatises. Hedayat made an early transcription of the radif—Mirza Abollah's as performed by his student Mehdi Soli—in 1928, though it was never published (Youssefzadeh 2003).

While the general orientation of Khaleqi's extensive scholarly work is best described as an extension of Vaziri's engineering of Western approaches into Iranian discourse, the former's *Sargozasht-e musiqi-e Iran* ("History of Iranian Music") in three volumes, published in 1954, 1956 and, posthumously, 1998, stands out as a major landmark in "home grown" Iranian musicology. A detailed historical account of Iranian music through the late Qajar period through to the mid-twentieth century, it culls a vast quantity of valuable information from rare written and oral sources, documenting the social and political milieu along with biographical and anecdotal sketches of a wide range of musicians, patrons, and other stakeholders. Its influence on subsequent scholarship of Persian music is profound, wherein its citation is ubiquitous among scholars of all stripes.[41]

Following the Reza Shah's prevailing policies of Westernization and government cultivation and control of culture, two music periodicals—*Muzik-e Iran* and *Majaleh-ye Musiqi-ye Radio Iran*—emerged in the 1950s that included articles and music and examples of short compositions. Articles on various aspects of music appeared regularly during the following decades in newspapers *Kayhan International* and *Tehran Times*. While these periodicals were aimed at a more general musical audience not scholarly *per se*, they evince the increased interest in public discourse about contemporaneous musical issues and have a clear scholarly value today in terms of documenting the latter. A familiar theme runs through much of this discourse:

> From 1946 onwards, in articles and editorials in contemporary journals, many
> of the great musicians, composers, songwriters and poets who flourished in
> Tehran during this period voiced their anxiety about the course of their na-

tional music (*musiqi-ye melli*), lamenting its decadence and decline, while un-
derlining the lack of support and at times interference in the development of
music by the Ministry of Culture. (Lewisohn 2008:80–81)

Although educated in the West as an architect and collaborating with French
scholars since the 1960s, Dariush Safvat's (b. 1928) contributions to the scholarship of Persian music present a decidedly conservative, emically Iranian perspective sharply contrasting Vaziri's agenda. A master setarist and student of Boroumand, Saba and Hormozi, Safvat is a staunch proponent of maintaining the traditional integrity of Persian music and particularly emphasizes its essential grounding in Sufi values. His writings have a fairly wide dissemination among both
Iranian and the Western scholars. We noted earlier Safvat's key role in the formation and early administration of the *Markaz*, which had a profound impact on
both scholarly and practical approaches to Persian music during the crucial decades before and after the revolution. Representing a younger generation following
Safvat's orientation but trained and active more exclusively in Iran is santurist
Majid Kiani (b. 1941), who played and continues to play a prominent role as a
government administrator of media, music education, and scholarly publication in
the postrevolutionary period.

In a scholarly parallel to the tendency commonly found among musicians,
there exists a significant musicological contribution from "amateur" scholars in
Iran, whose principal source of income is derived from other non-musical/non-
scholarly means: notably Sassan Sepanta's work on recording technology, Hassan
Mashun's historical research, and not to forget the above-mentioned contributions
of the politician Hedayat. Farhang Raj'ai presents the interesting variation on this
line of scholarship by being a professor of political science in Canada while col-
lecting, editing, and providing erudite commentary for the earliest recordings of
Persian music. Following nationalistic agendas operating under varying rationales
both before and after the revolution, the government has supported folk music
scholarship and field collection, particularly through the work of Fozie Majd,
Mohammad Taghi Massoudieh, the outstanding ethnomusicological work of Reza Darvishi and others. Financed by Iranian National Television, in 1972 Majd
established a research team that collected over 500 high-quality tapes of folk music from various regions of Iran, which since the revolution remain archived and
inaccessible to researchers, unfortunately (Youseffzadeh 2000:37).

In acquiring their art, every practicing musician is also *de facto* a
musicologist, historian and music theorist to varying degrees, even if they have
no interest to write up and publish their research and it remains as "oral
knowledge." Some Iranian musicians—notably Safvat, Kiani, and Tala'i—have
brought their knowledge into the scholarly forum, often making extremely
valuable contributions in the process. Shajarian has been engaged more or less
continuously in extensive research on various musical fronts since his childhood:
Qur'an recitation, radif, individual style/*sabk*, vocal technique, *aruz*, tasnif
repertoire, Iranian folk music (especially Khorasani), poetry, Sufism, organology,
acoustics, instrument design, and construction, to name the most immediate.

Some of this research has been published in the format of recordings, others in a small number of articles.[42] Shajarian's primary motivation has been clearly practical, towards that of artistic and aesthetic excellence, the transmission of tradition and demonstration of its potential for creative flexibility, by which he assumes the archetypal role and function of a traditional Ostad rather than that of an academic. His research activity through the 1960s and 1970s centered on radif, the *sabk* of great avaz masters, and tasnif repertoire.

Shajarian's Professional Activities in the 1970s

Despite his ultimate disillusionment with the medium, radio work and its exposure was the cornerstone of Shajarian's career; the success of his early appearances opened up further opportunities on other fronts, one of which was concertizing. He first performed in the prestigious Shiraz Arts Festival in 1969, alongside some of the biggest names in music from around the world. He was a regular presence at the festival through the 1970s, recording his 1976 performance of Rast Panjgah with Lotfi and his 1977 performance of Nava, again with Lotfi but this time the *Sheyda* ensemble as well, releasing both on Delawaz in 1998 under the titles *Rast Panjgah* and *Chere bi Chehre*. He appeared in other music festivals throughout the country throughout the 1970s with various musicians, including the Tus festival in 1976, which was established at the request of Persian musicians frustrated with the avant garde domination of the Shiraz festival who requested their own venue (see photo 4). His 1976 performance at the festival was recorded and released as by Lofti as *Chavosh 9* (and later by his *Sheyda* Institute under the title *Jan e Jan*). International performance opportunities also arose quickly following his early radio appearances. He performed with Ebadi on Iraqi national television in Baghdad in 1968. The year 1974 brought further international concerts with Ebadi in India, Pakistan, Afghanistan, and Turkey (see photo 3) as well as China and Japan with a group of artists chosen to commemorate the opening of flights between Iran and these countries (Abdollahi 2003:2069–70).

The success of his radio, television and concert work along with the income it provided allowed Shajarian to safely drop his stage name Siavesh Bidkani in 1971 and begin performing under his own name. Still holding his day job at the Ministry of Natural Resources while maintaining a very active performing career with a national and increasingly international profile, he was transferred to a position in the radio section of NIRT in 1975. He was selected as the artist to peform avaz on a widely distributed set of instructional discs produced in 1976 for the Institute for the Intellectual Development of Children and Young Adults,[43] demonstrating the radif. Alongside his busy performing and recording schedule, he took a teaching position in the Faculty of Fine Arts in the University of Tehran in 1975, which he held until the Music department's closure shortly following the revolution. He has occasionally taught there for short periods since the reopening of the department in 1990 (Nooshin 2001) and kept an increasingly large number of private students in the meantime. Over the past three decades these have included many of the top singers in the country: Shahram Nazeri, the late Iraj Bestami, and Sarāj; he worked more intensively with Kerāmati, Mozafar Shafi'i, Qasem Raf'ati, Ali Jahandar, and Hamid Reza Nurbakhsh (Shajarian et al. 2004:64; 224–25). Others from the younger generation include Ali Reza Ghorbani, Salar Aghili, Sina Sarlak and, of course, his son Homayoun, who has received the most complete transmission of his art through the means of traditional, noninstitutionalized mentoring. Shajarian has trained many women as well—such as Afsane Rasāyi and Azam Gholāmi—who remain much less known due to legal restrictions on women performing to "mixed audiences" in public (Shajarian et al. 2004:64).

Having established a solid career and securely plugged into an extensive professional network within the competitive Tehran music scene, Shajarian began to carve out a more autonomous professional niche for himself in the second half of the 1970s. As noted above, increasingly dissatisfied with the "unfavourable crowd" he had to work with, he distanced himself from his work with the radio and decisively cut all official ties with the establishment in March 1977 (Abdollahi 2003:2070), effectively abandoning his day job, which at this point was most likely entirely titular, in any event. Just under a year later he founded his own production company Delawaz ("Heart Avaz") for producing and releasing his own programs. Shajarian retains control over all artistic and business matters in these productions (Shajarian 1993:44). The move was bold, unprecedented, and visionary. From the micromanagement of government-controlled radio and television, privately produced cassettes would now become his main medium for addressing his by now enormous and dedicated audience (and the free market at large). His working paradigm was now freelance and free enterprise. He had declared and established for himself *auteur* status, with its concomitant freedom and power; this was an unprecedented achievement in the field of Persian music. With an uncanny prescience, he was ideally equipped to ride the unforeseen, oncoming energy surges of cassette culture and the raging madness of the revolution.

The mission statement published on the home page of Delawaz's English website (www.delawaz.com/en), aimed at a global audience, reads: "Delawaz Cultural Co. was founded in 1976 by Iranian famous musician & Vocalist, Mohammad Reza Shajarian to distribute Iranian Professional Traditional Music all over the world." The Persian site (www.delawaz.com) provides a more detailed and somewhat different message for Persian readers:

> Delawaz Cultural and Artistic Company was founded by the good offices/ambitions of Ostad Shajarian on Esfand 1, 1356 (February 20, 1978) to maintain the authenticity of Iranian vocal and instrumental music by preparing and distributing programs of musical "prophecy" (*mardomkhodāsāz*),[44] connecting the thinking of artistically knowledgeable people, colleagues, music masters, and introducing and arranging programs for young artists.

Shajarian recorded the double cassette album *Golbāng* in 1977 with his long-time colleagues whom he first encountered through the radio—Payvar, Houshang Zarif,

Ebadi, Bahari, and composer Hasan Yousefzamani—which becomes the first Delawaz release in 1978. In other ways his Delawaz enterprise fits comfortably into a well established social groove, as Iran had an active legacy of private associations and societies that promoted music beginning in the early-twentieth century, e.g., the *Anjoman-e Okavvat, Zahir al-Dawlat,* and Vaziri's *Kolub-e musiqi.* Still furthering his prospects for creating opportunities outside the pervasive grid of government control, Shajarian collaborated with Lotfi, Ebtehaj, Parvez Meshkatian, and Alizadeh in 1978 to found the *Kānune Chavosh* ("The Herald Society") for the purposes of cultivating various musical activities, including concert and record production, publication, radio and television programming for foreign markets and musical instruction (Abdollahi 2003: 2070). Shajarian did some teaching at the new organization.

AK

While many people were involved in its activities and foundation, *Chavosh* was primarily Mohammad Reza Lotfi's initiative and enterprise. Two different bands that existed before the revolution were based here: the 'Aref Ensemble (directed by Parviz Meshkatian and Hossein Alizadeh) and the Sheyda Ensemble (directed by Lotfi himself). The center had many functions but one of the most important was that it was a conservatory for studying traditional music. There were many different teachers for each instrument over the years. Sheyda was also a recording and production company, where some of the works produced were those of Shajarian, such as *Chavosh Six,* which is a memorable work from him. There was also a luthier workshop in the institute, making the most common traditional instruments. In its function, perspective, and activities *Chavosh* was like a private version of the state Conservatory. The "Chavosh movement" has had its own fluctuations and varying goals since the time of the Islamic Revolution of 1979, but it still continues to operate under Lotfi's guidance.

RS

Some observers separate the activities of Lotfi's official organization from a broader movement that followed in the wake of this initiative, denoting both a style of music and a subculture of musicians who believed in looking forward while retaining roots, and did not shy away from political engagement:

> Musical groups collectively known as the Chavosh (Herald) movement altered the way that players of classical Persian music viewed the world and related to their audiences. Like Western rockers, these performers were "modern"—in the sense that they chose as lyrics the lines of contemporary poets and they played in a style projecting impatience and idealism. And these were also "underground" bands—in the sense that their music stayed clear of the mainstream, defied the demands of the market, sought momentum in the energy of listeners and stayed true to the spirit of the times. (Sadighi and Mahdavi 2009)

The ethos of this more general movement encapsulates Shajarian's activities and orientation through the following decades, coming into ever sharpening focus and explicitness to the present.

The decade since he moved to Tehran in search of establishing a musical career had been hugely successful and productive for Shajarian. The year 1978 was a particularly busy one, marked by constructive optimism and bold initiatives. Change was in the air and he had deftly positioned himself to begin a new phase of productivity on his own terms. In August of that year he placed first in a national Qur'an recitation competition and began recording performances of his mature rendition of the sacred art (including the *Rabanna* discussed in chapter 2) he had practiced since his early childhood in Mashhad. He received this deeply prestigious accolade—that simultaneously holds great artistic, cultural, and religious significance—only a few months before the unforeseen cataclysm of the Islamic Revolution and the concomitant Iran-Iraq war, which would soon turn daily life in Iran into an unrecognizable nightmare.

Notes

1. (A)s both an idea and as historical reality contemporary Iran is the dialectical outcome of two diametrically opposed forces...While its racialized minorities (who are the majority of Iranians) and varied ethnicities are pulling it asunder, its drive toward an anticolonial modernity with which it has been blessed and afflicted pulls it together. What we witness today in Iran is a political culture that over the past two hundred years has been in continuous crisis—a crisis that has extended to its economy and polity alike, from the symbolics of its relations of power to the institutions of what it holds to be legitimate authority. (Dasbashi 2007:27)

2. Written in 1911 to challenge Russian machinations surrounding the expulsion of the American diplomat Morgan Shuster.

3. See Nettl 1978: 151ff. for a description of various concert formats in Tehran in the late 1960s.

4. Despite these reservations, held by a number of musicians and connoisseurs, Amir Koushkani's comments in chapter 1 stress that Payvar had an entirely legitimate authority with regard to Persian music.

5. See the photos in Wright 2009:13–14.

6. Mourning chants akin to avaz in the gushes of Hejaz and Gham Angiz.

7. http://payvand.com/blog/blog/2010/02/14/the-golha-project-digital-archiving-of-flowers-of-persian-poetry-and-song/.

8. Here is the passage from the liner notes:
   Ghorrat ol Ein, one of the few Iranian female poets before the twentieth century, is shrouded in mystery. Born in 1817, she was rebellious, brave and brilliant, a follower of the Baha'i faith and a women's rights activist. She quickly earned the scorn of the religious and political establishment and was killed by agents of the government at the age of 36. One of the most unique and creative female minds of recent times was lost. Only a handful of her poems survive and the one on this recording is her most well known. (*Faryad* liner notes)

9. "Concert Banned because of Presence of Women Musicians," February 24, 2010. http://www.freemuse.org/sw36684.asp.

10. Golbarg Bashi, "Iranian Feminism after June 2009," http://www.pbs.org/wgbh/pages/frontline/tehranbureau/2009/07/iranian-feminism-after-june-2009.html.

11. Interview on VOA Persian, broadcasted June 19, 2010; http://www.youtube.com/watch?v=wHiPVsJIJlY.

12. E.g., setaristsYusef Forutan, Sa'id Hormozi, and Dariush Safvat, and the vocalist Mahmoud Karimi, among others.

13. *Markaz-e hefz o esha'e-ye musiqi-ye Irani* ("The Center for the Propagation and Preservation of Iranian Music"), henceforth abbreviated as "the Markaz;" founded in 1968, it is discussed further below.

14. United Nations Development Programme *Human Development Report 2009*, http://hdr.undp.org/en/media/HDR_2009_EN_Complete.pdf (p.172).

15. Darvish Khan was both a conservative and a modernizer in various facets of his musical life: his pedagogical approach was largely conservative while his compositions, certain aspects of his style of tar playing and professional posturing were "renovating" or modernizing.

16. Following Vaziri both chronologically and ideologically, under Khaleqi's directorship (1949–59) the "side" of the *Honarestan* cultivating Persian music (*Honarestān-e musiqi-e melli*) was particularly vital and influential:

> The Conservatory's curriculum covered both the practical and the theoretical aspects of musical studies. Tuition was provided for everybody studying any Persian musical instruments of the classical tradition; students of Western instruments that had found wide application in Persian music, such as violin, clarinet and piano, were also enrolled tuition-free. On the theoretical side, Vaziri's theories on intervals and modes of Persian music, and the traditional precepts of the *dastgāh* system were the essential components of the course. In addition, Western musical notation, solfeggio, and tonal harmony were also taught. Subjects outside music, considered essential for a comprehensive education, such as language, history, geography, mathematics, etc., were also included in the curriculum. The Conservatory accepted both male and female students from the fifth grade through the six years of secondary school. (Farhat 2004a)

17. As detailed in Simms and Koushkani (2012), the *Markaz* was to play a key role in the rise in Persian music after the revolution.

18. Interview on VOA Persian, broadcasted June 19, 2010; http://www.youtube.com/watch?v=wHiPVsJIJlY.

19. Lord and Perry's seminal work in the former Yugoslavia in the 1930s and 40s was done with a clear awareness of its imminent demise.

20. Cf., Diana Taylor's notion of the archive and repertoire (2003).

21. For a more detailed discussion beyond this brief contextualization, see During 1988 and 1989:195ff.

22. During reports that this lost transcription was of Aqa Hossein-qoli's radif (2006:291–92). Another early transcription of Mirza Abdollah's radif based upon the performance of one of his students was made by Mehdiqoli Hedayat in 1928 but remains unpublished (During 2006:292; Zonis 1973:64).

23. This radif is actually a composite of several radifs. While lacking concrete evidence, some musicians claim possible intrigue surrounding the usurpation and inclusion of Vaziri's lost work in this radif.

24. Hossein Mehrani, *Shahnāvāz: The Improvisations of Ostād Ahmad Ebādi* (Tehran: Mahoor Institute of Culture and Art, 2000).

25. Solfege is widely used among West Asian and North African musicians, and indeed often cultivated to a highly advanced level. While commonly used to refer to notes among Iranian musicians, it has generally not been used by singers until quite recently.

26. Recordings are still often sold in Iranian grocery stores (this is also common in diasporic communites in the West).

27. There were six programs included under the umbrella title *Golhā*, each with a slightly different focus: *Golhā-ye jāvidān* (Eternal Flowers), *Golhā-ye rangārang* (Flowers of Many Colors), *Barg-e sabz* (The Green Leaf), *Yak shākha gol* (A Flowering Branch), *Golhā-ye sahrā'i* (Flowers of the Field), and *Golhā-ye tāza* (Fresh Flowers). The Gulha Project under the direction of Jane Lewisohn has recovered and digitized this monumental collection and is making it available online (www.gulha.co.uk).

28. Though how deeply they actually understand it may be another matter, according to Amir Koushkani.

29. A similar aesthetic emerged in American popular music of the 1930s and 40s that provoked a sense of initimacy between singer and listener, in stark contrast to the necessity of strong projection previously required when performing in a large space or making an acoustic recording.

30. There is a discrepancy regarding the date here as provided by various sources (e.g., Nasirifar 1990:402), including Shajarian himself, who provides 1966. However, Pirnia was still producing the program at the time and Shajarian clearly states that he was no longer doing so when he actually began work with the national radio. The audio is available on several internet sites and can be found through a Google search of "Barge Sabz 216" or "Barg Sabz 216."

31. Appendix 3 lists details of Shajarian's *Golhā* performances.

32. A point of further discussion in Simms and Koushkani (2012).

33. Interview in Persian, broadcasted June 19, 2010; http://www.youtube.com/watch?v=wHiPVsJIJlY.

34. The audio is available on several internet sites and can be found through a Google search of "Golhaye Tazeh 37."

35. Translation by Amir Koushkani.

36. The suffix "-*rā*" is a particle that marks grammatical objects, filled in with an asterisk in the second word-for-word line.

37. In the mythological love triangle of Khosrow, Shirin and Farhad, the latter is the chivalrous character embodying an all-consuming, self-sacrificing love, which remains unrequited. The story first appears in the *Shahnāme* but is retold by countless poets throughout history, the most famous version of which is by Nizami, and is found ubiquitously throughout Iranian folk culture. Farhad's axe refers to his task of carving through a mountain for the sake of his love for Shirin.

38. Persian music is by far the most studied West Asian art music tradition internationally.

39. I outline these important strains in Simms and Koushkani (2012) within the larger context of globalization.

40. See Shajarian's comments on this work on page 23 above; see also Kasmai and Lecomte 1991:251.

41. This despite Tabar's contention that Khaleqi's treatment (at least for volume I) is "very personal and without rigorous historical method" (2005:32).

42. Hossein Omumi Sr. noted the existence of these articles (personal communication, 1995). With the exception of Shajarian 1991, I have been unable to access or identify these, unfortunately.

43. Published with the English title *The Series of Music for Young Adults* (10 LPs produced by Kambeez Roshanravan for the Institute for the Intellectual Development of Children and Young Adults, Tehran, 1976).

44. The coinage of this novel term is not clear but probably arose from the teachings of Ostad Dadbeh and likely refers to artists who are divinely chosen to connect people to their higher potential.

As a young man in Mashhad, late 1950s. Ostad Shajarian has generously given permission to use this photograph.

With Ahmad Ebadi in Baghdad, 1968. Ostad Shajarian has generously given permission to use this photograph.

With Hossein Malik and Jahangir Malik in Istanbul, 1974.
Ostad Shajarian has generously given permission to use this photograph.

Performing (4th from left) with Lotfi (5th from left) and his Sheyda Ensemble
at the tomb of Ferdowsi in Tus, 1976. Ostad Shajarian has
generously given permission to use this photograph.

Chapter 4
Performing Avaz:
A Toolkit of Techniques, Materials and Creative Processes

OS
We understand this music [avaz] to be a kind of a language separate from the Persian language—it is a language on its own. It is exactly like the Persian language, it has rules, grammar, words or phrases that we call motifs, and sentences that maybe we can call melodic phrases, and these melodies are similar to the Persian language in that they are governed by rules that take shape with these phrases. And all these sentences together will be exactly like a speech or a written essay. So this music moves in this way and it moves very openly. It can speak about any topic; in fact it can even speak much better than ordinary language. (2010)

When we want to examine singers, for their methods and style of singing, we have to take into consideration these fifteen points:
1. Methods of how the voice is being used
2. How the singer manipulates his/her voice in the mouth
3. The kind of feeling or energy displayed on sustained tones
(hālat ejrā-ye keshesh-hā)
4. The timing of the avaz: its meter, speed, rhythm and its proportion to sustained notes
5. The form of sentence/phrase construction
6. The form of the relation of sentences to each other
7. The form of the usage of tahrirs
8. Poetry and its delivery and expression
9. The form of the poems and their relation to tahrirs
10. How the singer utilizes low-register and high-register singing

167

11. The relation between low-register and high-register
12. The technique or "tools" (advāt) of tahrir
13. The textures/weavings (bāft-hā) of tahrir
14. Sentence/phrase construction and its relation to the textures of tahrir
15. The usage of colour and the manner of voice in tahrir
(Shajarian et al. 2004:247)

Poetry, Music, and Their Combination

RS

This chapter examines exactly what Shajarian does as a singer, the very basis of his career and the reason for our interest in him: the art of avaz. Having posited the view that avaz performs an essentially narrative function in Iranian culture, this chapter reviews its structure, repertoire, and creative process from a wider narrative perspective. While corresponding to other Iranian narrative art forms, a key difference with avaz (and obviously more pronounced in instrumental music) is that an abstract melody is being generated, not a new linguistic text (though both may occur in genres such as *rowze khāni* and *ta'ziyeh*; the art of avaz rarely includes improvised texts). The lyrical mode of the poet takes a decisive narrative turn when a poem is taken up by a surrogate who "sings, or muses, or speaks for us to hear or overhear," thereby constituting the existence of a teller and a tale (Scholes et al. 2006:4). In bardic traditions the narrative is usually generated by the novel rearrangement of preset, stock materials running hierarchically from foreground motifs and figures of speech, to middleground themes, topoi, and scenarios, and ultimately to a background sequence linking the episodes into a foundational plot. Myriad options of arrangement, development, ornamentation, inclusion, and exclusion are possible in spinning out a unique rendition of the tale or an individual episode thereof.

The traditional narrative arts then consist of mastery of the preset vocabulary as well as its "grammar" for gaining fluency in generating unique renditions of a plot: its primary impulse is not creative but rather recreative; through constant rearrangement of more or less preset materials the narrator functions as "the instrument through which the tradition takes on a tangible shape as a performance" (Scholes et al. 2006:12, 53). The primary business of the narrator is the spontaneous construction of form—expanding on Aristotle's trite observation that not only plot but all levels of the performative structure (except perhaps the musical motive) require the formation or delineation of a beginning, middle, and end. The success of a given formulation hinges on striking a satisfying balance between the poles of expectation and suprise, playing it safe, and keeping things interesting, providing a coherent exposition of recognizable landmarks in the narration while adding spice and relief from over-predictability and potential boredom—all ideally tailored and appropriately responding to the specific audience and occasion.

Our focus here centers on looking at the resources inside a singer's creative "toolkit," an approach and metaphor (following Reck 1983) that aptly reflects the practical perspective of a great number of musicians around the world regarding their craft. The discussion here interpolates—as there is no emic tradition of explicating creative processes among Iranian musicians (Nooshin 2003:264)—what constitutes the essential tools of singers in general while specifically revealing what Shajarian has explicated regarding his own approach to the craft of avaz (to the extent that he was interested in doing so). For any musician a toolkit consists of materials, techniques, generative processes, and performance practices. In the case of a *khānande* the materials are poetry and the radif; the technique includes vocal tone, intonation, and diction; the generative processes include composition, improvisation, centonization, melodic decoration, and textual underlay; and for Shajarian we must add word painting and *morakab khāni* modulation between dastgahs. Performance practice includes the *jawab*-avaz format of accompaniment. The classical five-fold division of rhetorical practice provides a useful and accurate description of the craft of avaz:

> In the classical tradition of rhetoric, the subject has traditionally been characterized by a fivefold division of parts or areas of interest: the invention of the appropriate arguments for what one has the intention to say (*inventio*); the arrangement or ordering of the arguments in a purposive manner (*dispositio*); stylistic matters or the art of embellishment (*elocutio*); the actual performance (*actio*); and techniques for memorizing the speech (*memoria)*. (Hallden 2005:26)

Applied to avaz, *inventio* is predicated on the occasion, which guides the choice of poem, which in turn will suggest the appropriate dastgah for setting the poem. *Dispositio* occurs in aligning a given line of poetry with a specific gushe, and in deciding the overall form in the distribution and order of the avaz and instrumental modules (*pishdaramad, zarbi* pieces, tasnifs, etc.). The decoratation and development of the structural template of the gushe through the weaving of centonic units—the construction of sentences with musical words, to use Shajarian's metaphor—is the business of elaboration, *elocutio*. *Memoria* is central to mastering the radif and singers often memorize the poems they perform. The gig, gathering or recording date is obviously *actio*.

This chapter examines the process of how the toolkit is acquired and assembled, surveys the materials and processes in general and then revisits them with increasing detail in view of their function and operation at varying structural levels of the music, referring to this division with Schenker's useful borrowing from painting technique of the terms "background, middle ground, and foreground." Throughout we highlight the key role of flexibility in the implementation of the tools in order to see how avaz functions as a language (following Shajarian's description), and how its deployment becomes essentially automatic once mastered. The topics covered include a detailed view of many of those listed by Shajarian in the section above, which he holds to constitute the core of the art of avaz.

Acquiring the Toolkit

OS

Our song is close to the song of the nightingale and the canary. Our tahrirs are like the nightingale's in the mountain valley. We use the same technique but with our vocal chords' physique. I have worked a great deal with the nightingale's voice and I had a great many canaries. They sang for me and I had their voices in my ears. When I walked in nature, I always listened to the voices of birds.[1]

The stages of learning [avaz] from the beginning include: [first] technique, how to use the voice, then radif and methods/style, and then the same cycle again on a higher level. But if anyone wants to reach the end of this path [of learning avaz] and they don't have technique, their work will be lame and if they don't know the radif, their phrases, melodies, and sense for sequencing these won't progress. (Shajarian et al. 2004: 245)

Question: What is the best way to learn this music and the art of avaz—from tapes, notes, or orally (*sine be sine*)?

The best method is repetition. I mean if someone wants to become a good singer or musician, he must imitate his favorite musician to the highest degree. That means, he must completely overlook himself and not bring anything of his own to the table and try to imitate it completely. This is the best way of learning. For example, I have tried to learn English numerous times but could not. But a child can easily copy it from his parents without even knowing what verbs are, what adjectives are, and so on, and she can still speak the language flawlessly. So avaz and music is the same—why do you care what gushe this or that is? Just imitate. Try to sing exactly like your model. It is the same thing as a child does with language; even a child's accent becomes like her parents and her surroundings because of imitation. Nothing can substitute for imitation and nothing can be as influential as imitation.

What particular Ostad or school of singing has influenced you throughout your life?

They all have influenced me as a collective. Ever since my childhood I was always in love with sound, not music but singing, because music was never present in our house, as my father thought it was prohibited (harām). *When I turned 18 and went to college I became familiar with music and radio. Due to my love of music I could memorize whatever I heard, just like when you put a coin into your savings account, the melody would go into my being. Therefore, all these melodies came to my assistance later on in life and I could instantly, at any moment, use any one of them and even produce something else from them. It gradually turned into a language for me, a sort of internal language. I learned this language from my Qur'an recitals, Ostads, and more so from listening to instruments. I learned most of my phrases from the tar of Jalil Shahnaz. On top of that I have listened numerous times to all the radifs that have been recorded in Iran.*

Therefore all the motifs and phrases are in my head, almost as if it is my mother tongue.

When do you depart from your studies and stop imitating and are no longer concerned with theory (gushes, dastgahs, etc.) and only focus on performing?

Well, this is certainly a process that takes time, because I obviously started by imitating older masters and sang exactly like them—I mean exactly. *The first person I imitated that closely was my father: I learned the gushe Hejaz from him. I was little then and my father used to do* shabi-khāni *[i.e., taz'iyeh] and I learned Hejaz from him. Even today when I sing Hejaz, I sing like my Dad. Qur'an recitation was for me again an imitation of the great Egyptian reciters. When I later started avaz, I practiced Zelli's approach, Banan's style and I also practiced Taherzadeh's style very diligently. In a sense, if any of them were around today they would not be able to differentiate between themselves and me. This was the method I practiced. I mean I imitated their every single breath. I also focused a little on Eqbal Soltan and Taj Esfehani, but the ones I really liked were Zelli, Qamar, Banan for the lower range, and Taherzadeh. These were mainly the people I enjoyed listening to and imitating. When I was younger I imitated people like Zabihi.[2] I worked on all these singers and could sing just like them, so the combination of all of them together became some sort of a compilation in me and there was nothing else for me to go and learn. I mean there was a no longer a singer who attracted me and from whom I should to go and learn something. The collection of all of them together made me an artistic character—combined with my own taste, of course. I mixed their styles together with my own taste and with time it transformed into "Shajarian's style."*

What suggestions do you have for people who want understand and practice your art?

They must work hard and focus on what I have done, for example, learn why I sang a poem in a particular gushe and what I do with my voice when I sing, and then ask themselves whether I have delivered the poetry in the best way possible. If the answer is yes, then they should try to imitate this method and once they start to imitate, over a period of time they will capture this science just the same way that it happened for me. This knowledge will be part of them over time, but it is contingent on their ability, the way they practice, the way they have imitated their favorite singer, and how close they have come to him or her regarding their methods of tahrirs and delivery of the poetry. (2009)

What do you suggest to those people who do not have access to your avaz classes?

They have to see which singer their voice is closer to, and then get their albums and start practicing. I mean practicing part by part. For example, to sing each beyt twenty times and record their voice and listen to it and see which part of their voice is closest to the original [of the model singer]. Listening to your own voice is the best help, and you must train your ears. The first step of learning avaz is imitation, specifically imitating a singer whose voice is closest to yours.

(BBC 2007)

Ever since childhood I was in search of a good voice, I always responded to beauty and I absorbed it. So I tried to sing with correct principles, and I tried to imitate voices and I practiced and made my own voice. So I asked questions from whoever was around me, to guide me, until I went to Golhā on Pirnia's program. But even up until that time I had never had an Ostad, except what I heard on the radio or from my father.

In general if one has the preliminary talent, one can take or steal whatever sounds good [to them]. However, one takes this and filters it through oneself, and puts one's own logo on it, and then brings that out. This is part of the job of the artists. You see, we are not born singers and radif specialists, we learn these from our surroundings. It is like our language; our language and music have evolved together. I mean the potency that our language has, our music also has. If we change the music of our words, their meanings change as well. Music is divided between instrumental music and vocal, accompanied music. One is the music that is in service of the vocals and the other is the music that is on its own and has its own atmosphere and is open to interpretation. A music that cannot create an atmosphere or is not capable of creating different interpretations is a defeated music. Thankfully Persian music has all these possibilities.[3]

RS

While my purpose here is not to posit a crosscultural model or theory of musical acquisition, much of the following discussion could contribute toward this end. Like a child acquiring its native language (to use Shajarian's simile) musical acquisition begins with passive listening and assimilation, unconsciously "soaking it up" in the course of everday life. As a high proportion of *khānande*s emerge from families and subculture of religious singers, the vocal arts a child is often immersed within center on the sacred genres. It is noteworthy, however, that Ostad Shajarian expresses an explicit lack of interest in these (chapter 2 above). The stage of passive listening is followed by one of active listening where the neophyte develops an analytical ear and copies singers whom they admire. This process has been documented in detail within the jazz tradition by Berliner (1994), whose findings apply with remarkable consistency to a great number of other contemporary musical traditions around the globe. In the Iranian tradition, such close listening, exact copying and memorization is the essence of formal study of the radif. Generative sensibilites are gained inductively through memorizing the radif (often various versions), compositions, and listening to the improvisations of other musicians (i.e., unique, individualized realization of the models).This process also characterizes the acquisition process of the *naqqil* and bard: memorizing poetry, piece by piece, often with the help of a teacher, along with memorizing *tumar* plot summaries (Page 1979: 198). In the case of the bard this mimetic activity would of course include vocal and instrumental melodies and techniques as well. Through absoption of these models the artist inductively gleans structures, processes, and recombinatory possibilities that lead to creative, generative capabilities—renewing the music while retaining definitive features of the tradition.

This process is akin to the feedback of chaos theory and fractal geometry. The tradition reiterates itself through the particular consolidation of the models (which may be viewed as functioning as attractors in this analogy) of an individual artist entering the field, based on his or her subjective taste, who then spins out a novel variant of this idiosyncratic aggregate which may also include new contributions. The resulting quality of this unique outcome is what separates great artists from the simply competent or mediocre, and whether this expression becomes an attractor for others that is subsequently reiterated. Copying and taking from others is, very cross-culturally, what musicians do and have done since time immemorial. It is certainly not the absurd theft of "intellectual property," as fashionably denounced (often in turgid, elitist Postmodernese prose) by some critics, who impose and project upon these widespread normalities a Western capitalistic obsession with ownership and property rights.[4] Whether unaware or completely ignoring these futile, irrelevant pontifications, musicians continue to share, borrow, and take; they appropriate things they like, season them to their own taste and make them their own.

This *modus operandi* has increased exponentially through the mediation of recordings, which, as we saw in chapter 3, constitute a technological extension and intensification of the age-old notion of *poshte parde/poshte dari*—listening from "behind the curtain or door." Despite the derision that purists often level at musicians who "learn through lifting" from recordings, it is by now so widespread and integral to the acquisition process of great masters in traditions around the globe (and usually openly endorsed by them) that we must view much of the former as anachronistic, retroromantic fundamentalism or perhaps the defeated bitterness of disenfranchised gatekeepers. In the act of lifting and imitation we are "performing someone else," a mode in which we must lose our selves. Imitation and repetition is widespread in the acquisition of artistic, athletic and social skills and is efficacious because, unlike this book, it "directly transmit[s] performance knowledge without the need for a verbal explanation or theorizing. Such 'talking about' may be very helpful at a certain stage of acquiring performance knowledge, but it can hinder such acquisition if used too early or too frequently" (Schechner 2005:232–33). Recordings paved the way for the widespread, liberating phenomenon of selfstudy, of being an autodidact, the results of which run the gamut from dilletantism (both harmless recreation and shameful charlatanism) through various degrees of serious acquisition along the path to mastery. Of course, this is not to say that recordings are the sole means of acquisition and direct oral transmission and live mentorship is dead or unnecessary—far from it—but that the significance of "lifting" in the acquisition process is much greater than is generally admitted in much of our scholarship. The importance Ostad Shajarian places on lifting is also a function of his early Mashhad selfstudy initiatives: having no teacher, it was indeed a necessity that he later came to regard as intrinsically efficacious.

Both the materials and processes that stock the singer's toolkit are inherited from the tradition, some anonymous, others attributed to known individuals. Some of these tools are obligatory and constitute the fundamental level of attaining and demonstrating basic competence, others are quirky and selective, with the artist sampling and choosing according to their personal taste. The power of the individual underlies this latter aspect both in the selection of individuals drawn upon as influences, and then as the resulting new expression of the artist, who encodes and propels the former forward in his or her musical statements. This individual variation is crucial to the maintanence of the tradition, as it replenishes and enriches it, recasting the inheritance in the ever-changing present. Viewed crossculturally, stakeholders in most musical traditions will appreciate, even demand innovation provided the command of the foundational skills are in place. The most obvious and important feature of Shajarian's acquisition of avaz performance abilities is his eclectic range of influences and study: he absorbs information from a wide range of individual styles and sources, drawing on "all radifs," old recordings, living masters, and instrumental music. This general mode of acquisition seems typical of musical transmission in West Asian cultures; an individual's artistic identity is to a large degree a complex composite of her selection from the tradition.

Shajarian began his acquisition of avaz through systematic training in Qur'an recitation, autodidactic lifting from records and radio, and then traditional "live" instruction with various vocal and instrumental masters. He in turn became a vocal instructor both privately and in various institutions, notably *Chavosh* and the University of Tehran. In teaching, Shajarian utilizes his vast knowledge of a variety of radifs, *sabk* and Persian folk music. The main *radif* he taught through to the early 1990s was the authoritative version of Davami, but he supplemented this with his own versions of gushes, based on his extensive private research. His instruction with new students begins by focusing on their vocal tone, after which he selects a particular version of a *gushe* based on the individual student's type of voice and musical aptitude (personal communication, Siamak Shajarian, 1995). More recently Shajarian provides his students with teaching CDs of his own performances, editing out the *jawabs* and electronically transposing them to suit their vocal register (2010), bringing his pedagogical approach full circle with the generation of his students.

Vocal Technique

Vocal Production and Tone

OS
Question: What kind of physical characteristics does your voice have?
My voice can produce nineteen notes [i.e., two and a half octaves] *without any difficulty; however, fifteen notes are often enough for avaz. But there is another crucial aspect of avaz and that is the dynamic range, control and power of the voice. Another qualification is dynamics—the stronger a voice is the better it is, but we have to keep in mind that the notes must always keep their beauty. A strong voice, which is usually called a "valley voice," is a voice that can easily be heard from 200 meters away in an open space. This feature of the voice is usually called the audibility or range of the voice. So one feature is the audibility*

of the voice and another is its intensity and control. Another parameter is the color and "character," which is part of the quality of the voice. The quality of the voice means its color and character, its transparency and blurriness, its clearness and raspiness. Sometimes a voice that is raspy is much more beautiful and is often called a "muddy voice." But a muddy voice is not able to produce the high notes and usually only sings in the middle range. The fourth feature is control of the voice. The voice is exactly like a wild horse that needs to be tamed, so that it will obey you whenever you wish. If you do not tame a horse it would not obey, so one has to work with one's voice, otherwise the voice remains wild. The fifth feature is the fragrance of the voice that comes from within the artist. Fragrance contains the cultural aspects, the honesty and the "being" of the artist—therefore some voices are fragrant and some reek. Some are without any fragrance at all: these are all due to the spirituality of the voice. So these are the points that characterize different kinds of voices.

Now, the voice that comes out of the larynx can be controlled with different types of techniques. Each culture has its own unique way of controlling this voice and the singers of each country use these techniques to produce music. From classical singers to jazz and opera and even folksingers, each uses a particular technique. However, in Persian avaz there are no ascribed techniques for performing. Our singers use their voice however they wish, depending on their own backgrounds and tastes. None of the avaz teachers were ever concerned with strengthening the voice. They only taught radif and style, they never focused on how the student must produce the voice. The only teacher who had experience and enforced it was Ostad Boroumand. He was knowledgeable about the voice and could spot its flaws and correct the student. He was not a singer himself and his voice was very low but he could deliver what he intended to say and I always could understand him very easily.

You suggested that your voice is capable of producing nineteen notes, but in some of your works it is seen that you have started on the *chap kuk* [based on a tonic other than the main one associated with a dastgah] and ended there, so it seems that you are capable of producing more than nineteen notes.

When I say nineteen notes, I mean nineteen notes that are clear and are without any sort of shaking, so that I can easily produce a tahrir on any one of them. I may be able to sing higher but because it might not have the clarity of the note below it, I do not consider it. I mean that it would be outside of the beauty of my work. Some singers think that they should always sing high, but if they cannot sing high, they should not do it. When the voice starts shaking and turns unpleasant one should always stop at that point. The voice must only go as far as it is pleasant, there shouldn't be even one unpleasant note.

What really fascinates avaz enthusiasts is the fact that your avaz has a certain clarity and beauty even at a very high register.

That is due to the shape of my larynx and my hard work. I have been working on the core of my voice ever since I was a child, without even having a proper teacher. When I was introduced to Boroumand, I realized that this is the most important part of avaz. He did not criticize the way I was generating my voice, he

only cautioned me and asked why I sang like Banan when I had a stronger voice?
I shouldn't do that! I used to copy Banan's technique and at the time that was a
very good thing, but I do not do it anymore. Boroumand told me not to fabricate a
voice but to let it sing naturally and only occasionally revert to the other way. He
really approved of me and I worked for years to find my own voice.

The technique for Iranian avaz is such that a lot can be done with it the
second it is produced. The voice starts at the end of the windpipe and gets to the
chest and fills the throat and comes out of the lips—therefore there is so much
potential along its path. For my taste, I do not really like to do anything to the
voice from the point it is generated until it hits the end of the soft palate (uvula)
and throat. If we try to sing from the end of the vocal chords [the back of the
throat], the voice turns bad. It will sound like a sheep! The throat must be com-
pletely open, but when it hits the mouth—that is when I start playing with it. The
sound that is generated from the chest has amplitude but not quality and you will
tire very quickly. A good voice must hit the roof of the mouth when it is generated
from the larynx. The roof of the mouth gives the sound a particular intensity,
which is the best sound for Persian music. Even if one sings in the high register
for two hours one would still not get tired, just like the sound that is produced in
opera, although the techniques are a bit different. We do not use our diaphragm
to a great degree; we work with it in our mouth. We must also never put too much
pressure on our jaw and the lower lip must have a natural shape. The tongue is
very crucial because the sound is guided by the tongue—all these aspects change
the color and shape of the sound. The teeth are also very important and singers
must take good care of their teeth, because it becomes very noticeable when they
sing with false teeth. The nose, sinus, mouth, and the external shape of the mouth
are also important, as well as the shape of the lips and the extent to which they
are open.

The ancients (qadmā) have always said that the voice must come out in the
shape of a cone [i.e., wide from the bottom of the vocal apparatus and tapering to
the opening of the mouth], which is just the opposite of what is said to other sing-
ers in the world. The ancients were very concerned with the external shape of the
mouth. In Iranian avaz when the voice comes out, the mouth should not open and
close too often because most of the work takes place before the sound gets out.
When Pavarotti sings "ah," for example, his mouth is turned open at least six
centimeters but in Persian avaz it should not open more than the thickness of the
index finger. That means that the shape of the mouth should have a cone-like
structure. That means the "ah" should have the shape of the "oh" and the lips
should not open that much. The techniques that are used inside the mouth are
very important and they require practice. My suggestion for students who wish to
sing avaz is that instead of starting with Daramad of Shur, they should start by
learning the techniques of voice and how to generate it. (Gudarzi et al.
2000:117–120)

The lungs have not much to do with the quality of the voice. The lungs only
push the air out, they only blow. Then this air hits the vocal chords that are adja-
cent to the windpipe. Once the sound is produced, you can do all sorts of things

in the path that it is taking, like giving it different shapes or colors. Then, if we are talking about the head voice, the sound hits the roof of the mouth, and resonates to the roof of your head, so when someone touches your head they can actually feel it is vibrating; and the chest doesn't get tired either. The singer must know how to use their head voice, obviously. Furthermore, the singer must know how to carry his voice so that there is not too much pressure on his vocal chords. Once the sound is in the mouth, your tongue, teeth, lower jaw and cheeks all have a role in the color of your voice. Even the sinuses and nose have a large impact on the timbre and color of the voice.

Some people like my father, who had a very strong voice and was a Qur'an reciter, had a voice that Arabs call kheishoum *(nasal voice). This voice is formed in a way that it is projected from the nose. For example Umm Kulthum or Mustafa Esmail, who died thirty years ago and was a Qur'an reciter, these people could do this very grandly. My father could also do it and that is how I learned it. I put my voice in my nose and bring it out; this technique involves the sinuses and you control it in the space of your mouth. (2009)*

Basically whatever an artist learns is taken from the ancients and from his own surroundings. If I was not an Iranian and instead lived in the jungles of the Amazon, I would have never practiced this music. Instead I have learned the music from my surroundings and my predecessors, from their recordings. Therefore their voices each had their own effect on me. I have a very good talent for understanding the voice. When I was very little, around two or three years old, I use to go to some ceremonies with my father and listen to them and when they sang I could distinguish who had a good voice or the differences between each voice. So I have lived with avaz all my life. I also studied valuable singers through whatever recordings I could find, and copied and learned the characteristics of their voices.

So what made you choose this timbre for yourself?

Well, there are a few reasons. First of all, there were many different voices that I have worked with from different singers, and their accents and expressions have stayed in my ears. Some of their voices here close to my voice and others were a little farther. Also, Qur'an recitals from prestigious Arab singers influenced me a lot, like Um Kulthum. She is the best Arab singer, and there will never ever be a singer like her again with a voice like that. Another was Mustafa Ismael from Egypt, who also had strong technique and voice—I listened to these kinds of people. I even listened to Pavarotti and all other big singers from around the world and identified what they really had in their voice. From a collection of these voices and the physics of my own voice and abilities I tried to reach a conclusion that satisfied me. I think I reached it in those years that we previously talked about [ca. 1980–2000]. I use my sound with different intensities and control, and even when my voice is in the high register, it generally still has some bass element in it—there is a harmony of bass in it, in the high pitches. Therefore I will try to control all of this with my own ear at all times to reach a level that satisfies me, and this timbre satisfies me.

In the early 1990s you often experimented with the lower register of your voice.

Yes, this was deliberate because I prefer lower frequencies to higher. I am actually working on a bass santur;[5] contrebass and cello satisfy me a lot. Also the singers who have a bass sound attract me more than those who sing high.

Are you familiar with or do you like North Indian classical singing?

Yes, they sing bass. The voice has a high range, a low range and a middle range. Achieving the middle range comes very fast, but reaching the high range and the lower range needs a lot of practice. You can reach the high range in your younger years and but your lower range comes when you are older, after forty. Your vocal chords need to be more established from singing a lot, and they also need to be rougher and thicker to produce the bass sounds better.

Before microphones people had to sing very high. Have microphones influenced the way you sing?

Yes, microphones have allowed me to sing in the lower registers much easier. In the past I could not sing this low because no one could hear me. (2008)

> *In the* Payam Nasim *CD, the range is very wide. None of my students could sing both the bass notes and the high notes that were performed. If they performed the high notes they couldn't perform the low notes and vice versa. (2010)*

In your opinion what constitutes a good voice? How do you define a good voice without taking into account the language and poetry?

A good voice is constituted by what the singer does with his voice. When you look at an acrobat and you enjoy what he or she is doing with his or her movement, that is similar to what I enjoy in a voice and the way in which the voice is utilized. Also the type of voice is important and the way it is put to work, so that the best possible sound is brought out. The moment one opens one's mouth I can instantly tell how much control they have over their voice and how much technique is involved. In our music, however, it is the improvisation that gives it so much value because we do not rehearse a particular avaz: we create in the moment, we create tahrirs and construct sentences in the moment. (2009)

Intonation

As you know, in different dastgahs the intonation of A-koron, for example, may slightly change. This is more instinctive. The reason is probably because somewhere in Iran, in some region, somebody placed the A-koron a little lower and thereby made it much more attractive, and we subsequently followed suit and became accustomed to singing that A-koron a little lower. I have always followed this pattern to create variety. For example in Bayate Tork, if we sing the note B-flat and then want to go on D (which makes it Dashti), we try to sing that D a little lower. In Bayate Raje the relationship between the E flat and F changes ever so slightly so that Bayate Raje can be created and have its own unique and beautiful sound—to such an extent that when you enter Bayate Raje you never want to leave it. But if you keep it in its own classical system [tuning], the energy changes and the feeling of Bayate Raje does not surface.

Question: How do you deal with this in performance? Do you tell other musicians to change their notes slightly?

The musician should already know this and have the same energy as me when he wants to enter Bayate Raje. It must also be noted that it is more difficult for the instrumentalist to do this, because when I change the note "E" I can always come back to the original, but the instrumentalists can't be as flexible—if he changes his frets for that gushe, he will have difficulties later on in other gushes. So that's why sometimes it seems as if we are not in tune; this problem does indeed exist. There's nothing you can do!

Perhaps it's better to keep quiet, then, during some passages.

Yes, exactly—they realize this and they do not play, because it becomes irritating. These are the things that I have always considered and have sung. Dr. Barkeshli, who followed music from the point of view of physics, asked his pupil Mr. Naji, who plays and makes great tars and was the person who replaced Dr. Barkeshli at the Iranian Institute of Art after he passed away, to go and find out from Shajarian the most authentic scales of Persian music. He realized that I sing very accurately. He measured the scales on machines and realized that in certain gushes, some of my notes are different than other scales. So he told Naji to go and learn that particular gushe from Shajarian because he is the one who sings these scales correctly. So Naji recorded different dastgahs while I sang and he would take those recordings and measure them.

Usually when the ensemble goes on stage to do a sound check, I stand by the soundboard technician and will tell him, for example, to add more frequencies of 250 hz range or lower the frequencies at 2500 hz or the 6000 hz and instead add more frequencies of 800 hz. I mean, I really understand frequencies and when I suggest something to the operator he will instantly do it. Recently, one sound engineer told me that he has never encountered such sensitive ears in his life. Because he had a computer, and when I told him what to do, he could check it with his computer and realize that it was exactly right. This is why my expertise is in the voice and sound. (2008)

AK

Shajarian is very particular about sound quality and takes the acoustics of the hall and the particular sound system into account for every concert. In addition to making specific adjustments to the sound system, he will adjust the way he uses his voice to further enhance the particular environment and acoustic circumstances. Most singers rely on the equipment to do this but he goes a step further to adjust his technique to get the best sound possible. So he is paying attention to the acoustic occasion as well as the social occasion.

Diction

In spite of the clarity of diction Shajarian was capable of delivering in his early recordings—for example, on his debut performance on Barge Sabz #216 (dis-

cussed in chapter 3), where he seems to deliberately take care with the words—
most people couldn't make out the words he was singing in much of his work
before the revolution. Of course, everybody agreed that he was a good singer but
it was often difficult to understand his diction because he was eating the words.
But right now he is the only one presenting words with great care and clarity,
much better than anyone else.

He doesn't like to hear this about his earlier work but he said that Banan
once told him to "sing like you're speaking." Why does he give that advice? I'm
going to take one step back and try to interpolate the situation. If I'm a master
like Banan and I liked Mr. Shajarian, who is kind to me, I want to give him good,
honest advice. I will advise on something that he really needs. And the results are
evident: before the revolution, no one can decipher the words, but after the revolution he's articulating words exactly the way they are meant to be heard in the
Persian language. So that's the difference, a major change, it's in fact a major
achievement in his work.

We have to remember that Shajarian was a very good student and he was
trying to fulfill the wishes of his teachers. The first time he met Boroumand,
Boroumand told him that "you're not presenting the music very well the way
you're singing."[6] He's complaining. And the second time Shajarian sings for him,
he tries to fulfill his wishes. So I'm going one step back and watching this conversation and noting that Boroumand is making a recommendation and getting a
different result from it. That's Shajarian's character, to try to fulfill the demands
of the master. He's trying to make them happy, get their approval. He changes his
style at this time because he knows Boroumand is a good teacher. And coming
from Qur'an tradition, Shajarian understands the difference between Arabic and
Persian phonology. In that tradition presenting the text of the Qur'an is of paramount importance, it's your top priority and your singing is secondary. So when
he moves to Persian classical music, because he had that talent, he knows how to
apply this to *avaz*. He does it because he wants to fulfill this master's wishes and
follow the aesthetic thinking behind those wishes. "You have to sing radif *exactly*
the same as we show you because you are the protector of this music, you must
try to preserve this music. So if you want to get my approval you have to sing this
music exactly the way it should be."

I think that the most important person he got the radif from, his most important source is Boroumand. He learned radif from Mehrtash and Boroumand:
he got the core radif from Mehrtash but the presentation of it, with the words in
relation to poetry, he got from Boroumand (but not the word painting, discussed
below that came later). For one thing, Boroumand didn't want him to use a lot of
long tones. He wants Shajarian to sing one portion of the poem right away with
no rhythmic digression. He didn't like a lot of melismata between words. He says
"you're using a lot of long tones. Make it short and then you can use a *tahrir* later.
So do not add too much here—*keshesh nadeh* ("don't make it so long")—that's too
long for this poem." So, there's the proof that the poem was not very important in
that style because you're basically killing the poem with that kind of approach.
No one can follow what's going on with the text: there's the first line and then

one minute later the second and then another minute later the first again. Nobody can understand what he is saying. Boroumand helped him to clarify his use of text with the radif.

There are many local accents and dialects of Persian and it's interesting how singers who speak in a particular dialect will sing in the so-called "standard" pronunciation of Persian currently cultivated in central Iran and used for public broadcasting. The accents involve the lengthening or shorting of syllables and the color of certain vowels, so there are both rhythmic and tonal differences that usually get flattened out in avaz. Occasionally you can hear a singer and you can tell where they're from: Iqbal Sultan, for example, showed he was from Azerbaijan. When Ostad Shajarian is around people from Mashhad, he speaks with a Mashhadi accent, but this is otherwise only very slightly detectable in his usual speech, which is mainstream Tehrani Persian. His diction when singing with classical Persian is very clean.

There is a lot of flexibility for setting the words to a melody in avaz but you need to take care not to prolong syllables in a way that cuts the word, breaks its flow at a bad spot, thus distorting it. It's also a matter of balancing the whole of each phrase and the whole poem, keeping the pace of the words even, not rushing through some and over-extending others, shifting tempos in a random way. In Persian the word one aims for is *qarine*, "symmetrical, matching." You can and must have contrast in the delivery but it must relate to the unity of the whole. Some singers get caught up in each phrase and they aren't aware of the big picture, the overall form. Good singing should follow the model of the natural contours of clear speaking—proper accents, pronunciation, and rhythm. It should be consistent and natural.

Materials

RS

As noted in chapter 1, from the perspective of performance theory, the occasion is the main "proto-performance" of avaz, its starting point and impetus. Performances of avaz implement "proto-tools" through which musicians engage in the reiterated behavior that defines the art, craft, and tradition. The proto-tools or traditional preset materials used in avaz performance are classical poetry, the radif, and its substratum of a relatively small number of background melodic profiles or paths, short melodic themes and more generic motives (which Shajarian regards as being analogous to words in language) that constitute a more or less continuous centonic fabric.[7] Poetry obviously supplies a vast range of semantic signifiers—symbols, narratives, characters, philosophies, etc.—shared by Iranians, and arranged in infinite combinations. The form and structure of the radif functions in a corresponding manner to the plot, subplots, episodes, characters, and the idiomatic figures of speech found in the epic narratives from which a bard or *naqqal* improvises a unique performance. Of course, all narrative performance traditions have their proto-tools. Among them the bard's art is probably the closest to that of avaz, with a wider (and occasionally overlapping) repository of texts and the preset melodic materials resources of maqam (e.g., Blum 1972; Youssefzadeh 2002). *Ta'ziyeh* and *ru-howzi* have their own stock characters and plots, the *naqqali* their *tumar*, all of which have fed into the stock characters of Iranian film.[8] From structural outlines through to surface details, the "materials" are rendered with freedom through interpretation.

Corroborating common sense, neurologists both theorize and find mounting evidence that the establishment and storage of mental schemata—structural templates, prototypes or attractors—play a major role in musical cognition and generation (Levitin 2006). The traditional poetic forms of *ghazal*, *masnavi*, *dobeyti*, and *ruba'i* function as structural schemata for textual aspects of avaz and also play a significant role in shaping musical structure, while the radif provides the fundamental schemata for all levels of musical structure from background to foreground, in addition to its ingeniously embedded pedagogy of generative processes and grammar.[9] While scholars have questioned the validity of such a "vocabulary and grammar" model posited to describe language (e.g., J. Becker 2004:6–7), and more particularly its transposition as an analytical tool for musical traditions, it is an eminently useful and relevant approach for gaining an accurate yet clearly partial view of avaz performance. More importantly for our purposes here, Shajarian is adamant and unequivocal in his conception of avaz as a language.[10] There is, of course, never any "one thing" going on in the complex activity of musicking but rather multiple layers and strands of ever emerging phenomena: in this case the "vocabulary-grammar" paradigm is greatly complicated by intersubjective communication in a given occasion/performance context; the affirming of cultural (and increasingly crosscultural) identity; the myriad subjective emotional responses and perceived significations of the performance; and the mixing of musical and poetic media, among other factors. And just as the vast majority of humans over dozens of millennia have had complete generative competency in their languages without the slightest cognizance of what a suffix, direct object or subordinate clause is, we should not be surprised to find that musicians create and perform without conscious awareness of centonic materials and their usage (cf., Nooshin 1999:147ff., 385). Our explication and interpolation of vocabularies and grammars exist on an etic, theoretical level that is nonetheless empirically demonstrable and can be practically useful; the ultimate value of such explication is (rightly) a matter of subjective opinion. The following discussion on materials provides partial yet useful interpolations of the generative process of performing avaz. The perspective is synchronically centered on contemporary practice and is not asserting (nor excluding the possibility) that this interpretation was deliberately embedded by the Farahani family in their consolidation of the repertoire.

The Persian Poetic Tradition

It is both a trite understatement and a stereotype that Iranians love poetry. Definitively, poetry presents the primary resource of avaz. The richness and significance of poetry in Iranian culture, past and present, is remarkable by any standard, perhaps even unsurpassed. Dabashi argues that Iranian cultural and ethnic diversity defies the stereotyping so essential to nationalistic construction, and that Iranian identity is best understood or defined by literary humanism (*adab*), particularly the archetype epitomized by the itinerant Sa'di (2005: 12–31).

> The majority of Iranians are not "Persian," meaning the Persian language is not their mother tongue. But even a cursory look at the history of Persian literature shows that all the masterpieces of classical Persian literature were in fact created by poets and literati from "the provinces." Rudaki and Ferdowsi were from Khurasan; Nezami and Jami were from modern-day Afghanistan . . . if these poets were around today Tehranis would make fun of their accents, were they to recite their own poetry. Rumi's ghazals will not even rhyme properly sometimes unless we read them with what today Tehranis would condescendingly call an "Afghani accent." (Dabashi 2007:286–87, n.16)

While obvious to the Iranian listener, cultural outsiders interested in Persian music must not forget that it is the poem that presides as the main focus in a performance of avaz.[11] Of course the aesthetic impact of the poem is greatly increased with an effective musical setting: the art of avaz is, precisely, coupling and maximizing the effect of the two media with taste, skill, and inspiration.

Shajarian repeatedly maintains that there can be no good performance of avaz without an intimate understanding of the poem being sung (e.g., 1993:44; various quotes below); quite above and beyond matters of vocal technique and command of musical materials and parameters, a good singer must be able to choose poems to be set with "taste and talent" (Kasmai 1990:4). This comprises the fundamental rhetorical stage of *inventio*: the invention of the appropriate "arguments" to support the intention of one's statement. Among other qualities, Shajarian is distinguished from other singers by his deep literary knowledge of Persian poetry, which he acquired through methodical, diligent selfstudy and in consultation and dialogue with scholars, poets, writers, critics, and philosophers. He routinely spends much of his time and energy perusing and studying the huge Persian canon. Digging deeply, he mines the literature of ancient poems and reanimates them through his avaz, which is then recorded as a document that other musicians and listeners will draw upon for further performance applications. Shajarian's work thus functions as an important bridge between cultural knowledge as stored media and as embodied performance (Diana Taylor's archive and repertoire, respectively), propelling and propagating a vigorous feedback between the two. Moreover, from the

1980s onward Shajarian's use of the archive is immediately performative, for he takes great liberties in editing and arranging the contents of a poem or group of poems to suit his needs in setting them as avaz (detailed further below).

Shajarian's Selection of Poetry

Ostad Shajarian's profound knowledge of the literature and its hermeneutics directly informs his avaz and sets him apart from other *khānandes*.While Shajarian draws liberally from the vast legacy of Persian poetry, the majority of his selections are taken from the *ghazals* of Sa'di and especially Hafez. Among musicians and connoisseurs of avaz, Shajarian is often affectionately referred to as a "child of Hafez." Hafez is of course the most revered classical Persian poet in Iran[12] and, in addition to his general cultural cache, carries a particular intellectual prestige among the classical poets as well. There is an intrinsic musicality in Hafez's poetry, recognizable even to cultural outsiders, that makes it an ideal vehicle for avaz. In a letter of 1857, the renowned Khayyam translator Edward Fitzgerald wrote that Hafez's "*best* is untranslatable because he is the best Musician of Words" (Quoted in Avery 2007:15).

Other classical poets that Shajarian draws upon with some frequency include Attar and Baba Taher. While rarely drawn upon for the poet's work, his recording of Omar Khayyam (the date is unclear but likely in the 1970s) was hugely successful in Iran.[13] He occasionally sings modern poets such as Hushang Ebtehaj, Mehdi Akhavan (his most popular setting of contemporary poetry is Akhavan's *Zemestan*), Fereydoun Moshiri and others.While Shajarian's emphasis is not at all surprising, the relative paucity of avaz settings of Rumi is noteworthy;[14] though he turned to Rumi more frequently in the early 2000s for his albums released by World Village, targeting a North American audience. In general, he uses Rumi in tasnifs or Masnavis and only rarely as the main body of the avaz. Shajarian discusses the significance of Rumi in the film *The Voice of Iran,* noting his unique status to all of humanity and, while making a case for his overriding Persian-ness, feels that it's "best not to issue him an ID card."

Some reasonably hard statistics to back up this profile are provided in Table 4.1, showing the distribution of poets used in Shajarian's avaz recordings (excluding tasnifs) throughout his career. Much of the *Golhā* data (poetry for seventy-one of the one hundred programs he recorded that could be clearly identified) may reflect the producer's choices rather than Shajarian's. The *Golhā* data indicate one poem sung as avaz for each program, while the "Delawaz, etc." (some albums are not released by Delawaz)[15] data include different poems or excerpts of poems and poets on a single album. Based on these quirky properties the overall distribution is given below in Table 4.1.

Table 4.1. Distribution of Poets in Shajarian's Recordings

Poet	*Golhā* programs	Delawaz, etc.	Total
Hafez	32	46	78
Sa'di	23	28	51
Bastami	8	0	8
Ebtehaj	5	4	9
Rumi	2	5	7
Baba Taher	1	13	14
Attar	0	16	16
Other	n/a	13	13

Distribution in terms of percentages of the above recording categories:

Hafez	36.8%	39.7%
Sa'di	22.4%	26%
Attar	12.8%	8%
Baba Taher	10.4%	7%
Rumi	3.2 %	3.5%
Other	15.3%	13.6%

Table 4.2 provides a detailed view of the distribution of poets in Shajarian's Delawaz recordings (in chronological order). On this table each "x" indicates a separate poem performed (as far as can be determined).

Table 4.2. Distribution of Poets on Delawaz Recordings

Album Title: Persian/English	Hafez	Sa'di	Attar	Baba Taher	Rumi	Other
Golbāng 1	x	x				
Golbāng 2	x			x		
Bidad	x					
(Homayoun)	xx					

Title:	Hafez	Sa'di	Attar	B. Taher	Rumi	Other
Astan e Janan	xx			xx		
Serr e Eshgh		x		x	x	
Nava Morakab khani		xxx		x		
Dastan		xxx				
Payam e Nasim	xxx			x		
Del e Majnun	x	x			x	
Khalvat Gozide	x					
Delshodegan	xx					Moshiri
Asman e Eshgh			xxxx			
Yad e Ayam	xx					
Cheshme-ye Nush	x			x		
Jan e Oshagh	xx			x		
Gonbad Mina	xx			x		
Homayun Masnavi						'Iraqi (xxxx), Kashani
Saz e Ghesse Gu & Konsert	x					
Bozorgdasht Hafez	x					
Eshgh Danad	x			x		
Rosvayie Del		x	x			

Title:	Hafez	Sa'di	Attar	B. Taher	Rumi	Other
Shab e Vasl	x	x				
Moammaye Hasty	xxx					
Rast Panjgah	xxx					Nizami
Chehre be Chehre	x					
Shab, Sukut, Kavir			xxx	xx		
Sarv e Chaman (Switzerland & US)	xxx	x		x		
Aram e Jan		xx				
Ahang e Vafa	x	xx				
Bahariyeh	x					
Raz e Del						Ebtehaj (xx)
Entezar e Del	xx					
Bouye Baran					x	Moshiri
Peyvande Mehr		xx				
Zemestan Ast						Akhavan
Bi To Besar Nemishavad			xxx		x	
Faryad	x	xx				Moshiri (xx), Ghorrat ol Ein

Title:	Hafez	Sa'di	Attar	B. Taher	Rumi	Other
Ghoghaye Eshghbazan		x				
Soroud e Mehr	xx	x	x			
Saz e Khamoush	xx	x				
Ah! Baran	x		x			
Rendan e Mast	x	x				
Ghasedek		xx	x	x	x	

Delawaz album covers; Shajarian et al. 2004:317 ff.

Ostad Shajarian selects poetry according to the occasion for which the performance occurs, taking into account the particular audience, time of year, function, context, and general atmosphere of the performance. As noted in chapter 2, avaz enacts a secular version of the clerical practice of *monāsebat khāni*—the selection of texts appropriate to the occasion, an indispensible skill for religious singers. While his selection is sometimes made spontaneously right before a performance (particularly at small private gatherings[16]), his process is much more carefully calculated for his recordings and international tours, as discussed below. This underlines the importance of the social context of the performance and the definitive characteristic that an effective performance of avaz unites and harmonizes musical expression, poetic effect, and performance context. Ideally the performer establishes a powerful and focused correspondence: music reflecting the poem, and the poem reflecting the occasion.

OS

I am very interested in poetry that is about my people and the history of my people (2008). I am meticulous about the poetry I pick and its synthesis with music. Every time that I have a concert, I usually go through my books several times to find an appropriate ghazal and sometimes I am forced to change it over and over. This process is greatly dependent on my mood and my acquaintances and the people among whom I live. If I don't have good poetry in my hands I can't sing good-quality avaz. The idea behind choosing the poetry of Hafez is that each and every artist generally chooses to polish one particular precious stone for himself. So the poetry of Hafez is like that jewel for me.

The artist should search for a poem that has a message for his own particular time and present it. In my view, the meter and the structure of the poetry are not as significant as the implication and the meaning of the poetry. It is not important what the form is, it does not make a difference if it is ancient or classical or contemporary and modern poetry (Shajarian et al. 2004: 219, 221). The poems ones sings must be chosen with taste and talent, for the most appreciated singers are those who choose the most beautiful verses that express profound thoughts.[17]

What I personally like to do is to find a really good poem, usually from Hafez, Sa'di, Rumi or Attar—one of these four. Hafez and Sa'di are very highly regarded in their art of poetry and Rumi and Attar are very powerful from the viewpoint of mysticism. I always want to deliver my poetry to the listener in a way that she can really understand it, and be moved by the poetry in a way that she could never think was possible before. I am the one who gives it this powerful meaning through my technique. It is all based on the meaning of the poetry. Even when I compose tasnifs I sometimes reject very beautiful melodies just because they do not match with the meaning of the poetry. I want my poetry to be heard— that is usually my goal. For us Iranians, poetry has the highest status in art.

The hardest thing for me to do regarding my concerts is to pick my poetry. I mean, I really get frustrated, especially these last years. The reason is due to the fact that I have sung all the good poems from Sa'di, Hafez, Rumi, and Attar and now I have no poems to work with if I want to put a concert together. At the same time, I don't permit myself to sing inferior poets. Although you might be able to find one or two good lines in their poems, not all of it pleases me. I mean, I cannot even sing it. If the poem is not top-quality I cannot sing it. This is because I choose my poems for my concerts and my albums with the energy and the feelings of the people and society. Sometimes, two or three days before my concerts, I suddenly realize that my state and my energy towards my environment have changed or that I am in a place that has no energy. In these cases I immediately change my poems and choose one that fits with my new state. (2008)

The great poets like Hafez, Sa'di, Mowlana, Attar, and Khayam are like the diagram of our culture, as well as a mind set. So if I see something in my society that I want to express and take up, I will realize that this particular concept has been mentioned by Hafez in the most profound way. Because Hafez has expressed himself in a more beautiful way, I use his words. When I choose to talk about a particular issue, I go and search among the works of these poets, and when I absolutely sense that I have found what I'm looking for, I will present it. But I must emphasize that when I present it, the words are no longer Hafez's, they are my words because I am singing it. I go so deep into its form that they become my thoughts and my words, with a difference that I have borrowed them from Sa'di or Hafez. At that stage everything is in service of the poetry. I also have to present it correctly. Our poets have lived among their people and have expressed their concerns, and history is always repeating itself, so our youth are also interested in this poetry and also avaz, because it too expresses their concern.[18]

I think that good music does not need words. Good music can say what it wants to say without using words. But sometimes the combination of music and words are necessary. Imagine if I did not choose to use Hafez for my Bidad *CD. I probably could deliver the same feeling without any poetry. But the point is that the listener must be familiar with the music to understand its meaning. The language of music is of course a specialized field but even ordinary people can understand its meaning. Music is truly an amazing thing! The person who is a professional will understand its meaning and the nonprofessionals will also realize its message, so it really doesn't need any words.* (Shajarian et al. 2004: 228)

Poem Shaping the Structure of Avaz
RS

Once selected, the poem dictates the structure of the impending avaz in a number of ways. Diverse musical options are built directly into the poem. As noted by Ostad Shajarian, the semantic content of the text first and foremost prescribes the overall Affekt and hence selection of an appropriate dastgah, and for individual lines, selection of an appropriate gushe. The unfolding "narrative" of the poem (the term applies loosely here) suggests a dramatic profile which is mirrored in the musical setting through the use of range, dynamics, modulation between gushes, sectionalizing, and overall emotional intensity. Even ghazals, where each couplet can form a selfcontained, independent idea, usually string together such quasi-independent semantic entities in a manner that suggests continuity, leading to the final couplet which provides some sort of punchline—a conclusion, resolution or summarization—not unlike the last couplet of an Elizabethan sonnet. The length of the poem likewise affects the duration, proportioning, and pacing of the avaz, its density of text setting, amount of rhetorical repetition, and placement of instrumental modules (introductions, interludes, *zarbi* pieces, etc.). The poetic meter (*aruz*) controls, suggests and delimits the setting of melody in terms of foreground rhythm and phrasing hierarchy, though there is a wide range of flexibility, which we will examine in detail below in discussing the musical foreground.

In reference to observations of the radifs of Karimi and Davami, Hajarian further notes a correspondence with the placement of the ultimate rhyme or repeated words of a couplet that recur throughout the ghazal (*radif*) with the melodic forud of the dastgah. While on the one hand this would appear to be necessarily so by definition—the final line of text (containing the *radif*) will be accompanied by the final phrase of the gushe (which often includes the forud)—longer *shah* gushes, especially as treated in the improvisations of individual singers, have various potential stopping points before their ultimate conclusion, which may or may not include the forud[19] as it may in the radif. This observation from the radif is generally not a generative tactic used in avaz performance and brings us to a more fundamental issue regarding vocal radifs, avaz performance and contemporary scholarship. Following the tradition of Forsat's *Bohur al-Alhan*, Davami and Karimi personally conceived the radif as including the prescription of specific poetry for specific gushes, a position that has been taken up by a number of ethnomusicologists either explicitly or implicitly (e.g., Miller, Wright, and Hajarian). It is not shared by

Ostad Shajarian or the majority of musicians in our experience, despite Davami's and Karimi's huge influence as teachers. As we will see shortly, this is precisely the point: they were significant as teachers, not performers. The radif is a complex, non-linear entity, and there are indeed a small number of gushes with traditionally-assigned poems. As one would expect, Shajarian adheres to the traditional convention of poetry associated with particular *gushes*, e.g., performing Charbagh of Abu Ata to Esfahani's "*Che shavad be che reye zard-e man,*" or Sufiname of Esfahan to Hafez's "*Biyā Sāqi ān mey ke,*" and the like. But for the majority of musicians, and the vast majority of gushes in the radif, any poem may be sung to any gushe. All of these relationships are discussed in greater detail as they appear below in examining the main structural and practical layers of avaz from background to foreground.

AK

The meaning of the poem, regardless of the rhythm, rhyme scheme or other formal attributes, leads the singer to the specific gushe—the meaning directly relates to the scale (*māye*), the intervals, the sounds existing in the Persian musical tradition.

When you're choosing a ghazal to sing, usually one or two lines from the poem catch your attention and attract you to it. These lines of course become very important in setting the avaz. Some ghazals are developmental, where subsequent lines comment upon, complement and enrich earlier ones, like in an essay, but more often each line has its own meaning and can stand on its own. Mr. Shajarian will often reorder, mix, and omit beyts in his delivery of a given ghazal. Some lines feature individual words that are particularly strong and evocative—e.g., words like *'eshq*/love, *serr*/secret, Saqi/cupbearer, *torā*/you, *morā*/me, or the poet's name (*takhallus*)—even if the line within which they appear is not very important or profound. A good singer can identify the most important, climactic beyt or two and highlight them by setting them as the apogee of the performance. Singing loudly was a practical consideration in the preamplification period of public performance and it was of course regarded as an admirable quality, especially the ability to sing loudly and for a long time (cf., values of religious singers in Reckord 1987:98ff). I think those values remain today when people evaluate avaz singers; singers are aware of this and will set the climactic line of the poem with the highest register and volume.[20]

Shajarian didn't often use his bass register in his early work, especially juxtaposing his higher and lower registers because this could be viewed as a weakness. He started to explore his lower range in the 1980s (a noteworthy example is his setting of Nahoft on *Nava Morakab khani*) and more often from the 1990s and he often shifts between registers in the apogee of the performance for dramatic effect or experimentation.

Vocables and Interjections
RS
Avaz features vocables and interjections that are not part of the text of the poem being set. Entire sections of avaz (i.e., portions between instrumental *jawabs*) can consist of vocables alone; Shajarian often begins his performances with such nontextual expositions of the daramad. Extended tahrirs consist largely of these vocables, though they frequently begin with the last syllable of text and then continue as vocables. His most frequently used vowel, the long "ā," and the long "ō" is also common; he occasionally uses "ī" (ee), and in a few instances sustains "n" for a short stretch of notes. Initial attacks of "y," "d" or "n" are used for phrasing purposes, melodic emphasis and for change vowels in the course of a long tahrir, usually launched with an initial attack. "Akh" occurs frequently at the ends of subphrase, marking off a phrase component within a longer line. The vocable quality can be clearly subordinate to the melodic contour of the line and remain consistent through a phrase. In some performances he plays with the vowel modulation through the course of a phrase, adding an effective and expressive envelope of colour to the melodic line. This technique is likely what Shajarian referred to in his final point in his list of criteria for evaluating an avaz singer—point 15. *"The usage of colour and the manner of voice in tahrir"*—given at the beginning of this chapter. It is interesting to note that attention to the modulation of tone colour was a specialty of Shajarian's hero, Umm Kulthum (Danielson 1997: 93).

Following traditional practice, Shajarian's avaz also features standard verbal interjections that are not part of the poem but often appear both during extended tahrirs ending a line of poetry and in shorter intermediary tahrirs (cf., During 1995:101; Miller 1995:226). Miller (ibid.) reports that Karimi urged singers to be judiciously sparing in their use of such interjections. The most common interjections used by Shajarian are *Khoda* ("God"), *aziz-e man* ("my dear"), *jān* ("soul"), *dūst /dost* or *yār* ("friend"), and, especially from the 1980s onward, *dād* ("justice") and *bidād* ("injustice"). A single word or any combination of these may be used and repeated in a given phrase. While they traditionally function as generic "filler" syllables to alternate with vocables, Shajarian also seems to deploy them semantically in some performances, strategically juxtaposing them with a line of poetry to intensify the dramatic effect.[21]

Radif

OS
The radifs from the past have all been recorded and are available to everyone. Mousa Ma'roufi's radif is notated and has even been performed. There is also the avazi radif of Karimi that has been recorded and transcribed by Dr. Massoudieh. So these are available and one can use those for theory and style. But these are

mostly like formulae or a model: the art of the Iranian musician is to sculpt new
models out of the old ones.

Question: Are you still trying to record your own radif?

No, this has not been done yet, due to various personal problems that I have had.
However, I have sung this radif in different ways throughout my recordings. In
general, singing plain radif is not easy, since you do not have that right emotion:
it is a dry, dogmatic and classical (klāsik) process. I cannot do it. I enjoy it when
I am in the right mood and I start to sing, and I believe that students should turn
towards those kinds of recordings. Learning plain radif is just like learning dif-
ferent melodies, but the students also need to realize that avaz requires tech-
niques of performance, as well as a variety of expressions, and none of these
things are touched upon in plain radif recordings. The real radif happens in the
avaz that is sung on stage or in studio; its characteristics are more transparent in
those circumstances. I don't want students to just learn radif and become radif
experts. In that way they become like Karimi: they don't become singers, they
become radif experts. I want the student to know the radif along with the tech-
niques of singing. So these are the reasons why throughout the years I have
avoided recording my own radif. This way I force students to listen to my avaz
recordings, otherwise they would only listen to the radif and the radif on its own
does not contain that right energy.

But given your position in contemporary Persian music, recording your radif
would become an important historical event and would constitute a major statement and contribution.

My collection of avaz and my recordings have already been accepted and ad-
mired and, in a sense, everyone has already listened to my radif. The difference is
that they have heard it in different performances, in a good quality. At the same
time, there is a collection of the methods of all the past singers in my avaz. New
singers seeking to establish themselves cannot avoid my work.

Do you have any other use for the radif at this stage of your life?

No.

Is your understanding of Abu Ata, for example, different today from what it was
thirty years ago? Are you going deeper into it?

No, I still look at it the same way. But if you have noticed a difference in various
recordings of mine, it is because I always create variety in my works and never
repeat the same thing. I always have to introduce something new and change my
methods of construction, but my view with regard to Abu Ata has always been the
same throughout the years. If I am in a certain mood and want to express the
secrets of my heart and make a statement, I usually do it with Abu Ata.[22] (2008)

The radif is nothing but a formula—the singer must learn it and know it but
afterwards he must try and create on his own. So staying in the boundaries of
radif is not correct either. What is important is the method of singing and how it
is being delivered.

Are you planning on releasing your own radif?

Yes, I am thinking about it but I have performed the avazi radif, every gushe, in
my recordings although they are not all at one place because I wasn't trying to

*record radif per se. So I might have sung the same poem in different gushes. If,
however, one wants to learn my style he or she can find all the radif in my released works.*

 *I am waiting for a chance to record my own radif and name each gushe. But
I would rather sing a short version of the radif and explain where there are extra
features or parallels. If the student knows the melody, then that is all he needs to
know. In the radifs that are available at present sometimes some gushes are sung
one or two notes higher or lower and that confuses the student. This job requires
expertise because the characteristics that differentiate each gushe must be explained. But even more important is the method of avaz, which until now, no one
has paid any attention to. I want to show these methods on a CD or even a DVD
and have notes and suggestions for the students on how to approach it, so those
people who are outside of Iran and do not have access can benefit from it. (BBC
Persian 2007)*

RS

As mentioned in passing above, the radif may be fruitfully viewed as a script or
scenario containing narrative pathways, templates, building blocks, themes with
clear identities, and "plugs" (fragments, filler materials) analogous to plots, episodes,
characters, extras, motifs, decorative idioms and figures. The endless recycling of
these components accounts for a high level of redundancy. Avaz and Persian music
are based on schemata drawn from the radif, both structural and processual or
grammatical; study of the radif reveals a seemingling endless stream of options,
routings, arrangements, development, and variation of a relatively small body of
melodic and rhythmic materials. Through continued immersion in the radif the
student acquires the ability to often predict the set of idiomatic options of a given
phrase or gesture, inductively assilimating an underlying "grammar." There are
always subtle changes to detail and occasional surprises in the flow of the radif—a
coherent and yet essentially fractal quality—that make complete predictiblility
impossible and memorization difficult but generating idiomatic variations relatively
easy. Indeed, the point is clearly to assemble essential structural materials and
understand their idiomatic recombinative and transformational possibilities. While
involving considerably more than mere memorization, the latter is the practical key
to radif acquisition and is therefore also clearly analogous to the rhetorician's
practice of *memoria*, "techniques for memorizing the speech."

 Two important lineages of the vocal radifs exist. The most influential and
widely disseminated is that of Abdollah Davami (1891–1980), particularly as it
was transmitted through his pupil Mahmud Karimi (1927–1984). This radif is
characterized by its cogency and, particularly with Karimi's version,[23] inner consistency of dense transposition and recycling of motives, tahrirs, and entire phrases. The second line of vocal radif transmission is relatively little known. The repertoire preserved by Hatam Askari Farahani (b. 1933) extends back through his
teacher Seyyed Zia Rasa'i (a.k.a. Zakeri) to Seyyed Abdol Rahim, a nebulous yet
influential master active at the turn of the twentieth century. Askari deliberately
restricted his transmission of this very large repertoire to preserve its integrity

from the abuses that can be associated with published radifs (see During 1996). Askari finally recorded this radif but it remains unpublished as yet, with the exception of dastgah Nava (published by Soroush in 1992). It is characterized by its large size due to the greater number of gushes (some eight hundred!), their lengthier duration, and the inclusion of rhythmic types that are normally only associated with instrumental radifs. Askari's nephew Farhad Farhani maintained that the transmission of this radif included anecdotes describing the circumstances regarding the creation of particular melodies—a quasi-epical account of Persian music history (personal communication, 1998).

While the radif is clearly central to the performance of Persian music it has also been subjected to exaggeration and fetishization both among Iranian musicians and Western ethnomusicologists, though for different reasons. The radif is, after all, a relatively recent construction of the late-Qajar period. Among other important contemporary masters, Ostad Shajarian repeatedly maintains that it is not a closed system, that musicians can and indeed should add to it. This is in fact their "job": to fine-tune, update, and revise the definition of the oral tradition of narration. Individual contributions usually remain anonymous. Most creative musicians regard the radif as a flexible springboard for making "new" music according to their own taste and idiosyncracies while a staunch minority (and I'm only guessing here at the actual distribution of opinion among Iranian musicians) regard it with a fundamentalist view of unalterable, canonic sanctity. Some authors and musicians feel that this devaluation of the radif is a function of time, indicative of more recent values and that its position was paramount earlier in the twentieth century (e.g., During 1987a:140). Among other factors, this is true because the radif was at that time the latest innovation for musicians: cutting edge, new music that by the end of the fast-moving, densely-packed twentieth century verged on ossified nostalgia when held verbatim. It was still functional for many because it contained the tools and materials for creating music that spoke meaningfully to the present moment as both linear, historical time, and "vertical," spiritual depth.

The radif is unquestionably emblematic as a national monument in the realm of music, a fact in which the complex issues of postrevolutionary nationalism surely play a major role. As noted by Harris (2008), there is a tendency for the canonization of twentieth-century traditional Asian repertoires toward this kind of obsessive iconicity, and that the materials become larger, more complex and unified over time. Canonic length and complexity in Iran culminated in Ma'roufi's rendition, a massive composite of several sources and lineages, published in a lavish limited edition by the government in 1963. Since the revolution, the much more concise radifs of Davami (via Karimi) and Mirza Abdollah (via Boroumand) seem to have claimed the most canonical cache, especially judging from the proliferation of recent arrangements made for a variety of instruments. The quasi-fundamentalist view of the radif and evident widespread promotion of Davami's and Mirza Abdollah's through these publications seems at home with the expectations of conforming to unquestioned authority so vital to the maintenance of the floundering Islamic Republic. It is indeed a good idea for, say, a kamanche player to study Karimi's radif to get a deeper grasp of the repertoire, but is it really necessary to have a separate published arrangement of this vocal radif in order to do so?[24]

As for Western scholars, the unique function of the radif as both a repertoire and a "software" for creative acquisition presents an irresistible urge to subject it to all sorts of systematic analyses, feeding conveniently into a core activity of the scholarly enterprise. While much of this work is revealing and genuinely useful, it is vital to keep the overall point of the radif as a tool for performance in perspective, tempering the endless, admittedly fascinating obsession with its brilliant, fractal structure.[25] Radif analyses need to be read and placed in perspective with regard to the range of individual musicians' conceptions of the canon—from free spirits to fundamentalists. There's surely no shortage of dedicated native informants from camps of both extremes to substantiate one's research. I believe a more balanced, realistic view will reveal that most musicians fall in the middle or lean toward freedom of interpretation. Unanchored in this performance context, analyses can drift into reification of the type famously critiqued by Joseph Kerman among Western musicologists in the 1980s, an argument that is not too different from what musicians like Shajarian level against radif fundamentalists: the radif is not a thing unto itself but rather a means to the end of making music.

For most musicians, playing the radif is not considered performance. Despite the viewpoints of Karimi and Davami regarding the performance of the radif as an end in itself, they (and Boroumand) were not performers but rather guardians of transmission with gifts of prodigious memory. They were essentially, definitively teachers, their function was preservative not creative. This vocation, reflecting personal artistic dispositions, was crucial for the maintenance and transmission of the tradition throughout history but has been seriously undermined by the role of recording technology. While these Ostads are rightfully revered by all musicians for their dedicated transmission of a vulnerable tradition, especially through such a critical period of social change in Iran, as vocalists they were clearly not on the same artistic level as Taherzade, Qamar, Banan, Shajarian or other renowned performers. Ostad Ali Akbar Khan Shahnazi is a unique exception in being both a master of radif transmission and an inspired, creative performer.

Shajarian respects the rigour of the radif and he unquestionably did his homework in learning various versions, but his attitude toward it is emphatically one of freedom and subordination to making "new" music. Inspired musicality trumps theoretical propriety, just as it did when Davud Pirnia overrode the audition committee's recommendation to reject Shajarian for national radio broadcast in 1966. In retrospect this seemingly random turn of events was a bifurcation point for both Shajarian's career and Iranian music history. Had correctness won the day here, it's anyone's guess as to how Shajarian would have fared in the fickle, often irrational machinations and fortunes of the music business. Shajarian's "talented late-bloomer" status in terms of theoretical knowledge probably shaped his later attitude to the radif once he mastered it, with his characteristically diligent work ethic. As he unequivocally states above, his radif is presented and embedded in his recordings, a thoroughly practical orientation that subordinates theory and puts the music itself at the forefront, quite reminiscent of Bach's approach of combining supreme artistry with demonstrative pedagogy in his so-called didactic works,[26] which are at once artistic masterpieces and impeccable, vast theoretical models. Shajarian's recordings—such as the landmark recordings transcribed in this study— may therefore be regarded as the most significant contribution to the radif in the late twentieth century, feeding back, revising, updating and supplementing the older canonical models. It is already evident that his influence is a primary platform of feedback for the younger generation of *khānandes*.[27]

Processes

Composition and Improvisation

OS

Classical Iranian singing . . . is pure improvisation that depends on the singer's sensitivity and state of soul. . . . The singer of avaz must spend long years with a master studying the classical melodies known as the radif. Moreover, he must learn learn to improvise with talent and without limitation, so that, like an experienced orator, he can express himself without losing his breath or referring to a notated or composed melody in front of him. He is at the same time the composer and the interpreter, accomplishing both these tasks simultaneously. (Liner notes to Ocora 559097, 1990:3-4)

RS

While definitively based on a range of preset materials, both structural and decorative, the execution and delivery of Iranian narrative arts are quite consistently improvised. Across sacred and secular genres the *modus operandi* is improvisation: in *naqqali, ta'ziyeh, rowze khāni, pardi dari, ru-howzi,* and clerical homilies. The latter practice often exhibits the freest format, following the tradition of speeches made by Sufi sheikhs (as famously exemplified by Rumi's *Fihi ma fihi*) that were frequently extemporized free associations based on no single theme (de Bruijn 2009:292). It would be more surprising indeed if avaz did not follow these improvisatory approaches. From the practical artistic perspective of a performer, the concept and practice of improvisation is the clearest and most natural thing imaginable. From the scholarly perspective of a musicologist or anthropologist, however, it is an extremely complex subject that brings up a host of problems and issues, even when confined to one particular tradition. The topic of improvisation in Iranian music has received a considerable amount of attention, with most of the normative surveys including some discussion of it (particularly Caron & Safvat 1966, Zonis 1973, During 1984, During et al. 1991, During 1987a, Nettl 1992, Nettl and Foltin 1972); since these earlier studies Nooshin has reinvigorated the topic with several valuable contributions. It is clear from both scholarly and artistic perspectives that improvisation can mean many different things in Persian music.

Nooshin (2003) has drawn attention to the exclusive binary dualism intrinsic to the concepts of composition and improvisation in Western thinking, along with the inadequacy of this as a musicological category and the legacy of colonial subordination it both implied and maintained. Improvisation in this discourse emphasized difference over inclusion to the extent of functioning as an "icon of difference" (ibid.: 258, 247). The composition-improvisation dichotomy doesn't work particularly well with Western music (Schulenberg 1982: 80; Rink 1993; Blum 2001), let alone non-Western traditions, for the creation of music generally features aspects of both processes, which are more fruitfully viewed as a continuum rather than an either/or duality, following Nettl's early influential observations (1974). In a broad crosscultural view, both generative categories involve the variation and interpretation of preset structures. Borgo offers an elegant refinement in describing the situation:

> Composition and improvisation are not mutually exclusive, but neither are they synonymous with one another; they are interwoven and implicated in one another. Mike Heffley [2005:292][28] argues that composition and improvisation are two similar and equal generative forces in the same one music, pushed to either complimentary [sic] or conflicting roles, according to personal and social dynamics. (Borgo 2005: 190)

Like notation itself, Iranians appropriated the alien musical concept of "improvisation" from the West, and with increasing awareness in the past four decades, have employed the term *bedaheh navazi* as essentially synonymous with the Western notion (Nooshin 2003: 262).[29] It is interesting to note that the Persian term was adopted from the tradition of oral poetry (ibid.: 244), showing once again the integral relationship of these arts. Improvised verse or *bedihā-sarā'i* (sometimes referred to by its Arabic equivalent *ertejāl*) dates to pre-Islamic times and was considered the epitome of poetic talent and skill (Bagley 1985). Throughout history a sizable amount of this poetry was transcribed and preserved as miscellanea (often as *robā'ī* and the *qit'a* forms) included in collected works. The practice was cultivated by contests (*moshā'ara*) and continues today for various public occasions—commemorations, meetings, weddings, funerals, etc.—delivered on the spot and tailored to the occasion.

The views of Iranian musicians regarding improvisation highlight both rigorous training and an "idealized mystique" that has "encouraged Iranian musicians to think of their music in a broader global context," especially drawing stereotypical parallels to jazz and Indian music (Nooshin 2003:262). A primary variable in evaluating an improvisation is the degree or extent to which it is grounded in the radif, ranging from strict adherence with only subtle variation of ornamentation (decorating the model which remains consistent) to individualistic fantasies containing occasional vague references to its broader features (essentially disregarding the model). The normative ethnomusicological sources listed above provide further categorization and description of these degrees. The criterion of radif reliance goes a long way in defining an individual artist's style. During feels that improvisation is much more valued in modern times (particularly since the 1960s), by both musicians and the listening public, than in the Qajar period (1987a:35). It was in the Qajar period that the radif was conceived; some observers believe a primary impetus for this was to preserve the classical modal tradition during a period of tumultuous cultural change whereby the performance of radif with little improvisation was perhaps an "academism" conducive to preservation (During ibid.:136; Farhat 1980). The order of the day may have been to batten down all hatches and "stick to the script." Nooshin cautions that the history of the radif is "highly speculative and it is not at all clear that this repertory originally derived from improvisatory practice" (2003: 268).

On the other hand, the oral history of Persian music from the late Qajar period and through the early twentieth century is full of fantastic legends of the great performances of masters who would play one dastgah for an entire evening without repeating themselves, or would never play the same gushe the same way twice, and many other feats of improvisatory prowess (During et al. 1991: 205–06; 247). Wright notes that improvisatory performance practice attached to the radif saved it from becoming an ossified, "frozen music," as became the case with other West Asian, Central Asian, and North African modal canons in the twentieth century (2009: 12). In Persian music, improvisatory excellence is largely a function of the artist's level of inspiration at a given moment, which, as we have seen, is in turn greatly influenced by his or her environment and the receptivity of the audience. The result is the Iranian "silent *tarab*" feedback system discussed above, the ebbing and flowing dynamic of inspirational energy between the artist and the audience. This social feature of musical performance is particularly important in West Asian culture (both ancient and modern) in general, and, again, one which perhaps finds its ultimate precedent and archetype in Qur'an recitation.

It is not surprising that issues of authenticity would arise from expanded improvisatory practice, complaints of musicians stretching out too much (Nooshin 2003:262–3), having too much bulk and too little content, distorting the definitive "purity" of the tradition. While such notions as purity are ultimately an illusion, a transient synchronic construction, the controversy is a natural consequence of the existence of a healthy spectrum of individual aesthetic sensibilities within the artistic community—broadly described above as that of preservers, renovators, and innovators (the latter including both iconoclasts and visionaries). Individuals along the continuum of the spectrum have their own critical bandwidths of aesthetic acceptance and, depending on one's position, a particular performance can cross the line into taboo areas of "*harz navāzī*" (self-indulgent, wasteful babble; goofing off) or dull radif quotation, as the case may be. Across the spectrum, a good performance essentially requires a balancing act of expectation and surprise (Nettl 1992: 248ff.; 1974: 411) in a satisfying, tasteful manner. Subjective definitions of the heavily-loaded term "tasteful" seem to lie at the root of the inevitable conflict, in Iran (see During 1994a), as elsewhere. Authenticity was a relatively new issue in twentieth century Iran, one that was exponentially complicated by the Islamic Revolution and the ensuing nationalist/fundamentalist politics.[30]

The creative process operative in Ostad Shajarian's avaz is the result of a complementary engagement of what is conventionally viewed as compositional and improvisatory practices. And while the compositional side of this involves the solitary activity associated with the Western conception of the process, it also involves considerable collective interaction and activity (discussed shortly). The avaz featured on his recordings and in his tour performances is carefully worked out, reworked and refined, often over a period of months. In terms of both process and final product, they are more like the conventional notion of set compositions with variably embellished delivery (cf. Nettl 1992: 252). Works such as *Bidad*, *Zemestan Ast*, and *Dastan* are precisely defined, clearly recognizable, repeatable entities quite distinct from generic improvisations in Homayun or Chahargah. Indeed, when listening to Ostad Shajarian's recordings with him, he will sing the oncoming phrase over the previous *jawab* from memory without preparation. And yet, as the *Dastan* comparative transcription in our companion volume (Simms and Koushkani 2012) reveals, alternate recording "takes" vary considerably. As with improvisatory practices in early Western opera singing, the composition is set but the singer improvises an individual rendition of the piece through ornamentation and cadenzas; avaz practice allows much greater latitude for inserting decoration and improvised flourishes. As we proceed to outline Ostad Shajarian's creative process in the following sections, we note that his craft may be fruitfully viewed in relation to the rhetorican's activities of invention and disposition, which are composed in the conventional sense, while the elaboration is improvised during the action of the performance. The comparative transcription of two complete performances of his work *Dastan* (ibid.) provides a detailed illustration regarding the complex relationship of these processes.

AK

Since the revolution Shajarian works in a particular way before he makes a concert or records, which begins by finding out what is going on in Iranian society. He looks carefully. He looks for the best poem, one he thinks is really suitable to the social situation, and then he starts to work on the music for it: he essentially composes his avaz. It's like a composition, he decides which gushes are set to which verse, where to place the climax of the piece, what the appropriate pacing is. This process takes place over a period of months, maybe four months. He told me "I take my time," and that's his working process. He doesn't simply choose the poem the night before and then improvise the first thing that comes to his mind. He sings it in different places—in his garden, in private performances, gatherings—and he thinks deeply, shaping the avaz. He rehearses the music with different accompanists and sometimes he gets some ideas from people who are particularly knowledgeable about poetry and social or political matters. After that he starts to rehearse with the group he'll be recording or touring with and they create the introduction, zarbi sections, overall arrangement, etc.

He chooses the poem and then he works on it. And why? This is one of our subjects, discussed in detail below: word painting. He tries to create the best music for that poem. He consults with experts to understand the poem so that by the time he turns to the music, he understands the poem very well. He works out the musical details according to his own feelings, taste and sensibilities regarding Persian classical music. You have some autonomy when you're doing this, for example, things such as choosing the space left between words. He has become a master of that. How he pauses and where in the phrase he places this. Earlier in his career Shajarian never used a lot of bass tones but he gradually moved toward more use of his low register. Previously, most singers thought it was impressive to show off and sing loudly and in a high register but that was against Shajarian's beliefs and what he was working on. So his techniques and his aesthetic ideas are related as he creates his art in the occasion.

Varying and Elaborating Templates

An essential generative process in the performance of avaz (both vocal and instrumental) is the variation and development of structural templates that exist at the levels of the foreground phrase and middle ground gushe, activity subsumed under the rhetorician's category of elaboration. As just noted above, the primary generative mode here is improvisation. Tactics, gestures, and techniques are encoded in the radif and used but not explicated in the practical discourse of musicians. Ethnomusicologists[31] have observed these to include, among other possibilities: segmentation and sequencing of phrases and tahrirs; the expansion or contraction of the number of notes and/or range of a phrase (or tahrir) through successive repetitions; varied ornamentation or articulation in repeating a phrase, which can range from extremely subtle and fractal-like[32] to explicit; varying rhythmic density, placement and balance of long-held notes vs. florid movement; shifts of tempo; transposing rhythmic melodies into free rhythm and vice versa; paraphrasing melodies; transposing melodies into different scales; among instrumentalists, the antiphonal alternation of register; the selection of phrases from a gushe and the amount of development devoted to each; the selection and arrangement of variant phrases derived from different radifs of the same gushe; the inclusion and variation of phrases or other ideas (e.g., articulation, ornamentation, rhythmic features) lifted from other singers.

Nooshin notes that processes involving repetition are the most important elaboration devices and offers a detailed description of various techniques of melodic extension, sequence, and contraction (1996:290–314, 355ff.). The radif also inductively supplies a number of archetypal templates for phrase structures or types that musicians may draw upon in constructing their musical discourse, which can be varied and combined (Nooshin 1996 320–26); arch shapes are the most common though phrase shape and contour is, of course, also determined by the character and structure of the gushe.

"Free metering"

Aruz, the Persian meters of prosody, and the relative rhythmic weight of words in declamation and normal speech (not always the same thing in practice) also function as templates that are varied through the free rhythm. Free meter is a direct bridge, an overlapping, intermediary zone between the music of avaz and the poetry. It is a definitive feature, indeed the *modus operandi* of avaz: the primary means of motion, propulsion, and frequently the suspension of the unfolding of the poem and the music. Singers have a wide range of latitude for taking a line of prosodically conceived poetry and "free metering" it. I prefer considering it as a verb rather than a static, bounded noun, as we are dealing with a process and a dynamic force, something more akin to sailing, surfing, or lobbing volleyballs. Exactly how one free-meters a line depends on one's skill, knowledge, experience, priorities and intensions. It is ultimately a spontaneous, intuitive skill: calculation is necessary, but will be distractingly obvious if overdone and work against establishing a natural flow, which is the whole point. In terms of calculation and options involved, some of the variation/elaboration techniques listed immediately above apply to free metering. Along with mode, free metering sets the atmosphere of the performance, its tempo and "tone" (the latter in terms of verbal discourse or even drama), and free rhythmical play can influence the meaning expressed in a line.

AK

I know many people who dislike nonmetric music—avaz sung or played instrumentally. I often see from the stage when I am performing that audiences get bored at these points of the program, the energy goes down. They get more engaged with ensemble *zarbi* pieces, especially upbeat *rengs* and *tasnifs*. Perhaps the free meter of avaz is more advanced and they don't understand it. We bring more flexibility to music with it, it allows for more freedom: hence the name free meter! For example, you can momentarily go into a passage that establishes a five-beat cycle or some other regular accents in perhaps a different pulse rate. You have a lot of potential there if you pay attention. If the performer and audience are communicating well, you have a lot of creative space, unlike a rhythmic cycle where you are chained to those six beats. Free meter is an excellent tool for evoking various shades of meaning of the poem. It is an intentional tool to facilitate close interaction with the multidimensional meanings within the poem. Finally, the symbolism of free meter is quite deep: you are "outside of time." It's from Hafez's time, it's from today and it's from the time the CD you are listening to was recorded.

"Word Painting"

Let the music follow the sense of the words.—Emperor Chun (China, c. 2300 BC)[33]

Melody is the sensual life of poetry. Do not the spiritual contents of a poem become sensual feeling through melody?—Beethoven[34]

OS
[Upon reviewing the centonic analysis from Simms 1996]
You have to be careful since there are two issues here and you are only consider-ing one. What you have analyzed is only based on the music and tahrirs and their constructions but all these are in relation with the meaning of the poetry and it is because of the poetry that I have decided to launch a certain tahrir at a certain point. Therefore it has to be analyzed in this way, this is the correct way. But if you only analyze a tahrir on its own and without the poetry, then some of its sig-nificance will be lost. Whatever happens with regard to all of my techniques is due to the meaning of the poetry. So in relation to the meaning of the poetry I choose a certain musical setting, and then the tahrir that you hear is again in relation to the construction of that melody, which is in relation to the poetry. Hence, you cannot just look at it from the technical perspective. (2008)

Music is the soul of the poem and the life of the spoken word. Through musical expression of a poem, each word takes on its unique meaning and significance. Hence, to fully express the meanings in a poem, one chooses a maqam, gushe, or melody in harmony with the poem. (CD notes to Kereshmeh KCD–107 [1996], p. 3)

Poetry and music, in the long history of this ancient land, have always been like two wings of a bird that enable it to fly. But music should be independent from poetry because it is poetry that is in need of music. Music is the blood that rushes into the veins of the poetry and it is the life that flows in the body of words. When these two join each other, their beauty and influence reach their highest potential. Music should be the interpreter or translator of the poetry in a beauti-ful and attractive way. (Shajarian et al. 2004: 228)

Those composers are successful who are constantly dealing with poetry and understand the musicality in words. I believe that if a singer does not understand the musicality of words, then why should he even sing? If he does not know it, then stop singing! Those singers who are in command of the music of the poetry can more easily combine words and music together because their training has been with poetry. This is not to say that singers should be composers, but they must be familiar with poetry and its music and meaning. In fact, any musician must be familiar with poetry, whether a composer, singer or instrumentalist. (ibid.:223)

AK

Shajarian's album *Rast Panjgah* (1975) was an important recording for him in terms of its music. The poem worked for him but his target was basically musical: presenting the dastgah Rast Panjgah, which is difficult to sing and based on obscure parts of the radif. The recording *Rast Panjgah* represents a major change in Ostad Shajarian's style and is a very good example of the absence of word painting in his oeuvre. But after the revolution, in *Bidad* he says, "I was thinking about a poem, and I wanted to find music for that poem, where each word would be presented in a proper way, and contributing to an escalating argument."[35] He wanted to take it from Hafez and make it to suit his own needs. This kind of job is more difficult because you have to manipulate the music. You must be a greater expert in order to set the music in a flexible situation compared to simply bringing out the obvious outline of the poem. I believe this to be the source of all the invention of Shajarian's avaz. He's engaged in word painting as deep as possible in relation to its *iham*, which is such a definitive aspect of Persian poetry. So he used this approach, combining it with his technique and vocal ability, the repertoire for the radif, and working on it for several months around that poem, finding the best musical means to convey his painting of the words.

Question: These are just images we're using but what is the relationship between word painting and theatricality, bringing out the drama and the theatre of this? Painting is a visual image but there is also a quasi-dramatic quality involved. Different arts emphasize different means. In the end, Ostad Shajarian's tool is his voice. When he performs in concert, he's not actually using a lot of devices like other people. He probably thought that this was the right way—not showing anything, any emotion, not showing any emotion in his face or using body movement. His voice presents that theatricality. But more recently this theatricality has become physically more prominent, with Shajarian moving a little bit more now compared to before, using his hands and then showing facial expression in relation to the wording.[36] But you certainly see this kind of thing in *rowze khāni* and *madih khāni*, which Shajarian is familiar with. Listen to his *Rabbana* when he sings "*faghfir lana*" which means to forgive, to ask for forgiveness from God. Listen carefully to that portion, he's adding a cracking, a crying texture to his voice[37] at the ending of the words—that's word painting. This conveys feeling and helps signal to the audience that this is the time you can cry.

If you listen to the famous religious singer Moazen Zadeh Ardabili give the *azan* (call to prayer) and his setting of particular words in other sacred recitations, he used a sobbing effect like his voice is breaking for words referring to a specific person or referring to separation and longing, which is something you can hear Shajarian using as well. In Persian culture this sound creates a lot of emotion: it induces you to cry. Using these musical gestures is helping your audience, directing them as to how to listen to the music. So in Iran after the revolution, if someone uses these tools to actually protest something, it's pretty potent. In *rowze khāni* that person singing is actually crying with his singing but without tears. All of this is part of the art of word painting.

Sometimes Shajarian breaks the tradition when he feels he's not on the right path in serving of the poem, which lends more creativity to his work. For example, there aren't a lot of melodic leaps in the radif tradition but in some of his work we find that he's leaping around.[38] The reason he does that is because he wants to support the chosen meaning of the poem, he wants to break the flow and modify the original conjunct character of the melody. He introduces these sudden changes to focus attention on the essence of the music itself.

RS

On its own, without words, music is abstract not denotative. Avaz brings semantic content to melody, just as the great recycler Handel would set words to his instrumental melodies that would propel them into a new aesthetic dimension. From another angle, the strategic choice of mode and deployment of free metering can serve to spin or enhance the meaning of a poetic text in a manner similar to the way in which body language and nonverbal cues in human communication convey a surprisingly high portion of meaning in relation to language, according to recent scientific discoveries. Within a strictly linguistic domain of a nontonal language like English (i.e., unlike Chinese or Mandinka where the tonal placement of a given phoneme directly signifies meaning), accent, pitch, duration, tone colour, dynamic, attack, articulation, etc., all figure into conveying meaning. The words "you're going out" can signify various shades of quite different meaning by manipulating these parameters.

Whether using the metaphors of painting or drama, which are so integrally related here, avaz functions to animate the words of poetry silently entombed on the page. It's important to qualify that the term "word painting" as proposed by Amir Koushkani and used throughout this study is generic and devoid of the specific usage it carries by musicologists of Western music to denote melodic gestures miming specific words—such as ascending melodies for "and He ascended into heaven," descending for "He descended into hell" or repeated leaping intervals to illustrate the words "up and down," recapitulating the music for "as it was in the beginning" and other clichés that especially characterize music of the late Renaissance and Baroque periods. While not entirely out of the question and indeed occasionally occurring in avaz, this mimetic approach is not what is meant by the term in the context of this study. It rather refers to evocation of the inner meaning of the text with a corresponding musical ambiance or engagement of signifiers (some with a specific cultural meaning that may border on the Western notion of word painting), more of an x-ray of the words than an illustration.[39] In Shajarian's avaz, word painting also serves to elicit specific layers of *iham* embedded in the poem. Evocation and animation necessarily involve qualities of dramatization and ultimately persuasion, and hence rhetoric. The term implies a nice ambiguity of words painting the music and/or music painting the words.

This conception of the relationship between music and lyrical content is widespread in West Asia and beyond. Egyptian Qur'anic reciting places emphasis on "heightening the meaning" of the words via their recitation (*taswir al-ma'na*), which was effectively transferred to secular song by Umm Kulthum (Danielson 1997:57,

141ff.), aspiring to the ideal that "the meaning of the text be the focal point of the rendition and that the singer draw out and enhance the poem somehow or other" (ibid.:148). American composer Harry Partch was a paradoxical conservative icono-clast, radically rejecting just about everything that Western art music had passed on to him while trying to restore what he termed the "Corporeal" ancient Greek primacy of the text and music's service to it (1974:15–17). Latin texts didn't count and are denounced as "Abstract" because the text must be immediately intelligible to the listener.[40] While Shajarian is explicit in his conception of text and music, we have seen that the field of Persian music is large, diverse, and predicated on the personal aesthetic dispositions of individual musicians. In his study of the avaz of Touraj Kairas, Wright remains sceptical about the role of the poetic text as a driving force in the aesthetic experience of avaz for both performers and listeners, presenting evi-dence that relegates it to the back seat while purely musical parameters take charge (2009:121–24). Indeed, Shajarian's staunch position on the matter emphatically de-fines his style and differentiates him from other singers.

The deliberate coupling of text and music to enhance meaning is evident in other Iranian narrative performing traditions. Characters in *ta'ziyieh* singing shift modes as the action demands but also employs specific voice stylings and/or modes to differentiate roles[41] (especially differentiating good guys from bad), denotations that are clearly understood by the audience (Shahidi 1979:44). "It is a fundamental assumption of *ta'ziyeh* and of Iranian performing arts more generally that humans who have been properly socialized are able to communicate through singing, wailing, groaning, sighing, and the like, not just through speaking" (Blum 2005: 86). The performance practice of the *bakhshi* and *parde-dari* both involve the individual narrator shifting roles or characters through the use of varied vocal gestures and stylings. Shajarian likewise shifts and manipulates voice in this quasi-theatrical manner, denoting various roles within a poem, e.g., speaking "upward," as a darvish or supplicant speaking to God; or "downward" as a principled human denouncing the injustice of another, regardless of social standing; or a peer-to-peer conversational or soliloquy mode, among others. Williams notes that such use of various "voices" characterize the exposition of the *Masnavi*, wherein Rumi continuously oscillates between seven different voices of narration: authorial, storytelling, analogical, speech and dialogue, moral reflection, spiritual discourse, and hiatus (2006:xxiff.).

Shajarian began to use abrupt shifts of register to evoke dramatic qualities of the text in the 1982 recording *Nava* (*Morakab khani*) that he employed more frequently in later work. While often clearly evident in his performances, he explicitly notes that his tahrirs are strategically placed and constructed in support of the meaning of the text—a practice that has a particularly powerful dramatic effect. Shajarian occasionally sets a text to a gushe whose proper name evokes or resonates with the content of the text—his most famous and brilliant example being *Bidad*. In the Nahoft ("secret") section of *Nava* (*Morakab khani*), his voice is hushed and mysteriously rarified in his lower register, strongly contrasting with the previous section. This type of intertextual allusion is akin to, though likely not consciously influenced by, the neighbouring tradition of musical punning in the Ottoman *kâr-i nâtik* form and the Western notion of word painting.

Specific examples of Shajarian's word painting are described by Amir Koushkani in the commentary accompanying the discussion of Shajarian's landmark recordings in Simms and Koushkani (2012). His readings are of course subjective but also provocative and informative, showing levels of depth that are easily missed. Following Boroumand's admonition to Nettl (1983:259), this is surely a dimension of avaz that I will "never understand." At the very least, Amir's glosses (which frequently retranslate lines of poetry) are representative interpretations of an educated, informed Iranian who has spent his life with the tradition—the music, literature, and spiritual practice—and who knows the performer on a personal level. While still a single opinion, it is significant, carrying greater weight than those of a casual listener in the absence of the artist choosing to divulge these detailed insights. Even if we had the good fortune of acquiring the latter, we're dealing with *iham* here and "there ain't no answer."

Beyt Ordering, Editing and Rhetorical Repetition

Once selected, Shajarian draws freely upon the contents of the poems he sets in a creative, rhetorical process of *disposition*: *beyts* are reordered, omitted, lines may be later repeated after intervening *beyts*, and fragments of different poems are spliced together,[42] among the most common alterations. His use of the ghazal is performative and clearly endorses the view of the *beyt* as an independent unit. Indeed, as we have seen, the poem is no longer the poet's but rather Shajarian's, to "say what he wants to say" in the same way a director adapts Shakespeare to a contemporary production or film. Shajarian's album *Astan e Janan* is particularly illustrative of extensive *beyt* reordering, while *Nava (Morakab khani)* furnishes a good example of how reordering can be put into the service of word painting.[43] Occasionally single words differ from standard sources (not hugely surprising given the complications of variant readings and editions[44]). These micro changes may be merely coincidental and unintended. It is quite likely that Hafez himself suggested to Shajarian the fruitful possibilities of rearranging *beyts*. In the film *The Voice of Iran*, Shajarian relates how Hafez used the same words as other poets but changed their ordering, which brought out new meaning whereby he "stitches heaven and earth together." His practice would thus appear to be an extension of word painting on a higher structural level.

Like most singers, Shajarian's avaz is characterized by the free use of the rhetorical repetition of *beyt*s, groups of words, and individual words, a heightened form of punctuation in which the word or words are given greater musical and semantic emphasis. It most frequently occurs with either the first or last words of a *misra* but is applied to any word in the line that he feels should be highlighted to enhance meaning in the direction of his spinning of the text. The repetition is improvised and varies from performance to performance—the repetition of key words and expessions is likewise idiomatic in *ta'ziyeh* [Shahidi 1979:48], while the performance practice of Qur'an recitation includes options of repeating individual verses. This strategic use of repetition occurs much more frequently in Shajarian's later work. Presumably the early studio and radio recordings were made under time constraints, allowing much less freedom in this respect, but it doubtlessly reflects his interest in making a persuasive statement with a poem and word painting it that arose in the 1980s. His use of rhetorical repetition is indeed one of the primary means of word painting, evoking different shades of meaning from a given line through deploying varied emphases, melodic designs, ornamentation, and occasionally different modal environments.

Modulation: *Morakab khāni*

Paralleling his free usage of poetic texts, Shajarian brought a useful tool to bear on avaz, one that blows open the structure of the radif as conventionally conceived: *morakab khāni* or "composite, compound" singing. *Morakab khāni* tears down any rigid, grid-like view of the organization of the radif, a declaration of independence from its prescribed modulations and boundaries in favor of a more dynamic exploration of the infinite possible routings of its aggregate contents. This modulatory freedom actually harkens back to the fourteenth-century *kolliyāt* and *kull al-nagham* genres in the Iranian musical tradition, and was still somewhat known in the nineteenth century when the radif was formulated and came to dominate musicking (Feldman 1996:298). It also has a heritage with the performance practice of Qur'an recitation. Shajarian's superior musicianship and exploratory personality enabled him to exploit the limitless frontiers offered by the technique in service of expanding the expressive capabilities of avaz. His brother Siamak observed that Shajarian is able to modulate to any gushe "without hestation" (personal communication, 1995). A definitive characteristic of Shajarian's avaz, it is unclear how his practice is related to more esoteric practices of avaz outside the public sphere. Khatam 'Askari, for example, practiced *morakab khāni* modulation in the 1990s, regarding it in terms of Sufi doctrine as a musical expression of unity and the "fusion of all differences" (During 1996:354n.36). *Morakab khāni* modulation brings Persian music closer to the modal conception, practices and freedom of contemporary Arab and Turkish *maqam/makam*, and for avaz opens up considerably the potential for evoking the Affekt of individual lines of poetry. Rigid adherence to the prescriptions of the conventional modulation sequence of gushes in a given dastgah is clearly a limitation in this regard. Expressing the meaning of a poem is Shajarian's top priority in his mature conception of avaz.

Shajarian explained another practical advantage or reason for deploying *morakab khāni*. In the past some of his performance contexts have been such that musicians dictated the dastgah of a performance based on their compositions at hand, whereby he engaged modulations in his avaz to perform the poem according to his sensibilities and taste rather than being locked into that of the somewhat randomly determined *pishdaramad* and *zarbi* compositions (personal communication, 2008).

OS

Question: What is the role of modulation in Persian classical music today?

Modulation allows us to pass from one dastgah to another in order to better express the emotion of a poem. To sing a ghazal, it's first necessary to discover its music, the music of the chosen poem. I go on the music of the words in order to decide on the modulations and what allows the best expression of the sense of the words. You know that the goal of a singer is to render to the words their signification, and there are not a lot of singers that do this. (Kasmai & Lecomt 1991:249)

AK

The idea of *morakab khāni* comes from Mirza Abdollah and Aqa Hossein-qoli themselves, who were instrumentalists. I believe we have only five dastgahs in Persian music—Mahur, Homayun, Chahargah, Segah and Shur—and the idea of Rast Panjgah and Nava is really a lesson in possibilities of *morakab navazi* of these five dastgahs. Traditionally we are told that these two additional dastgahs were reserved for teaching to advanced students at the end of their radif studies, and were therefore regarded as advanced dastgahs. I remember, for example, Ostad Houshang Zarif saying that Rast Panjgah was part of the *radif 'āliz* (advanced radif) of Ostad Ali Akbar Khan Shahnazi. But they're not dastgahs in my view; they are a combination of these five dastgahs. Recall that early-twentieth century culture looked down on music as an activity for educated people: it was a kind of disgrace to be a musician, who was regarded as a lowly servant even fifty years ago in our society. Most of the great musicians of the Qajar period who established dastgahi music were eager to maintain their own traditional style of musical education, without wishing to expose themselves to Western influences. Their goal at that time, musically speaking, was to preserve the tradition and create a pedagogical system around that tradition. Ostad Abdullah Davami is an example of one of those masters who made sure that everything known was preserved intact. They didn't like change and felt it was their duty to keep the music in its original condition. Of course, there are still musicians today who adhere to this idea. But right now if you want something to stay the same you simply record it and put it in the library, it's going to stay exactly the way you played it and you don't have to worry about it. The concept of "keeping the music the same" doesn't have the same meaning in our era as it did before recording.

But the idea of *morakab khāni* is already in the so-called dastgahs of Nava and Rast Panjgah. After all of the chaotic times and improvised musical transmission, with its lack of uniform pedagogical system, a talented and hard-working artist such as Ostad Shajarian comes along and shows how this technique can be exploited by a vocalist. Most musicians had their hands full enough learning the basic dastgahs and were not ready to go onto this next level of understanding and creative freedom. There was a sense of approval by old teachers regarding *morakab navazi*, which is a different and open way to organize the gushes of the radif. Shajarian was the first vocalist known to present the dastgah Rast Panjgah at the Shiraz Festival of 1975; in all of the *Golhā* programs, I don't remember anyone else doing this. The very title of his cassette *Nava (Morakab khani)* seems to be transmitting this message to us. This is reinforced by his album *Cheshme-ye Nush*, recorded with Lotfi in 1995, which is in Rast Panjgah and likewise presents an exploration of *morakab khāni*, including a substantial departure to Nava.

Words, Sentences and Centonic Weaving: Basic Melodic Motion and Phrase Construction

RS

Parry and Lord's groundbreaking work on formulaic composition in oral epics, conducted and published in the 1930s–1960s, spawned a wide range of applications, adaptations and hypotheses among musicologists working with disparate musical traditions. Formulaic composition is clearly operative in the earliest documented evidence we have: i.e., the cuneiform sources of epic and mythic narration in various ancient Mesopotamian languages dating from the late 3rd millennium BCE, where the technique appears to have been both generative and social (Dalley 2000: xvi ff., 41–42). Distribution of the technique is vast through both time and space, from myriad national epics around the globe and in Western music through plainsong, Baroque *Figurenlehre* theorists,[45] and bebop. Some literary scholars regard the recurrence and reconfiguration of verbal figures as a tell-tale signifier of oral composition (Scholes et al. 1965: 20ff, 50).[46] Like pottery or carpet designs, the repertoire of specific formulae in a given musical tradition (along with the specific microintonation of intervals) is a marker of that tradition and its people, habitually associated with conceptions of ethnicity, and more recently, nationalism. Emblematic of a collective tradition, they are supraindividual, and yet paradoxically the means by which artistic individuality is expressed. Referring to pattern in Japanese visual arts, Yanagi notes:

> Most beauty is related to laws that transcend the individual. . . . The difference between former times and ours is that the individual remained unobtrusive until recently. All used the same patterns without any question of jealousy. . . . In a good pattern man is faithful to laws; one detects in it a true humility. It is good to the extent that it is free of any arrogance or personality. A very strange consequence of obedience to these laws is the increased freedom that then results. The acceptance of limits creates an ease of mind. (1972:117)

I will not dwell upon the theoretical aspects of this well-worn theme nor propose any general theoretical advancement here other than drawing attention to yet another variation, merely noting its empirical existence and describing its "behaviour" or functioning in Shajarian's avaz, which exemplifies a much wider practice among

Persian musicians. As per his words at the opening of this chapter, Shajarian explicates his conception of the process in linguistic terms in a way that is remarkably akin to seventeenth-century theorists of *Figurenlehre* and *musica poetica*: motives are words that the artist links together to form sentences in a process of sentence construction (*jomlebandi*).[47] The primary structural and generative feature at the foreground of avaz is indeed the dense weaving or stringing together of short melodic motives from a rather small repertoire of such stock figures, a process conventionally denoted as centonization (from the Latin *cento*, "patchwork") by scholars of Western plainsong. It is a microrepertoire considerably scaled down and more subtle than the larger structural levels of mode (scale, melody type) or tune family yet functioning in a selfsimilar fashion. Likewise, the restored behaviour for which musical repertoires are a vehicle—we constantly reperform the same scales, modes (and their components), and particular compositions—is evident in the musical foreground, the constant reperformance of a microrepertoire. It is indeed more intensified on this structural level (or fractal scale) as the recurrence of centonic units constitutes the basis of the higher levels.

The formulae of epic singers are verbal, based on narrative themes or events (which could be viewed as roughly analogous to the gestalt of a gushe) and formulae predicated upon prosody, syntax and semantic content: specific formulae recur in very specific contexts. Semantic and syntactic parameters are linguistic and have no equivalents in musical melody. Trietler's seminal adaptation of epic formaulae to plainsong shows how the text influences the placement of some formulae, which function as recitation, cadence, tenor and finalis tones (1974:351), a practice that has clear parallels in avaz, with the *aqaz, shahed, ist,* and *qarar* functions that were conceptualized and explicated in the late Qajar period.[48] Syntactic context is much more ambiguous for instrumental music or nontexted vocal music (i.e., employing only vowels or vocables).[49] I will identify some melodic contexts and functions in the operation of formulae in the detailed description of Shajarian's practice below. Nooshin's analysis and remarks regarding formulaic composition in Persian music are particularly insightful from the performer's perspective:

> Whilst . . . musical creativity may involve a process of "abstracting" certain underlying "rules" which can be reapplied creatively by musicians (much as in spoken language), it is also important to note that memorised formulae (of varying lengths) also play an important role in musical composition/improvisation (as well as in spoken language). Within improvised musical traditions, formulae may be used as "fillers" whilst the musician works at the next creative step, as well as forming the basis for the creation of new formulae.

> (I)mprovised performance in Persian classical music (and with implications for other musical traditions) transcends the simple memorisation of alternative versions of phrases and their subsequent selection and rearrangement in performance (in a similar way to behavioral explanations of language), but the active analysis and recreation of the music through the abstraction of compositional rules and their creative reapplication in different contexts and

with different musical material. Moreover, the system has its own evolving dynamic, and procedures and material can take on a perpetually generative character . . . (P)rocedures may be creatively combined to generate new procedures which when applied to musical material, produce new ideas which themselves become the basis for further development. In this way, the performance tradition comprises an ever changing kaleidoscope of patterns, in which no two musical expressions are the same. (Nooshin 1996: 65; 384–85)

As a result, "like the speaker of language, a musician can perform musical permutations which are both "grammatically" correct and at the same time novel" (ibid.:63), which may be a more clinical way of describing Safvat's notion of an improviser possessing the "soul of the radif . . . whatever we play is 'pure radif' and 'nothing but the radif'" (During 1991:246).

While the most essential step of formulaic analysis is to establish what the individual component units are, some scholars of other musical traditions question the separability or isolation of motivic particles from the overall flow of the melodic lines and run into problems with their cataloguing of the former (Smith 1984:144ff.). Despite the fact that the dovetailing of units can often be interpreted in alternate ways, Iranian practices do not present a particular problem in this regard. A striking feature is the surprisingly small repertoire of units that recur with great density in a very elastic deployment. Lord maintained that formulae are "the symptom, not the cause, of formulaic composition" in epic singing (ibid.:152) and Treitler similarly held that the centonization evident in plainsong did not constitute a generative practice. However, our experience and analyses are corroborated by Shajarian's explicit comments that centonic processes indeed perform a generative function in avaz.[50] Empirical observation and emic performance sensibilities reported by other musicians further support the assertion that centonic weaving is the melodic *modus operandi* of avaz, the fibre of all elaboration of templates and the essential means of melodic motion. The centonic analysis presented in detail below, in the section on the foreground layer, excavates and explicates the basis of this important structural and processual level, isolating the motifs that form its basic vocabulary (according to Shajarian's own analogy). The vocabulary remains largely intuitive and subconscious for most artists, whose business and interests are very practical: to make good music. Upon outlining the analysis to Ostad Shajarian, he at once acknowledged its operative basis but also qualified its significance.

OS
[upon perusing our centonic analysis, presented in detail below]
So you mean you have transcribed the power or ability (tavānāi) *in the art, in the work. So what we talked about was a formula or a model that you can find in books. So I and other artists use these models to unfold our creativity and artistry. So this is an argument about composition, but there is something even more important than composition. That is the creativity that takes place in the moment, and only those artists who are able can achieve that. It is improvisation* (bedāhe khāni). *Improvisation is about being in the right state of mind and singing some-*

thing new that even if one is asked to repeat it later on, one can probably not do it and will instead sing something else. (2008)

Question: When you are drawing upon the style of instrumental melodies and tahrirs do you have one particular instrument in mind?

No, no, there's no particular instrument. This kind of sentence construction is like language, it just flows by itself. I don't even know what I am going to sing until the exact moment. When I start singing they come right after one another. I never think about it before hand, once the poem is finished I think about what kind of sentence construction I should put together and even when I start the tahrir I don't know what's going to happen in the middle or at the end. They just come right after one another until it ends. (2010)

Borrowing from Instrumental Idioms

RS

As mentioned in passing in chapter 1, the relationship between vocal and instrumental styles in Persian music is complex and ultimately unknowable, so interwined and mutually arising are their idioms. More than most singers, Shajarian has consciously integrated instrumental idioms into his avaz, from learning santur in his late teens to his early instruction with Ebadi in phrasing, his aborption of instrumental radifs (*"I studied them all"*), to his great love of repeatedly declared indebtedness to Jalil Shahnaz with regard to phrase construction.

Accompanying Avaz

The dialectic of *saz o avaz*—singing and solo instrumental accompaniment—is an essential, dynamic feature of performing avaz. Like a great jazz musician, Shajarian has played with "everyone" in the Persian music scene at one time or another. During his early tenure with national radio, Shajarian performed regularly with the top instrumentalists of the time, many of them at least a generation older than him. Among the more prominent, these included: Ahmad Ebadi, Reza Varzande, Habibollah Badi'i, Asghar Bahari, Jalil Shahnaz, Mohammad Musavi, Jahangir Malik, Hasan Nahid, Farhang Sharif, Houshang Zarif, Javad Ma'ruffi, Hasan Kasa'i, Mohammad Reza Lotfi, and Nasir Farhangfar. As his career solidified to the point where he could be more selective about his accompanists, he had a tendency to play for stretches of several years (averaging around five years) with a particular lineup, resulting in something of a periodization of his work. In most cases the leader of the ensemble (inevitably the tar or santur player) also supplied composed material—*pishdaramads, tasnifs*, interludes and *rengs*. The following summary maps out prominent accompanists who constituted a more or less regular ensemble for a given period of touring and recording. It's important to emphasize that the situation is very much more fluid and complex than the following tidy profile suggests:

Setar: Ebadi (1960s–1970s)
Tar (and often doubling on setar): Farhang Sharif (1970s), Lotfi (1970s; mid to late 1990s), Pirniakan (late 1980s, 1990s), Alizadeh (early to late 2000s), Derakhshani (late 2000s)
Santur: Meshkatian (1980s), Payvar (1970s)
Ney: Musavi (early 1980s), Jamshid Andelebi (1990s), Abdolnaqi Afsharnia (1980s, 1990s)
Kamancheh: Kalhor (2000s)
Tombek: Farhangfar (late 1970s, 1980s), Mortaza 'Eyan (late 1980s–early 1990s), Homayoun Shajarian (from the early 1990s)

Shajarian has mentioned on several occasions that he finds Lotfi's accompaniment particularly inspiring and, though he doesn't explicitly say so, it's quite evident from his recordings that Meshkatian's were as well.

OS
[Saz o avaz is like] two people sharing a common language, they converse; each person aware of the one's place in the conversation, only speaking as the dialogue demands. Although the instrument does not utter words, the musical phrases chosen by the instrumentalist are in accordance with the poem being recited.[51]
Question: You have sung with many different musicians, from Payvar and Meshkatian to Pirniakan and Alizadeh. What factors determine who you will perform with? What is the dynamic of exchanging of ideas between you and them when performing?
First of all, I never get an idea or an opinion from any of the instrumentalists. I'll do my own work and it is the musician who must get ideas from me and respond to me. It has just happened this way, they wanted to play with me and I agreed to play with a certain instrument. Therefore, in terms of energy or feeling [hess] we tried to be close with each other and put on a performance. In the past, every time that my ensemble has changed, it has been due to various reasons. For example, it has happened in the past that I have worked with one ensemble for many years and then I have decided to work with another composer, and this situation has happened with the other ensembles too. This was to create variety— for example, it's like when you one day feel like eating a different food and another day a different one again. In a sense, I test those bands and try to find their taste, because each musician has a different taste. This change also creates variety in composition and performance, and it is also interesting for me to be involved with different ensembles and people.
What are the main criteria for a successful partnership?
There are several things. The first is to be an able musician from the technical perspective. Second is their creativity and knowledge to allow them to be in sync with me. Thirdly, they have to have a respectable attitude towards me and to be

likeable. If they do not have the right character, it does not matter how great their technical skills are, I will not approach them. So it is not only that we work together but also we feel together, we have an emotional bond with each other. It has happened in the past that I have worked with one musician but then due to certain events our feelings towards one another changed, and we could not work with each other anymore. So it is both an emotional relationship and an artistic and technical relationship.

How do you choose your instruments for accompaniment? Do you prefer tar and kamanche to other instruments?

Not really, but you know that tar is a better sounding instrument and a more complete instrument compared to other Persian instruments—it completely satisfies you from any angle. Therefore I always like to have one tar in my works. I usually set the tar either with a ney or a kamanche, because we don't have any other sustained-note (kesheshi) *instruments. Then I have to determine the degree to which those instrumentalists are compatible with each other, how they can function together as a pair. (2008) [With accompanists] you should theoretically combine a plucked* (mezrabi) *instrument with a sustaining one. For example ney with santur, or kamanche with santur.* (BBC 2007)

When I take the stage with two musicians and a tombak, this is in my view the best Iranian format, practiced since a long time . . . if instead of two you have three, it's no longer the same thing. It's like in traditional wrestling, there is a logic that excludes having a third partner. When two musicians speak through their playing, it's very beautiful. The singer enters into a dialogue, sometimes with one sometimes with the other. It's my preferred style because, it must be also said, the feelings of two musicians can harmonize better than those of ten. . . . Moreover, it's easier to get on the same wavelength with one instrumentalist than with two. One can better match one's feelings. I even think that if one day I were to be on stage alone, I would focus better and that the result might be surprising, provided there is no incident in the hall, that there would be perfect silence. The presence of many musicians with different sensibilities and techniques always disconcerts me. The mere fact that the sound of instruments is different can be troubling enough to make me lose my concentration and the hāl I may have attained. If the musician is trying to be the close to me, my feelings, it is easier for me to sing than if there are two, three or four musicians. (Kasmai and Lecomte 1991: 251–52)

Producing a Record Release

The typical production or creative process of an individual concert, a tour program or a record release begins with Shajarian observing society, and consequently having a message, "something to say" in response to his observations. Having established this he then labouriously scours the literature for a poem that provides a suitable vehicle for conveying his statement. Once the poem is selected he begins to workshop, craft, and fine tune his avaz over a fairly long period of several months in rehearsal and small private gatherings (cf., Schechner 2005:232). The composition of his avaz thus involves an essential element of collective feedback and collaboration from which he will ultimately and exclusively choose what he feels to be the most successful of the options explored. He usually defers to the group leader (usually also a composer) for supplying the framing instrumental compositions and perhaps the tasnif(s), though for the latter he occasionally draws on the "classics" from the repertoire or composes them himself.[52] The overwhelming majority of Shajarian's Delawaz albums are live recordings and he has a policy of recording all of his concerts as candidates for possible release; his archive of these must be vast.

Concerts were suspended shortly after the revolution and through the 1980s Shajarian took recourse in a process of recording the *saz o avaz* privately in his home studio and then getting a composer—Parviz Meshkatian at this time—to supply suitable framing compositions for a particularly successful performance.[53] Some of his landmark recordings from the period, including *Bidad Homayun* and *Nava (Morakab khani)*, were produced in this manner. Shajarian encountered this process in his radio work, where it was standard practice to record the various components of a *Golhā* program—the instrumental solos, *saz o avaz,* orchestral pieces, vocal tracks for orchestral tasnifs, poetry recitations, and announcements—separately, sometimes over a period of several months and edit the final show together later for broadcast (personal communication with Jane Lewisohn, 2010). While the programs each had a cohesive unity, the individual performers of the various parts would have no idea as to what and who might be included in the final production. In some of Shajarian's more experimental Delawaz recordings that featured large orchestras and elaborate polyphonic arrangements such as *Golbāng, Jan e Oshaq, Gonbade Mina,* and *Dud e Ud,* it appears that the avaz was performed and conceived in a traditional manner quite separate from the ensemble writing, recording and editing, resulting in a juxtaposition of styles.

Since the 1990s the postproduction work of Delawaz albums has been a family business. Homayoun Shajarian is regularly credited (or cocredited) with editing and mixing, while Ostad Shajarian's daughter Mojgan does all graphic design and her husband Mohammad Ali Rafiei manages the performing rights and business matters. While collaboration is essential to Shajarian's creative and production processes, he retains complete control over all aspects of Delawaz releases, making him a veritable auteur of avaz. The 1991 album *Payam e Nasim/Message of the Breeze* is the epitome of his autership, as he has composed all of the framing composions: the pishdaramad, tasnif, and reng (a second tasnif is an anonymous classic of his choosing). He also maintains that this album features all of his techniques in avaz.

Two Delawaz projects departed substantially from his usual working routine outlined here—*Night, Silence, Desert* (1998) and *Zemestan Ast* (2001)—wherein he was presented with precomposed music for which he was to supply avaz. While somewhat harkening back to his early radio days working with music presented to him from composers, in these works he had complete license to set the avaz as he wished.[54]

AK

Ostad Shajarian has an amazing ear for editing. I once played a recording for him that was very carefully edited with precise cross-fades and every technical measure taken to make it unnoticeable but he could tell immediately. He could feel the different energy, "spirit," and microrhythms of the spliced sections. Most of his albums are recorded live and his avaz is subjected to very little editing. For example, he may not like the energy of a particular jawab and will cut and paste an alternate take of that phrase from another concert on the tour. His singing is amazingly consistent, especially in front of a large audience.

Layers

Based on Shajarian's own technical remarks, which like many artists tend to be rather general, along with empirical structural observations and the authors' performance sensibilities, this section presents a detailed, interpolated view of Shajarian's creative/generative process. Revisiting in greater detail some topics outlined above, the discussion proceeds from the background to foreground layers of the music, outlining the structural and creative choices available and/or necessary at each stage, the materials upon which these are based, and other relevant variables.

Macro-form, Structural Background

The radif consists of aggregates of melodies nested within each other like Russian dolls, or to use a computer analogy, files within various levels of folders: while there are some "nonaligned" gushes, most cluster as variants or satellites of hierarchically superior shahgushes, which in turn unite to form a dastgah or avaz, the aggregate of which in turn constitutes the entire repertoire of Persian music, the radif. Each dastgah has its idiosyncratic formal approach or performance practice, indeed Nettl has argued that each may be fruitfully regarded as a different form (1992:252): e.g., Chahargah is a fairly predictable sequence of events, Mahur a less predictable selection from a wider menu of gushe choices, while Shur and Esfahan are more open to free-wheeling development. From the narrative perspective assumed in this study, the radif is musically analogous to the bard or storyteller's complete repertoire of stories and national epics, each dastgah corresponding to an individual story wherein subplots and episodes function analogous to shahgushes and gushes. The dastgah supplies the outline of the musical "plot" in the form of its progression of gushes, which provide the scale/modality, modulation scheme, and structural contour of the musical background—its narrative skeleton[55]—along with a *dramatis personae* of identifiable melodic motives and middle ground progressions, with their various entrances and exits.[56]

Like the existential reality of life itself, the performance of avaz is based on a series of choices (cf. Zonis 1973:99ff.; Nooshin 1999:68–70) from the vast repertoire of classical poetic literature and the radif. After selecting a poem—and for Ostad Shajarian, this will always be based on the specific occasion of the performance—the singer must choose an appropriate dastgah and then, which gushes will be employed for which *beyt*s in its recititation and to what extent each will be developed. Through this balance of free will and fatalism, of choosing from a preset menu, the background outline of a particular performance is established. For Shajarian this is a creative process that partakes of rhetorical categories of both invention (devising, establishing a meaningful statement) and disposition (arranging materials to effectively convey the former). His working process includes experimentation, deliberation and revision and is therefore essentially compositional in the conventional usage of the term.

Alignment, Coupling of Dastgah and Poem

OS

There are two things to highlight regarding poetry [in relation to selecting melodic modes]: the poetic rhythm and the meaning, the content of the words. Many singers chose and still today choose their dastgah as a function of the rhythm of the poem. For example, when the singer wants to perform Segah, he/she uses the same rhythm, which limits freedom. . . . What matters is the meaning of the poem. When I open a book of Hafez's poetry, the meaning of the poem suggests to me which dastgah would best move the listener. If I want to complain and lament separation from a loved one, I won't sing in Chahargah but would choose the atmosphere of Abu Ata or Afshari or a portion of Mahur where I would be able to express myself. But I must say at the same time that if one day I felt like singing the same poem in Chahargah I would do it in a way that would express a deep sense of the words. I'd like to say that a singer must have the power, the capability to sing a poem—even in a dastgah that is not particularly convenient to convey the meaning of the words—to interpret this dastgah in a manner that says what he/she wants it to say. (Kasmai and Lecomte 1991: 250–51)

I have always lived with music and music is the language of my heart. This is partly because of my training with various Ostads and partly because of listening to good music. Following this, I have entirely immersed myself with this language and it has produced results and music that have become part of me. All the different phrases that I have heard from different musicians and the different techniques of singers and their expressions, all this comes to use in delivering the poetry and shows how familiar a singer is with poetry. I always try to convey in my avaz exactly what the poet has intended[57] and this emphasis on poetry has resulted in bringing together both music and poetry in me. So when I open a book of poetry I instantly find its music, just like when you open a newspaper and start reading. When you read the newspaper you know exactly what the article is about and when I read poetry, I know exactly what it says and I can sing it in the form of avaz. I doubt that there is anybody else who can do this, unless they have read the poetry a few times and then put it to music. I mean, I used to be like that too, I used to predict how I was going to sing a particular poem, but I don't need to do that anymore. The second I hold the poetry in my hand I can tell what dastgah it must be sung in and I instantly start singing. (2009)

Question: How do you choose the dastgah for your avaz?

In general, each of our dastgahs can evoke a certain emotion better than others. For example, if we want to describe a particular event, we choose a maqam that is expressive. Or if we want to complain about something and say something with anger, we choose a maqam and a poem that contains those characteristics. For example, the poem that I choose, always already says what I want to say and then I choose a maqam that can properly fit with that state. So for instance, if a particular poem fits with Afshari, I will never sing it in Chahargah. Because Chahargah will damage the poem and cannot provide that state of complaint that is needed. Or if you want to sing something that is regretful and sorrowful, about something that you have lost—for example if someone has lost his country—this must be done in Bayate Esfahan, because Bayate Esfahan can produce that regretful and sorrowful feeling of loss. Hence I will never sing this in Bayate Tork, because that has a different expressive power. I always follow these guidelines.

Is this your own finding or have you learned this through an Ostad?

No this is my own. I have heard about merging music and poetry together but only in a general matter, not in a specific way of how to accomplish that. I have thought about it myself and have achieved it on my own. My conclusion is that we musicians, from singers to instrumentalists to composers, have to think we are composing for a film. We have to imagine a certain event and then compose music for that. Therefore, that scene's message will become much more apparent if we choose the right music for it. Our duty as musicians is to compose the music of the film of life—this life in relation to the events that happen, which constantly changes. We should then choose our poetry in relation to that topic and choose the music in relation to the same. (2008)

RS

Table 4.3 charts out the distribution of dastgahs through Shajarian's oeuvre of recordings;[58] though the results are very rough, they are overall indicative of his preferences, frequency of usage and recorded legacy. Given the production process of *Golhā* programs, much of the data here may reflect more the choices of the program producers than Shajarian himself, especially for the early dates. Statistics for the Delawaz and other albums is much more complex and misleading, as many of these performances include *morakab khāni* modulations outside of the dastgah that begins the performance. There are at least eight instances of fairly major departures from home base, which are listed here only by their opening dastgah (details of these modulatory journeys are given below). Occasionally an entire album is devoted to one dastgah but more frequently the recordings were initially conceived and released as cassettes and contain two separate "pieces" set in different dastgahs for each side of the cassette.

It comes as no great surprise that Shur and Mahur receive the most performances under both columns. Afshari and Segah are also performed with relative frequency. The big decrease in the frequency of Abu Ata in the Delawaz/other recordings is surprising, given that Shajarian has expressed a particular liking of this mode. Esfahan is also relatively under-represented in his later work.

Table 4.3. Distribution of Dastgahs in Shajarian's Recordings

Golhā programs (100 performances)		Albums (Delawaz and other)
Shur	8	10
Abu Ata	13	3
Dashti	7	6
Afshari	11	8
Bayate Tork	9	5
Nava	2	4
Segah	12	7
Chahargah	6	4
Homayun	10	6
Bayate Esfahan	7	2
Mahur	11	10
Rast Panjgah	0	3
Shushtari/Mansuri	1	n/a
Dashtestani	1	n/a
Unknown	3	

Background "Intensity Curves"

In discussing the narrative nature of avaz in chapter 1 I noted Shajarian's mastery of dramatically shaping large-scale musical time in his avaz, which frequently evokes an almost symphonic narrative quality. Shajarian's performances consist of episodes of varying lengths that take on the character or function of sustained plateaus, transitions, and climaxes. The latter are more or less obvious and marked in a number of ways: reaching the highest pitch of the performance (in modal terminology, the *oj* region of the dastgah), higher dynamics, particularly poignant poetic content, and intense emotional expression. The climaxes usually conclude with a comparatively elaborate *forud* (modal descent back to the daramad) in order to return to the regular register, marking an initial release of tension. The material following the *forud*, which can be proportionately substantial, is of a much more relaxed nature: less emotional intensity, lower dynamics and tessitura, more syllabic setting of text, and fewer tahrirs.[59] The proportional placement of this climax in the course of a performance serves a dramatic function and outlines the large-scale formal organization of an *avaz* performance, aptly described by Nettl as an "intensity curve" (Nettl and Foltin 1972:180) but could also be considered as a dramatic curve. This background structure is of course apparent in the serial organization of the radif itself, where the overriding defining feature is "tonic" pitch level, however, and not the other expressive parameters considered here, which can manipulate the musical and dramatic effect of the former considerably. Hajarian notes that, quite logically, this musical climax is usually aligned *beyt ul-ghazal*, the "best" couplet of a ghazal as denoted by tradition or the singer's subjective taste (1999:174ff.).

Short performances, like *Golhā* #37 and (Abu Ata from the 1996 sample), often emulate the radif model, featuring a gradual building of intensity with a relatively quick release, like a Hollywood film or detective novel. This could be schematized (cf., Zonis 1973:45) as:

While many dastgahs follow this archetype, others—like Shur, Bayate Tork, Afshari and to some extent Mahur—do not correspond to it so neatly.

A remarkable feature of many of Shajarian's longer performances is the relatively long release of tension after the climax of the piece, which often occurs halfway through the performance or even earlier, e.g., *Bidad, Dastan, Yad Ayam,* and *Zemestan Ast.*[60] By Western aesthetic standards and sensibilities, these climaxes can seem somewhat early in the unfolding of the work. The entire curve, including the placement of climactic points, is of course integrally related to the contents of the poem, the lines of which Shajarian frequently reorders in order to express his "message." The postclimax phase of these longer performances often serves to highlight the narrative progression of the text, which is much more densely distributed. More than one *beyt* may be recited between *jawabs* here, whereas before the climax a single *misra* may be sung between two *jawabs*. Shajarian often uses a second poem at this point, which is recited in a comparatively short period of time.

Like the poems themselves, Shajarian's performances show a wide variety of both basic shape and varied detail of the latter. Some performances feature multiple climaxes—*Nava (Morakab khani)* no less than four of them. The Afshari concert from Paris has a novel concave profile, beginning and ending with much intensity; *Astan e Janan* a long "ramp up" along its first third to oscillation throughout its later two-thirds. And so on. Figure 4.1 shows some abstract and very approximate representations of the background curves of the avaz performances (i.e., excluding framing instrumental pieces) discussed in this study (including Simms and Koushkani [2012]) and from Simms 1996. Presented in chronological order, Shajarian's earlier performances follow the archetypal radif curve more closely than in his later work.

*Golbāng (Esfahan)

*Golbāng (Mahur)

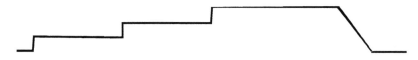

Bidad

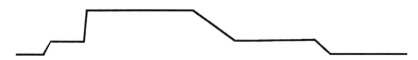

Homayoun

Astan e Janan

Figure 4.1. Background "intensity curves'"

Nava Morakab khani

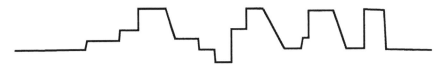

Dastan, *Khalvat Gozide, *Golbāng (Dashti)

*Afshari

Yade-Ayam

Zemestan Ast

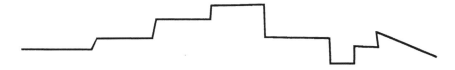

Figure 4.1 (continued). Background "intensity curves"

Further to examining this background level of structure, it is instructive to determine the varying proportions that Shajarian's avaz occupies in some of the albums examined here, stripped of instrumental compositions, tasnifs, and improvised *jawabs*, which averages out to be roughly one quarter of an album's duration:

> *Golhā-ye tāze* #37: 9' of avaz in a 30' total[61]
> *Bidad*: 11' avaz of 35' total
> *Homayoun*[62]: 16' of 39'
> *Astan e Janan*: 28' of 75'
> *Nava*: 24' of 55' (highest proportion)
> *Dastan*: 14' of 57'
> *Yad e Ayam*: 11' of 56' (lowest proportion)
> *Zemestan Ast*: 12' of 40'

Middle Ground: Aligning *Beyt* and Gushe; Gushe Selection

If the progression of gushes establishes the formal background of an avaz performance, the middle ground is a function of the musicial activity at the level of the individual gushe. At this layer of structure and strategy the main compositional work is again one of rhetorical *dispositio*: aligning a line of poetry with a specific gushe or phrase within a gushe; and choosing which melodic phrases of longer gushes to concentrate upon and indeed, in many cases, which variants from the radif (of various masters) will be employed. In the case of masters like Shajarian, new melodies of their own creation will also be used. As we also noted above, he will occasionally repeat the same line of poetry to a different gushe, a variable that will also come into play at this stage of decision making. The "performance examples" throughout this study (including Simms and Koushkani [2012]) provide details regarding the alignment of *beyt* and gushe in specific recordings. This section presents an overview of Shajarian's selection of gushes throughout his oeuvre of Delawaz recordings, simultaneously providing insights into the middle ground (the individual gushes selected) and background (their progression) of his avaz.

OS
Question: What steps do you take to develop your style and especially your avaz?
I never sit down and write the phrases I use in my avaz or think about the tahrirs I should use or what techniques I must employ, unless I am in a situation that I must explain at least to some extent what I will be doing, like in a concert situation. For example, I say I will be singing this beyt *in daramad, but I would not say what phrases I will use for that daramad, I usually leave it up to the day of the performance. I usually have a general idea of my avaz—which lines go better with what gushes— but that's it, I leave the rest to my feelings during the day of the concert, or when I'm in the studio. When I hear you play Segah I listen to it*

and think to myself what poem I must use and when I start to sing I don't even know how I am going to finish my phrase. It is like when we talk, I don't usually know how I am going to finish my speech but the conversation usually gets to a point that it ends on its own. Of course, this is not easy, but I am very familiar with poetry and that makes it easier. (2009)

RS

Not surprisingly, as with most performers of Persian music Shajarian's selection of gushes centers on *shahgushes* for the dastgah being set. As a master of *morakab khāni*, he frequently and seamlessly inserts novel modulations into the main flow of *shahgushes* as either brief diversions or as a full-blown section (e.g., in the performances *Homayoun, Astan e Janan*). Within the recordings examined in detail in this study (Table 4), only *Dastan* stays within a single dastgah (i.e., Chahargah). These modulations are usually made via the gushe Oshaq (appearing in all performances except *Dastan*) to gushes of Shur and its satellites; Shajarian shows a particular proclivity for the gushe Qarache,[63] which is generally followed by Ravazi, giving the impression that he conceives of the two as a coupled unit. This practice reflects the fact that all dastgahs/avazes of the radif have a modulation to a gushe set in the modality of Shur (or very close to it, as in the case of Delkash of Mahur). The following listing of his gushe selection for performance examples included in this study (including Simms and Koushkani [2012]) is taken from recording notes, presumably supplied by Shajarian for the Delawaz releases[64]; semicolons indicate groupings by the track, as presented on the recording. The gushes are listed in their order of performance. There are a few surprises that would pass by otherwise unnoticed by just listening: e.g., in *Homayoun* he includes Yatim Segah, Abu Ata and the juxtaposition of Hijaz and Bayate Kurd (which are closely related); *Astan e Janan* includes a gushe Quchani; and most baffling of all, the inclusions of Bozorg and Masnavi-ye Segah in *Dastan*, though the latter designation may be simply a printing error.

Table 4.4. Gushes in Recording Sample (including Simms & Koushkani 2012)

Golhā-ye tāze #37 (Homayun): Daramad, Chakavak, Bidad, Bayate Raje, forud.

Bidad: Bidad, Bayate Raje, Oshaq, Qarache, forud, Bidad to Shushtari, Shushtari 2; (instrumental interlude) then continue with 2nd Shushtari, forud to Homayun, Daramad Homayun.

Homayoun: Daramad 1, Daramad 2, Yatim Segah, Chakavak1 & 2, Bidad; (instrumental interlude); Bidad, Bayate Raje, Oshaq; (interlude); Oshaq, Qarache; Qarache, Razavi, Daramad 2, Hejaz, Jame Daran, Bayat Kurd 1 & 2, Abu Ata & forud to Ushaq, forud to Homayun, Shushtari, forud to Homayun.

Astan e Janan: Daramad Bayate Tork, Gushayesh, Dad, Shekaste, Shahabi, Qatar, Kurde Bayat, Hazin?,[65] Oshaq, Baste Negar, forud, Shur, Quchani, Sarangi, Shur, Khosrow va Shirin, Gham Angiz, Deylaman, Dashtestani/forud, Shur.

Nava (Morakab khani): Daramad, Gardaniye, Naghme, Gavesht, Bayate Raje, Oshaq, Qarache, Razavi, Salmak, forud, Daramad Nava, Nahoft, Oshaq, Rohab, forud/Baste Negar, Gardaniye, Bayate Tork, Gushayesh, forud be Nava, Rohab, Segah, Muye, forud, *eshare*/allusion to Nava.

Dastan: Daramad (phrases 1 & 2), Muye, Zabol, Hesar; Hesar, forud, Pahlavi, Jame Daran & forud; Mokhalef (phrases 1&2), forud, Mansuri, forud; Bozorg? & Masnavi-ye Mokhalef; Bozorg?, Masnavi-ye Segah?, Orjuze (a.k.a. Rajaz).

Yad e Ayam: Daramad Khara, Daramad Shur, Razavi, Ashiq Kosh, tahrir Naghme, Salmak, Qarache, Razavi, tahrir Javad Khani, Hosseini, forud; Ashiq Kosh.

Zemestan Ast: Dad; Bidad; Iraq; Dad; Shushtari, Homayun, Dad & Bidad.

Source: Delawaz recording liners (except *Golhā-ye tāze #37* by RS).

The tables on the following pages present the distribution of dastgahs and gushes in Shajarian's Delawaz recordings,[66] as indicated by the information published with the recordings (most but not all albums supply this). I have supplied the designations for the *Golbāng* recordings, which are clearly identifiable. Table 4.5 shows the appearance of gushes for each performance that belong to the main dastgah according to the radif, while Table 4.6 indicates the appearance of gushes that normally lie outside the main dastgah. Albums that involve a large proportion of *morakab khāni* modulation are discussed further below. Aside from the expected shahgushes, some further exotic designations appear in Table 4.6, e.g., Kermānji (in *Payam e Nasim*), 'Āsheq Kosh (throughout the albums in Shur), Shekaste Qafqāz/ "Caucasus" (in *Aram e Jan*), and "*parse khāni*" (in *Bouye Baran*). Most of the modulations of Table 4.6 are to Shur and its satellites. There are gushes that are conspicuously absent in Table 4.5: e.g., Sayakhi in Abu Ata, Shekaste and Qatar in Bayate Tork,[67] Hesar of Segah, Qara'i appears in only one Afshari performance. The tables do not indicate the order in which the gushes appear through the performance, concealing many interesting and unpredicable routings. Gushes often skip ahead of their usual placement in the radif, only to appear somewhat late in the game according to the protocol of the radif. In *Anhang o Vafa*, even the daramad is delayed; likewise *Bouyeh Baran* begins with Mokhalef of Chahargah while *Golbāng 1* begins with Rak of Mahur. The latter case may be viewed as a performance of Rak as opposed to Mahur, in the same manner as his famous rendition of the gushe *Bidad*.[68] Razavi appears unexpectedly early on in *Moamayi Hast, Yad Ayam*, and *Asman e Eshq* (which is in Segah, not Shur). Shajarian creates some interesting clusters and juxtapositions of materials, such as the modal "attractor" of Hijaz, Dashti, and Bayate Kurd in *Peyvande Mehr* or combining elements of Rast Panjgah and Nava in *Faryad* and *Chashme Nush*. The latter combination would seem to lend weight to Amir Koushkani's comments regarding these dastgahs above. *Shab o Vasl* demonstrates the use of Delkash for introducing gushes from Shur, thus further intensifying this definitive modal shift in the plot of Mahur.

Table 4.5. Distribution of Dastgahs and Gushes in 42 Recordings

*Asterisk denotes *morakeb khāni* performances (discussed further below); only gushes within the dastgah are listed here.

Shur

	D. Khara	Daramad	Salmak	Shahnaz	Qarache	Razavi	Hosseini	Other
Khalvat Gozide		x	x	x	x	x	x	Ushaq kosh, Bozorg
Yad Ayam	x	x	x		x	x	x	Ushaq kosh, tahrir Naghme, tahrir Javad Khani
Moamayi Hasti		x	x		x	x (1,2) x (1,2)		Dobeyti
Peyvande Mehr (A)		x	xx		xx	x (1,2)		
Saz Ghesse Gu (B)		x (1,2)	x, x		x	x	x	

Abu Ata

	Daramad	Sayakhi	Hijaz	Gabri	Khusrow o Shirin	Sarang
*Payame Nasim	x (1, 2)		x (1,2)			
Eshq Danad	x (1-3)		x (1,2)		x	
Abu-Ata Concert,	x		x	x	x	
Peyvande Mehr (B)	x		x			

Dashti

	Daramad	Oshaq/Oj	Gham Angiz	Dashtestani	Gilaki	Deylaman	Sarang
Golbāng 2 (B)	x	x			x		x
Gonabade Mina (B)	x (1,2)	x					
Raz e Del	x (1,2)	x, x				x	x
Saz e Khamoush	x			x			

Afshari

	Daramad	Jame Daran	Qara'i	'Iraq	Rohab	Masnavi	Other
Entezare Del (A)	x	x				x (Masnavi Bozorg)	
Arame Jan	xx	xxx		xxx	x		
Bouye Baran (B)		x		x	x	x	Hazin, Bayate Raje
Paris 1989 (OCR release)	x	x	x	x	x		Nahib, Hazin, Massihi

Bayate Tork/Zand

	Daramad	Shekaste	Qatar	Masnavi	Other
Astan e Janan	x	x	x		Gushayesh, Dad, Shahabi
Dele Majnun	x				Gushayesh, Feyli
Soroud e Mehr	x			x	'Iraq

Nava

	Dar-amad	Gard-aniye	Naghme	Bayate Raje	Neysha-burak	Nahoft	Nahib	'Iraq	Rohab	Other
Nava Morakeb Khani	xx	xx	x	x		x				Gavesht, Oshaq
Chehre be Chehre	xx	xx	x	x	x	x	x	x	x	Oshaq, Majosli, Buselik
Bi To Ba Sar Nemishavad	x				x	x				Masnavi Nava

Chahargah

	Daramad	Zabol	Muye	Hesar	Mokhalef	Mansuri	Other
Dastan	x (1,2)	x	x	x	x (1,2)	x	Pahlavi, Jame Daran, Bozorg?, Masnavi Mokhalef, Orjoze (Rajaz)
Bouyeh Baran (B)		xx	x	(1,2)	x (1-3)	x	

Segah

	Daramad	Zabol	Muye	Hesar	Mokhalef	Maghlub	Other
Asmane Eshgh	x (1-3)	x	x		x (1-3)	x	Pas Mokhalef, Dobeyti in Segah, Pahlavi and Maghlub
Entezare Del (B)							
Rosvayie Del	x (1-3)	x	x		x (1,2)		
Ghessegu (A)	x	x	x		x	x	
Jan e Jan	x	x	x	x	x		Masnavi Mokhalef, Hodi, Pahlavi

Homayun

	Daramad	Chakavak	Bidad	Bayate Raje	Oj/Oshāq	Shushtari	Other
Bidad			x	x	x	x (1, 2)	
*Homayoun	x (1, 2)	x (1, 2)	x	x	x	x	
*Homayun-masnavie	x	x	x		xx	x	

Bayate Esfahan

	Daramad	Bayate Raje	Oshaq/Oj	Jame Daran	Suz o Godaz
Jane Ushaq (A)	x		x	x	x
Golbāng 1 (A)	x	x	x		x

Mahur

	Dar-amad	Dad	Gush-ayesh	Khav-aran	Hesar	Feyli	Shek-aste	Del-kash	Neyriz	'Iraq	Rak	Other
Golbāng 1 (B)			x							x	x	forud
Golbāng 2 (A)	x		x					x		x		
Serre Eshgh	x	x	x			x	x, x	x	x (Saghir & Kabir)	x	x	Dobeyti, Masnavi Mahur
Sarve Chonan	x		x	x	x		x (1,2)	x		x (1,2)		
Shab va Vasl	x	x, x	x		x		x	x, x				Keresh-meh
Ahang Vafā	x	x	x (1,2), x	x	x			xx			xx	Nahib, Safir Rak
Bahariye	x	x	x	x			x					

Rast Panjgah

	Daramad	Parvane	Qarache	Ruh Afza	Bahr e Nur	Sepehr	Other
Cheshme-ye Nush	x (1,2)	xx				xx	Panjgah
Rast Panjgah	x	x	x	x		x	Bayate Ajam, tahrir Javad Khani, Tarz, Leyli & Majnun, Neyriz Saghir & Kabir
Faryad	x						Neyriz

Source: Delawaz album liners (except *Jan e Jan* from Sheyda album liner; *Paris 1989* from Ocora album liner; *Abu-Ata Concert* from Kereshmeh Records album liner; *Golbāng* designations by RS).

Table 4.6. Inclusion of Gushes Outside the Main Dastgah

Dastgah/Album	Gushes included outside dastgah
Shur:	
Moamayi Hasti	Hijaz, Masnavi of Dashti
Peyvande Mehr	Ushaq Kosh, Abu Ata, Dashti, Hijaz, Kurd, Bayate
(side A)	Raje (Oj of Dashti), forud Sarang
Saz Ghesse Gu (B)	Hijaz, Oj
Abu Ata:	
Eshq Danad	Jame Daran, Kurd (1,2), Oj, Esfahanek, Dashtestani (twice)
Abu-Ata Concert	Kurd, Dashtestani (twice), Chupani
Peyvande Mehr (B)	Dashti, Kurd, Bayate Raje (Oj of Dashti), forud Sarong, Shur
Dashti:	
Gonabade Mina (B)	Qarache, Razavi
Raz e Del	Bayate Raje, Qarache, Razavi, Abu Ata, forud to Salmak
Saz e Khamoush	Khosrow o Shirin
Afshari:	
Aram e Jan	Shekaste Qafqāz, Shur, Buselik
Bouye Baran (B)	Bayate Raje, *"parse khāni"*
Bayate Tork/Zand:	
Soroud e Mehr	'Iraq
Nava:	
Without You	Kurde Bayat, Masnavi Nava
Segah:	
Asmane Eshgh	Qarache, Razavi (1, 2)
Rosvayie Del	Razavi (1,2), Neyshasburek,
Ghessegu (A)	Forud to Jame Daran
Homayun:	
Bidad	Qarache
Beyate Esfahan:	
Jane Ushaq (A)	Buselik, Qarache

Mahur:
Serre Eshgh   Qarache, Razavi,
Sarve Chonan   Qara'i, Pas Hesar, Baste Negar, Jame Daran (twice)
Shab va Vasl   Qarache, Razavi, Hosseini, Jame Daran, Baste Negar
Ahang Vafa   "Beyat Lar" ?, Dashti, Baste Negar, Qarache, Razavi,
                         Jame Daran (twice), Hijaz
Rast Panjgah:
Faryad   Dashti, Abu Ata, Shushtari

Source: Delawaz recording liners (except *Abu-Ata Concert* from Kereshmeh Records album liner).

Table 4.7 shows the progression of modulations in Delawaz recordings (designations from the album notes) that are primarily performances of *morakab khāni*, according to whether they are "one-way" or "round trip" modal journeys from their departing dastgah. As with the practice of modulation in Turkish and Arab *makam/maqam*, there are varying degrees of weight or establishment of a new mode—a "passing" modulation that inserts gushes into a larger chain of modes (typical of examples listed in Table 4.6) versus a "full blown" modulation wherein a new dastgah is established through the appearance of constituent gushes of the new dastgah and perhaps a forud. The latter sequence of centers is indicated in parentheses before the list of the sequence of gushes. In general, Shajarian freely shuffles the orderly deck of the radif to create novel modal progressions, treating the radif as a flexible resource for creating new forms in a manner that reflects the compositional approach of *taksim/taqsim*.

Table 4.7. *Morakab Khāni* Modulation Gushe Sequences

"ROUND TRIP" MODULATION

Nava (Morakab khani)
(Nava-Bayate Tork-Segah-Nava):
Daramad, Gardaniye, Naghme, Gavesht, Bayate Raje, Oshaq, Qarache, Razavi, Salmak, forud, Daramad Nava, Nahoft, Oshaq, Rohab, forud/Baste Negar, Gardaniye, Bayate Tork, Gushayesh, forud be Nava, Rohab, Segah, Muye, forud, *eshare*/allusion to Nava.

Dele Majnun
(Bayate Tork, Afshari, Bayate Tork):
Daramad Bayate Tork, Gushayesh, Abol Feyli, Delkash, Qarache, Razavi, forud, Daramad Bayate Tork; Afshari, Jame Daran, 'Iraq, forud to Afshari; Masnavi Afshari, forud to Bayate Tork.

Homayoun
(Homayun-Shur-Kurde Bayat-Abu Ata-Homayun):
Daramad 1, Daramad 2, Yatim Segah, Chakavak1 & 2, Bidad; Bidad, Bayate Raje, Oshaq; (interlude); Oshaq, Qarache; Qarache, Razavi, Daramad 2, Hijaz, Jame Daran, Bayat Kurd 1 & 2, Abu Ata & forud to Ushaq, forud to Homayun, Shushtari, forud to Homayun.

Homayun Masnavi
(Homayun-Afshari-Homayun):
Daramad Homayun, Chakavak, Qarai, Rohab, 'Iraq, Nahib Hazin, Jame Daran & foroud; Bakhtiari, Ney Davud; Deylaman Homayun; Oshaq and forud to Homayun; Masnavi Homayun & Bidad & Oshaq, Shushtari.

Bahariye
(Mahur-Chahargah-Mahur):
Daramad Mahur, Gushayesh, Dad, Khavaran, Shekaste, Chahargah (1, 2), Zabol, Shushtari (1, 2), forud to Mahur.

Cheshme-ye Nush
(Rast-Shur-Nava-Bayate Esfahan-Rast)
Daramad Rast 1,2, Parvane, Naghme 1,2; tahrir Buselik and Sepehr; Panjgah and Sepehr; Salmak, Dashtestani, forud Parvane, 'Iraq and forud-e Nava, Gardaniye, Rohab; Nahoft, forud in Nava; Nahoft, return to Rast; Jame Daran; Bayate Raje; forud in Esfahan; Naghme Esfahan (tasnif), forud to Rast

"ONE-WAY" MODULATION

Astane Janan
(Bayate Tork, Kurde Bayat, Shur, Dashti):
Daramad Bayate Tork, Gushayesh, Dad, Shekaste, Shahabi, Qatar, Kurde Bayat, Hazin?, Oshaq, Baste Negar, forud, Shur, Quchani, Sarangi, Shur, Khosrow va Shirin, Gham Angiz, Deylaman, Dashtestani/forud, Shur.

Payame Nasim
(Abu Ata-Kurde Bayat-Dashti):
Daramad (1, 2), Hijaz (1, 2), forud; Daramad Kurde Bayat (1, 2), Dashtestani, Quchani, Germānji, Gham Angiz, Sarangi, Deylaman.

Ghoghaye Eshghbazan
(Shur-Dashti-Afshari):
"*Bedahe khani*"/improvisation in Shur and Hijaz, Dashtestani and Deylaman, Avaz in Deylaman, Afshari, Qara'i.

Source: Delawaz album liners.

In the majority of cases the transfer of modal center stays within the *māye*/scale of Shur, i.e., the movement in between Shur and its satellite avazes—in the process perhaps reuniting branches of a family that went their separate ways in the late Qajar period. Common bridging or pivot modulations are Hijaz, Kurd, Delkash, Oshaq, and Qarache-Razavi for transfers within the *māye* of Shur; Zabol and Shustari for affecting shifts between Chahargah and Homayun. There is in fact a pervasive exploitation of the modal ambiguities of Abu Ata, Bayate Kurd, Hijaz, and Dashti—a modal attractor of the radif that could also include Bozorg, Nahoft, Husseini, and other related gushes. It is very easy to slide between these and, indeed, difficult to maintain their individual identities, in the same way that neglecting nuances and details of closely related ragas in Indian music can distort their individual identities. It seems, however, that Shajarian is deliberately playing with their vague boundaries as part of his modal rhetoric. Viewing his choice of gushes from figures 4.4 and 4.5 together, Shajarian shows clear proclivities for Jame Daran, Qarache-Razavi, Dashtestani, Deylaman, Kurd, and Abu Ata, i.e, for modes in the orbit of Shur, the proverbial "mother" dastgah of the radif.

Foreground

Principles of Textual Underlay
The relationship between prosody and musical setting in avaz has received considerable attention in the scholarship of avaz. In terms of Western ethnomusicological research, Tsuge's study (1974) did the preliminary spadework, focusing entirely on this very topic. The core of Tsuge's findings was summarized most concisely and effectively in an article (1970) published before the completion of his dissertation. Tsuge established and explored the principle that the rhythm of avaz is based on the classical poetic meters of *aruz*, the prosodic system systematized by the ninth-century writer al-Khalil. This quantitative system used the conjugation of the Arabic verb *fa'ala* (*fa'ulon, fa'ilon, mafa'ilon*, etc., indicating respectively: o - - , - o - , o - - -) as a mnemonic paradigm. It is explained in detail in many studies (e.g., Tsuge 1974; Weil 1960; Elwell-Sutton 1976). Following from this first principle, Tsuge asserted that the "primal unit" of avaz is the phrase, comprised of recurring elements—initiation, accent, tahrir, etc.—and that the phrase unit corresponds with a foot of the poetic meter, usually an iamb (Tsuge 1970:221–22). Phrases usually begin with an iambic unit and syllables preceding this initial accent are generally "neutral" in duration. The distribution of text articulation is generally more dense at the beginning of phrases. Phrases usually end with tahrirs, a model phrase consisting of "accent–prolongation–tahrir" (Tsuge 1970:222–24).

Massoudieh's transcription of Karimi's radif is introduced with an analysis that cites the most important relationships between the musical structure of avaz and a poem (1985:36ff.). The first is of course the relationship between the poetic meter and melodic rhythm. Massoudieh corroborates Tsuge's thesis that the scansion of long and short syllables generally corresponds to the melodic rhythm, noting the frequent exceptions that long syllables are often of unequal duration, being variously set to multiple tones or tahrirs (ibid.:36–38).[69] The next relationship is that existing between linguistic intonation and melodic contour, where once again we find a general correspondence (ibid.: 38–40). As the intonation of spoken Persian is generally descending, especially at the ends of phrases (this is even more pronounced in recited poetry), we find frequent initial melodic leaps at the beginnings of phrases to establish a relative pitch height. Stressed syllables are usually reflected by musical accents.

During (1995) corroborates many of the above findings and offers further interesting insights. The article draws on ideas from Tala'i (1983), an interesting experiment During conducted with singer M. Manuchehr Anvar, and During's first-hand experience with avaz in general. Most importantly, he emphasizes the wide margin of variance to which a poem may be subjected while remaining acceptable within the boundaries of performance. The *aruz* of a poem is not always clearly apparent when it is sung; performance conventions include flexible rules by which the strict and unalterable prosody may be freely interpreted (During 1995:102–03). Metric structure is only "suggested" in various places throughout the performance. This liberal, elastic treatment of *aruz* mirrors the tendency, noted decades ago by Parry, of singers privileging formulaic expression, i.e., idiomatic delivery, over metrical exactitude (Lord 1948:35). One would expect even more such discrepancies in avaz, where musical virtuosity is more at play, than in the more literally narrative emphasis of an epic singer.

In addition to factors of syntax that may influence the rhythmic setting (particularly in choosing syllables to elongate or emphasize verbs at the ends of phrases), During identifies some basic, flexible rules that govern the elongation or contraction of syllables. As observed by Massoudieh, the actual duration of long syllables may vary considerably and irregularly beyond the 2:1 ratio implied by *aruz* theory. While long syllables may be shortened as well (or equalized to short syllables), the converse should not occur, in which short syllables are elongated (During 1995:105). The structure of metric feet can be altered for semantic or emphatic purposes: individual words and their rhythmic setting may overlap the poetic feet, or may be segmented into feet of various kinds that differ from the *aruz* (ibid.:104–5). A final level of transformation further relinquishes certain aspects of the *aruz*: During suggests that contemporary art music is moving increasingly towards easing up on, or even removing, the contrast between long and short syllables (1995:105).

While *aruz* structure is suggested in textual underlay and rules exist to account for its embellishment, flexibility and a wide margin for acceptable performance variation prevails. It is undoubtedly this freedom that inspired one of the greatest Western scholars on Sufi poetry to report that "Persians themselves do not care much for the rhythmical stress when reciting poetry" (Schimmel 1992:51). During notes that "in the most erudite and rigorous form, which is that of the vocal *radif*, it is easy to find a number of irregularities that are difficult to justify" (1995:114). He also stresses the obvious (but usually understated) fact that discrepancies in the performance practice of improvising textual underlay are also due to the plurality of individual styles and aesthetic approaches that make up the classical tradition, which is not homogeneous (ibid.:113). We are also reminded that these discrepancies are generally on a rather rarefied level of detail, and that in general, the style of avaz is "extremely consistent with regard to meter" (ibid.).

Normative research has thus established what one might well expect: that the rhythmical structure of avaz is intimately, perhaps at times even definitively, related to the poem being sung on many levels but while avaz is a musical shadow of the poem, there is a wide margin of tolerance and freedom for variation. It is common sense to assume that the rhythm of a poem will be reflected to some degree in its musical setting—it would be much more remarkable if this were not the case. The extended theoretical ruminations regarding the relationship between poetic meter and musical rhythm all beg the issue of the intrinsic differences between poetic composition versus avaz performance. While the poems were composed using *aruz*, this does not necessitate that performances, affected as they are by the individual performer and the occasion, slavishly adhere to it. It seems that *aruz* was more a scaffolding or springboard for creative expression, not a rigid container.[70] It is thus logical that musical performances—the creative interpretation by one artist of the creative expression of another—often follow the outlines of *aruz* but frequently deviate from it as well.

OS

Before aruz *the poetic meters were called* atanin *like "tan-tananam" but after the arrival of Islam they used Arabic words like* fa'ilun. *The prosody is not Arabic, it's Persian but they put Arabic words to it instead of Persian. These kinds of rhythmic patterns in poetry do not exist in the Arab world. They do not have music like this because these* atanin *are ours: instead of* mafa'ilun mafa'il *you used to say tan-tananam tan-tanam, tan-tananam tan-tanam. The music in this is ours; these patterns were part of the music that has now changed into this other system. The music contained in it is ours, it doesn't matter if you use* mafa'ilun *or say tan-tananam. Everyone thinks these are Arabic but it's not true, I can sing a gushe for each of these rhythmic patterns and none of them are Arabic.*
Question: When you are singing avaz, are you conscious of the *aruz* or is your treatment of the rhythm of the text more intuitive?
Well, I had thought about it in the past and spent much time studying to learn the meters, but I don't think about it anymore, it is very automatic now, it comes by itself. What is important to me now is the meaning of the poetry, its message, and how to deliver that. The poetic rhythm is not so important for me anymore. When I am reading a poem, the first two misras *have* aruz, *so you must technically read it and move on to the next* misra. *But most of the time when I finish the first* misra *I hold its last word and attach it to the next word and finish it. Or sometimes when I finish the first* misra, *perhaps two words of the second* misra *are related to the first, so I stick them there, and then I sing the rest of the second* misra. *I mean, I play around and break the* aruz. *(2010)*

Textual Underlay in Shajarian's Avaz

AK
Ostad Shajarian says (on p. 203 above) that if a singer doesn't understand the rhythm of the poem he shouldn't sing! So he knows *aruz*, I'm sure he studied that. But he has a good understanding of the rhythm of the poem. The rhythm of each word is important. Great composers of tasnif have a thorough knowledge of literature. For example, Meshkatian's knowledge of literature was very unique and noteworthy. So these artists know poetry and its rhythm very well. They know how they can present a word. Words are very flexible in Persian and can be easily manipulated and create different meanings. They know that. So the art of *iham* is transferable to music if you know it very well. Shajarian does that very well in his avaz, and of course in avaz you have much more flexibility if you understand the rhythm of the poem.

Knowing the science and tools of *aruz* is more useful for poets than singers of avaz. In the case of composers of tasnif, knowing the *aruz* of the poem you are trying to set is probably helpful to ensure that you are not displacing the syllables of the word incorrectly. But if you are a Persian speaker and know music but not *aruz*, you can intuitively discern the rhythm and pulsation of the poem, even if it's written in a difficult *aruz*. While it's of course good to know *aruz*, you can still be a good singer of avaz without having it in your toolkit. On the other hand, I think it's necessary to know music—understanding melodies and musical rhythm—in order to be a good poet. We believe that Hafez was probably a musician, not because the title Hafez used to denote musicians or sifting through historical evidence (although that may well exist), but rather because there seems to be a hidden music embedded in his poetry.

RS
Shajarian's practices of textual underlay generally corroborate the principles established by previous research (especially During 1995). It is generally syllabic with short intermediary melismata and long, frequently extensive tahrirs at the ends of phrases; long penultimate tahrirs are also common before these extended cadential ones. Phrases correspond to the *misra* (with very few exceptions) and the *beyt*. Phrases are frequently subdivided into shorter components—sometimes no longer than a single word—arising from rhetorical punctuation and repetition (see below). The text is characteristically distributed more densely at the beginnings of phrases, giving way to the more melodic focus of the cadential tahrirs. A more declamatory delivery style, however, characteristic of the "postclimax" section of a performance, features a more even distribution of text throughout the phrase, with attenuated tahrirs. Shajarian shows the tendency to use neutral/short durations at the beginning of phrases (cf. Tsuge 1970:222ff. and During 1995:113) and frequently upon the repetition of a phrase, first setting it using durational contrast and then repeating it with more equalized rhythmic units. The function here is clearly dramatical. He

occasionally omits or elides syllables and usually will do so consistently if repeating the same *misra*.

Shajarian's setting often adheres reasonably closely to the *aruz* but does not rigidly correspond to it; there are frequent inconsistencies and disruptions that suggest a very free treatment of the meter. Occasionally the relationship is extremely obscure, with no apparent relation to the meter; this type of free setting usually does not last for very long, and he will soon reestablish a closer outline of the meter. Short syllables of *aruz* are generally more consistently and clearly maintained than long syllables in his setting. A final general observation regarding the comparisons below is that Shajarian's setting of the last foot of a *misra* is usually consistent, and frequently corresponds to the *aruz*.[71]

The following examples (some taken from the sample of Simms 1996) illustrate this wide range of settings, from fairly close correspondence to degrees of variation and eventual freedom from the meter.[72] Each example presents the transliterated *misra*, an English translation, the *aruz* scansion of the poem, and compares the latter with one or more settings of a *misra*. The number in parentheses indicates which section of avaz the *misra* occurs in within Shajarian's performance. The symbols used to denote the musical renditions of the lines are the following:[73]

- a "short" setting of a syllable (generally a sixteenth note) is indicated by a "o"
- a "long" setting (an eighth or dotted eighth note) by "-"
- an "over-long" setting (a quarter note or more) by "=="
- a tahrir melisma by "vvv"
- a semi-colon represents a fermata or caesura, and a question mark denotes an unclear or missing syllable
- an asterisk denotes a standard textual elision in scansion, resulting in a musical elision as well
- the avaz section from which the example is taken is given in parentheses before the *misra*.

Occasionally Shajarian outlines the *aruz* with great clarity; this is especially typical in gushes that are conventionally performed with minimal improvisation, such as Hodi-Pahlavi, Charbagh, Deylaman, Sufināme, or any Masnavi:

Hodi-Pahlavi: man hamān neyam ke gar kosh beshnavi
                    "I'm that very ney, which, if you listen well"
(1)   man ha mān ne yam ke gar kosh besh na vi
aruz: -   o   -   - | -   o   -   - | -   o   -
performed: -   o == == ==   o ==   -   -   o =

The following examples are taken from two alternate performances of Shajarian's landmark *Dastan*, abbreviated here as DB (a performance in Bonn) and DI (from Iran).[74] While comparing Shajarian's individual settings to the *aruz*, it is interesting to note his consistency and variation in treating the same *misra*. The first examples show virtually identical settings, characterized by consistent elisions:

goftam bebinamesh magaram darde eshtiyaq
"I said that if I saw her, unless my pain of eagerness"

(3) goft am be bi na mesh   ma ga ram dar de   esh ti yāq

```
aruz:  -   -   o | - o   -     | -   o    -    -   o | -  o   -
DB :   -   -   o - -   ==;   -  ==   ?   -    -   ?  o  ==
DI:    -   -   o - -   ==;   -  ==   ?   -    -   ?  o  ==
```

sāken shavad bedidam u mushtāqtar shodam
"...dwells, (but) I saw her and became even more filled with longing"

sā ken sha vad be did a mu mush tāq* tar   sho dam

```
aruz:  -   -   o  | -   o  -   o | o    -   - o |   -    o  -
DB:    -   -   o  vvv o  -   -   ?  o    ==     -    o vvv
DI:    -   -   o  vvv o  -   -   ?  -    ==     -    o vvv
```

The following example is virtually identical in four settings (the *misra* is repeated rhetorically in both performances):

chun shabnam oftāde budam pishe aftāb
"I fell like dew before the sun"

(4)   chun shab nam of* ta de bu dam pi she āf* tāb

```
aruz:       -   -   o  | - o   -   o | o    -    -   o  | - o   -
DB & I:     -   -   o   ==   -  o   o   ==   ==   ?    ==  vvvv
```

Rhetorical repetition again provides four versions of the following *misra,* showing a more typical degree of variation in setting:

az dar darāmadi u man az khod be dar shodam
"When you entered the door, I lost myself"

(1)   az dar dar ā ma di u man az khod   be dar sho dam

```
aruz:  -   -   o  | - o   -   o | o    -    -    o | -    o   -
DB:    -   -   o  ==  o   ==  -   -    ==   ==    o   -    o  vvvvv
       -   -   o   -  o   ==  ?  o    -    -;    o   -    o   ==
DI:    -   -   o  ==  o   ==  -  o    -    ==    o   -    o  vvvvv
       -   -   o  ==  -   ==  -  -    ==   ==    o   -    o   ==
```

gui kaz in jahān be jahān-e digar shodam
"It's as if I had gone from this world to the next!"

gu i kaz in ja hān be ja hā ne di gar sho dam

```
aruz:  -   -   o  | - o   -   o | o    -    -   o | -   o  -
DB:    -  vvv; o  o  o   -   o   o   ==   ?   o   -   o vvvvv
DI:    -  vvv; o  o  o  o   o   o   ==   ?   o   ==  o vvvvv
```

gusham be rāh tā ke khabar midahad ze dust
"My ear to the ground, I wait for news from the friend,"

gu sham be rāh   tā ke kha bar mi da had ze dust

```
aruz:  -   -   o  | - o   -   o | o    -    -   o | -   o  -
DB:    ==  -   o vvv;   -  o   -   ==   ==  ?  ?   o  ==
DI:    ==  -   -  vvv;   o  -  o   ==   -   -   -   o  ==
```

The following settings show more contrast:

> sāheb khabar biyāmad o man bi khabar shodam
> *"When the messenger came I lost my senses"*

```
(2)       sā heb kha bar   bi yā ma do man bi kha   bar   sho dam
aruz:     -  -  o  | -   o  -  o | o  -    -  o  | -   o  -
DB:       -  -  o  ==    o == o  ==  ?    o  -    ==   o vvv
DI:       -  -  -  -     -  == -  -   -    -  o    ==   -  ==
```

> kavval nazar be didan-e u dide var shodam
> *"It is to her that I owe my eyesight!"*

```
(8)       kav val na zar   be di da ne u   di de   var sho dam
aruz :    -  -  o  | -   o  -  o | o  -  -  o  | -   o  -
DB:       -  -  -  vvv  o  -  o  o == -  -  -    -   o  vvv
DI:       -  == -  -    o  == o  o  -  o  o      o   o  ==
```

Having looked at some alternate settings from different takes of the same piece, I will conclude with some examples of *misras* repeated rhetorically in the same take. The following examples from *Golha-ye taze* #142 in Abu Ata[75] are remarkable for their variety. Note the variable placement of caesuras in the following example.
Golha-ye taze #142:

> avval kasi ke lāfe mabat zanad manam
> *"I am the first one to boast of love and friendship"*

```
(2)       av val ka si   ke lā  fe ma bat za nad ma nam
aruz:     -  -  o  -  |  -  -  o  -  | -  o  -  o  -
a)        -  ==  -  -  -  ==  o  -  ==; o == == ==
b)        -  -  -  -   ==; == ==; -   ==  o == - vvv
```

Caesura placement corresponds in the following example, falling on the fifth syllable of both executions of each *misra*. Note the inconsistency of the short syllables in relation to the *aruz* (falling on the fourth syllable in the first *misra*, and the third for the second *misra*), which is ideally the same for the entire poem.
Golha-ye taze #142:

> dardi-ist dar delam ke gar az pish-e āb-e chashm
> *"There's a pain in my heart before the tear is shed"*

```
(5)       dar di-ist dar de lam ke gar az   pi she āb e chashm
aruz:     -  - o  o  - |  - o  -  o  -  |  -  o  -  o  -
a)        -   == - o  ==;  -  o == -  o  - o  ==
b)        -   == == o  ==;  o  -  -  -  o  -  - ==
```

> bar giram āstin beravad tā be dāmanam
> *"And I hold fast: to either the sleeve of apathy or to my skirt"*

```
          bar gi ram ās  tin  be ra vad tā be dā ma nam
aruz:     -  - o  o  -  | - o  -  o  -  | -  o  -  o  -
a)        -   == o  ==  ==; o  -  ==  -  -  -  == vvv
b)        -   -  o  -   ==; o  o  -   -  -  -  == ==
```

The performance of *Bidad* is characterized in particular by a free and varied setting of the text. The first example illustrates again the tendency to neutralize syllables when repeating a *misra*.

>yāriyan dar kas namibinim* yāran-rā che shod
>
>*"We don't see friends among the people, what happened to friends"*

(1)	yā	ri yan	dar	kas	na	mi	bi	nim*	yā	ran	rā che shod
aruz:	-	o -	-		-	o	-	-		- o	- -		- o -
a)	-	o -	-	==	o ==	o	==;	- -	- o vvv
b)	-	- -	-	- -	- ==	==	vvv	- -	- o vvv

Another example from *Bidad*, the first half showing how the short syllables in the *aruz* are maintained relative to each setting:

>sad hazārān gol shekoft o bānge morqi bar nakhāst
>
>*"Hundreds of thousands of roses bloomed but no birds called out"*

(9)	sad ha zār	ān gol	she koft	o	bān	ge mor qi bar	na khāst
aruz:	- o - -		- o -	-		- o - -		- o -
a)	- - == == ==	- ==	-;
b)	- o == == ==	o -	-;	-	o - ==	-	o vvv

The musical phrase of this setting concludes at the end of the second phrase of the 9th section with the first half of the next misra (*andelibanrā che pish amad*); the following musical phrase, which begins the *forud* to Homayun, carries the final half (*hazārān rā che shod*). This is a particularly clear example of the kind of overlap that is possible between musical and poetic phrasing; in this case, it highlights the text "What happened to the hundreds of thousands?"[76]

The performance of *Yad e Ayam* (along with *Homayoun*) features a high incidence of rhetorical repetition.The text setting shows a great variety of treatment, some of which (with the exception of the first example) virtually obliterates the *aruz*. Shajarian is unapologetic about these liberal settings: *"Well, these kinds of things happen in avaz. We get rid of the rhythmic pattern. But I am never consistent with them; these things are always changing (2010).* While "the analysis" is probably best left at that, even in these rather extreme cases we see the greatest consistency in the placement of short musical durations.

Yad e Ayam:

>kofr-e zolfesh rah-e dīn mizad o ān sangīn del
>
>*"The blasphemy of his locks struck the way of faith and that stone heart"*

12)	kof re zol fesh	ra	he	dīn mi zad	o	ān	san gin del
aruz:	- o - -		o o -	-		o o -	-		- -
a)	- - == ==;	- - == == ==	? -	- - vvv
b)	- - == == ;	- - == == -	? ==	- == vvv

dush miyāmad o rokhsāre bar āfrukhte bud
"He came last night and his face was all aglow"

(2)	dush*	mi	yā	ma	do	rokh	sā	re	bar	āf	rukh	te	bud
aruz:	- o	o	-	o	o	-	-	o	o	-	-	-	-
a)	==	==	==	-	==;	-	-	o	o	-	-	-	==
b)	==	-	==	-	o	-	-	-	o	-	-	-	vvv

The following *misras* prominently feature equalized syllables:
jān-e (y)'ushāq-e sepande rokh-e khod midānest
"He'd known the soul of love, the rue of his own face"

(5/6)	jā	ne	y'u	shā	qe	se	pan	de	ro	khe	khod	mi	dā	nest
aruz:	-	o	-	-	o	o	-	-	o	o	-	-	-	-
a)	-	?	-	==;	?	o	-	-	-	-	==	-	-	vvv
b)	==	?	==	==	?	o	-	-	-	-	-	-	-	vvv

del basi khun bi ham āvard vali dide berikht
"The heart brought much blood, but the eye poured it out"

(9/10)	del	ba	si	khun	bi	ham	ā	vard	va	li	di	de	be	rikht
aruz:	-	o	-	-	o	o	-	-	o	o	-	-	-	-
a)	-	-	==	-	-	?	-	==;	-	==	-	-	-	vvv
b)	-	-	-	-	-	?	-	==	o	-	-	-	-	==

A new poem with a contrasting *aruz*[77] is sung at section 15, providing further examples of how the meter is outlined yet open to variation.
be mozhgān-e siyah kardi hazārān rakhna dar dinam
"You made a thousand holes in my faith with your black eyelashes"

(15/16)	ba	mozh	gā	ne	si	yah	kar	di	ha	zār	ān	rakh	nadar	di	nam
	o	-	-	-	o	-	-	-	o	-	-	-	o	-	-	-
a)	o	-	-	==	o	-	o	-	-	-	==	-	o	-	-	vvv
b)	o	-	-	==	-	-	-	==	o	-	-	-	-	-	-	vvv

agar bar jā-ye man gayri gozinad dust hākem ust
"If you chose a stranger in my place, she is the judge"

(19)	a	gar	bar	jā	ye	man	gay	ri	go	zi	nad	dus	t*	hā	kem	ust
	o	-	-	-	o	-	-	-	o	-	-	-	o	-	-	-
a)	-	-	-	-	-	==	-	-	-	-	==	?	-	-	==
b)	o	-	-	-	o	-	-	o	-	-	-	==;	?	-	-	==

The examples examined here show Shajarian's practice of textual underlay to largely corroborate the theoretical principles established by Tsuge, During, and others. The most fundamental feature is that the *aruz* is outlined but with a wide margin of possible variation. While the extremes of close correspondence to considerable distortion occasionally occur, the majority of Shajarian's avaz fall in the middle. Alternate settings of the same text occasionally show contradictory treatment of the same syllable; short syllables are set with the greatest consistency and function as the primary means of outlining the *aruz*. The use of equal or neutral durations is common, especially when repeating the same *misra*. Textual content also plays a role in the placement of over-long settings, caesuras, and tahrirs; this can also vary, and functions as a form of semantic emphasis. While this analysis provides insights and brings some precision to understanding Shajarian's textual underlay, we must keep its significance in perspective. For Shajarian, the quasi-mathematical grid of *aruz* is unquestionably subordinate to his expression of the meaning of the text, a priority by which we thereby enter into the nonlinear, intuitive realm of dramatic narration.

Words, Sentences (and Centonization)
The middle and background structural level of melody are generated from, and governed by, the modal definitions or prescriptions of the gushe being performed, which are subject to a wide range of variation and development, improvised according to the artist's tastes and creative abilities. Foreground details of melodic construction, elaboration, and ornamentation, as well as rhythmic features, articulation, and textual underlay—all components of the rhetorical domain of *elocutio*—are likewise improvised. A fundamental, perhaps even definitive feature of avaz is the improvised creation of tahrirs. Like so much else in this tradition, the process of learning how to do this is implicitly contained in the study of the radif, through inductively assimilating materials, idioms, and stylistic parameters that are subsequently creatively rearranged and varied. Though not explicated in traditional pedagogy, the process of improvising tahrirs and creating much of the foreground decoration of lines carrying text is essentially centonic. To the best of my knowledge Sadeghi (1970) seems to be the first scholarly study to have explicitly acknowledged and discussed this important feature of Persian music. I came to the same centonic conclusions independently through my study of setar performance (see Simms 1992:148ff.), which are further corroborated by Amir Koushkani's experience as a performer and my earlier study of Shajarian's recordings (Simms 1996), from which the following analysis is taken.

The most important feature of the centonic repertoire—a vocabulary of "words" in Shajarian's conception—is that the same units appear in all modal environments, and thus represent a primary melodic structural level of the radif, though one not explicitly recognized in traditional music theory. They are abstract, androgenous melodic shapes devoid of any modal implications. As with Sadeghi's identifications (1970: 84–85) and my own (1992:150), the repertoire of centonic units frequently recurring in the 1996 sample of Shajarian's avaz, especially within his tahrirs but in other parts of his phrase construction as well, is surprisingly small. I do not claim to have a definitive count here, as there are many different, equally valid ways to define a "word" or "unit" and, in any event, would question the ultimate value of such strictly quantitative data. With these reservations in mind, it is reasonable to propose that Shajarian's repertoire consists of approximately twenty units, shown in Figure 4.2, many of which could be viewed as variants or derivatives of each other (e.g., those listed below as 3b, 3d and 1e; or 1c and 3c., etc.). In spite of the derivative similarities, in the list of figure 4.6 I have identified motives that seem to function as discrete, independent units. In presenting this analysis my interests and goals are craft-oriented and practical (i.e., describing how I view Shajarian's avaz) rather than advancing centonic theory or engaging in a rigidly quantifiable science. As noted above, Shajarian acknowledged the general thrust of the analysis but politely implied that it was a rather obvious matter of compositional craft. While he may discuss technical aspects related to it with his advanced students, he had no interest in going into such details with us, preferring to steer our focus to larger issues of expressing the meaning of the text. I am left (perhaps appropriately) explaining empirical observations and my ideas that follow from it.

I arbitrarily present the motivic repertoire here roughly according to the basic melodic function or characteristic of each unit. Most units travel directionally but some are stationary, decorating a single pitch rather than propelling a specific direction. We emphasize throughout this study the intrinsic flexibility operative in creating avaz along with the intrinsic ambiguity of its "meaning." An individual unit can function in more than one way: 1d, for example, is also used in sequential descent, likewise for 4a. The units consist of three to six notes, though the majority are four and especially five. The ubiquity of the rhythmically asymmetrical five-note units is especially remarkable, Shajarian showing a clear preference for using them. The units are frequently found in tahrirs, as listed here in Figure 4.2, in flowing sixteenth notes. But just as they are modally androgenous melodic shapes, they are also rhythmically flexible and found in a great variety of rhythmic configurations throughout his avaz (some examples are given in Figure 4.3 below on page 252).[78]

Figure 4.2. Repertoire of motifs/words (centonic units)

While Shajarian clearly uses some units more than others, and seems to have particular favourites (e.g., 1e, 3d, 3f), all are prototypes/archetypes of the tradition, and are found in the authoritative radifs. Many of these units are identified by Sadeghi (1970:84–85)[79] and most are identified by Miller, who lists a lexicon of motives, though without any commentary (1999:278–79). Virtually all of the units I identified in a simplified teaching version of the radif of Kamel Alipour (Simms 1992:150) are found in Shajarian's collection, further indicating their wide currency among a broad range of sources. They appear to be the primary archetypes of Persian melodic structure. On the other hand, they are quite generic, appear to have a common heritage with both Turkish and Arab classical music, and are even found in fourteenth-century Italian Istampies, the first notated repertoire of European instrumental music (a crosscultural connection that is likely mere coincidence).

In order to demonstrate the traditional provenance of Shajarian's repertoire, Figure 4.8 lists at least one occurrence of each unit in Karimi's authoritative vocal radif, most units are easily found throughout it.[80] Units are identified by gushe title, page number (Massoudieh's 1985 edition), and staff number counting downward from the top of the page.

Table 4.7. Cross Referencing Shajarian's and Karimi's Words/Units

Shajarian Motive	In Karimi: (Gushe page #/staff#)
1 a	throughout
b	Gilaki (throughout); Bakhtiari 126/1
c	Bayate Raje 130/9
d	Feyli 169/6
e	Bozorg 52/4; Owj 134/10
2 a	throughout
b	Bidegani 95/3
3 a	Bidad 120/5
b	Bidad 120/5; Hijaz 70/3
c	rare in Karimi; found throughout Boroumand's instrumental radif
d	Razavi 50/11
e	relatively rare (Gushayesh 166/1)
f	Chahargah 153/3
g	rare; found throughout Boroumand
h	rare
i	Hijaz 70/11
4 a	Shushtari 124/1
b	Nahib 181/4

5 a	Owj 47/2; Owj 47/3
b	Raje 121/1
c	Shekaste 170/2; Rak Hindi 184/1
d	throughout

Source: Massoudieh 1985.

In Karimi's radif, particularly in tahrirs, the units frequently recur in varied modal transpositions, but in more or less the same rhythmic and melodic configurations. The configurations are relatively regular, the units are clearly linked or separated, and often in symmetrical sequences. The pedagogical benefit of this is to ingrain the archetypal idiomatic combinations in the student's memory. By contrast, the striking feature of Shajarian's tahrirs is their seemingly infinite variety. While they may share an overall contour and use similar unit configurations, no two are ever quite the same. This is accomplished by a variety of centonic procedures, some of which function to link and combine, others to interrupt a regular sequence or combination, a practice described by the great medieval philosopher and proto-ethnomusicologist al-Farabi as *tafsil* (with reference to medieval Arabic rhythmic modes [*iqat*]). These processes constitute the primary options for basic melodic motion in the construction of sentences or phrases (*jomlebandi*).[81]

Units can be repeated (Figure 4.4a), used in regular, symmetrical sequence (Figure 4.4b), and combined into compound units. Shajarian often creates interesting compound units that seem exclusive to an individual performance, and therefore suggest an improvisatory, nonmemorized formulation. These units are often asymmetrical groupings of seven or nine notes (Figure 4.4c).

A note or short combination of two or three notes can be added to a centonic string, often as a prefix or conjunction (Figure 4.4d); similarly, a note or short combination can be added as an infix (Figure 4.4e). Units characterized by repeated notes may vary the number of repetitions. This is particularly evident in the treatment of unit 2 (a and b)—probably the most fundamental and ubiquitous tahrir figure traditionally known as *qalt* ("rolling")—which can be performed in regular groupings of twos and threes (Figure 4.4f) or rhythmically displaced variations of 1-2-2-2-2, or 1-3-3-3-3, or any number of combinations of twos and threes (Figure 4.4g).

These procedures are characteristic of Persian music and are learned inductively from the study of the radif, where they are found in a wide variety of contexts. They are of course not exclusively Iranian, and indeed have an extremely wide distribution, found in a vast array of music ranging from European art music (e.g., Haydn, Stravinsky) to African musics and jazz. Perhaps the most explicit theoretical treatment of such procedures is found in the South Indian theory of *yati*, where they form a complex but integral and practical feature of Karnatak music.

Figure 4.3. Rhythmic Flexibility of Units

Golbang (Dashti): 8.5

Homayun: 15

Yad Ayam: 6.2

Figure 4.4. Motivic Processes

4.4a
Hodi: 3

Golhâye tâze #37: 8

4.4b
Dastan (Iran): 26

Hodi: 4

4.4c
Homayun: 4

Because of the enormous variety of Shajarian's tahrirs, it is impossible to make a definitive model that would apply to all of them. I will suggest, however, a common structure that is fairly common, especially in his early period. This tahrir will often begin with the flowing sequence or repetition of particular units from the repertoire (from Fig.4.2; denoted below as A or B), which is typically interrupted by one or a series of longer note values (another example of al-Farabi's *tafsil*). The *qalt* figure (unit 2 from Fig. 4.2), in any of its simple or longer versions, is often used to lead into the final cadential figure, which is generally one of the varieties identified by Massoudieh (1985:19). A schematic model follows:

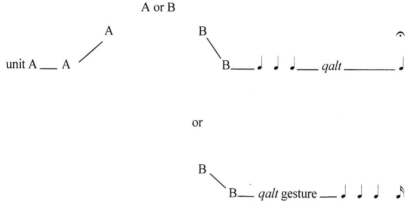

The modal prescriptions of gushes, the repertoire of centonic units, when viewed in all their flexibility, and the procedures for their development and variation provide analytical tools that can account for much of the exterior structure of Shajarian's melodic design. Implied within the radif and explicated here, they provide a tool kit for creative activity. The repertoire of units and procedures can be applied to a large majority of his tahrirs from the 1996 sample. Figure 4.5 provides a detailed motivic analysis of an excerpt from the album *Bidad* (1984)[82] to illustrate the dense distribution of the units. As noted in appendix 3, the choice of beaming throughout this study is largely based on highlighting this centonic structure in Shajarian's music.

As informative and potentially useful as these insights may be, however, they only shed light on an underlying structural level that is still quite incomplete in terms of the overall musical experience, as Shajarian was quick to point out: *"What is important in these tahrirs are the expressions* [i.e., timbre, timing, dynamics, articulation, energy, etc.] *that are given to them. So sentence construction is one topic and the colour of those sentences is also another topic" (2010).* As is their integrated musical impact upon the listener and their contribution to the enhancement of the poem, the total experience of avaz. Given this larger context it is probably relevant to consider the function of the centonic repertoire with respect to word painting as well—that the foreground motives serve the text and evoke feeling.[83]

Figure 4.5. Motivic analysis from *Bidad*

8: Qarache

mehr - bā - ni   ke   sar   ā - mad   shah - ri - yā

rān - rā   che   shod

a

ha   ye   hi   de   ye   hi

le   ye   hi   da   le   ye   hi   de   le   ye   hi   da

Gesture and "Dramatic" Implications

No view of avaz performance would be complete without including discussion of the physical gesture of performance and its dramatic implications for the audience. Like other aspects of musicking, gesture in performance is predicated on both cultural expectations and individual personality. However it may be regarded within a particular musical culture, it is a tool of performance. Godlovitch notes how in Europe during the common practice era, Italian musicians were renowned for extroversion and display while the French cultivated a studied reserve (1998:158n. 23). Individuals function within these cultural conventions and even when the latter may allow and even value expressive gesture, such as the jazz tradition, a performer like Keith Jarrett can push the collective threshold of acceptability to its limits. Perhaps resonating with the interests of performance studies, ethnomusicologists have been paying more attention to gesture in the past decade—how it relates to instrumental technique (During 2001a) or what it might tell us about communication between musicians and/or their audience (Clayton 2008). In contrast to these studies that analyze clearly, if not highly extroverted gesture, what does it signify when there's virtually no gestural or locomotive movement at all, as is the case with Shajarian's performance of avaz? His comportment on stage is static, ascetic, and minimalist. His singing is full of passion and drama and yet he sits absolutely still, in an erect posture with his hands on his knees or thighs, not unlike a typical meditation stance. Occasionally one notices a very subtle rotation of his planted hand while singing, a quick glance at an accompanist or an equally subtle swaying of his head or upper body during a *jawab*. While many vocal techniques employ a widely opened mouth, this is not the case in Persian avaz, where even for high pitches and dynamics the mouth opens very little. Over the course of a concert one realizes quite quickly that there's really nothing to watch—so just focus on listening.

This gestural minimalism is in fact a common feature of Persian music performance culture (During 2001a:41–42) but even considering the acceptable range of individual variation within these collective standards, Shajarian leans toward restraint.[84] The downplaying of gesture in *asil* music and avaz contrasts noticeably with the conventions of vocal delivery in other Iranian narrative performance traditions—*rajaz khāni*, *rowze khāni*, *ta'ziyeh*, *naqqali*, and bardic recitation—where performers are generally animated through facial gestures, along with a range of conventional, acceptable head, shoulder, arm, and hand movements. If anything, *asil* performance standards here align with the behavior expected of Qur'an recitation.

For most observers, there is indeed a great incongruity between the intense emotional engagement of Shajarian's singing and his totally restrained movement, resulting in a unique, quasi-dramatic tension of understatement. On the one hand this highlighting the balance or superimposition of energies is used to great effect by virtuosos of many traditions—including African and Western art music—of making impossibly difficult technical feats seem easy and effortless. For many, this aesthetic of "the cool" is the very essence of virtuosity. There are other factors operating in Iranian culture that come into play that harken back to ancient arguments of the *samā'* polemic and illustrated by recent reports of crowds at rock concerts being policed for excessive body movement (Nooshin 2005). The view here appears to be that there are good uses of music— the spiritually and intellectually uplifting—and there are bad ones that appeal to our lower passions, are body-centered and ultimately sexual. Music appealing to the head and heart is fine, but to the body is not. Depending on the particular branch and individuals involved, the behavior induced by Sufi *samā'* could manifest in both directions, as evidenced by myriad reports and iconographic evidence throughout history of ecstatically entranced dervishes dancing with abandon. There has always been considerable suspicion regarding this, particularly outside of Sufi circles, reflecting the great risk of social rejection when engaging in inauthenticated *rend* behavior. Qureshi observed that the most extroverted, ecstatic movement frequently corresponded with members of low social status among attendees of *qawwali samā'*; those of high social and religious standing rarely exhibited the same (1986:128–29).

Shajarian's comportment in performance and the silence he demands (and receives) in his concert protocol reflect Western classical concert conventions that denote a serious, interiorized, reflective occasion. At a fundamental level, however, this protocol is not unrelated to *samā'* as serious "head and heart" music, ideally inducing a transpersonal state that Mircea Eliade (1969) described as enstasy.[85] Washburn describes enstasy as a "mature contemplative state":

> The implosive absorptions (trances, engulfments) of regression in the service of transcendence and the explosive dissolutions (transports, ecstasies) of re-generation in spirit lead eventually to more poised and lucid contemplative states that combine absorption and infusion without being subject to the violence of implosion or explosion. . . . Unlike implosive absorption, which is a dark, dense, and inert condition, enstasy is a state that is luminous, spacious, and pneumatically alive. And unlike ecstasy, which is a wildly expansive and intoxicated condition, enstasy is a state that is stable and discerning. Mature contemplation, like so many other features of integrated life, is a synthesis of opposites. It is a synthesis of fusion and infusion, absorption and expansion, composure and inspiration. (Washburn 1994:301–02)

While Shajarian describes occasionally attaining some ecstatic, transporting states of *hāl* when performing, which he highly values, his general demeanor reflects the deliberate cultivation of an enstatic experience, an intense but decidedly "sober" engagement in *samā'*.

We noted in chapter 2 that, like Western concerts, there is a clearly understood separation of the domains of listening and applause among Shajarian's audiences: the former being strictly enstatic, the latter ecstatic beyond anything encountered at a concert of Western art music. Shajarian receives these cued applauses with slow, gentle bows, eventually placing both hands over his heart upon repetition. During his 2010 tour,[86] though perhaps originating earlier, he also faced individual segments of the house successively and briefly raised his arms up, hands over his head with palms open in a gesture of a championship salute, eliciting a thunderous roar with each repetition.

AK

I've seen many major singers perform, either live or on television and video recordings, and none of them were ever demonstrative with their gesture or trying to show-off, because culturally, it wasn't approved of by the masters. The Persian word *sangin* means "heavy" but it also has the meaning of someone who is mature. A person who acts *sangin* is considered to be mature. Iranians generally admire people who comport themselves discreetly, who are not showing off and moving and acting a lot when they speak. If you use a lot of hand gestures, move your shoulders and laugh a lot, in most parts of Iran they don't like it and call it *sabok*, which literally means "light" but in actual fact the sociocultural connotation is much more intricate: what is meant is "too forward and unrestrained in mannerism." "You shouldn't listen to this guy, he's so *sabok*." So Shajarian is aware of these cultural boundaries and he wants to present himself as *sangin*. He's heavy. You can trust him, he has centuries of authenticity, humility, maturity and tradition behind him.

One of the first things my teacher (Pirniakan) told me when I studied tar is exactly what his teacher, Ali Akbar Shahnazi, told him: you have to hold the *mezrab* (plectrum) in such a way that no one can see it. So you hold it inside your hand covering it with your first finger. If no one can see it, then you are holding it right. Never show your *mezrab*. You see Kayhan Kalhor playing with a lot of movement but you do not hear any vibrato or other aural effect resulting from it; he's exaggerating intentionally. He's undertaken training outside the tradition and he wants to show that and he works authentically with this new culture right now. But with older musicians, for example, if you wanted to present this kind of extroverted movement twenty or even ten years before the Islamic Revolution, no master would approve of that. But right now people like watching performances on satellite TV and DVDs, so there is a shift to the visual aspect of performance.

They're adding to their visual presentation and I really like it, actually, because I think performers should be allowed to show their emotions. Alizadeh does that a little bit. Ostad Lotfi is trying to gradually, showing some Sufi-inspired motions like he's doing his meditation and *zikr*. Something happened after the revolution and these are the things that are showing changes in stage demeanor. Shajarian is coming from that older culture and it's very difficult for him. It seems that he still thinks that if he moves, if he shows any theatricality, it will be regarded as *sabok*. He is showing expressive gestures a little bit. But his art after the revolution was largely in the service of the poem and then creating music that makes that poem his voice. It's not Hafez's poem protesting social conditions anymore, it's his voice.

Forud/Bridge

RS

Ostad Shajarian had already assembled the toolkit examined in this chapter by 1980 but deployed it quite differently afterward. The Islamic Revolution and concomitant war with Iraq changed everything for Iranians and marked a decisive shift in Shajarian's approach to avaz and sociopolitical action in the face of these crises. This key period of Shajarian's rise to national superstardom and his subsequent entry onto a global stage, assuming an unprecedented public profile as both an artist and activist for freedom in Iran, is the subject of our companion volume (Simms and Koushkani 2012). We conclude this part of our study by noting the figure of pivotal influence in Shajarian making this monumental shift in his career and life: Ostad Gholam Reza Dadbeh, whom Shajarian met in 1979 and studied with until the master's death in 2002. Dadbeh's teachings included, among other things, pre-Islamic Iranian doctrines that emphasized *mehr*, "kindness," and *farhang-e pulmani*, "the culture of being a bridge for others."[87] Shajarian would now use his exceptional vocal gifts along with the vast experience and tools that he acquired through diligent study to both reflect the collective feelings of Iranians and to act as a guiding light through the storm of post-revolutionary Iran with his avaz.

OS

More than my father it is necessary to point to Ostad Dadbeh [in my development]. *He made much more of an impression on me than my father did. Encountering Ostad Dadbeh transformed me. Moreover, he had an excellent effect on my artistic personality. He transformed me. I had the groundwork but he gave me an explanation for the important affairs and problems of humanity. From that time my artistic work followed the ideals of humanity, which are the ideas of the world. In an orderly manner we had sessions with him and were filled with his conversations and teachings. Only now do I see how much we acquired and what is obtained in the history of being. This background reveals the secret of many things. I felt that the secret of art became revealed to me. For example, it explains what the purpose of a melody and music is, what the essence of art is, what kind of secret it is revealing. . . . We have a keepsake from Dadbeh (may his memory remain with us!) in his recording of Barg-e Sabz 115 with the santur of Reza Varzande, singing Dashtestani with a sound and method of singing that is really "the voice of heaven." He taught me how to know all phenomena in the world of people, how to discover the essence* (pey bebaram) *of the people of my land, and how to put those things into action.* (Shajarian et al. 2004:114, 151)

Notes

1. From the film *The Voice of Iran* (2003).
2. Seyyed Javad Zabihi, the singer of religious chant in the Pahlavi period introduced in chapter 2, well-known through his national radio broadcasts.
3. Interview in Persian, broadcasted June 19, 2010; http://www.youtube.com/watch?v=wHiPVsJIJlY.
4. Granted there are always legitimate exceptions to such sweeping statements. There are indeed minority cases where music is "owned" by individuals (such as some North American aboriginal traditions) and occasional abuses have occurred where large amounts of money have been made by the unacknowledged sampling of short excerpts of traditional music by powerful and (already) wealthy Western musicians. But given the widespread, *natural* tendencies of musicianly behaviour around the globe, both of these categories represent a small minority.
5. This instrument was realized shortly afterward and named the *tondar*. This instrument and his other work designing and crafting musical instruments are discussed in Simms and Koushkani (2012).
6. From a recording of a lesson of Shajarian with Boroumand that circulated among musicians in Tehran in the 1980s.
7. "The *radīf* is not only a repertoire but also a model (*olgiū*, "matrix"), a collection of rules, an aesthetic framework (*chahār-chūb*)" (During 2002: 860).
8. Unsurprisingly, most of these have archetypal origins and political connotations. Tehranian identifies the conventional roles of the headman, shaman, hunter, clown in Iranian cinema with the archetypal figures of the shah (tyrant), the "innocent imam" (embodying justice against oppression), the *lutiljavanmard* (chivalrous man, hero of oppressed, fighting injustice), and the *rend* (wise fool, jester) (Tehranian 2004:195).
9. See Nooshin 1996:52ff. for an excellent overview of theoretical approaches to the relationship of linguistic and musical creativity.
10. The gist of his quote opening this chapter also appears in a 2002 interview in the film *The Voice of Iran*.
11. Quite naturally, this is indeed often forgotten by non-Persian speaking enthusiasts. Questions of etic perceptions, conceptions and other matters concerning the cross-cultural reception of avaz are discussed in Simms and Koushkani (2012).
12. Though Rumi, whose poetry is much more suited to translation (corroborating Fitzgerald, Shajarian comments that Hafez is essentially untranslatable), holds this distinction globally. In the past decades Rumi has apparently risen to become the biggest selling poet in English, paralleling and surpassing the Khayyam craze in Victorian England.
13. OS: "*Music is a part of our life; it is the essence of our language. Iranians are clever, they know about Omar Khayyam, they understand him. They do not talk about him but he is present in our lives, he lives with us.*" From a recent BBC special on Khayyam posted at: http://www.youtube.com/watch?v=vIAvWWzscqs.
14. The predilection for Hafez and Sa'di and relative paucity of Rumi can also be seen in Karimi's *radif* (i.e., Massoudieh 1985). Of the 133 gushes, Miller (1995:232) counts 51 poems by Sa'di, 46 by Hafez, 7 by Jami, 7 by Rumi; the remaining 20 are a mixture of various lesser known poets. While Shajarian does sing Rumi (increasingly so since the late 1990s), Sharam Nazeri has distinguished himself by drawing upon Mowlana for his avaz.

15. These albums are discussed in Simms and Koushkani (2012), where full discographical information is also provided.

16. This is a standard practice at such gatherings. However, at a Toronto concert in the mid 1990s, Mohammed Reza Lotfi selected poetry by leafing through a book right on stage, reading as he performed it, reflecting a more intimate and spontaneous *majles, khānegah* or *sama'* orientation of his solo performances during that period.

17. Liner notes to the album *Iran: Mohammed Reza Shadjarian; Musique classique persane*, (Ocora 559097, 1990), p. 4.

18. Interview in Persian, broadcasted June 19, 2010; http://www.youtube.com/ watch?v=wHiPVsJIJlY. Acccessed June 28, 2010.

19. It is important to distinguish that there are at least two types of *foruds*: short ones that included signature melodic material from the daramad and longer ones that are gushe-specific and return to the modality and ambitus of the daramad (at which point they frequently tag on the former short *forud*). Furthermore, dastgahs such as Shur have a number of short *foruds* that can occur unpredictably while others (such as Chahargah) are are uniform and consistent.

20. Cf., Hajarian 1999: 173–74, who notes the formal correspondence, referring to the "most important or favourite" couplet of the poem as the *beyt ul-ghazal*.

21. E.g., see the discussion of word painting in *Bidad* and *Nava* in Simms and Koushkani (2012).

22. In an informal interview with RS in 2002, Ostad Shajarian explicitly identified Abu Ata as his personal favourite, the most efficacious mode for attaining *hāl*.

23. Regarded by many as a simplified version of Davami's radif (During 1996:364n.52).

24. Jamshid Andalebi's arrangement for ney of Mirza Abdollah's setar radif is another, earlier curiosity that ignores the fundamental idiomatic incompatibility of these two instruments; ney players are much better served emulating vocal radifs (though admittedly, Hasan Kasa'i taught radif to his students via singing and playing setar). More to the point is the convention of ney players, following Kasa'i, as being the real "free wheelers" of the contemporary tradition, exhibiting a greatest degree of personal expression with regard to radif materials, featuring a marked tendency to idiosyncratically develop at great length a limited number of gushes.

25. I speak from personal experience here, having conducted exhaustive analyses of the motivic and background structures of Mirza Abdollah's and Karimi's radifs in the late 1990s that remain unpublished. While some of the results of this work enhanced my performance abilities and understanding of cognate maqam traditions, I eventually sensed the danger of imposing rigorous linear order on this essentially nonlinear musical entity and questioned the significance of such scrutiny in view of the kind of Persian music that I actually found inspiring to listen to. One must know the radif but other factors are involved in order to make "good music" from it.

26. E.g., the Klavier Übung series, Well-Tempered Clavier, Inventions, Art of the Fugue, etc.

27. Discussed further in Simms and Koushkani (2012).

28. Mike Heffley, *Northern Sun, Southern Moon: Europe's Reinvention of Jazz* (New Haven:Yale University Press, 2005).

29. Blum notes that, despite centuries of practice, both the concept and word/s for improvisation were also new entities when they gained currency in nineteenth-century Europe (1998).

30. Examined in detail in Simms and Koushkani (2012).

31. Notably Zonis (1973:105–114), Nettl (1974, 1987:40, 1992), During (1984 and 1987:138ff.), and Nooshin (1996, 1998), along with my own practical experience.

32. Described as "non-repetition" by During (1984); cf. Nettl (1992: 249).

33. Cited in Partch 1974:10.

34. As quoted by Bettina Brentano von Arnim (in Godwin: 1987:201).

35. Paraphrasing from an insert included in the original release of the album *Bidad*, which contained a short essay written by the radio broadcaster Bahman Bustan.

36. This is discussed further at the end of this chapter.

37. Marked in the transcription in chapter 2 at 1:39 and 2:07. Um Kulthum used this technique (known in Arabic as *baḥḥa*) to great affect and was particularly appreciated by her audience (Danielson 1997:93)

38. E.g., both individual phrases within of *Nava [Morakab khani]* (this album is discussed in detail in Simms and Koushkani [2012]), as well as its background contour in general (discussed further below in this chapter).

39. In this way it is more akin to how jazz improvisers think about the lyrics of a tune they are improvising upon to help them evoke the right emotional content (Berliner 1994:203, 255).

40. Partch argued that the explosion of popular music in America during the 50s and 60s was partially explained by the fact that it provided such a relevant, Corporeal music to a public that was otherwise lacking the same in other genres of Western music (1974:52, 58). It is interesting to note that for many composers of Western popular music, text serves the melody in their working process: lyrics very often came after the chords and tune are set, tailored to the rhythm and phrasing of the latter (e.g., McCartney's iconic "Yesterday" began as "Scrambled Eggs"). In avaz, melody serves the text in the same manner as leider or opera are composed in Western art music, starting with the libretto or poem.

41. E.g., the gushe *Rak* is associated with the role of Abdollah, son of Imam Hussein— hence the proper name *Rak-Abdollah* in the radif (Tabar 2005:41).

42. But in these cases the integrity of each poem is upheld: unlike his treatment of *beyts* within a poem, he never "crosses back" to an earlier poem once it is left.

43. See performance example 4 in Simms and Koushkani (2012).

44. Hafez is particularly problematic as there was no reliable edition of his works made in his lifetime; rather we are left with thousands of scattered manuscripts presenting enormous difficulties in authentication and variant readings (see Arberry 1962:9ff.).

45. Who explicated it at great length (see Bartel 1997).

46. This latter view has not gone unchallenged (see Finnegan 1992:69–70) and indeed within musical practices formulaic composition is found in both oral and literate/notational contexts. It seems likely that it arose in oral contexts and was carried over and used creatively by composers in notated practices.

47. The extended language metaphor for creating music is of course widespread in many other cultures and is particularly well-documented by Berliner (1994) with regard to the jazz tradition.

48. These functions were likewise conceptualized for Turkish makam and Arab maqam in the late-nineteenth century, possibly in part due to Western influences among indigenous theorists.

49. As an example from another traditional practice Smith quite logically, if self-evidently, proposes that in formulaic composition found in jazz soloing, the syntactic context at play is the chord progressions of the tune (1983:156).

50. This is another point whereby Shajarian's practice coincides with Baroque conceptions of *musica poetica*.

51. Liner notes to the CD *The Abu-Ata Concert*, (Kereshmeh KCD–107, 1997), p. 3.

52. Shajarian's tasnif compositions are discussed in Simms and Koushkani (2012).

53. This period is discussed in detail in Simms and Koushkani (2012).

54. These works are discussed further in Simms and Koushkani (2012).

55. Cf., the *naqqal*'s *tumar*, the stock plots of *ta'ziyeh* and *ru-howzi*, the stock modal prescriptions of the *bahkshi*'s *maqam*, etc.

56. This allegory is most explicit in Ottoman theoretical treatises, wherein *makam*s are conventionally delineated in a narrative prose idiom. I thank Münir Beken for bringing this to my attention.

57. This statement contradicts Shajarian's more frequently expressed perspective that he appropriates poems to convey his own ideas. Presumably both intentions are operative, perhaps at different times and to different degrees.

58. Again, a comprehensive discussion and discography of Shajarian's recorded oeuvre is presented in Simms and Koushkani (2012).

59. This is sometimes the result of finishing a performance with a Masnavi section, which is characterized by these features. Masnavi is a generic treatment of a gushe (classified as a *tekke* in Farhat's terminology [1991]) where modal properties are retained but set to a specific rhythmic pattern. Where the *tekke* kereshme is in a clear hemiola, the Masnavi is based on a free treatment of the Masnavi rhythm (the *aruz Ramal Musaddas*: - o - - | - o - - | - o -).

60. Cf., Nettl's "tapering off" formal type in the instrumental performances he reviewed (1974:408).

61. The radio program format is of course quite different from that of the albums.

62. The spelling is rendered here as it appears transliterated on the album, which differs from the transliteration of the dastgah as it is used in in general throughout this study (i.e, lacking as "o" in the final syllable).

63. As an accomplished reciter of the Qur'an Shajarian has mastered Arab maqams not found in the radif. It is interesting to note that his frequent performances of the gushe Qarache feature a wide upper vibrato on the third degree of the mode that somewhat evokes the atmosphere of maqam Saba.

64. The notes for *Bidad/Homayoun*, as released in 1996 by al-Sur (*Mohammad Reza Shadjarian. Vol I: Bidad, Homayoun.* Al Sur, ALCD 191) present some minor variants. It appears that Shajarian was consulted for these liner notes.

65. A question mark indicates a gushe listed on the album but not clearly apparent in the recording.

66. Note that *Eshq Danad* and *The Abu-Ata Concert* are the same recordings, the former released on Delawaz, the latter on Kereshmeh Records. While the designations differ slightly, Shajarian appears to have been consulted for the information on the Kereshmeh release. Shajarian was likewise consulted for the notes of the Ocora release of the Paris 1989 concert. See Simms and Koushkani (2012) for full discographical information.

67. The sample is small in this case, and both of these gushes in fact appear in the *morakab khāni* piece *Astan e Janan*, which begins in Bayate Tork.

68. Discussed further in Simms and Koushkani (2012).

69. In some ways, this variable treatment is analogous to the variation inherent in the qualitative or relative notation of rhythm in Persian music—some notes are "longer" than others, but the precise relationship can vary considerably.

70. In this respect, it is not unlike drawing upon the radif when freely improvising.

71. This is analogous to the melodic consistency of initiations and endings noted below.

72. I sincerely thank Prof. Maria Subtelny for her expertise and assistance with the poetic scansions, which are taken from Simms 1996.

73. The useful format of these comparative diagrams is taken from During (1995).

74. See the full, comparative transcription of both versions in Simms and Koushkani (2012).

75. See Simms 1996 for a full transcription.

76. See the notes and transcription in Simms and Koushkani (2012).

77. The corresponding musical rhythm of this meter, when interpreted strictly, is found in various parts of the radif, with each foot repeating an ascending melody (e.g., it is an integral motif in Hesar of Chahargah and the second Daramad of Shur [Boroumand's *radif*]).

78. In this figure and in Figure 4.4, the numbers following the title of the album from which the example is taken indicate the avaz section of the performance. Likewise in Figure 4.5, the numbers denote avaz sections.

79. E.g., my 1c corresponds to Sadeghi's 3, 1d with his 19, 2a with 4, 3a with 10, 3b with 13, 3h with 14, 4a with 9, 5c with 11 and 18, etc.

80. The point here is to demonstrate that Shajarian didn't invent these units: neither did Karimi or Davami. They are in the "public domain." Shajarian was a highly accomplished singer of avaz by the time he started studying radif with Davami in the early1970s and would have absorbed this centonic repertoire through other, earlier means.

81. Nooshin (1996, 1998) provides a typology of common sentence structures derived from a large sample of recordings.

82. This iconic album is discussed in Simms and Koushkani (2012).

83. Crossculturally, this notion again harkens back to the conceptions of Baroque *musica poetica* theorists and is famously exemplified in Bach's *Orgelbüchlein*, wherein the mood of each chorale text is evoked by the rigorous engagement of a specific motive.

84. This relative observation also excludes the few rare individuals from "the old school" of avaz (e.g., Sodeyf) who would underline their melodic lines with hand gestures (During 2001:43).

85. Greek for "standing inside onself," as opposed to ecstacy, "standing outside oneself."

86. The context of this is discussed in Simms and Koushkani (2012).

87. Dadbeh and these ideas are discussed further in Simms and Koushkani (2012).

Appendix 1
Contemporary Conventions
of Avaz Performance

While there are plenty of good introductory texts offering an overview of the performance tradition of Persian music, this appendix presents an abbreviated, basic orientation for those readers unfamiliar with it.

> Despite . . . signs of modernity, most Iranian musics remain attached to what musicians have defined as the immutable frames or axes of tradition. The slight changes in intervals foreseen by Vazīrī have been adopted only in theoretical treatises, modes have been preserved, and, even more curiously, no mode or modal type has been added for more than 150 years. The main instruments are still those of the nineteenth century, scarcely changed, despite the appearance of many new instruments, both Western (piano, violin, flute) and Eastern (*'ūd, qānūn,* and *rabāb*). Poetry and song still mobilize the public, and the sung *ghazal* remains the center of any musical performance, so much so that instrumentalists, breaking with the traditional separation of functions, have also begun to sing *taṣnif-hā*, solo or in a group, at the end of their concerts. (During 2002:863)

The Radif

The radif is a collection of two to three hundred (depending on the rescension of a particular line of transmission) melodies called gushes (pronounced 'gū•sheh). Some as short as ten seconds, others lasting a few minutes; most are in free rhythm but some are metrical; each are given a proper name. These melodies are memorized by musicians and used as models upon which they improvise and compose. The melodies are organized in an explicitly holonic fashion into specific groupings within which they have a specific order, which is reasonably consistent between the various rescensions. This organization can be introduced effectively to neophytes through an analogy to computer terminology wherein the gushes are individual files. The total aggregate of 200 to 300 files on a hard drive is the radif, which are distributed into seven folders known as dastgahs. Two of these main dastgah folders contain subfolders known as avaz: the main dastgah folder Shur has four avaz subfolders and Homayun has one, making a total of twelve folders and subfolders within which the individual gushe files are situated. While identical or similar file names exist within the various folders, the contents of these files are never identical. Files within each folder are often chunked into groupings of related contents. Some files are more important than others.

The "Suite" Tradition and Its Components and Accompaniment

Supposedly established by Darvish Khan, contemporary practice Persian music consists of a juxtaposition of improvised and composed, nonmetric and metric, instrumental and vocal sections that form a kind of suite. The key aesthetic consideration appears to be contrast. The improvised, nonmetric avaz sections are framed by various composed instrumental forms such as the introductory *pishdaramad*, the up-tempo *chaharmezrab*, the dance-like *reng*, and the vocal *tasnif*, strophic or through-composed metrical settings of poetry, and occasionally short compositions that function as interludes between avaz sections. An entire suite can last anywhere between twenty to sixty minutes and generally follows the scheme: *pishdaramad/chaharmezrab*; avaz; interlude/*tasnif*; avaz; concluding *tasnif* and/or *reng* (see Zonis 1973 and During 1984 for detailed descriptions of these forms). Shajarian's performances generally follow this format, though he began experimenting with the ordering in the early 2000s. Avaz sections are central in the scheme of the suite, while the composed sections primarily function to highlight the avaz and are more or less optional.

Excluding vocal radifs, avaz is almost always accompanied by a traditional Persian instrument, most often tar, setar, ney, santur or kamanche (for descriptions of these instruments, see During 1984; Zonis 1973). The accompanist instantaneously mirrors the melody of the singer, and provides instrumental interludes (*jawabs*, lit. "answers") between couplets or single *misras* (hemistiches). Avaz accompaniment is a demanding practice which requires fast reflexes and an excellent memory, as the accompanist must duplicate or mirror the singer instantaneously; this results in a slight delay and heterophonic (theoretically, quasi-canonic) overlap of the two lines. The accompanist must also remember the overall shape of the avaz phrase, which she then paraphrases during the *jawab* interlude. While such a paraphrase is expected, it is acceptable to present completely contrasting material, so long as it maintains the modal identity of the sung phrase. *Jawabs* function to provide musical and dramatic relief from the intensity of the avaz, rest for the singer, and allow the listener time to reflect on the poetic content of the sung phrase. Operating similar to the composed sections of a full performance of contemporary Persian music but scaled to a lower structural level, *jawabs* function to frame and highlight sections.

"Free Meter"

The rhythmic structure of avaz is nonmetrical and complex. While metrically free, short portions often have a definite sense of pulse, the tempo of which can vary considerably between successive portions. Other more complex sections are based on the rhythm inherent in the text and are difficult to define in terms of musical rhythm. The density of rhythmic articulation varies from what may be very loosely interpreted as sixteenth notes to dotted whole notes. Tahrirs, the extended melismata that idiomatically employ the glottal *tekye* appogiatura, are largely based on a fast steady pulse, and therefore highly rhythmical. They are textless, usually sung to a long "ā" or "ō" vowel.

Phrase Construction

Melody is generated and regulated by the modal theory of dastgah, with the gushe functioning as the most directly practical hierarchical level of the modal system. A gushe is a model "composition" containing all the definitive modal characteristics such as ambitus, functional pitches, chromatic alternation, background melodic contour and motivic materials. Once memorized it is the basis from which the performer improvises, developing the model from his inductive understanding of the modal parameters. Having selected the dastgah beforehand, the singer then chooses from the gushes (submodes) that collectively constitute the dastgah. While the choice is theoretically free, in practice it is predetermined by the conventions of performance. These conventions are not explicitly articulated in theory, but invariably include certain important submodes (*shāh gushes*). While these choices are often made beforehand (additional preset or "compositional" parameters of the performance), spontaneous choices could, and some connoisseurs might say should, be included.

With the selected melodic materials and the poem at hand, the singer proceeds spontaneously to weave the two into a distinct third entity. In the process of setting the poem afresh, the singer draws upon the experience and models of many memorized gushes, which in a vocal radif include guidelines for stylistically idiomatic textual underlay. The acquisition of the skill of text setting is, like that of nontextual, purely melodic improvisation, a process of creatively reconstructing and rearranging the poem with the tools and knowledge inductively learned from the radif.

Phrases are generally constructed in the following archetypal manner. The text of the poem may be preceded by a short or long exposition of a key motif of the gushe sung to a vocable, perhaps concluding with a tahrir. This may be followed by singing the text, perhaps to the same motif, which will usually proceed to a more declamatory delivery of the text focusing on a single pitch with neighbour notes and short melismatic punctuations. A tahrir is invariably performed at the end of each couplet, and occasionally even after the first *misra* or some point halfway through a *misra*. These final tahrirs function cadentially and can be extremely extended—Shajarian will often include several phrases within a tahrir, some of which contain sixty or seventy articulated pitches on a single breath.

Appendix 2
Transcription of Avaz and
Translation of Poetry

"It is the mark of an educated mind to rest satisfied with the degree of precision that the nature of the subject admits, and not to seek exactness when only an approximation is possible." Aristotle, *Nichomachean Ethics*

RS

The use of Western notation in Persian music dates to the early twentieth century, though its use for Western-style military music in Iran dates to the second half of the nineteenth century. It was appropriated by Iranian musicians since this time and is now widely used in transmission, pedagogy, composition and scholarship. Contrary to the backlash against transcription that was fashionable among ethnomusicologists in the 1980s and 1990s, most Iranian musicians have no such qualms about its usefulness in their musicking. While we never discussed the topic with Ostad Shajarian, he clearly appreciates the transcription of his music and probably likens it to his own extensive work and recommendations for "lifting" with great precision from recordings. Our purposes for including transcription in this study are for reasons that apply to ethnomusicology in general and those specific to Shajarian's music. As I've outlined elsewhere (Simms 2004:5) regarding the former, transcription serves to make certain structural features more discernible to readers, allows for comparative and analytical observations outside the flow of time, facilitates memory of musical materials, and helps one locate and follow a series of musical events in a long performance. I neglected to add that transcription facilitates scholarly discourse regarding the structure of a specific music with some degree of precision and it can help us, to some degree, in our pursuit of musical performance. Regarding Shajarian in particular, given his high position of authority regarding the radif, his deliberate avoidance of recording "his radif," and his explicit statement that his radif is in fact contained within his albums, Amir Koushkani and I feel that transcriptions of the latter are in and of themselves a significant contribution to radif studies. I have prepared full transcriptions of Shajarian's avaz from the albums excerpted in our study (including numerous works examined in Simms & Koushkani [2012]) published by Delawaz, which we

271

view as extending the line of core radif publications—Saba, Ma'ruffi, Boroumand, Karimi, Davami and Shahnazi—begun in the 1950s. As mediated music Shajarian's recordings already straddle "the archive and the repertoire," and we are making his music more archival by transcribing it, following emic Iranian proclivities for archiving the radif.

The transcription format is based on the appropriations of Iranian musicians over the past decades to suit their music (see Tsuge 1974:44–109), incorporating a few new symbols for phrase markings and approaches to layout. Standard symbols from Western notational practices are used for articulation (vibrato, slurs, glissandi, accent, "ghost notes"), mordents and grace notes and denote essentially the same performance techniques. A mordent appearing to the right of a note indicates that it is executed after the initial attack of the note. Conventional Iranian symbols for the *tekye* glottal appoggiatura "o" and *koron* "quartertone" flat ♭ are retained.

In calibrating the degree of detail to include while remaining intelligible, I have opted for a compromise that leans decidedly toward the prescriptive pole of the prescriptive-descriptive continuum. Performances appearing in my 1996 dissertation were carried over—digitally copied, corrected and thoroughly revised—for the present study. These revisions and the performances contained in this study but not in the dissertation were transcribed using the software Transcribe!. This software exposes a level of ornamental detail easily missed in regular listening that nonetheless contributes significantly to the overall effect of Shajarian's singing and marks his style. This is particularly true with regard to his frequent use of ghost notes to very subtly punctuate the initiation and termination of phrases. Transcription of the formidable *Rabbana* also engaged the software Melodyne Editor. All transcriptions were done by me; portions of the material were later edited by Amir Koushkani.

Any discussion of avaz transcription must begin with acknowledging that it is impossible to notate this music accurately, especially with regard to rhythm and ornamentation. Avaz is characterized by a qualitative flow of musical time that eludes the quantitative grid of Western notation. Having seen that avaz is essentially the shadow of a spiritual radiation, a dynamic quality, it seems wholly appropriate that the music eludes any absolute, rigid, quantification and concretization. Likewise, it is impossible to convey features of timbre and articulation that are so essential to Shajarian's art. As with any system, a transcriptional approach is both defined and limited by itself, and will eventually and inevitably lead to its own contradictions (see Grigg 1994: 267ff.). It is clearly a limited means to an end. For this study, it serves as a roadmap, however crude (as any transcription of avaz must be), to the recordings. It is a means by which we can identify melodic and rhythmic motives, developmental processes, and the relationship between text and music.To this end, perhaps the metaphor of the transcription as a series of footprints is more useful: the transcription can only serve to retrace the steps of where and how a living activity occurred, leaving traces that allow us in some way to reconstruct a journey, or better still, a dance. A transcription is of course an analysis in itself, and in this study the process generated many of the ideas and analyses. The analysis, however, and especially the choices made to convey graphically what is perceived aurally, must remain more a creative than a scientific undertaking; choices are constantly made that are not entirely rational nor open to rational solutions.

While this modified notation appears identical to European notation, with the addition of a few new ornamental and chromatic symbols, it cannot be read as such with regard to rhythm. It assumes familiarity with the sound and style of the music and, more specifically, an understanding of the orally transmitted performance and interpretive practice employed with the notation. The principle difference for *avaz* is that rhythmic durations, indicated by flags, beams, dots and note values, are qualitative and not quantitative: an eighth note is therefore "shorter" than a quarter note; a dotted sixteenth note is "a bit longer" than a sixteenth note.

The difficulties of accuracy here are obvious, and are compounded by the fact that the rhythmic flow can at times be related by simple mathematical proportions. Differentiation between free sections and proportioned sections is not indicated in my notation, and would indeed result in a level of complexity that stands at antipodes to the free flowing, spiritual basis of the music. Likewise I have made no attempt to indicate the relative pulse rate in proportioned sections, which frequently change quite noticeably between adjacent phrases and even subphrases. Related to the issue of tempo, I have felt a frequent shift between duple/quadruple and triple pulse rates in Shajarian's avaz, a trait that seems idiomatic to the music. I have notated this by using eighth note triplets and dotted sixteenths, the most common occurrences. Usually the shifts are too brief to be considered as a definite entry into the triple grid.

It goes without saying that, like any transcription, what I present is my opinion about the music, with all the subjective limitations that this entails; far from being definitive, the musical *iham* is clearly open to alternate interpretations and perceptions. The most significant adaptation I have made affects the choices of beaming and flagging notes. This is the result of my bias and assumptions regarding the centonic structure of the music, how notes corresponded to syllables within words of the text, and how I feel rhythmic accents and agogic stress. Following Shajarian's comments on the "language" of Persian music and the centonic analysis, I have beamed notes into motivic groups throughout the transcriptions, which can be readily identified in the flow of the music and matched with their archetypes presented in chapter 4. The transcription, therefore, is also a blow-by-blow motivic analysis. Long strings of notes are often subdivided into their component motivic structures. The graphic representation of the motivic groups may be viewed as neumes, notes that belong together as units and not merely an aggregate of discrete pitches. Without pressing the analogy too far, I am relating to the notion posited by some scholars of early Christian chant that neumes were largely mnemonic, prescribing general melodic direction and perhaps stock centonic units (Burstyn 1990:136). Difficulties arise with this systematization, of course, because there are often conflicts between rhythmic weight, stress, and motivic grouping. In these cases I have usually opted for the centonic grouping in the belief that the units are primarily melodic shapes and they subsequently allow for greater rhythmic variety and flexibility. Inevitably some excerpts seemed too forced, in which case I left the grouping as I perceived it in the musical flow. Beaming also reflects how I feel rhythmic and agogic stress, with relative weight falling on the first note of each beamed or flagged unit.

This is of course a subjective practice, clearly open to alternative interpretations and perceptions. Again, if a formulation seemed too forced, I opted for a representation that seemed to go with the musical flow.

In general, the underlying pulse rate for each beamed unit remains constant, though this rate often changes slightly from unit to unit, as discussed above. As the fastest pulse level is found in the tahrir melismas, I have chosen this, notated as sixteenth notes, as the main calibrating standard for the rhythmic values. As mentioned above, these are at times mathematically related but frequently not, and it is best to follow the principle of relative and not divisive time value throughout. Extended tahrirs, which are characteristically (if not definitively) proportional, are an exception to this principle. With regard to repeated notes and long strings of notes in tahrirs, Shajarian often detaches these (sixteenth notes in my transcriptions) without the use of *tekye*, but with a lighter glottal stop. This is not indicated, but implied by the absence of slurring and the *tekye* symbol.

Another frequently encountered difficulty in assigning rhythmic values occurs in sections that appear to have a constant pulse rate but include held note values of five or seven beats, i.e., values that cannot be notated without ties. In order to keep the transcriptions intelligible, I have arbitrarily rounded these off to the lower value (so that a clear duration of ten beats is notated as eight: i.e., a half note). Such asymmetrical values seem idiomatic to avaz as they are frequently found in motivic groups, especially groups of five, where they are however easy to notate as a string of eighth or sixteenth notes.

Some of the greatest difficulties in assigning rhythmic values occur in sections of avaz that are primarily declamations of the text. These sections are usually melodically static, often confined to a single reciting tone with occasional neighbour notes. Tahrirs, while melodically complex, are easier to transcribe because their rhythmic structure is clear: they either flow in a constant stream or have clear proportional values. The declamatory sections of avaz defy the concretization of notation and therefore represent the most rhythmically inaccurate portions of the transcription. It seems appropriate that these sections direct focus to the poem itself, the mystical experience, which likewise cannot be explicated or "pinned down." They must definitely be approached as approximate and relative, qualitative, and not mathematically divisive. I have again used flagging and "neuming" to indicate how I feel stress and accent.

I have also tried to clarify musical phrasing through the use of layout and barlines. Avaz sections, meaning the entire segments sung between long *jawabs*, are separated by barlines and generally offset (barring awkward spacing) as new paragraphs in the layout; each section is given an ordinal number for identification in the accompanying analysis. Phrases within the section are separated with dash on the first staff line. Commas indicate short pauses, which usually delineate sub-phrases.

We have used existing translations of poetry (with occasional minor stylistic adjustments) where these are available and suitable; otherwise we have translated the poetry into free, idiomatic English verse. It is obviously impossible to translate a poem, especially a great poem, and reproduce its effect—preserving and revealing the nobility of language and thought of the original—let alone its rhythm, rhyme, and double meanings. Our translations alter minor words, especially prepositions and verb tenses in order to flow and to be more idiomatic in English. These translations are not meant to be great literary achievements (although some turned out quite respectably) nor distorted over-extensions of poetic license. They are intended to lie somewhere between these extremes, conveying a sense of the meaning and content of the original to those who do not read Persian.

Appendix 3
Shajarian's *Golhā* Performances
1967-ca.1976

These data were obtained through the kind courtesy of Jane Lewisohn at The Gulha Project (www.gulha.co.uk), whom I sincerely thank. Dates of recording or broadcast are not available due to the treatment of the source materials (which were stored in boxes featuring the royal emblem) in the post-revolutionary period. A comprehensive discography of Shajarian's recordings on Delawaz and other recording labels is provided in Simms and Koushkani 2012.

Program/number	Dastgah	Poet
Barge Sabz		
216	Afshari	Hafez
242	Bayate Tork	?
245	Segah	?
246	Afshari	?
247	Homayun	?
248	Chahargah	Hafez
249	Shur	?
250	Esfahan	Hafez
251	Abu Ata	Hafez
255	Shur	?
258	Segah	Sa'di
261	Afshari	Sa'di
271	Abu Ata	Sa'di
279	Bayate Tork	Hushang Ebtehaj (Sayeh)
283	Segah	Tawhidi Shirazi
287	Mahur	'Imad Khurasani
288	Bayate Tork	Fursat al-Dawla Shirazi
292	Homayun	Sayf Farghani
306	Segah	Sa'di

Golhā-ye tāze

13	Mahur	Hafez
23	Abu Ata	Rahi Mu'ayyiri
25	Esfahan	Farukkhi Yazdi
31	Mahur	?
37	Homayun	Hushang Ebtehaj (Sayeh)
42	Bayate Tork	Sa'di
48	Chahargah	Hafez
53	Chahargah	Sa'di
54	Dashti	Shahriyar
58	Bayate Tork	Hafez
60	Bayate Esfahan	Sa'di
65	Abu Ata	Rahi Mu'ayyiri
66	Abu Ata	?
71	Homayun	Sa'di
72	Bayate Tork	?
75	Afshari	Mowlana (Rumi)
77	Mahur	Firidun Mushiri
85	Shur	Hafez
87	Bayate Esfahan	Hafez
92	?	Hafez
97	Segah	Sa'di
100	Homayun	?
102	Dashti	Sa'di
104	Abu Ata	?
106	Mahur	Hafez
107	Segah	Hafez
121	Mahur	Hafez
123	Homayun	Hafez
125	Homayun	Sa'di
128	Bayate Esfahan	Abu Sa'id Abu'l-Khayr
133	Shur (Naghmeh, Razavi, Hosseini)	Sa'di
138	Bayate Tork	Hafez
140	Chahargah	Hafez
142	Abu Ata	Sa'di
144	Bayate Tork	Hafez
147	Segah	Sa'di
151	Homayun	Furughi Bastami
		Baba Tahir
		Nizami Ganjavi

153	Segah	Hafez
154	Afshari	?
156	Afshari	Hafez
158	Shur	Hafez
160	Mahur	Sa'di
162	Abu Ata	Hafez
166	Shur	Sa'di
171	Chahargah	Sa'di
176	Dashti	?
178	Afshari	Hafez
180	Homayun	Fakhr al-Din 'Iraqi
182	Abu Ata	'Umar Khayyam
185	Mahur	Hafez
187	?	Hafez
190	?	Hushang Ebtehaj (Sayeh)
192	Shur	?

Golhā Rangarang

472	Bayate Esfahan	Sa'di
519	Mahur	Furughi Bastami
524	Mahur	Furughi Bastami
541	Afshari	Pizhman Bakhtiyari Farukkhi Yazdi
544	Abu Ata	Nizami Ganjavi
562	Dashti	'Ali Sadarat (Nasim)
	Abu Ata	Furughi Bastami Hafez Furughi Bastami Hafez
567	Dashti	Majmar Zavara'i (Esfahani)
572	Abu Ata	Gulbun Hafez
574	Dashti	Furughi Bastami Rahi Mu'ayyiri
575	Bayate Esfahan	Hafez
578	Segah	Nadir Nadirpur
580	Afshari	Rahi Mu'ayyiri Hushang Ebtehaj (Sayeh)
580	Nava Afshari	Rahi Mu'ayyiri Hushang Ebtehaj (Sayeh)

Golhā-ye
Sahra'i
63   Dashtestani   ?

Yek Shakhe
Golhā
402   Dashti   Hafez
407   Segah? Abu Ata?   Furughi Bastami
410   Afshari   ?
412   Shustari Mansuri   Pizhman Bakhtiyari
                                                Khursandi Shirazi
                                                Rahi Mu'ayyiri
413   Chahargah   Sa'di
417   Bayate Tork   Fursat al-Dawla Shirazi
                                                Salman Savaji
                                                Mowlana (Rumi)
418   Homayun   Rahi Mu'ayyiri
                                                Hafez
425   Bayate Esfahan   Sa'di
439   Mahur   Sa'di
446   Mahur   ?
447   Nava   Sa'di
450   Bayate Esfahan   Hafez
457   Segah   'Imad Faqih Kirmani
                                                Hafez

Appendix 4
List of Recording Sample Used in Simms 1996

Asterisks denote transcriptions from the dissertation sample not revised for this book (some performances of which were referred to in chapter 4).

1. *Golhā-ye tāze* #37; dastgah Homayun, 1974
2. *Golhā-ye tāze* #142; Abu Ata, 1970s
3. *Golbāng vol. 1* (Delawaz); Bayate Esfahan, 1977
4. *Golbāng vol. 2* (Delawaz); Mahur, 1977
5. *Golbāng vol. 2* (Delawaz); Dashti 1977
6. *Hodi/Pahlavi: *The Series of Music for Young Adults; Chahargah* (series of 10 LPs produced by Kambeez Roshanravan for the Institute for the Intellectual Development of Children and Young Adults, Tehran; 1976)
7 & 8. *Bidad Homayun* (Delawaz); Bidad 1982, Homayun 1984
9. *Khalvat Gozide* (Delawaz); Shur, 1980
10. *Mohammed Reza Shajarian and Ensemble 'Aref* (World Network/WDR, LC-6759); Chahargah, 1987
11. *Dastan: Konsert e Shajarian* (Delawaz); Chahargah, 1987
12. *Iran: Mohammed Reza Shadjarian; Musique classique persane* (Ocora C-559097 [HM 83]); Afshari, 1989
13. *Yad e Ayam: Konsert-e Shur Amerika* (Delawaz); Shur, 1992

Glossary

'Aref Qazvini: (1882–1934) Singer and composer of politically charged, nationalist tasnifs in the *Mashrute* period.

aruz: System of classical prosody in Persian poetry.

asil ("authentic, rooted"): A common epithet used to denote traditional Persian art music.

attractor: In chaos theory and fractal geometry, a point around which other points in a dynamic system organize themselves or to which they are drawn (water pouring into a drain is a commonly used simplification).

avaz ("voice"): 1) Nonmeasured vocal rendition of traditional poetry based on the radif; vocal or instrumental improvisation in the style of the radif; 2) a secondary modal system derived from a dastgah (i.e., Abu Ata, Dashti, Afshari, Bayate Tork are derived from Shur, Bayate Esfahan from Homayun), in this sense also known as *mote'alleqat* and *naghmeh*.

bakhshi: Epithet for a traditional bard in various parts of Iran, particularly Khorasan.

beyt: A couplet of poetry.

chaharmezrab ("four strokes"): A fast instrumental piece, usually in compound meter and characterized by an ostinato plectrum pattern; may be composed or improvised.

daramad ("coming in"): The first and most important gushe of a dastgah that establishes the fundamental modality of the latter.

dastgah ("apparatus"): A classical mode or modal system represented by an ordered series of gushes; there are seven dastgahs (Shur, Mahur, Homayun, Chahargah, Segah, Rast Panjgah, and Nava) and five "secondary" dastgahs (Abu Ata, Dashti, Afshari, Bayate Tork, Esfahan). *Dastgahi* is a Persian adjective referring to this system. See appendix 1.

Farahani family: A "dynasty" of musicians, primarily tar and setar players, associated with the Qajar court and credited with establishing and transmitting the radif. Important members include Ali Abkar (1810–1855), his sons Mirza Abdollah (1843–1918) and Aqa Hossein Qoli (1853–1915), and their respective sons Ahmad Ebadi (1906–1992) and Ali Akbar Khan Shahnazi (1897–1985).

feedback: When a system or equation feeds back into itself in a cyclical, ever transforming, and nonlinear manner (e.g., microphones picking up the signal of amplifers, pointing a video camera at a monitor). See reiterated/restored behaviour.

forud ("descent"): A melodic device of varying lengths that brings about a return to the modality and tessitura of the main mode of the dastgah. Ostad Shajarian often uses these to modulate to another dastgah.

ghazal ("gazelle"): A short form of Persian classical poetry, usually of mystical-erotic content, consisting of monorhymed couplets, commonly used for avaz texts.

gushe ("corner"): A submode, subsection, and melodic formula of a dastgah; characterized by a particular and narrow ambitus, a functional hierarchy of modal degrees, specific thematic material, and occasionally chromatic alterations of the main mode (creating the effect of a modulation); gushes have proper name designations and vary in length from a few seconds to several minutes. See appendix 1.

hāl ("state"): A temporary state of grace, transcendence, and ecstacy; used by musicians to denote inspiration and depth in perfomance.

iham: The multilayered, ambiguous, polysemous quality exploited in Persian poetry.

jawab ("answer"): Instrumental interludes that frame sections of *avaz* singing.

kereshme ("coquetery"): A genre of *gushes* characterized by a hemiola rhythm.

khānande: A singer of avaz.

khaneghah: Meeting place for Sufi groups.

majles: A small, private musical gathering, usually held in a private home.

maktab: A "school" or style of singing or playing, usually associated with a particular city.

maqam: Umbrella term for West Asian melodic modes, used by Iranian musicians to denote either scale or mode.

Mashrute/Constitutional Revolution: (1905–1911) A popular revolt by Persian citizens against the corruption of the Qajars, resulting in the democratic infrastructure of the Constitution of 1906 and the creation of a parliament (*majles*).

Masnavi: The great poem of Jalal ad-Din Rumi (thirteenth century); avaz settings of texts from Rumi's *Masnavi* (also transliterated as *Mathnawi*), characterized by a particular rhythmic treatment.

Mirza Abdollah: (1843–1918) Tar-player of the Farahani family who became the most important transmitter of the radif

misra: A hemistich of poetry.

Mohammad Reza Pahlavi: (1919–1980) Was installed as Shah in 1941 after his father Reza Shah was forced to abdicate. Continuing the modernization agenda of his father, he cultivated a close relationship with the United States as a supplier of oil and "policeman" of West Asia. He was deposed by the Iranian people in the revolution of 1979.

morakab khāni: Modulating from one *dastgah* to another in the same performance.

motreb: An urban minstrel in traditional Iranian culture, used with decidedly derogatory connotations of "low-life," cheap musicking.

oj: The melodic apogee of a dastgah, as it occurs in a particular gushe.

Ostad: Prestigious/honourific title given to master artists in the Muslim world.

Pahlavi dynasty: (1925–1979) So-called dynasty established by Reza Shah, consisting of him and his son Mohammad Reza.

parde-dari: art of narrating stories, especially regarding Karbala, while pointing to scenes on a large painted tableau.

pishdaramad ("before the daramad"): A composition that initiates the performance of a dastgah, characterized by a moderate triple meter and based on important gushes of the dastgah.

Qajar dynasty: (1794–1925) Dynasty of Turkish origin that established Tehran as the capital of Iran in 1795, grew increasingly bankrupt and ineffectual through the nineteenth century and was *de facto* rendered obsolete with the Constitutional Revolution until it was dissolved in 1925.

radif ("series, row"): 1) The entire aggregate of gushes, organized into twelve dastgahs in the late nineteenth century, that constitutes the repertoire of Persian classical music. It is traditionally memorized exactly as transmitted to students by their teacher, and then becomes the basis for improvisation and composition. According to various sources it consists of 200 to 300 gushes comprising four to six hours of music. 2) In poetry, a refrain of one to three words used to end *beyts* throughout a ghazal.

reiterated or restored behaviour: A term used in Performance Studies to describe the repetition of actions, rituals, routines in art and daily life that are consciously or unconsciously "rehearsed."

reng: A dance piece in moderate or fast compound meter, often concluding the performance of a dastgah.

ru-howzi: A tradition of improvised theatrical farce performed in public.

Reza Shah: (1878–1944) Military man who took over power as the Shah in 1925 following the total collapse of the Qajar dynasty. He pursued policies of authoritarian modernization and nationalism but was deposed by the British and Russians in 1941.

sabk: The style or methods of a particular artist.

samā': In Sufi orders, the use of music, both ritualized and spontaneous, for spiritual development.

self-organization: The dynamic wherein complex and chaotic systems spontaneously display order on a higher level (such as urban sprawl, the economy, a traffic jam).

self-similarity/scaling: The recurrence of a similar pattern on various levels of organization in a complex system or fractal (e.g., a cauliflower or a cloud where various component parts resemble the whole).

shāhgushe ("king gushe"): The most essential and definitive gushes of a dastgah.

tahrir: Extended melismata that employ *tekye* ornaments.

takhallus: A poet's name or pen name appearing in the final *beyt* of a poem as a "signature."

tasnif: A composed, metrical, and frequently strophic setting of a classical poem.

tekye ("lean"): Glottal flip appogiatura; definitive ornament of avaz.

Bibliography

Abazari, Youseff Ali, et al. 2008. "Secularization in Iranian Society." *Media, Culture and Society in Iran: Living with Globalization and the Islamic State*, ed. Mehdi Semati, 238–54. London: Routledge.

Abdollahi, Mehnāz. 2003. "Sāl Shomār-e Mohammad Reza Shajarian (Chronology of Mohammad Reza Shajarian)." *Daftar-e-Honar.* 10/15:2068–71.

Anderson, Benedict. 2006. *Imagined Communities: Reflections of the Origin and Spread of Nationalism* (Revised edition). London: Verso.

Anwar, A. 1985. "Anjoman-e Okowwat." In *Encyclopaedia Iranica*, Online Edition, 15 December, http://iranica.com/articles/anjoman-e-okowwat-or-okuwat-the-society-of-brotherhood-a-non-political-sufl-type-society-officiatty-founded-on-15-saban-1317121-de-cember-1899-y-m-irzu-ait-khan-zahir-al-dawla-to-promole-the-ideals-of-equity-and-brotherhood-in-iran.

Appiah, Kwame Anthony. 2006. *Cosmopolitanism: Ethics in a World of Strangers.* London: Allen Lane.

Arberry, A.J. 1962. *Fifty Poems of Hafez* (second edition). Cambridge: University of Cambridge Press.

Ardalan, Nader and Laleh Bakhtiar. 1973. *The Sense of Unity: The Sufi Tradition in Persian Architecture.* Chicago: University of Chicago Press.

Attar, Farid ud-Din. 1984. *The Conference of the Birds.* Translated by Afkham Darbandi and Dick Davis. New York: Penguin.

Auslander, Philip. 2006. "Musical Personae." *The Drama Review* 50(1):100–119.

Avery, Kenneth. 2004. *The Psychology of Early Sufi Samā': Listening and Altered States.* New York: Routledge Curzon.

Avery, Peter, trans. 2007. *The Collected Lyrics of Hafiz of Shiraz.* Cambridge: Archetype.

Bagley, F.R.C. 1985. "Badīha-sarā'ī," In *Encyclopaedia Iranica,* Online Edition, December 15, http://iranica.com/articles/badiha-sarai-composition-and-utterance-of-something-improvised-badih-usually-in-verse.

Bahktiar, Laleh. 1976. *Sufi: Expressions of the Mystical Quest.* New York: Thames and Hudson.

Barkeshli, Mehdi. 1963. *La musique traditionnelle de l'Iran.* Tehran: Secretariat d'Etat aux Beaux Arts.

Bartel, Dietrich. 1997. *Musica Poetica: Musical-Rhetorical Figures in German Baroque Music.* Lincoln: University of Nebraska Press.

Baudrillard, Jean. 1983. *Simulations.* NewYork: Semiotext(e).

BBC Persian. 2007. *"Matn-e kamal pāsokh-e Shajarian be porsesh-haye shoma* (The Complete script of Shajarian's responses to your questions)." 25 April, www.artmusic.ir/news/show.asp?CC=24&Id=12405.

———. 2010. *"Rabbana-ye Shajarian o vākonesh-hāye moāfeq o mohkālef* (Shajarian's Rabbana and opinions for and against)." 17, August, www.bbc.co.uk/persian/arts/2010/08/100809_144_rabana_shajarian.shtml.

Becker, Ernest. 1973. *The Denial of Death.* New York: Free Press.

———. 1975. *Escape from Evil.* New York: Free Press.

Becker, Howard Saul.1982. *Art Worlds.* Berkeley: University of California Press.

Becker, Judith. 2001. "Anthropological Perspective on Music and Emotion." In *Music and Emotion: Theory and Research*, ed. Patrick Juslin and John Sloboda, 130–160. Oxford: Oxford University Press.

———. 2004. *Deep Listeners: Music, Emotion and Trancing.* Bloomington: Indiana University Press.

Behnam, Jamshid. 2004. "Iranian Society, Modernity and Globalization." In *Iran: Between Tradition and Modernity*, ed. Rahim Jahanbegloo, 3–14. Lanham: Lexington Books.

Berliner, Paul. 1994. *Thinking in Jazz: The Infinite Art of Improvisation.* Chicago: University of Chicago Press.

Bharier, Julian. 1972. "The Growth of Towns and Villages in Iran, 1900-66." *Middle Eastern Studies* 8/1:51–61.

Blackmore, Susan. 1999. *The Meme Machine.* Oxford: Oxford University Press.

Bloom, Harold. 1973. *The Anxiety of Influence: A Theory of Poetry.* New York. Oxford University Press.

Blum, Stephen. 1972. "Musics in Contact: The Cultivations of Oral Repertoires in Meshhed (Iran)." PhD diss., University of Illinois.

———. 1972a. "The Concept of the 'Āsheq in Northern Khorasan." *Asian Music* 4/1:27–47.

———. 1974. "Persian Folksong in Meshhed (Iran) 1969." *Yearbook of the IFMC.* 6:86–114.

———. 1998. "Recognizing Improvisation." In *In the Course of Performance: Studies in the World of Musical Improvisation*, eds. Bruno Nettl with Melinda Russel, 27–45. Chicago: University of Chicago Press.

———. 2001. "Composition." In *The New Grove Dictionary of Music and Musicians,* ed. Stanley Sadie, 6:186–201, London: Macmillan.

———. 2001a. "Iran, §III: Regional and Popular Traditions." In *Grove Music Online. Oxford Music Online*, www.oxfordmusiconline.com. /article/grove/music/13895.

———. 2002. "Hearing the Music of the Middle East." In *The Garland Encyclopedia of World Music Volume 6: The Middle East*, eds. Virginia Danielson, Scott Marcus and Dwight Reynolds, 3–13. New York: Routledge.

———. 2002a. "Iran: An Introduction." In *The Garland Encyclopedia of World Music Volume 6: The Middle East*, eds. Virginia Danielson, Scott Marcus and Dwight Reynolds, 823–38. New York: Routledge.

———. 2005. "Compelling Reasons to Sing: The Music of Ta'ziyeh." *The Drama Review* 49/4:86–90.

Borgo, David. 2005. *Sync or Swarm: Improvising Music in a Complex Age.* New York: Continuum.

Boubakeur, Hamza. 1968. "Psalmodie iranique." In *Encyclopedie des musiques sacree, vol. 1*, ed. Jacque Porte, 388–403. Paris: Editions Labergerie.

Boyce, Mary. 1957. "The Parthian "Gōsān" and Iranian Minstrel Tradition." *Journal of the Royal Asiatic Society of Great Britain and Ireland* 1/2:10–45.

Braudy, Leo. 1986. *The Frenzy of Renown: Fame and Its History.* New York: Oxford University Press.

Briggs, John and David Peat. 1989. *Turbulent Mirror.* New York: Harper and Row.

———. 1999. *Seven Life Lessons of Chaos: Spiritual Wisdom from the Science of Change.* New York: HarperCollins.

Burckhardt, Titus. 1967. *Sacred Art in East and West: Its Principles and Methods.* London: Perennial Books.

Burstyn, Shai. 1990. "The "Arabian Influence" Thesis Revisited." *Current Musicology* 45–47:119–146.

Campbell, Joseph. 1988. *The Power of the Myth*. New York: Doubleday.

Caron, Nelly. 1968. "La musique Shute en Iran." In *Encyclopedie des musiques sacree, vol. 1*, ed. Jacque Porte, 430–40. Paris: Editions Labergerie

Caron, Nelly and Dariouche Safvat. 1966. *Iran: Les Traditions Musicales.* Paris: Buchet/Chastel.

Caton, Margaret. 1974. "The Vocal Ornament *Takiyah* in Persian Music." *UCLA Selected Reports in Ethnomusicology* 2/1:42–53.

———. 1982. "'Abdallah, Mirza" in *Encyclopaedia Iranica*, Online Edition, December 15, 1982, available at http://iranica.com/articles/abdallah-mirza.

———. 1983. The Classical Tasnif: A Genre of Persian Vocal Music. PhD diss., UCLA.

———. 1986. "'Aref Qazvini, ii. 'Āref's Music." In *Encyclopaedia Iranica*, Online Edition, 15 December, http://iranica.com/articles/aref-qazvini-poet.

———. 1988. "Banan, Golam-Hosayn." In *Encyclopaedia Iranica*, Online Edition, 15 December, http://iranica.com/articles/banan-golam-hosayn.

———. 1994. "Darvīš Khan." In *Encyclopaedia Iranica*, Online Edition, 15 December, http://iranica.com/articles/darvis-khan.

Chalisnova, Natalia. 2009. "Rhetorical Figures." In *Encyclopaedia Iranica*, Online Edition, 20 July, http://iranica.com/articles/rhetorical-figures.

———. 2009a. "Persian Rhetoric: Elm-e Badi' and Elm-e Bayan." In *A History of Persian Literature, Vol. I: General Introduction to Persian Literature*, ed. J.T.P. De Bruijn, 139–71. London: I.B. Tauris.

Chehabi, Houshang. 1999. "From Revolutionary Tasnif to Patriotic Surud: Music and Nation-Building in Pre-World War II Iran." *Iran* 37:143–154.

———. 2000. "Voices Unveiled: Woman Singers." In *Iran and Beyond: Essays in Middle Eastern History in Honor of Nikki R. Keddie*, eds. Rudi Matthee and Beth Baron, 151–66. Costa Mesa, CA: Mazda Publishers.

Chelkowski, Peter (ed.). 1979. *Ta'ziyeh: Ritual and Drama in Iran.* New York: New York University Press.

Chelkowski, Peter and Hamid Dabashi. 1999. *Staging a Revolution: The Art of Persuasion in the Islamic Republic of Iran.* New York: New York University Press.

Chittick, William. 1983. *The Sufi Path of Love: The Spiritual Teachings of Rumi.* Albany: SUNY Press.

Clayton, Martin. 2008. "Toward an Ethnomusicology of Sound Experience." In *the new (ethno)musicologies*, ed. Henry Stobart, 135–70. Lanham, MD: Scarecrow Press.

Cook, Nicholas. 2001. "Between Process and Product: Music and/as Performance." *Music Theory Online: The Online Journal of the Society for Music Theory* 7(2).

Conquergood, Dwight. 1992. "Ethnography, Rhetoric, and Performance." *Quarterly Journal of Speech* 78:80–123.

Curtis, Glenn E. and Eric Hooglund. 2008. *Iran: A Country Guide*. Washington: Federal Research Division of the Library of Congress.

Daftar-e-Honar. 2003. 10:15, March 21. (Issue dedicated to Shajarian).

Danielson, Virginia. 1997. *The Voice of Egypt: Umm Kulthūm, Arabic Song, and Egyptian Society in the Twentieth Century.* Chicago: University of Chicago Press.

Dabashi, Hamid. 1999. *Narrative and Truth: The Untimely Thoughts of 'Ayn Al-Qudat Al-Hamadhani.* Surrey, UK: Curzon.

———. 2001. *Close Up: Iranian Cinema, Past, Present and Future.* New York: Verso.

———. 2001a. "For the Last Time: Civilizations." *International Sociology* 16:361–68.

——. 2004. "Blindness and Insight: The Predicament of a Muslim Intellectual." In *Iran: Between Tradition and Modernity*, ed. Rahim Jahanbegloo, 95–116. Lanham: Lexington Books.

——. 2005. "Ta'ziyeh as Theatre of Protest." *The Drama Review* 49/4:91–99.

——. 2007. *Iran: A People Interrupted*. New York: Norton.

——. 2009. *Post-Orientalism*. New Brunswick, NJ: Transaction.

Dalley, Stephanie, trans. 2000. *Myths from Mesopotamia: Creation, The Flood, Gilgamesh, and Others*. Oxford: Oxford University Press.

Davis, Dick. 1992. *Epic and Sedition: The Case of Ferdowsi's Shahnameh*. Fayettevile: University of Arkansas Press.

Debano, Wendy. 2005. "Introduction: Music and Society in Iran, a Look at the Past and Present Century." *Iranian Studies* 38/3:367–72.

De Bruijn, J.T.P. 1988. "Badī' (1)." In *Encyclopedia Iranica*, Online Edition, 15 December, http://iranica.com/articles/badi-1-rhetorical-embellishment.

——. (ed). 2009. *A History of Persian Literature, Vol I: General Introduction to Persian Literature*. London: I.B. Tauris.

——. 2009a. "Classical Persian Literature as a Tradition." In *A History of Persian Literature, Vol I: General Introduction to Persian Literature*, ed. J.T.P. De Bruijn, 1–42. London: I.B. Tauris.

Del Giudice, Margerite. 2008. "Ancient Soul of Iran: The Glories of Persia Inspire the Modern Tradition." *National Geographic* (August) 214/2:34–67.

Ditmars, Hadani. 2009. "Persian Melodies: Vancouver Has Become the Hub of Classical Persian Music Where East Meets West." *The Walrus* Jan/Feb 2009:62–66.

During, Jean. 1975. "Elements spirituels dans las musique traditionelle iranienne contemporaine." *Sophia Perennis* 1/2:129–54.

——. 1977. "The Imaginal World and the Art of Iran." *World of Music* 19/3–4:24–34.

——. 1982. "Revelation and Spiritual Audition in Islam."*World of Music* 24/3:68–84.

——. 1982a. "Music, Poetry, and the Visual Arts in Persia." *World of Music* 23/1:72–88.

——. 1984. *La musique iranienne: Tradition et evolution*. Paris: Editions Recherche sur la civilisation.

——. 1984a. "La Musique traditionelle Iranienne en 1983." *Asian Music* 15/2:11–31.

——. 1985. "Theorie et pratique des gammes iraniennes." *Revue de Musicologie* 71/1–2:79–118.

——. 1987. "Acoustical Systems and Metaphysical Systems in Oriental Traditions." *World of Music* 29/1:19–31.

——. 1987a. "Le Point de vue du Musicien: Improvisation et communication," and "L'Improvisation dans la musique d'art iranienne." In *L'Improvisation dans les musiques de tradition orale*, ed. Bernard Lortat-Jacob, 33–45 and 135–41. Paris: Selaf.

——. 1988. "Conservation et transmission dans les traditions musicales du Moyen-Orient : Les donées nouvelles." *Cahiers de Musiques Traditionelles* 1 :100–111.

——. 1988a. *Musique et extase: L'audition mystique dans la tradition soufi*. Paris: Albin Michel.

——. 1989. *Musique et mystique dans les traditions iraniennes*. Paris: Institute Francais de Recherche en Iran.

——. 1989a. "Les Musiques d'Iran et du Moyen-Orient Face a l'Acculturation Occidentale." In *Entre l'Iran et l'Occient: Adaptation et assimilation des idées et techniques occidentals en Iran*, ed. Yann Richard, 193–223. Paris: Editions de la Maison des sciences de l'homme.

————. 1989b. "Boḥūr al-alḥān. Evaluation." In *Encyclopaedia Iranica*, Online Edition, 15 December, http://iranica.com/articles/bohur-al-alhan-treatise-on-persian-music.

————. 1991. *Le Repertoire modele de la musique iranienne: Radif de tar et setar de Mirza Abdollah, Version de Nur Ali Borumand*. Tehran: Soroush.

————. 1992. "L'oreille islamique: Dix annees capitales de la vie musicale en Iran 1980–1990. " *Asian Music* 13/2:135–64.

————. 1992a. "What is Sufi Music? " In *The Legacy of Mediaeval Persian Sufism*, ed. Leonard Lewisohn, 277–87. London: Khaniqahi Nimatullahi Publications.

————. 1994. *Quelque chose se passe: Le sens de la tradition dans l'Orient musical*. Lagrasse: Verdier.

————. 1994a. "Question de goût: L'enjeu de la modernité dans les arts et les musiques de l'Islam." *Cahiers de musiques traditionnelles* 7: 27–49.

————.1995. "Vers et Melodie, Recitation et Chant: Elements du Dossier Persan." In *Pand-o Sokhān: Hommage a Charles-Henry de Fouchecour*, eds. C. Balay, C. Kappler, Z. Vesel, 95–115. Tehran: IFRI.

————.1996. "La Voix de Esprits et Face Cachee de la Musique: Le Parcourse du Maitre Hatam 'Asghari. " In *Le Voyage Initiatique en Terre d'Islam: Ascensions célestes et itinéraries spirituels*, ed. Mohammad Ail Amir-Moezzi, 335–73. Paris: Peeters.

————. 1996a. "'Ebādī, Ahmad." In *Encyclopaedia Iranica*, Online Edition, 15 December, http://iranica.com/articles/ebadi-ahmad.

————. 2001. "Sufi Music and Rites in the Era of Mass Reproduction Techniques and Culture." In *Sufism, Music and Society: In Turkey and the Middle East*, eds. Anders Hammarland, Tord Olsson and Elizabeth Özdalga, 149–68. Istanbul: Swedish Research Institute.

————. 2001a. "Hand Made: Pour une anthropologie du geste musical." *Cahiers de musiques traditionnelles* 14:39–68.

————. 2002. "Tradition and History: The Case of Iran." In *The Garland Encyclopedia of World Music Volume 6: The Middle East*, eds. Virginia Danielson, Scott Marcus and Dwight Reynolds, 853–64. New York: Routledge.

————. 2005. "Third Millenium Tehran: Music!" *Iranian Studies* 38/3:373–98.

————. 2006. *The Radif of Mirza Abdollah: A canonic repertoire of Persian music*. Tehran: Mahoor.

————. 2006a. "Du samâ' soufi aux pratiques chamaniques: Nature et valeur d'une experience." *Cahiers de musiques traditionnelles* 19:79–92.

————. 2009. "New Challenges for the Musical Tradition in Contemporary Iran." In *Proceedings of International Musicological Symposium "Space of Mugham,"* 124–29. Baku: Şərq-Qərb.

————. 2010. *Musiques d'Iran: La tradition en question*. Paris: Geuthner.

During, Jean and Sultonali Khudoberdiev. 2007. *La Voix du Chamane: Etude sur les Baxshi Tadjiks et Ouzbeks*. Paris: L'Harmattan.

During, Jean, Zia Mirabdolbaghi and Dariouche Safvat. 1991. *The Art of Persian Music*. Washington: Mage.

Eliade, Mircea. 1969. *Yoga: Immortality and Freedom*. Princeton: Princeton University Press.

Elwell-Sutton, Laurence. 1976. *The Persian Metres*. New York: University of Cambridge Press.

D'Erlanger, Baron Rodolphe.1938. *La musique arabe, t.III*. Paris: Paul Geunthner.

Elsner, Jurgen (ed.). 1989. *Maqam, Raga, Zeilen melodic Konzeptions und Prinzipien der Musikproduktion: Arbeitstagung der Study group 'maqam' beim ICTM vom 28. Jun ibis 2. Juli 1988 in Berlin*. Berlin: ICTM.

Ezzaher, Lahcen. 2003. *Writing and Cultural Influence: Studies in Rhetorical History, Orientalist Discourse, and Post-Colonial Criticism* (Comparative Cultures and Literatures, vol. 18). New York: Peter Lang.

Farhat, Hormoz. 1980. "Iran I." In *The New Grove Dictionary of Music and Musicians,* ed. Stanley Sadie, 9: 292–300. New York: Macmillan.

———. 1991. *The Dastgah Concept in Persian Classical Music.* Cambridge: Cambridge University Press.

———. 2004a."□aleqi, Ruh-Allah." In *Encyclopaedia Iranica,* Online Edition, 14 January 14, http://iranica.com/articles/kaleqi-ruh-allah.

———. 2004b. "Vaziri, Ali Naqi." In *Encyclopaedia Iranica,* Online Edition, 14 January 14, http://iranica.com/articles/vaziri-ali-naqi.

Farmer, George Henry. 1954. "Persian Music." In *Groves Dictionary of Music and Musicians,* 5th Edition, ed. Eric Blom, 6: 676–82. London: MacMillan.

Faruqi, Ishmail and Lois Ibsen Faruqi. 1985. *Cultural Atlas of Islam.* New York: Macmillan.

Feld, Steven. 1981. "'Flow like a Waterfall': The Metaphors of Kaluli Musical Theory." *Yearbook for Traditional Music,* 13:22–47.

Feldman, Walter. 1996. *Music of the Ottoman Court: Makam, Composition and the Early Ottoman Instrumental Repertoire.* Berlin: VWB-Verlag fur Wissenschaft und Bildung.

Finnegan, Ruth. 1992. *Oral Poetry: Its Nature, Significance, and Social Context.* Bloomington: Indiana University Press.

Firuzi, Mohammad Ali (ed.). 2003 [1382]. *Ghazaliāt Sa'di.* Tehran: Qoqnoos.

Gabler, Neal. 1998. *Life the Movie: How Entertainment Conquered Reality.* New York: Knopf.

Geertz, Clifford. 1973. *The Interpretation of Cultures: Selected Essays.* New York: Basic Books.

Gerson-Kiwi, Edith. 1963. *The Persian Doctrine of Dastgah Composition.* Tel-Aviv: Israel Music Institute.

Gluck, Robert. 2007. "The Shiraz Arts Festival: Western Avant-garde Arts in 1970s Iran." *Leonardo* 40/1:20–28.

Godlovitch, Stan. 1998. *Musical Performance: A Philosphical Study.* London: Routledge.

Godwin, Joscelyn (ed.). 1987. *Music, Mysticism and Magic: A Sourcebook.* New York: Arkana.

Grigg, Ray. 1988. *The Tao of Being: A Think and Do Workbook.* Atlanta: Humanics.

———. 1994. *The Tao of Zen.* Boston: Charles Tuttle.

Gudarzi, Mohsen, Mohamad Javad Kashi and Mohsen Ali Asghar Ramezanpour. 2000. *Raz-e Mānā: Didgāh-hā, Zendegi va Āsar-e Ostad-e Avaz Iran Mohammad Reza Shajarian* (The Eternal Secret: Viewpoints, Life and Impressions of the Master of Iranian Avaz, Mohammad Reza Shajarian). Tehran: Nashr Ketab Fara.

Guenon, Rene. 1972. "The Language of the Birds." In *The Sword of Gnosis,* ed. Jacob Needleman, 299–303. Baltimore: Penguin.

———.1980. "The Arts and Their Traditional Conception." *Studies in Comparative Religion* 14/3–4:195–98.

Haery, Mahmoud. 1982. "Ru-Howzi: The Iranian Traditional Improvisatory Theatre." PhD diss., New York University.

Haim, Soleyman. 1963. *The Shorter Persian-English Dictionary.* Tehran: Beroukhim.

Hajarian, Mohsen. 1999. "*Ghazal* as a Determining Factor in the Structure of the Iranian *Dastgah*." PhD diss., University of Maryland, Baltimore.

Hallden, Philip. 2005. "What Is Arab Islamic Rhetoric?: Rethinking the History of Muslim Oratory Art and Homiletics." *International Journal of Middle East Studies* 37/1:19–38.

Harris, Rachel. 2008. *The Making of a Musical Canon in Chinese Central Asia: The Uyghur Twelve Muqam.* Aldershot: Ashgate Press.

Hayles, N. Katherine. 1990. *Chaos Bound: Orderly Disorder in Contemporary Literature and Science.* Ithaca, NY: Cornell University Press.

———. (ed.). 1991. *Chaos and Disorder: Complex Dynamics in Literature and Science.* Chicago: University of Chicago Press.

Hedges, Chris. 2009. *Empire of Illusion: The End of Literacy and the Triumph of Spectacle.* Toronto: Alfred A. Knopf Canada.

Hickmann, Hans. 1961. *Musicgeschicte in Bildern. Bamd II. Musik des Altertums. Lieferung 1. Ägypten.* Leipzig: VEB Deutscher Verlad für Musik.

Hillmann, Michael. 1976. *Unity in the Ghazals of Hafez.* Minneapolis: Bibliotheca Islamica.

Hinnells, John. 1985. *Persian Mythology.* New York: Peter Bedwick Books.

Hobsbawm, Eric & Terence Ranger (eds.). 1992. *The Invention of Tradition.* New York: Cambridge University Press.

Jahanbegloo, Rahim (ed). 2004. *Iran: Between Tradition and Modernity.* Lanham: Lexington Books.

Jargy, Simon. 1971. *La Musique Arabe.* Paris: Presses Universitaires de France.

Johnson, Steven. 2001. *Emergence: The Connected Lives of Ants, Brains, Cities and Software.* New York: Scribner.

Kasmai, Sorour. 1990. Liner notes to CD *Mohammad Reza Shajarian: Musique classique persane.* Ocora 559097.

Kasmai, Sorour and Henri Lecomte. 1991. "Le Pelerinage aux Sources: Mohamed Reza Shajarian au Tadjikistan." *Cahiers de Musiques traditionelles* 4:247–53.

Katschi, Katschi. 1962. *Der Dastgah.* Regensburg: Bosse.

———. 1967. "Das Intervallbildungsprinzip der persischen Dastgah Shur." *Jahrbuch für musikalische Volks-und Volkerkunde* 3:70–84.

Khaleqi, Ruhollah. 1955. *Sargozasht-e Musiqi-ye Iran* [Tale of the Music of Iran]. 3 vols. Tehran: Chapkhāne Ferdowsi.

Khaleghi-Motlagh, Djalal. 2010. "Adab i. Adab in Iran." In *Encyclopaedia Iranica,* Online Edition, 21 January, http://iranica.com/articles/adab-i-iran.

Khan, Hazrat Inayat. 1983. *The Music of Life.* Santa Fe: Omega Press.

Koch, Klaus-Peter. 1980. "Persia". In *New Groves Dictionary of Music and Musicians,* ed. Stanley Sadie, 14:549–52. New York: Macmillan.

Lawson-Tancred, Hugh, trans. 2004. *Aristotle: The Art of Rhetoric.* New York: Penguin.

Levin, Theodore. 1996. *The Hundred Thousand Fools of God: Musical Travels in Central Asia and Queens, NY.* Bloomington: Indiana University Press.

Levitin, Daniel. 2006. *This Is Your Brain on Music: The Science of a Human Obsession.* New York: Plume.

Lewis, Franklin. 1995. "Reading, Writing and Recitation: Sana'i and the Origins of the Persian Ghazal." PhD. diss., University of Chicago.

———. 2008. *Rumi: Past and Present, East and West.* Oxford: Oneworld.

Lewisohn, Jane. 2008. "Flowers of Persian Song and Music: Davud Pirniā and the Genesis of the *Golhā* Programs." *Journal of Persianate Studies* 1:79–101.

Lewisohn, Leonard. 1997. "The Sacred Music of Islam: Samā' in the Persian Sufi Tradition." *British Journal of Ethnomusicology* 6:1–33.

Locke, David. 1989. *Drum Damba: Talking Drum Lessons. With Abubakari Lunna.* Crown Pt., IN: White Cliffs.

———.1991. *Kpegisu. With Godwin Agbeli.* Crown Pt., IN: White Cliffs.

Lord, Albert. 1948. "Homer, Parry, and Huso." *American Journal of Archaeology* 52/1:34–44.

———. 1970. *The Singer of Tales.* New York: Atheneum.

Manateqe Azad. 2001. "Biography of Mohammad Reza Shajarian, Renowned Iranian Singer." *Manateqe Azad: Economic, Social, Cultural (Monthly)* June 2001, No. 119:20–22. (http://netiran.com/Htdocs/Clippings?Art/010628XXAR01.html. Accessed July 2, 2002).

Marcus, Scott. 1992. "Modulation in Arab Music: Documenting Oral Concepts, Performance Rules and Strategies." *Ethnomusicology* 36/2:171–95.

Markoff, Irene. 1986. "Musical Theory, Performance and the Contemporary *Bağlama* Specialist in Turkey. " PhD diss., University of Washington (Seattle).

Ma'roufi, Musa. 1963. *Les systems de la musique traditionnelle de l'Iran (Radif).* Tehran: Secretariat d'Etat aux Beaux-Arts.

Mashhun, Hassan. 1994. *Tārikh-e musiqi-ye Iran* (The History of the Music of Iran), Tehran: Nashr-e Simorgh.

Massoudieh, Mohammed Taghi. 1968. *Awaz-e Shur.* Regensburg: Bosse.

———. 1971. "Die Melodie Matnawi in der persischen Kunstmusik."*Orbis Musicae* (Tel Aviv) 1/1:57–66.

———. 1973. "Tradition und Wandel in der persischen Musik des 19. Jahrhunderts." In *Musikkulturen Asiens, Afrikas und Ozeaniens im 19. Jahrhundert*, ed. R. Gunther, 73–94. Regensburg: Bosse.

———. 1985 (1978). *Radif vocal de la musique traditionelle de l'Iran.* Tehran: Sorouche.

———. 1988. *Musiqi-e Mazhabi-e Iran. Jeld-e Avval: Musiqi-e Ta'ziyeh* (Religious Music in Iran. Volume One: Music of the Ta'ziyeh). Tehran: Soroush.

Miller, Lloyd. 1995. "Persian Music: A Study of the Form and Content of Persian *Avaz, Dastgah* and *Radif.*" PhD diss., University of Utah.

———. 1999. *Music and Song in Persia: The Art of Avaz.* Salt Lake City: University of Utah Press.

Mir-Hosseini, Ziba. 1994. "Redefining the Truth: Ahl-i Haqq and the Islamic Republic of Iran." *British Journal of Middle Eastern Studies* 21/2: 211–28.

Mirian, Shahram. 2007. "*Goftgui Sedayeh Alman ba Mohammad Reza Shajarian: Musiqi hamvare zaban-e ā'etrāz mardom bude ast* (Sedayeh Alman interview with Shajarian: Music has always been the voice of complaint for people)." *Sedayeh Alman, Deutsche Welle.* 7 June, http://www.artmusic.ir/news/show.asp?CC=24&Id=12965.

Movahed, Azin. 2003. "Religious Supremacy, Anti-Imperialist Nationhood and Persian Musicology after the 1979 Revolution." *Asian Music* 35/1: 85–113.

Musavi, Mohammad. 2003. Liner notes to CD *A Century of Avaz, vol.1.* Mahoor M.CD-133.

Nakjavani, Erik. 2005. "Delkaš." In *Encyclopaedia Iranica*, Online Edition, 20 July, http://iranica.com/articles/delkas.

———. 2008. "Qamar-al-Moluk Vaziri." In *Encyclopaedia Iranica*, Online Edition, 15 December, http://iranica.com/articles/qamar-vaziri.

Nasirifar, Habib Allah. 1990. *Mardan-e Musiqi-ye Sonati va Navin-e Iran* (The Men of Classical and New Music of Iran). Tehran: Intisharat Rad.

Nasr, Seyyed Hossein. 1964. *Three Muslim Sages: Avicenna, Suhrawardi, Ibn 'Arabi.* Cambridge: Harvard University Press.

———. 1966. *Ideals and Realities of Islam.* London: George Allen and Unwin.

———. 1976. "The Influence of Sufism in Traditional Persian Music." *Studies in Comparative Religion* 6/4:225–34.

———. 1987. *Sacred Art and Islamic Spirituality*. Albany: SUNY Press.

Nederveen Pietrse, Jan. 2004. *Globalization and Culture: Global Melange*. Lanham: Rowman & Littlefield.

Nelson, Kristina. 1985. *The Art of Reciting the Qu'ran*. Austin: University of Texas Press.

Nettl, Bruno. 1970. "Attitudes Towards Persian Music in Tehran, 1969." *Musical Quarterly* 56:183–97.

———. 1974. "Thoughts on Improvisation: A Comparative Approach." *The Musical Quarterly* 60:1–19.

———. 1974a. "Aspects of Form in the Instrumental Performance of the Persian *Avaz*." *Ethnomusicology* 18:405–14.

———. 1978. "Persian Classical Music in Tehran: The Processes of Change." In *Eight Urban Musical Cultures*, ed. Bruno Nettl, 146–185. Urbana, IL: University of Illinois Press, pp..

———. 1983. *The Study of Ethnomusicology: Twenty-nine Issues and Concepts*. Urbana: University of Illinois Press.

———. 1985. *The Western Impact on World Music: Change, Adaptation, and Survival*. New York: Schirmer Books.

———. 1992. *The Radif of Persian Music: Studies of Structure and Cultural Context*. Champaign, IL: Elephant and Cat. http://www.scribd.com/doc/9307940/The-Radif-of-Persian-Classical-music-studies-of-structure-and-cultural-context-by-Bruno-Nettl.

Nettl, Bruno, with Bela Foltin, Jr. 1972. *Daramad of Chahargah: A Study in the Performance of Persian Music*. Detroit: Detroit Monographs in Musicology, no. 2.

Nettl, Bruno and Ronald Riddle. 1973. "Taqsim Nahawand: A Study of Sixteen Performances by Jihad Racy." *Yearbook of theInternational Folk Music Council* 5:11–50.

Nicholson, Reynold, trans. 1976. *The Kashf al-Mahjub: The Oldest Persian Treatise on Sufiism by 'Ali B. Uthman al-Jullabi al-Hujwiri*. London: Luzac.

Niedzviecki, Hal. 2006. *Hello, I'm Special: How Individuality Became the New Conformity*. San Francisco: City Lights Books.

———. 2009. *The Peep Diaries: How We're Learning to Love Watching Ourselves and Our Neighbors*. San Francisco: City Light Books.

Nooshin, Laudan. 1996. "The Processes of Creation and Recreation in Persian Classical Music." PhD, diss., University of London.

———. 1998. "The Song of the Nightingale: Processes of Improvisation in Dastgāh Segāh (Iranian Classical Music)." *British Journal of Ethnomusicology* 7:69–116.

———. 2001. "Shajariān, Mohammad Rezā." In *Grove Music Online. Oxford Music Online*, http://www.oxfordmusiconline.com.ezproxy.library.yorku.ca/subscriber/article/grove/music/48512.

———. 2003. "Improvisation as 'Other': Creativity, Knowledge and Power—The Case of Iranian Classical Music." *Journal of the Royal Musical Association* 128: 242–96.

———. 2005. "Subversion and Countersubversion: Power, Control, and Meaning in the New Iranian Pop Music." In *Music, Power and Politics*, ed. Annie J. Randall, 231–72. New York: Routledge.

——— (ed). 2009. *Music and the Play of Power in the Middle East, North Africa and Central Asia*. Surrey: Ashgate.

Norberg-Hodge, Helena. 1992. *Ancient Futures: Learning from Ladakh*. San Francisco: Sierra Club Books.

Noury, Manouchehr Saadat. "Notable Iranian Female Poets." http://www.irandokht.com/

editorial/print.php?area=pro&sectionID=8&editorialID=2237#.

Page, Mary Ellen. 1977. "Naqqali and Ferdowsi: Creativity in the Iranian National Tradition. PhD diss., University of Pennsylvania.

———.1979. "Professional Storytelling in Iran: Transmission and Practice." *Iranian Studies* 12/3–4: 195–215

Parsinejad, Iraj. 2003. *A History of Literary Criticism in Iran (1866–1951)*. Bethesda MD: Ibex.

Partch, Harry. 1974. *Genesis of a Music (2nd ed)*. New York: Da Capo Press.

Payvand. 2006. "Iran's tar virtuosos Shahnaz and Darvish Khan honored." 18 August, http://www.payvand.com/news/06/aug/1201.html.

Payvar, Farmarz. 1996. *The Vocal Radif and Old Tasnif According to the Version of Abdollah Davami*. Tehran: Mahoor.

Pirnia, Daryush and Erik Nakjavani. 2001. "Golhā, Barnāma-ye." In *Encyclopaedia Iranica*, Online Edition, 15 December, http://iranica.com/articles/golha-barnama-ye.

Postman, Neil. 1986. *Amusing Ourselves to Death: Public Discourse in the Age of Show Business*. New York: Penguin.

Pourjavady, Nasrollah. 2009. "Genres of Religious Literature." In *A History of Persian Literature, Vol. I: General Introduction to Persian Literature*, ed. J.T.P De Bruijn, 270–311. London: I.B. Tauris.

Powers, Harold. 1980. "Language Models and Musical Analysis." *Ethnomusicology* 24/1:1–60.

Qaneeifard, Erphane. 2003. *Sorush-e Mardom: andishe-ha va 'eqlid-e Mohammad Reza Shajarian darbare' avaz va honar-e musiqi* (The Inspiration of Society: The Collection of Shajarian's Opinion About the Iranian Classical-Music [sic])" Tehran: Dadar.

Qureshi, Regula Burckhardt. 1986. *Sufi Music of India and Pakistan: Sound, Context and Meaning in Qawwali*. Cambridge: University of Cambridge Press.

Racy, Jihad. 1991. "Creativity and Ambiance: An Ecstatic Feedback Model from Arab Music." *World of Music* 33/3: 7–28.

———. 2003. *Making Music in the Arab World: the Culture and Artistry of Tarab*. Cambridge: Cambridge University Press.

Rajai, Farhang. 1994. *Ganj-e Sukhteh: Pizhuhushi dar musiqi 'ahd Qajar* (Burnt Treasure: An Inquiry into the Music of the Qajar Period) [text accompanying cassettes]. Tehran: Aheya' Kitab.

Rashid, Subhi Anwar. 1984. *Musikgeschicte in Bildern. Bamd II. Musik des Altertums. Lieferung 2. Mesopotamien*. Leipzig: VEB Deutscher Verlad für Musik.

Reck, David. 1983. "A Musicians Toolkit: A Study of Five Performances by Thiragukarnam Ramachandra Iyer." PhD diss., Wesleyan University.

Reckord, Thomas. 1987. "Chant in Popular Iranian Shi'ism." PhD diss., University of California at Los Angeles.

Reynolds, Dwight. 2002. "Learning Epic Traditions." In *The Garland Encyclopedia of World Music Volume 6: The Middle East*, eds. Virginia Danielson, Scott Marcus and Dwight Reynolds, 339–46. New York: Routledge.

Ringer, Monica. 2000. "The Discourse of Modernization and the Problem of Cultural Integrity in Nineteenth-century Iran." In *Iran and Beyond: Essays in Middle Eastern History in Honor of Nikki R. Keddie*, eds. Rudi Matthee and Beth Baron, 56–69. Costa Mesa, CA: Mazda Publishers.

Rink, John. 1993. "Schenker and Improvisation." *Journal of Music Theory* 37:1–54.

Rouget, Gilbert. 1985. *Music and Trance: A Theory of Relationships Between Music and Possession*. Chicago: University of Chicago Press.

Sabur, Dariush. 1992. *Az Nur Ta Nava: Gholamhossein Banan, Ostad-e Avaz-e Iran* (From Light to Melody: Gholamhossein Banan, Ostad of Iranian Avaz). Tehran: Kitabforush Tarikh.

Sachs, Curt. 1940. *History of Musical Instruments*. London: Dent.

Sadeghi, Manoochehr. 1971. "Improvisation in Nonrhythmic Solo Instrumental Contemporary Persian Art Music." MA thesis, California State College at Los Angeles.

Sadighi, Ramin and Sohrab Mahdavi. 2009. "The Song Does Not Remain the Same." *Mid East Report Online*. 12 March, http://www.merip.org/mero/mero031209.html.

Safvat, Dariouche. 1984. "Musique et Mystique." Translated by Jean During. *Etudes Traditionelles* 483:42–64, 484:94–109.

Said, Edward. 1979. *Orientalism*. New York: Vintage Books.

Sardar, Ziauddin. 2004. *Desperately Seeking Paradise: Journeys of a Sceptical Muslim*. London: Granta Books.

Schechner, Richard. 2006. *Performance Studies: An Introduction*. New York: Routledge.

Schieffelin, Edward. 1998. "Problematizing Performance." In *Ritual, Performance, Media*, ed. Felidia Hughes-Freeland, 194–207. London: Routledge.

Schimmel, Annemarie. 1992. *A Two-Colored Brocade: The Imagery of Persian Poetry*. Chapel Hill: University of North Carolina Press.

Schneider, Marius. 1957. "Primitive Music." In *The New Oxford History of Music Vol. 1*, ed. Egon Wellesz, 1–82. London: University of Oxford Press.

———. 1982. "On Gregorian Chant and the Human Voice." *World of Music* 26/3:3–21.

———. 1986. "The Nature of Praise Song" and "Acoustic Symbolism in Foreign Cultures." In *Cosmic Music: Three Musical Keys to the Interpretation of Reality*, ed. Joscelyn Godwin, 35–85. West Stockbridge, MA: Lindisfarne Press.

Scholes, Robert, James Phelan and Robert Kellog. 2006. *The Nature of Narrative*. Oxford: Oxford University Press.

Schulenberg, David. 1982. "Composition as Variation: Inquiries into the Compositional Procedures of the Bach Circle of Composers." *Current Musicology* 33:57–87.

Sepanta, Sassan. 1987/1366. *Tārikh-e Tahavol-e Zabt-e Musiqi dar Iran* (A History of Sound Recording in Iran). Esfahan: Enteshārat-e Nimā.

Shahidi, Anayatullah. 1979. "Literary and Musical Developments in the Ta'ziyeh." In *Ta'ziyeh: Ritual and Drama in Iran*, ed. Peter Chelkowski, 40-63. New York: New York University Press.

Shajarian, Mohammad Reza. 1991/1370. "Dar kenār-e Ostād Dawāmī (Being Beside Ostad Davami)." *Kelk* 22:156–64.

———. 1993/1372. "*Hamishe va Hamchenān 'Khāk rāh-e mardom mehrbān va 'aziz hamutan hastam'*" (Always and Accordingly "I am the Dust on the Path of the Kind and Dear Compatriots"). *Fazelat* [Sal-e dovvom, Mehr 1372] 16:40–47.

Shajarian, Mohammad Reza, Kazem Motlaq, Mehdi Abedini & Hamid Javaharian. 2004. *Hezar Golkhāneye Avaz* (A Thousand Orchards of Avaz). Qom: Faragoft.

Simms, Rob. 1992. "Form and Meaning in the Sehtar Pedagogy of a Persian Sufi." MA thesis, York University.

———. 1996. *Avaz in the Recordings of Mohammed Reza Shajarian*. PhD diss., University of Toronto.

———. 2004. *The Repertoire of Iraqi Maqam*. Lanham, MD: Scarecrow Press.

Simms, Rob and Amir Koushkani. 2012. *Mohammad Reza Shajarian's Avaz in Iran and Beyond, 1979–2010*. Lanham: Lexington Books.

Smith, Gregory. 1983. "Homer, Gregory and Bill Evans? The Theory of Formulaic Composition in the Context of Jazz Piano Improvisation." PhD diss., Harvard University.

Storr, Anthony. 1991. *The Dynamics of Creation.* New York: Penguin.

Stravinsky, Igor. 1970. *Poetics of Music (In the Form of Six Lessons).* Cambridge: Harvard University Press.

Tabar, Hassan. 2005. *Les transformations de la musique iranienne au début du XXe siècle.* Paris: L'Harmattan.

Tala'i, Dariush. 1983. Musique et poesies persanes: Analyse du rhythme dela musique traditionelle traverse la prosodie. Memoire de maitrise, Universite de Paris VIII.

———. 1995. *Radif-e Mirza Abdollah: note nevessi amuzeshi va tahlili* ["The Radif of Mirza Abdollah: A Pedagogical and Analytical Transcription"]. Tehran: Nubahar.

———. 1999. *Traditional Persian Art Music: The Radif of Mirza Abdollah.* Costa Mesa, CA: Mazda.

Tavakoli-Targhi, Mohamad. 2004. "The Homeless Texts of Persianate Modernity." In *Iran: Between Tradition and Modernity,* ed. Rahim Jahanbegloo, 129–57. Lanham: Lexington Books.

Taylor, Diana. 2003. *The Archive and the Repertoire*: *Performing Cultural Memory in the Americas.* Durham: Duke University Press.

Taylor, Rogan. 1985. *The Death and Resurrection Show: From Shaman to Superstar.* London: A. Blond, 1985.

Tehranian, Majid. 2004. "Power and Purity: Iranian Political Culture, Communication and Identity." In *Iran: Between Tradition and Modernity,* ed. Rahim Jahanbegloo, 185–206. Lanham: Lexington Books.

———. 2008. "Epilogue: Wither Iran?" In *Media, Culture and Society in Iran: Living with Globalization and the Islamic State,* ed. Mehdi Semati, 257–69. London: Routledge.

Thackston, W.M., trans. 2008. *The Gulistan of Sa'di: Bilingual English and Persian Edition with Vocabulary.* Bethesda, MD: Ibex.

Thaut, Michael. 2008. *Rhythm, Music and the Brain.* New York: Routledge.

Treitler, Leo. 1974. "Homer and Gregory: The Transmission of Epic Poetry and Plainchant." *Musical Quarterly* 60/3:333–72.

Tsuge, Gen'ichi. 1970. "Rhythmic Aspects of *Avaz.*" *Ethnomusicology* 14/2:205–27.

———. 1974. "*Avaz*: A Study of the Rhythmic Aspects in Classical Iranian Music." PhD diss., Wesleyan University.

Tucker, Vincent. 1996. "Introduction: A Cultural Perspective on Development." *European Journal of Development Research* 8/2:1–21.

———. 1999. "The Myth of Development: A Critique of Eurocentric Discourse." In *Critical Development Theory: Contributions to a New Paradigm,* ed. Ronaldo Munck, 1–26. New York: Zed Books.

van Gelder, G.J. 2009. "Traditional Literary Theory: The Arabic Background." In *A History of Persian Literature, Vol. I: General Introduction to Persian Literature,* ed. J.T.P. De Bruijn, 123–38. London: I.B. Tauris.

van Ruymbeke, C. 2009. "Hellenistic Influences in Classical Persian Literature." In *A History of Persian Literature, Vol. I: General Introduction to Persian Literature,* ed. J.T.P. De Bruijn, 345–68. London: I.B. Tauris.

Varela, Francisco J., Evan Thompson, and Eleanor Rosch. 1991. *The Embodied Mind: Cognitive Science and Human Experience.* Cambridge: MIT Press.

Volk, Konrad. 1994. "Improvisierte Musik im alten Mesopotamien." *Improvisation* 2: 160–202.

Washburn, Michael. 1994. *Transpersonal Pysychology in Psychoanalytic Perspective.* Albany: SUNY Press.

Weatherford, Jack. 2010. *Indian Givers: How the Indians of the Americas Transformed the World* (second edition). New York: Random House.

Weil, Gotthold. 1960. "Aruz." In *Encyclopedia of Islam*, eds. H. Gibb et al., 1:667–77. Leiden: E.J. Brill.

Wilber, Ken. 1996. *A Brief History of Everything.* Boston: Shambhala.

———. 1997. *The Eye of Spirit: An Integral Vision for a World Gone Slightly Mad.* Boston: Shambhala.

———. 2000. *A Theory of Everything.* Boston: Shambhala.

———. 2000a. *Integral Psychology.* Boston: Shambhala.

Williams, Alan, trans. 2006. *Spiritual Verses: The First Book of the Masnavi-ye Manavi by Jalāl al-Dīn Rūmī.* London: Penguin.

Willoughby, Heather. 2000. "The Sound of Han: P'ansori, Timbre and a Korean Ethos of Pain and Suffering." *Yearbook for Traditional Music* 31:17–30.

Wilson, Peter. 1980. *Angels.* New York: Pantheon.

Wolf, Eric. 1997. *Europe and the People without History.* Berkeley: University of California Press.

Wright, Owen. 2009. *Touraj Kiaras and Persian Classical Music: An Analytical Perspective.* Surrey: Ashgate.

Yanagi, Soetsu. 1972. *The Unknown Craftsman: A Japanese Insight into Beauty.* London: George Allen and Unwin.

Yarshater, Ehsan. 1974. "Affinities between Persian Poetry and Music." In *Studies in Art and Literature of the Near East,* ed. Peter Chelkowski, 59–78. Salt Lake City and New York: University of Utah and New York University.

Youssefzadeh, Ameneh. 2000. "The Situation of Music in Iran since the Revolution: The Role of Official Organizations." *British Journal of Ethnomusicology* 9/2:35–61.

———. 2002. *Les Bardes du Khorasan Iranien: Le bakhshi et son repertoire.* Louvain: Peeters.

———. 2003. "Hedayat, ii. As musician." In *Encyclopaedia Iranica*, Online Edition, 15 December, http://iranica.com/articles/hedayat-mokber-al-saltana-ii.

———. 2004. "Singing in a Theocracy: Female Musicians in Iran. In *Shoot the Singer!: Musical Censorship Today,* ed. Marie Korpe, 129–34. New York: Zed Books.

———. 2004a. "Ḥosaynqoli, Āqā." In *Encyclopaedia Iranica*, Online Edition, 15 December, http://iranica.com/articles/hosaynqoli-aqa.

Zaehner, R.C. 1965. "Zoroastrian Survivals in Iranian Folklore." *Iran* 3: 87–96.

———. 1992. "Zoroastrian Survivals in Iranian Folklore II." *Iran* 30: 65–75.

Zeranska-Kominek, Slawomira. 1990. "The Turkmen Bakhshy: Shaman and/or Artist." In *VII European Seminar in Ethnomusicology: Historical Developments and Recent Trends,* eds. Max Peter Baumann, Arthur Simon, and Ulrich Wegner, 497–508. Wilhelmshaven: Noetzel.

Zonis, Ella. 1973. *Classical Persian Music: An Introduction.* Cambridge, MA: Harvard University Press.

Sound Recordings

Musavi, Mohammad, ed. 2003. *A Century of Avaz: An Anthology.* Tehran: Mahoor Institute of Culture and Art, M.CD. 133, 134 & 135.

Rajai, Farhang, ed. 1994. *Ganj-e Sukhteh: Pizhuhushi dar musiqi 'ahd Qajar* ("Burnt Treasure: An Inquiry into the Music of the Qajar Period") [Five cassettes and text]. Tehran: Aheya' Kitab.

Film/DVD

The Voice of Iran: Mohammad Reza Shajarian—The Copenhagen Concert 2002. Director, Christian Braad Thomsen, 2003. (Concert and interview)

Index

accompaniment, of avaz, 22, 213–15, 268
adab, 4, 6, 7, 11, 40, 54n1, 145, 183
aesthetics, 4, 6, 9, 13, 16, 17, 20, 33, 47,
    49, 57n48, 58n55, 85, 93, 97, 101,
    103, 106, 109, 120, 121, 131, 160,
    165n29, 180, 183, 201, 205, 221, 258,
    261n7; personal continuum of, 10, 31,
    35, 36, 40, 46, 47, 48, 50, 57n47, 132,
    199, 206, 240. *See also* innovators,
    preservers, renovators
Affekt, xii, 91, 101, 190, 208; modes and
    mood, 101–03, 137, 193
Akhavan Sales, Mehdi, 6, 42, 99, 185,
    187
Alizadeh, Hossein, 133, 162, 214, 259
angels, 9, 70, 106, 107, 108, 110
Anjoman-e Okhavvat 128, 162
'Aref Qazvini, 6, 22, 26, 95, 98, 121–22,
    128, 150, critical writings of, 158
Aristotle, 88, 90, 92, 96, 101, 168
art-craft relationships, 48
aruz, 89, 239–40, 242–47, 264n59
Attar, 13, 22, 51, 52, 113, 184, 185,
    186, 189
authenticity, 48–54
avaz, acquisition of, 134, 137, 138, 139,
    140, 141, 143, 170–74; ambiguity in
    structure of, 9–10; as a language
    167, 182, 210–13, 247–56; as narra-
    tive performance, 15–16, 18, 81,
    197, 206, 217, 220; background
    structure of, 217, 220–24; definition
    of, 2–3; foreground structure of,
    238–56; history of, 27–31; influen-
    tial masters of, 37–38; middle
    ground structure of, 224–38;

performance conventions of, 267–
    69. *See also maktab*, rhetoric
'Ayn al-Quzat, 85–86

Bahjat al-Ruh', 19
Banan, Gholamhossein, 26, 38, 52, 127,
    134, 138, 146, 171, 176, 180,
Barbad, 29–30, 34, 90
bards/bardic tradition, 15, 16, 30, 34,
    56n34, 68, 81, 82, 93, 109, 130,
    139, 168, 172, 181, 206, 217, 257,
Be Yad e Pedar (album), 69, 71, 114n2
Bikchekhani, Ostad, 22
Bohur al-Alhan, 23, 190
Boroumand, Nur Ali, 127, 133, 134,
    135, 138, 140, 141, 159, 175, 176,
    180–81, 195, 196, 207, 250, 261n6,
    265n77

celebrity, 11, 34–35, 40, 97, 139
centonic processes, in avaz, 152, 169,
    181, 182, 201–13, in Shajarian's
    avaz, 247–56, 273–74
chaharmezrab, 14, 26, 268
chaotics, xii, 15, 32, 46
Chavosh Institute and movement, 162,
    174
Chehre be Chere (album), 125, 187, 230
clerical culture (*mollahs, ulema*), 62, 64–
    66, 77, 91, 188, 197 ; rhetorical tradi-
    tions of, 89
concerts, in Iran, 16, 20, 69, 94, 122, 124,
    125, 128, 131, 133, 160, 162, 163n3,
    216, 258
"cultural purity," 41–42, 44, 45, 57n48,
    89, 157, 199

301

About the Authors

Rob Simms is a multi-instrumentalist and author of *The Repertoire of Iraqi Maqam* and co-author (with Amir Koushkani) of *The Avaz of Mohammad Reza Shajarian in Iran and Beyond (1979–2010)*. He is Associate Professor of Music at York University in Toronto.

Amir Koushkani is a performer (solo and in collaboration with other musicians), composer, arranger, and instructor of the traditional Persian stringed instruments tar and setar. He is a PhD candidate in ethnomusicology at York University, Toronto.